CW00494228

Land of the Golden Mouths

To Ann

With love from
Helen (Chang Yuen-Shiu)
15 June 2012

Land of the Golden Mouths

STORIES OF MODERN CHINA 1840–1976

VOLUME 2

Chang Yuen-Shiu

Copyright © 2010 Chang Yuen-Shiu

The moral right of the author has been asserted.

Apart from any fair dealing for the purposes of research or private study,
or criticism or review, as permitted under the Copyright, Designs and Patents
Act 1988, this publication may only be reproduced, stored or transmitted, in
any form or by any means, with the prior permission in writing of the
publishers, or in the case of reprographic reproduction in accordance with
the terms of licences issued by the Copyright Licensing Agency. Enquiries
concerning reproduction outside those terms should be sent to the publishers.

Matador
5 Weir Road
Kibworth Beauchamp
Leicester LE8 0LQ, UK
Tel: (+44) 116 279 2277
Email: books@troubador.co.uk
Web: www.troubador.co.uk/matador

ISBN
VOLUME 1 – 978 1848762-466
VOLUME 2 – 978 1848763-104

British Library Cataloguing in Publication Data.
A catalogue record for this book is available from the British Library.

Typeset in 11pt Times by Troubador Publishing Ltd, Leicester, UK
Printed in Great Britain by the MPG Books Group, Bodmin and King's Lynn

Matador is an imprint of Troubador Publishing Ltd

*I dedicate this book to the memory of Peter Bishop
who tried tirelessly and unsuccessfully to improve
my poor English for more than 45 years.*

Contents

VOLUME 2

Land *of the* Golden Mouths

VOLUME 2

68

Seventy Per Cent Expansion

As Chiang was preparing his fourth offensive against the Communist districts in Jiangxi in the autumn of 1932, the Japanese were advancing from Manchuria into north China. The Comintern instructed the Chinese Communist Party to make use of this crisis to form an anti-Japanese alliance with any Chinese armed forces. On 17 January 1933 Mao, as Chairman of the Chinese Soviet Central Government and Zhu De, as Chairman of the Chinese Red Army Military Commission, issued a manifesto calling for the immediate termination of attacks on Soviet districts and the protection of democratic rights. They also expressed their willingness to sign a ceasefire agreement with any armed forces in order to fight jointly against the Japanese imperialists and the Nationalist Party.

The Communist Party's attempt to isolate the Nationalist Party only strengthened Chiang's anti-Communist military policy and before long his fifth offensive was on the move. With the Red Army now in peril, the Communists began to climb down. On 10 April 1934, another Communist manifesto declared that the CCP would even be prepared to join forces with the Nationalist Party to fight the Japanese invaders and that it hoped desperately that Chiang would stop attacking Soviet districts.

However, there was no let-up in Chiang's 'civil war first' policy. Nationalist planes continued bombing the Red Army in their new bases around the remote borders where three provinces, Shaanxi, Gansu and Ningxia, met. In reality Mao's policy was just like Chiang's; it was also 'civil war first'.

Mao was now determined to overthrow Chiang's government by force and on 10 October 1936 the Red Army gave a mobilisation order, pledging to crush Chiang's forthcoming onslaught. The Chinese Communist movement was then at its nadir. By the autumn of 1936 the CCP controlled only two counties, with an army of under 20,000 men. North Shaanxi was sparsely populated, making it very difficult to find new recruits, but there was definitely no chance of a second Long March. On 1 July 1951, the party's 30th anniversary, it published figures revealing the vicissitudes of Communist membership. During the first period of cooperation between the Nationalist Party and the Communist Party there had been 19,000 members, but in the aftermath of Chiang's 1927 purge in Shanghai, Communist membership had reduced sharply to just 10,000. At the time when the party had set up its Soviet districts throughout the country, the Red Army had contained about 300,000 Communists. When the Long March was over, more than 80 per cent of the Communists had gone. However, the situation changed drastically with the outbreak of the Sino-Japanese War and party membership shot up to 1.21 million.

As soon as Hitler received the news of the Xian Coup, he promptly invited Wang Jing-Wei, the pro-Japanese politician who was convalescing in south Germany, to Berlin. After these clandestine talks, the plane which had taken Wang to Berlin took him on to an Italian port, where the following day he boarded a liner to sail back to China. The secret meeting between Wang and Hitler was discovered by a Tass reporter in Berlin who reported it back to Moscow. Stalin, paranoid as always, assumed that the two were hatching an anti-Russia plot, so he instructed the Chinese Communist Party to find a way to send Chiang back to Nanking before Wang arrived in Shanghai. The Comintern directive stressed that the CCP should seek the Nationalist Government's cooperation to fight the Japanese together, while keeping the Red Army independent, that the CCP should try to expand and re-equip the Red Army and that it should stock up on food.

Acting on these instructions, the Communist Party entered into negotiations with the Nationalist Party and on 10 February 1937 it announced four pledges: first, the CCP would terminate its policy of armed uprising to overthrow the Nationalist government. Secondly, it would rename its Soviet district governments as special district governments, rename the Red Army as the National Revolutionary Army and put both under the direct guidance of the Nanking government. Third, it would hold general elections in the special districts and fourth, it would cease confiscations of land and would commit itself to carrying out the policies of Sun Yat-Sen, as well as fighting the Japanese.

It seemed as though the Communists had abandoned their dogma of reform through violence and had decided to accept Sun's methods. The country was overjoyed and the Communists were soon allowed to operate legally in Nationalist government areas. The CCP now had its own newspapers in Chongqing and it began to publish books and open bookshops as a means of strengthening the propaganda war. The Red Army set up offices in Chongqing, Chengdu and Xian. Meanwhile a group of

Communists, including Mao, Chow En-Lai, Wang Ming, Qin Bon-Shan and Tung Bi-Wu, were appointed by the Nationalist government as members of the National Political Council, a kind of wartime parliament. However, all the Communist political and military infrastructure remained intact and under the CCP control.

The leading Communists in Yan'an soon threw themselves into a comprehensive review of the failure of their earlier cooperation with the Nationalist Party in 1927, in order to make the best use of the renewed alliance. They came to the conclusion, first, that in 1927 they had not had enough public support and had not had their own army; they had obviously parted with the Nationalist Party too early. Secondly, the Communists who had joined the Nationalist Party at that time had acted too rashly, antagonising the Nationalists. The Communists had been naive and immature; their foolish deeds had included showing Wang Jing-Wai the secret telegraph from the Comintern which had instructed the CCP to organise workers and peasants to take over the Nationalist Party. Thirdly, the premature breakaway had been a great disadvantage to the party, since once they were forced underground they had limited opportunities to convert the larger population.

The party leadership now decided that until they were strong enough they should avoid conflicts with the Nationalist Party, so as to give themselves a chance to pursue their own political activities openly. The true Communist intentions were revealed in a confidential lecture delivered by an important cadre, Chang Ho, in Yan'an's Anti-Japanese University. Its main points were, first, that cooperating with the Nationalist Party did not mean selling out the interests of the proletariat. The purpose was to cover up the CCP's covert attempts to win over the masses and overthrow the capitalist regime. Secondly, the present compromise aimed to win the release of political prisoners, freedom of speech and assembly. Thirdly, the present compromise also aimed to isolate the Nationalist Party and to topple its one-party rule. The Communist leaders understood very well that an anti-Japanese policy would win sympathy from the Chinese people and win new recruits for the Red Army and the party, as well as increasing conflict among the imperialists and at the same time protecting Russia.

Chang Ho also pointed out that the Communist Party's slogan, 'a democratic republic', was something which every party and faction in the country desired and to form an alliance with these other parties was the only way to isolate the Nationalist Party. Once a democratic republic was formed, the party could use any means, open or covert, to expand the army of the proletarian revolution in order to enforce the dictatorship of the proletariat.

The CCP should use its anti-Japanese policy and differences between other parties to split them, neutralise them and win them over. Land reform was the bedrock of the class struggle, a policy which must not be abandoned. With the revolution at a low ebb, the anti-Japanese policy could be brought to the forefront and land reform could be put to one side. When the revolution reached its high tide, the land reform revolution would be brought to the forefront again.

The Nationalist security agents who had infiltrated Yan'an obtained a copy of this confidential lecture at the beginning of the two parties' second attempt at cooperation and it shocked the senior Nationalists. The Communist representative, Chow En-Lai, who at the time was stationed in Hankow, was at great pains to try to minimise the damage. He issued an open letter in which he admitted that the papers were genuine; however, things were not as they seemed, he said, since there were mistakes in Chang Ho's lecture which had already been criticised.

His explanation did not dispel the suspicions in the Nationalist Party. In fact the tactics described in the lecture were an accurate description of the Communist Party's ensuing manoeuvres. Chow En-Lai spent most of his time in Chongqing during the eight-year Sino-Japanese War using his highly accomplished diplomatic skills to secure support from the Communists' sympathisers, individuals as well as parties and at the same time to undermine the sceptics.

There was never a great deal of hope for the second period of cooperation between the two parties. In 1937 Mao told his Red Army that the Sino-Japanese War provided an extremely good opportunity for Communist expansion. Their policy should be 70 per cent expansion, 20 per cent fighting the Nationalist Party and 10 per cent fighting the Japanese. Later, at the 1959 Lu Mountain Conference, Lee Yui, Mao's private secretary, had the job of noting down all Mao's remarks. In his memoir *The True Record of the Lu Mountain Conference*, he recorded a central committee meeting on 31 July where Mao had spoken about his policy towards the Sino-Japanese War: 'Some comrades had first thought that the less land the Japanese occupied, the better; they only came round later to the unified view that it was patriotic to condone the Japanese occupying more Chinese land, as otherwise it meant loving Chiang Kai-Shek's country. There were the Nationalists, the Japanese and us in the country; a story of three kingdoms.'

The Communist Party's policy during the Sino-Japanese War concentrated on expansion. The Red Army actively confiscated guns and recruited young fighters, as well as small guerrilla and militia groups and the

Communists also worked hard on any non-Communist troops. The nearby Shanxi warlord Yan Se-San became a prime target and they succeeded in persuading Communist commanders in Yan's armies to lead 20,000 of their men away to join the Red Army. Those reluctant to go with them risked their lives.

When Chiang left north China, some provincial and county government officials were instructed to stay on in the villages and mountains behind enemy lines to continue administering their areas, while some Nationalist troops were also left behind to conduct guerrilla warfare against the Japanese in cooperation with local militias and partisans. However, when they came into contact with the Red Army, friction all too often flared up. The Nationalist armies left behind were mostly a farrago of ill-equipped mobs who were frequently mauled by the highly motivated Red Army. Sometimes when the Nationalist Army was fighting the Japanese with support from guerrillas, the Red Army would stand back in order to attack whoever survived the fight. Confidential Communist papers called this a 'triangle fight'; Red Army commanders used the two enemies to destroy each other. With the help of this tactic, all of north China behind enemy lines gradually came under Communist control and as they gained new territory the Communists established local governments, issued their own currency, mobilised young people to join the Red Army and eliminated 'bad elements'.

Within three years the Red Army's numbers had swollen to half a million, with the ostensible purpose of fighting the Japanese. The Communists demanded again and again that the Nationalist government should take into account the increased size of the Red Army, so that they could be paid more money for maintenance and be given more arms and ammunition; currently the Nationalist government was paying the Communists to maintain an army of just 45,000 men. The Communists also demanded that the land which they had already occupied should be assigned to them.

Chiang could no longer afford to solve the problem through large-scale military action, because this would destroy the alliance against Japan. The Chinese people would not accept civil war when the country was threatened by Japanese encroachment. Chiang instead adopted a new strategy to constrain the Communists; he dispatched his elite armies to lay siege to the Communist districts in Shaanxi, Gansu and Ningxia provinces and Yan'an was turned into an isolated no-go area.

The appearance of Yan'an also changed. The Nationalist government flags which had been flying on the city walls for the last two years as a symbol of cooperation now disappeared and Nationalist government badges were torn from uniform caps. Conversation and classroom lectures, at meetings or on wall posters, was now always geared to the struggle against the Nationalist Party and Yan'an seemed to have forgotten about the war with Japan.

Communist troops were still roaming freely everywhere, disobeying the instructions of the Nationalist government. In early 1941, Chiang deployed 100,000 men from his regular army in south Anhui province to ambush the 9,000 men of the Communist New 4th Army. The fighting was over within a week and 7,000 men of the New 4th Army were killed, with 2,000 breaking away. The Communists protested loudly over this tragedy; they were determined that no one should forget the annihilation of their New 4th Army. They were equally determined to ignore the fact that they themselves had never hesitated to do the same to Nationalist troops. Relations between the two parties were sinking steadily, but they did not snap entirely. The Communists still needed the Nationalist Party; they were still not strong enough to progress on their own.

A few months later, in June 1941, the German army suddenly struck at Russia. If Germany and Japan joined forces to attack Russia, then Russia would be in dire trouble and unable to offer the CCP any help. The CCP therefore wanted China to intensify its fight against Japan, in order to prevent the Japanese from venturing into Russia. The Communists' official newspaper, *Liberation Daily*, began to soften its hostility to Chiang and in September 1942 and again in January 1943, Mao sent Lin Biao, a former Whampoa cadet, to see his old headmaster Chiang in Chongqing to pledge that the Communists would follow Sun Yat-Sen's policy and fight the Japanese under Chiang's leadership. He also asked Chiang to lift the blockade in north Shaanxi, supply the Red Army with arms, ammunition and medicine and grant them equal pay with Chiang's Central Army.

Lin Biao's ambitious requests got nowhere. On 22 May 1943, the Comintern was dissolved. Mao was worried that Chiang would now regard the CCP as having been discarded by Russia and would take the opportunity to exert more pressure on them. In early June, after declaring his opposition both to warlords and to the occupation of China, Chiang told Chow En-Lai and Lin Biao that if the CCP gave up its troops and abolished all Soviet governments by August, then it would be given the legal status that had always been denied to it.

The Communists rejected outright any transfer of control of the Red Army, which by now had more than a million men, to the military commission of the Nationalist government. There was absolutely no way it would let go of its political capital and the negotiation between the two parties was destined to fail.

The Red Army (the 8th Route Army or 18th Army Corps) had few large-scale battles with the Japanese on its record. The Communist *Da Kung Daily* reported that Lin Biao's 115th Division had won a great victory over the Japanese at Ping Zin Gate on 25 September 1937. It claimed that more than 4,000 Japanese had been killed. However, this figure has been pared down in recent years by Communist historians to just 1,000 and many believe that the figure of 1,000 is still exaggerated. According to Japanese records, Lin Biao had done nothing more than ambush their transport unit. The really big battle fought by the 18th Army Corps started in August 1940. Early that spring the Japanese started an operation to smother the Communist areas in north China. They gradually pushed forward, building strongholds one after another to fortify their new occupation. After four months the Japanese had overrun scores of Communist-controlled counties and two were still left untouched. However, Communist forces managed to filter through Japanese battle lines and re-established themselves in rural areas with popular support.

To counter the Japanese offensive, Zhu De, the commander-in-chief of the 18th Army Corps and his deputy, Peng De-Huai, launched a counter-attack in north China around the Tai Hun mountain range. They sabotaged railways and retook some key positions, killing the enemy. On 20 August fighting broke out in several areas, catching the Japanese by surprise and in the first three days the 8th Route Army recaptured half a dozen Japanese strongholds, including the Jen Jin coal mine. The Japanese had given this mine particularly strong fortifications, with high walls and electric fences, because it produced high quality coal, most of which was sent to Japan. Peng De-Huai had originally planned to use 22 regiments for the operation, but once the fighting started other regiments voluntarily joined the fight along the 1,000 km front. The 8th Route Army captured a number of Japanese positions and fought hard in Yang Cheun city, in a battle which lasted seven days and nights and in which the defending Japanese troops, who were supported by 100 aeroplanes, armed Japanese residents in the city in an attempt to shore up their defences. Meanwhile the Japanese positions along the Yu-Leu highway in the heart of the Tai Hun Mountains were picked off one by one by the 8th Route Army.

In the eight-year war with Japan, large numbers of Communist-run cottage factories and offices sprang up in villages all over the Tai Hun Mountains, which have an average height of more than 1,500 metres. There were paper mills, soap factories, printing workshops and banks, as well as two arsenals producing grenades, shells and rifles. Rails removed from sabotaged railways were carried up mountain paths to the arsenals to be melted down and reused, killing two birds with one stone. The front-line headquarters of the 8th Route Army were also situated in the Tai Hun Mountains.

The Japanese struck at Communist areas with a vengeance, carrying out their 'three-all policy' – loot all, burn all and kill all – and the Tai Hun Mountains bore the brunt of their aggression. Japanese cavalrymen would make sorties into the mountains with their horses' hooves wrapped in cattle hide to muffle their sound. Sometimes parents hiding in caves were driven to strangle their own babies to stop them crying. By the end of 1940, the mountains swarmed with Japanese troops and thick black smoke hung over villages as bombers pounded them without respite.

This campaign, consisting of more than 1,800 battles fought by the 200,000 men of the 8th Route Army's 105 regiments, continued for over three months and became known as the 'one hundred regiment campaign'. Chinese casualties came to 20,000. At first it was regarded as a great victory and for three days Yan'an held celebrations in its honour. Mao even declared that if a similar opportunity arose again, he would want more campaigns of the same kind. Soon, the draconian Japanese reprisals made Mao change his mind; he decided that in fact the 'One hundred regiment campaign' had been a grave mistake. He laid all the blame for it on Zhu De and Peng De-Huai, claiming that they had made the decision to launch the campaign alone, thereby revealing to the Japanese the true strength of the 8th Route Army. Peng's wife, Pu Oun-Shiu, maintained that the campaign had been approved by Mao and the party central committee, because she had seen a telegram from Yan'an, which Peng had kept in his jacket pocket for several days, giving permission for the campaign to proceed.

The Japanese pursued their three-all policy from 1941 to 1943 and Central Hebei, Shanxi and the area between Hebei and Chahar were all left devastated, with the 8th Route Army losing 100,000 soldiers. The population in the Communist-controlled areas of north China dropped by half from 100 million to 50 million. After the 'one hundred regiment campaign', Mao decided that the Communists should keep their heads down. From then on the Red Army took no more part in any big battles against the Japanese, although Communist forces were active behind enemy lines.

By the summer of 1945, in addition to the Red Army's one million soldiers, the Communists had also organised 2.2 million militiamen and had established 19 'liberated districts' in north, central and south China, with a total population of 95.5 million. Most cities, roads and railways controlled by the Japanese were surrounded by Communist forces. In all, during the eight-year war Nationalist government troops fought in 22 major battles, some 1,000 important battles and nearly 40,000 small clashes with the Japanese, paying the price of 3.2 million casualties. The final death toll of Communist military casualties against the Japanese was 600,000. The CCP repeatedly claimed that only the Communists had fought the Japanese, while the Nationalist troops had never taken part in the fighting; so the 3.2 million Nationalist soldiers who gave their lives for their country were all forgotten for the political convenience of the CCP.

69

The 'United Front'

The 'united front' was an important strategy, or trick, used by both the Russian and Chinese Communist parties to advance the revolution. It had two purposes, one external and the other internal. Its external purpose was to win over friends and to isolate enemies. The internal purpose was described by Lenin himself. When he returned to Russia from Germany after the 1917 February revolution, he suggested creating a 'united front'. When his colleagues asked why they should ally themselves with undesirable people, his answer was that it was to give them the rope to hang themselves.

The policy of the Chinese Communist Party towards a united front was not simply a replica of the Russian original; it was devised specially to suit China. Chow En-Lai pointed out that Lenin had conceived the idea of cooperating with other political parties but had failed because of their hostility towards the Soviet regime, whereas the Chinese Communist Party had succeeded in pulling together all other political forces for its benefit. Mao said many times that they had learned from 18 years' experience that the party's three great weapons were 'the united front, armed struggle and the party establishment'.

Mao laid down the principle of the united front, which was to forge links with other small democratic parties but at the same time 'struggle' with them, which meant making them support the CCP. It was Chow En-Lai who directed all the practical operations. Mao would not permit anyone to meddle with his army or the party, as both were in his powerful grip, but he allowed Chow a free hand on the united front. Chow judiciously stayed clear of army and party affairs, spending most of the eight years of the Sino-Japanese War in Chongqing trying to trap his quarry; this greatly helped him escape the fate of being liquidated by Mao.

During the second period of cooperation between the Nationalists and the Communist Party, the Communists were allowed to work openly in Nationalist areas. Nearly all Communist activities were now geared towards forming the united front. They kept in close touch with the press, making friends with some people and attacking others, particularly those in the upper echelons. Some Nationalists were very sceptical about the outlook of working with the Communist Party, while the Communists were worried that the sceptics might influence the Nationalist Party policy and damage the standing of the Communist Party.

Chow En-Lai often told his Nationalist colleagues, either in person or through the sympathisers of the CCP that 'a great and noble person like Chairman Chiang Kai-Shek' should be the leader of all the parties and of the whole country and not just the leader of one party. This implied that those selfish scepties wanted to keep the brilliant leader for their own party. Mao also showed his skill in the art of flattery to benefit the Communists when, on 29 September 1938, he wrote to Chiang, saying 'Your Excellency is leading the whole nation in fighting an unprecedented national revolutionary war and every Chinese person adores you.' Even after the New 4th Army incident in 1941, the Communist Party was still stressing – on 7 July 1942, the fifth anniversary of the Sino-Japanese War – that 'the whole nation should unreservedly support Chiang's leadership in the Sino-Japanese War.'

Apart from striving to win sympathisers inside the Nationalist Party, the Communists also worked tirelessly on all the other small political parties and in October 1941, after considerable manipulation by the Communists, the Alliance of Chinese Democratic Political Parties was born. Although members of this Alliance wanted the Communist Party to join them to make it into a more powerful political body, the Communists preferred to stay out of it but nevertheless use it for their own ends. The Nationalist Party was now outnumbered by two to one.

The Communist refusal to join the Alliance caused dissatisfaction and division and a couple of member parties left. After reorganisation, the Alliance was reborn as the Chinese Democratic League. This new set-up was open to individuals rather than parties and many distinguished intellectuals became members. It managed to absorb nearly all the political forces outside the Nationalist Party and the Communist Party and from day one it worked under the influence of the CCP. After Chow had instructed his party's Hong Kong office to give assistance to the Alliance, it launched its own newspaper, the *Kwang Ming Daily*, in Hong Kong in late 1941. Several Communists were sent to join it in order to ensure that it echoed Communist policy faithfully.

One of Mao's calculated moves was his demand for a coalition government. This suggestion not only struck at the Nationalist Party's unpopular one-party rule, but also functioned like a magnet, attracting many left-wing intellectuals and the small, ambitious political parties to the

Communist Party. These new members formed a chorus calling for the immediate termination of one-party rule and they made ferocious attacks on the Nationalist government. All this was of course very useful to the Communist Party, whose underground operatives in return looked after the wellbeing of these junior partners. Whenever the intellectuals were in difficulty, anonymous and mysterious characters would suddenly appear, giving them badly needed money, finding them jobs, helping them to flee from Japanese-occupied zones and even arranging for one wife to have an abortion.

By the time the Second World War was approaching its end, the Communists had succeeded in discovering the political stance of all the important people in Chongqing, both inside and outside the Nationalist Party. The Communist Party had successfully identified its friends and it had also infiltrated, undermined and split the Nationalist Party. The focus of the united front was now diverted to America. After eight years of ruinous war China badly needed American aid and American opinion became more important to the Nationalist government. The Communist Party now transferred their best foreign-language talents to Chongqing to work under Chow. There were about a dozen of them, all of whom later held important government positions in Communist China. Among them were Wang Bin-Nan and his German wife. Wang Bin-Nan later became the Chinese Ambassador to Poland and headed the team to negotiate with the Americans in Panmunjon during the Korean War. Two others, Chel Kwan-Hua and Chang Han-Fu, later became respectively foreign minister and deputy foreign minister, while a fourth, Lew Cheng-Gee, eventually headed an organisation in charge of relations with the overseas Chinese. This high-calibre team, helped by Sun Yat-Sen's widow Madam Soong Ching-Ling, concentrated all its energies into driving a wedge between the Americans and the Nationalist government and winning American sympathy.

One of the reasons Chiang did not take further action against the Communist New 4th Army was his wariness over the possible American reaction. Immediately after Chiang had eliminated the New 4th Army in 1941, President Roosevelt sent his assistant, Dr Laughlin Currie, to see Chiang, taking with him a letter from the president making a favourable comment on the Communist Party and urging the Communists and Nationalists to work more closely together to fight their common enemy, Japan.

The Americans could see what was happening in Chiang's government, but not what was happening far away, in blockaded Yan'an. The impression they gained of the Communist Party came from the astutely

438

polished Chow and his devoted team. Owen Lattimore, who had become Chiang's political adviser on the recommendation of President Roosevelt, together with two officials at the US embassy in Chongqing, John P Davis and John S Service, frequently met with Chow, who repeatedly invited the American government to send representatives to visit Yan'an. The Communists were hoping to obtain a share of American aid. Disillusioned by Chiang's government, the Americans advised their State Department not to ignore the Communist Party and they pronounced Chiang's government to be hopeless. The American government had to interfere to force the Nationalist government to lift the siege around the Communist districts and allocate lend-lease supplies to the Chinese Communists, who the Americans considered to be democratic fighters driven by nationalism and supported by the populace and not really true Communists at all.

American journalists in China had long disapproved of Chiang and their dislike of his regime was much aggravated after Stilwell's departure. B Atkinson of the *New York Times* and Theodore White of *Life* magazine both filed stinging reports about Chiang and many American pundits were predicting that the Communist Party would triumph over the Nationalist government; in the future there would be two Chinas, a feudal China ruled by the Nationalist Party and a democratic China ruled by the Communist Party. President Roosevelt could not ignore all these opinions completely.

As Chiang's defence in central China was collapsing in 1944, Stalin urged that Communist forces should be used to fight the Japanese. Under American pressure Chiang eventually agreed that US representatives could visit the Communist district in north Shaanxi and in July 1944 an American delegation including John Service went to Yan'an, where they held talks with Mao, Zhu De and Chow.

Mao, in a recent speech in Yan'an, had denounced the Nationalist Party for its reactionary collusion with American imperialists, saying that they were making use of peace talks to mount an attack on the Communist Party; the Communists therefore had to be prepared for self-defence. Mao had also pointed out that Stalin's slogan 'Defeat Germany in one year, Japan in two years' was the creative idea of a genius who had brought encouragement and hope and had lifted the morale of all mankind. If some people felt angry that Stalin's slogan had not been realised, they should direct their resentment towards the British and American imperialists who were reluctant to open up a second theatre, thereby inflicting further years of torment on China.

When Mao, Zhu De and Chow met the American visitors, they spoke with a very different tune, expressing their complete willingness to cooperate with America during and after the war. After the meeting John Service again advised the State Department that America should work with the Nationalist liberals and the Communists to reform the Chinese government. He spoke highly of the great achievements and the democratic spirit of the Communist Party and said he believed they would not oppose American interests in China. He therefore recommended equipping and training the Communist troops without worrying about the reaction of the Nationalist government. The CCP also invited Stilwell to visit Yan'an; its hand of friendship was stretched out to all Americans. Stilwell in return had many a good word to say about the Communist Party in his diary. In building up a rapport with Stilwell, the Communists successfully put further pressure on Chiang.

From 1943 onwards even some senior Nationalists privately began to reveal their deep dismay about the government's incompetence, nepotism and corruption and about Chiang's opinionated, autocratic rule. When Sun Yat-Sen's son, Sun Kor, made a speech on 5 May 1944 on the subject of political and economic freedom, his criticism of the Nationalist government irritated Chiang, who promptly accused Sun Kor of defaming his government, of cooperating with the Communists and of using Russian backing to usurp his position as head of the government.

Chiang had a habit of turning his friends into enemies, whereas the Communist Party's united front policy won friends and goodwill. Chiang was alienating his government from the people and driving them into the Communist camp.

70

Elephant's Tusks

Before the outbreak of war with Japan, Chinese government revenues came mainly from coastal areas; 54.3 per cent from import duties and 26.4 per cent from salt tax, mainly from the salt farms along the coast in the provinces of Hebei, Shandong, Jiangsu and Guangdong, while another 13.7 per cent came from textile and flour mills in several of the larger cities along the coast. The coastal areas were lost in the early stages of the war, removing most of the Chinese government's sources of income. But although revenue was greatly reduced, military expenditure continued to rise, until it swallowed up an average of over 63 per cent of the government's entire revenues every year.

The Chinese government encouraged businesses in the east to move inland to southwest China to escape the Japanese advance and to this end it offered subsidies, loans and cheap transport, which it could now hardly afford. Chinese agriculture had already been showing signs of stagnation before the war and the country needed to import wheat and rice. The bad harvests in 1940 and 1941 pushed up the price of rice, starting a chain reaction which affected many other goods. Annual inflation rose to 153 per cent and briefly reached 280 per cent. Speculators started hoarding goods and raw materials and even national financial institutions such as banks, post offices and government officials joined in the profiteering. When the government tried to bring inflation under control by suspending industrial loans, production, already sluggish, came to a complete halt.

By now junior army officers and other ranks were being paid between one thirtieth and one fiftieth of what they had earned before the war. Some servicemen turned to smuggling, sometimes even supplying the enemy with goods from inland. Ordinary people were similarly hard hit by inflation. The government fixed the exchange rate at 20 Chinese dollars to one US dollar, but soon the rate soared to 450 to one on the black market. Only the powerful and privileged could still purchase American dollars at the official rate from the banks, thereby making enormous profits. Many soldiers, aggrieved at their own financial hardship, lost the will to fight and this factor played a considerable part in the major Nationalist government defeat in central China in 1944.

The already crisis-ridden Chinese economy suffered further destruction from the Japanese economic blockade, pillage and sabotage. In occupied areas the Japanese appropriated crops, minerals and products such as tea and silk. Sometimes the items were seized by Japanese troops and sometimes they were requisitioned; at other times they were purchased in bulk through cooperatives. The Japanese restricted Chinese access to 'military materials', in other words metal, timber, paper, rubber, paint, cement and other materials. In some areas food was rationed, but the Japanese would make sure they had enough while the Chinese almost starved. The Japanese also set up banks in occupied areas, printing worthless money and banning Chinese currency.

The war often forced the Chinese to damage their own economic resources. When the Chinese Army retreated, they would often sabotage mines and destroy crops to stop them from falling into Japanese hands. The Chinese authorities urged peasants in occupied areas to grow less cotton so as to provide fewer raw materials for Japan and they stopped almost all trade with the occupied areas.

While China was fighting the Japanese invasion, another invasion, by Russia continued unchecked. In early 1943 Stalin became worried that the Japanese might attack Russia and as a precaution he evacuated all the mining and aeroplane manufacturing equipment from Xinjiang province. In June the Xinjiang warlord Sing Xee-Choy fell out with Stalin and in September Nationalist government troops moved into Xinjiang. The Russians in response organised riots in Xinjiang, supplying the rioters with weapons through Outer Mongolia and in May 1944 the Russian ambassador Aleksandr Panyushkin left China, together with the Russian military advisory delegation. As a concession Chiang transferred Sing away from Xinjiang, but this did not stop Russia from making more trouble. In November 1944 a riot took place in Ili and in January 1945 the Russian Army helped the rioters to seize the town; 4,000 Chinese soldiers died in the engagement. Obviously, helping China to fight the Japanese was not a Russian priority.

In February 1945 Roosevelt, Churchill and Stalin met in Yalta to discuss the political settlement in post-war Europe. In exchange for a Russian agreement to fight Japan in Asia, Roosevelt and Churchill accepted the following Russian terms. First, Outer Mongolia would maintain its status quo, which meant it would remain under Russian control. Secondly, the

442

Chinese naval base at Lushun would again be leased to Russia. Thirdly, the Chinese city of Dalian would be 'internationalised' and Russia would have special privileges there. Fourthly, Russia would regain a preponderant interest in the Chinese Eastern Railway and the Southern Manchurian Railway.

These concessions to Russia, at the expense of Chinese sovereignty, were negotiated by the Americans and British while leaving China in the dark.

Although the Russian Communists had declared in 1919 that they would renounce Tsarist Russia's pillage and exploitation in China, after the Russian Red Army had pursued the Russian White Army into Outer Mongolia it had stayed on to organise the secession of Outer Mongolia from China. Stalin reneged on the 1924 Sino-Russian Treaty in which the Russians had acknowledged that Outer Mongolia was part of China and that the Chinese Eastern Railway belonged to China. Both Roosevelt and Churchill meanwhile forgot their four-year-old Atlantic Charter, which had acknowledged the principle of no national boundary changes without the consent of the country concerned.

Stalin's plan was that, two or three months after the German surrender, he would secretly move 25 army divisions across Siberia to the Far East. He asked the British and American governments to say nothing of this to the Chinese until his military manoeuvres were complete and his troops were at the Manchurian border. China had been in this situation before; the Yalta deal reminded the Chinese people only too well that the diminution of Chinese sovereignty enshrined in the 1919 Paris peace talks was still continuing in 1945.

The awkward job of informing Chiang of the decisions made in Yalta by the three real superpowers fell to President Roosevelt, who in mid-March told the Chinese ambassador to America, Wai Tao-Ming, a quarter of the truth in order to test the Chinese reaction to this sellout. He was also concerned about Stalin's real intentions in China and sent Patrick J Hurley to Moscow in April to seek reassurance. Stalin and Molotov pledged Russia's full support for American policy in China; they would acknowledge Chiang as the leader of the only legal government in China, they would respect Chinese sovereignty in Manchuria and they would support American efforts to mediate between the Nationalist government and the Communist Party in order to build a united and democratic China. But Stalin insisted on China agreeing to the Russian demands first; only after this treaty had been signed would Russia declare war on Japan. He wanted the Chinese foreign minister, T V Soong, to go to Moscow before July to begin negotiations.

443

President Roosevelt died in mid-April 1945 and in late May the Russian government repeated the same pledges to his successor President Truman's envoy, Harry L Hopkins. On 22 May Patrick Hurley, now the American ambassador to China, told Chiang about the clause of the Yalta Treaty concerning China, but Chiang was unwilling to comply. Hopkins, Hurley and the American ambassador to Russia, Averil Harriman, separately urged Chiang and other senior Chinese officials to sign the Sino-Russian Friendship Treaty without delay. They pointed out that Russia had already agreed to enter the Sino-Japanese War; once the Russians had entered Manchuria it would be difficult to get them out, and by then they might well have come up with further demands. The Russians had stressed repeatedly that they would support Chiang's government and would have no contact with the CCP. After this deal was concluded the hope was that, with America as witness, the Russians would not break their promises.

Soong led his negotiating team to Moscow on 30 June. Chiang's son Chiang Ging-Kuo, a Russian expert who was among its members, described his team's position by saying that 'a weak country has no diplomacy. Other countries are chopping knives, but we are fish or meat, putting up with all the blows and seeking a way to survive. All we can do is to take the blows which will do the least harm.'

Negotiations began on 2 July, with Stalin browbeating the Chinese delegation. He wanted to designate Lushun and Dalian as Russian military zones and to assume ownership of the Chinese Eastern Railway, the Southern Manchurian Railway and their subsidiaries. He also wanted China to acknowledge Outer Mongolia as an independent country. If the Outer Mongolian problem was not solved, there would be no more negotiations.

On 6 July Chiang sent a telegram to Soong saying that the Chinese government would offer the people of Outer Mongolia a referendum after the war with Japan. If they voted for independence, they could have it. But that was unacceptable to Stalin. He told Chiang Ging-Kuo, 'I haven't asked you to help us. If your country has the power, you can fight the Japanese yourselves, then I would not submit any demands... I want Outer Mongolia purely for military strategy... If a military power attacks Russia from Outer Mongolia and cuts off the Siberian Railway, we would be finished.' Chiang Ging-Kuo argued that neither China nor a defeated Japan would be able to attack Russia from Outer Mongolia, but Stalin replied that a third party could do so. When asked whether he meant America, Stalin answered, 'Of course'.

The Sino-Russian negotiations made slow progress. Soong did not want to put his signature on the treaty and be remembered as the man who had sold out China and he accordingly resigned as foreign minister, to be replaced by Wang Si-Je. On 6 and 8 August 1945 two American atomic bombs exploded in Japan, causing 200,000 casualties. Although this figure was far smaller than the number of Chinese casualties in the Rape of Nanking, it was large enough to persuade Japan to consider surrender. Stalin now realised he would be unable to claim that Russia had defeated Japan and so he abandoned his blackmail that the deal must be in black and white before he entered the war against Japan. Instead, at midnight on 8 August, he sent a 600,000-strong army into China, declaring war on Japan the following day. On 10 August he warned Soong that it would be better for the Chinese government to reach an agreement with Russia as soon as possible, otherwise the CCP army would invade Manchuria.

On 13 August, the Allies received Tokyo's offer of unconditional surrender and, at the same time, China and Russia held their ninth discussion about the treaty, originally intended as an incentive to lure Russia into the war. Japan formally announced its unconditional surrender on the following day and the Sino-Russian Friendship Treaty was finally signed on the same day.

In the end the Chinese government had had to make considerable concessions, giving away three million square kilometres of Outer Mongolia and control of the two cities of Lushun and Dalian, with the two railways, in exchange for Russian promises that they would respect Chinese sovereignty and the entirety of Chinese territories. The Russians also promised that they would not interfere in Chinese internal affairs, in Xinjiang or anywhere else, that Russian armed forces in China would begin to withdraw three weeks after the Japanese surrender and that the withdrawal would be completed within three months.

Soong later said that this treaty would bring 30 years of peace and cooperation between China and Russia. It recalled the words of Lee Hong-Cheng in 1896; after signing a secret treaty in St Petersburg giving Russia special privileges, Lee Hong-Cheng was so pleased with his achievements that he told people that he had bought China 20 years of peace. Within two years, the bear returned, growling and biting for more treats. Half a century later, Soong did considerably worse than Lee Hong-Cheng. His 30 years turned out in reality to be less than three months; the bear again came back howling for more 'friendship'.

The Japanese commander-in-chief in China, General Okamura, surrendered to the Chinese on 9 September. During the eight-year Sino-Japanese War, the Nationalist government had recruited 12 million soldiers and 14 million labourers. The total number of Chinese military and civilian casualties was over 20 million, with 100 million people made homeless.

Property destroyed in the fighting was estimated to be worth between $500 and $800 billion.

There is an old Chinese saying: 'Elephants get killed because of their tusks'. In the same way China attracted avaricious predators.

71

A Chinese Ally

By the end of 1944, Stalin had obtained more American aid to support his army, one-and-half-million-strong and he now moved it to the Far East, where it was deployed along the 4,000 km Sino-Russian border, preparing to sweep into Manchuria and Inner Mongolia. The American government had satisfied most of Stalin's requests, giving him 40,000 vehicles and 200,000 tons of fuel, thereby enabling most Russian soldiers to ride into Manchuria in American vehicles.

At that time the Japanese Guan Dong Army had a total of 750,000 men in Manchuria; in addition it could call upon the collaborating Manchurian army, the Mongolian army and the Japanese Army in Korea, making a total of 1.2 million men. Towards the end of the war, the quality of the Guan Dong Army had deteriorated to such an extent that it was no longer an elite force, the pride of the Japanese Army. All the well-trained and battle-hardened units had been transferred to reinforce the Japanese Army in its ill-fated battles in the Pacific or else sent home to protect the motherland against the threatened landing of Allied forces. Most units still remaining in China were newly formed, inadequately trained and composed of men either too old or too young. Their military equipment, which was generally inferior to that of the Russians, was also depleted, since half had been shipped back to Japan. According to Japanese figures, when the Russians moved into Manchuria the Guan Dong Army had only 160 working tanks, 155 military planes and 500 training aircraft – although the Russians published a set of vastly inflated figures after the war, claiming that the Guan Dong Army had more than 1,100 tanks and 1,800 military planes.

The Guan Dong Army had built large numbers of military shelters and bunkers along the eastern and northern borders of Manchuria, but they were mainly for attack rather than defence and there were very few defensive structures behind the border. Consequently, once the Russian Army had broken through Japanese lines, it was an easy journey to the centre of Manchuria. The desolate, sparsely inhabited and seemingly endless grassland of Inner Mongolia, to the west of Manchuria, was neglected by the Japanese. They never dreamed that the Russian Army, far better equipped and fully mechanised, with 2,000 tanks, would drive into the undefended desert and grassland and push forward into Manchuria.

While the Japanese military leaders in Tokyo were arguing about whether to fight on or to surrender after the atomic bomb blasts, their instructions to front line troops in China was anything but clear. On 9 August, the day Russia declared war on Japan, the ill-prepared headquarters of the Guan Dong Army decided to evacuate all Japanese residents to North Korea. This should have presented no problem, since all railways were under Japanese military control. The evacuation was led by the commander-in-chief's family and he was followed by army officers with their families, valuables and any loot, taking over the trains at the expense of civilians and ordinary soldiers. On the following day railway stations swarmed with Japanese people, with tearful women and children begging the guards to let them board the trains, leading to scuffles with the military police. It was a chaotic and desperate scene which reflected the end of the Japanese dreams of a good life in a conquered country.

The Russian Army, commanded by Marshal Rodin Malinovsky, advanced into north China in three columns. When Japan formally surrendered on 14 August, the Russian right column ignored the order from Allied headquarters to cease fire and instead continued to advance in order to rendezvous with the CCP Army. Several CCP armies in north China had already received orders from Yan'an to move quickly into Manchuria; they were not going to miss this golden opportunity for expansion. Most of the Communist forces were spread around north and east China among the Japanese-occupied areas, whereas the Nationalist government's main forces were far away in southwest and northwest China. The Russian Army met the CCP troops to the north of Zhangjiakou (Kalgan), an important city which was soon seized by CCP troops with the help of Russian cavalry. The Japanese Army had been using Zhangjiakou as its headquarters for Inner Mongolia and the military supplies stored there in vast quantities were captured by the Red Army troops of Lin Biao and Hor Lone. In under two months they were able to build up a well-equipped, modern army of 200,000 men. The 100,000-strong Communist army commanded by Lor Yung-Wun and Leu Jing-Chao was also supplied with weapons captured from Japanese troops by the Russians and as more CCP forces arrived they were in turn equipped by the Russians. It was estimated that the weapons the Russians seized in Manchuria were sufficient to equip 800,000 men and a large proportion of them were handed over to Chinese Communist troops, who soon spread out over Manchuria.

The Russians had recognised Chiang's government as China's legal government and had promised him that Russia would not support the CCP. On 14 September 1945, one month after the Japanese surrender, a Russian military plane paid a surprise visit to Yan'an, bringing a colonel from the Russian Far East military command to meet the Chinese Communist leadership. Mao and Chow were currently away in Chongqing holding talks with Chiang and in their absence Liu Shao-Qi was left in command. The Russian colonel, as Malinovsky's representative, expressed sympathy for the CCP Army, but said he had to ask them to leave Manchuria, as Russia's reputation was at stake. Liu Shao-Qi detected double-dealing and he suggested that the CCP troops could enter Manchuria but not using the names of either the CCP or the 8th Route Army. This solution was accepted by the Russians and senior Chinese Communists were invited to go to Manchuria to ensure smooth cooperation between the Russian and Chinese Communist armies. A group of senior Communists, including Chan Yun and Peng Zhen, accordingly left for Manchuria in the same Russian military plane. It was known that all Russian policies concerning China, down to the salaries of Russian advisers in China, had to be approved by Stalin himself and it was obvious that the policy of quiet military cooperation between the two Communist parties had been decided by Stalin.

As soon as the Chinese Communist troops marched into Manchuria they gave themselves new names, such as the Manchurian People's Autonomous Army, the Manchurian Democratic Union Army and the Manchurian People's Liberation Army and so on. When the Nationalist government discovered that the Chinese Communist troops had already entered Manchuria they protested many times over the Russian breach of trust, but the Russians replied that the armies were the Manchurian people's autonomous and democratic armed forces engaged in fighting the Japanese and that they had nothing to do with the Russian Army. Soviet Russia had no intention of interfering in Chinese internal affairs.

Although some Japanese units in north Manchuria fought back fiercely against the Russians for about a week, on the whole the Guan Dong Army did not put up much resistance, particularly in the south. The Russians were worried that American marines could enter Manchuria via Dalian port and they were therefore in a great hurry to occupy the important areas before the arrival of the American army in order to wield greater bargaining power. In less than a week the Russian Far East armed forces took over the whole of Manchuria, as well as neighbouring Ehol province. Before the end of the week the Guan Dong Army had surrendered.

Instead of being occupied by the Japanese, Manchuria was now occupied by the Russians, who were known as China's allies. Russian soldiers committed all kinds of atrocities, beating and shooting Chinese people with trigger-happy abandon. Their victims in Harbin included a senior CCP commander, Lu Dong-San, who was robbed and killed. The widespread Russian rapes recalled the notoriety they had earned during the Boxer riot in 1900 as the most enthusiastic rapists. Russian terror shook Manchuria from north to south, with many women cutting off their hair to make themselves unattractive, while Japanese women in PoW camps shaved their heads and pretended to be men. In cities such as Changchun and Dalian, the streets were deserted from 4 or 5 p.m. When there were no women to grab in the streets, drunken Russian soldiers smashed open the doors of local residents to look for women and sometimes all the female members of a family would fall victim, including seven-year-old girls. The CCP turned a blind eye to all these Russian outrages, concealing them from the rest of the country.

In late September and early October 1945 the Nationalist government dispatched a delegation, headed by General Shon Sae-Fei and his deputy, Lt General Tung Yan-Ping, to Changchun to discuss the transfer of Manchuria back to China. The Nationalist government's undercover agents in Manchuria emerged to inform them of the true state of affairs in Changchun. The Russians would only allow Communists and Communist forces to operate in Manchuria, though the rule was slightly relaxed in Changchun itself because of the presence of the Nationalist delegation. There were two Communist newspapers in Changchun, both of them hostile to the Nationalist government; Nationalist Party agents had applied to launch their own newspaper, but they were unable to get permission from the Russians.

Shon held four meetings with Malinovsky between 13 October and 5 November, with each meeting more difficult than the last. The Chinese had hoped to have a smooth transfer of power, with Chinese troops moving into areas immediately after a Russian withdrawal, leaving no vacuum in between, so as to maintain public order. They sought Russian permission to fly in a small number of troops to big cities including Dalian, Harbin, Changchun and Shenyang and at the same time bring in larger numbers of troops by sea to land at Dalian. Shon asked the Russians to allocate them trains and ships to transport the Nationalist troops.

Malinovsky replied that Dalian was a commercial port and the Chinese Army could not land there either by sea or by air. It belonged to the military port of Lushun, so the Chinese request to inspect the city could not be approved. Furthermore, trains serving the lines through Changchun had been either sabotaged by the Japanese or taken to Korea; there were very few trains and steamships in service, so the Russians were unable to assign any of them to the Nationalist troops. The Chinese Army would be only allowed to fly into Harbin, Changchun and Shenyang two days before the Russian withdrawal.

The Chinese delegates argued that Dalian and Lushun were both Chinese territory and the Chinese government had the right to inspect anywhere on Chinese soil; but the Russians tried to prevaricate by saying they "would have to seek instructions from Moscow", which meant it would be the last time they talked about this matter. When the Chinese argued that the two days which the Russians were proposing to allow them for flying in troops to the cities was not enough and they should be allowed seven days, Malinovsky's answer was, as usual, that he would 'have to seek instructions from Moscow'.

At the final meeting, Malinovsky insisted that Chinese troops would not be allowed to land at Dalian. If the Chinese tried to land at Yingkou city, north of Dalian, then Russia could not be held responsible for their safety because a certain armed force was already there. Shon accused the Russians of being uncooperative; after more than a month of futile discussion, they had made no progress on the transfer of power in Manchuria. Malinovsky showed their heated exchange by banging the table and saying he would have to report to Moscow. Shon also banged the table and replied that he would also have to report to his superiors.

Less than three months after signing the Sino-Russian Friendship Treaty, the Russians finally revealed the motive behind their non-cooperation. On 15 November, at a discussion of economic affairs, the Russian military representative and economic adviser, Sladkovsky, handed over to his Chinese counterpart, Chang Kung-Cheun, a document declaring all the industrial equipment in Manchuria to be Russian property. It also listed 154 major Manchurian resources which were to be run by the Russians, in cooperation with the Chinese. It was clear to the Chinese that this cooperation would be in name only and that in reality the Russians wanted everything. Chang replied that economic matters had to wait until after Russia had handed Manchuria back to China. Sladkovsky made it clear that if the Russians were not given what they wanted, they would not discuss any Russian military evacuation from China. After all, he said, 'the Russian Army came to liberate the Manchurian people, Russian blood has been spilt on Chinese land, so shouldn't you give us a little economic benefit in return?'

Malinovsky soon sent his unequivocal message to the Chinese saying that Russia regarded all the important Manchurian industrial resources as spoils of war – the electricity industry, coal mines, iron mines, steel industry, machinery industry, chemical industry, brick factories, cement factories and salt mines, as well as eight airfields. They were generously prepared to allow the Chinese to have 50 per cent of them as Chinese capital for joint enterprises, but all managing directors and general managers would have to be Russians, although their deputies could be Chinese.

The Nationalist government disputed the Russian definition of war spoils. It decided that the Russians could not be trusted; even if they were given all these economic benefits, they might still refuse to leave Manchuria. The Nationalist government resisted the Russian demands, saying they would discuss economic affairs at a later date.

Meanwhile the Americans were helping to transport the Nationalist Army to north and east China, while at the same time 53,000 American marines landed to guard Peking, Tianjin, the important Kai-Ren coalmine and the railway between Peking and Shanhaiguan, in an attempt to halt Russian expansion. When Nationalist troops tried to land at the ports of Yingkou and Huludao in Liaodong Bay, north of Dalian, in late October they were shot at by Communist forces on shore and had to turn back. In late November, the Nationalist Army fought its way ashore successfully in Qinhuangdao and Huludao, capturing the two ports and so enabling reinforcements to land.

The situation in Changchun was getting more and more dangerous for the Nationalist government staff. On 29 October, the Russians sacked the Changchun police chief and replaced him with a Communist. Communist troops were converging near Changchun; some of them had already infiltrated the city and shooting in the Changchun suburbs went on day and night. The Nationalist delegation now decided there was no useful purpose in remaining in Changchun and, after obtaining permission from the central government, they prepared to leave, leaving behind a small group headed by Tung Yan-Ping to maintain contact with Malinovsky. The rest of the delegation returned to Shanhaiguan, the gateway to Manchuria in Yu county. This small town contained 42 Nationalist government department offices crowded together, all waiting to go to Manchuria.

The Chinese frustration caught the Russians by surprise and soon they became more cooperative. Some Communist newspapers in Changchun were closed down and others began to show less vociferous hostility towards the Nationalist government. Stalin himself tried to steer Chiang to the neutral ground between America and Russia and made some attempts to please him.

In September 1945 Stalin recalled three Russian representatives stationed in Yan'an, who took away with them their radio transmitter to show they had no more contact with the Communists. On 19 November, the Russians formally informed the Manchurian Bureau of the CCP that all Chinese Communist offices and troops had to remove themselves within three days from the big cities of Manchuria, so that the cities could be handed over to the Nationalist government. At the same time Chinese Communist forces were banned from obtaining more war materials from the Japanese army warehouses controlled by Russian troops.

When the Russian army commander in Shengyang, a presumptuous major general, went to inform Peng Zhen, the head of the CCP Manchurian Bureau, that all the Communists were to leave Shenyang, Peng and his colleagues urged him to reconsider. The major general said bluntly that these were his orders. They were to leave Shenyang and if they refused to go he would use his tanks to expel them. The meeting ended in a blazing row; Peng demanded to see Malinovsky, who refused to see Peng and in turn suspended all contact with the Manchurian Bureau.

Instructions from Yan'an arrived quickly, ordering the Manchurian Bureau to agree to the Russian demands, since after all the Russian officers were only following their government's orders and the CCP was keen to avoid clashes with the Russian Army. The Manchurian Bureau accordingly left the big cities voluntarily, instead setting up bases in rural areas. Some of the leading Chinese Communists would not forget this Russian perfidy.

Wu Shiu-Cheun, the second chief of staff of the so-called Manchurian Democratic Union Army and later on the deputy foreign minister of Communist China, recalled in his memoirs that they had been told on 4 October 1945 by Russian Army officers that there was a big Japanese arsenal near Shenyang which could be handed over to the Chinese Communist Army. The Communist central leadership acted on this information, ordering the 8th Route Army in Shandong province and a division from the New 4th Army to hurry to Shenyang to take over the arsenal, leaving their own weapons behind. By the time the troops arrived at Shenyang in mid-November the Russians had changed their minds; they now said that because of international considerations, it would not be possible for the CCP army to take over the arsenal.

On 10 December 1945, Stalin invited Chiang Ging-Kuo to visit Moscow. The Chinese, Stalin said, had to understand that the Americans were using China to pursue their own interests. They would sacrifice China when it suited them. Russia, on the other hand, was willing to supply China with machinery, vehicles and any other goods the country needed. At the same time the Russians hoped China would provide them with minerals and agricultural produce. They could help China build heavy industries in Manchuria and develop the economy in Xinjiang. But most importantly, the Chinese must absolutely not allow American soldiers into China. If even a single American soldier was present in China, it would be difficult to solve the problem of Manchuria.

On 6 June 1946, Stalin invited Chiang to visit Moscow or to meet him at the border. Chiang said that Stalin was used to playing dirty tricks; this invitation was designed to alienate China from America and he would not be duped. The Russians were angry that their economic extortion was having no effect and the calm between Russia and Nationalist China did not last long.

The American General G Marshall had put forward a plan to form three-man military teams, each containing one American, as a means of solving the disputes between the Chinese Communists and the Nationalist government. On 10 January 1946 one of these new teams arrived in Shenyang and overnight the Russian attitude turned ugly; from then on, the path leading to the transfer of power in Manchuria was full of thorns. Communist newspapers in Changchun, closed down a few months earlier, were now resurrected and Chinese Communist troops were given free passage on the Russian-controlled railway from Harbin to Changchun, boarding the trains in full military uniform and disembarking in civilian clothes to find their way into Changchun city. When Tung Yan-Ping asked the Russians for an explanation for this, the Russians replied that they had no information about these matters.

The Chinese Communist armed forces in Manchuria were constantly many times bigger than the Nationalist security forces. They now started to make surprise attacks on Nationalist positions and on the railways; in many cases, when these attacks were over Russian servicemen were found among the Communist casualties. On 13 January, 20,000 Communist troops took control of the Anshan power station in order to prevent electricity from being sent westwards into Nationalist areas. On 15 January, 1,000 Nationalist security troops found themselves disarmed by Russian guards when they returned to Changchun city after completing some work in a suburb; all were sent to a Prisoner of War camp. The following day, a senior Nationalist mining engineer, Chang Sen-Fu, was murdered.

In January 1946, Chang was ordered to negotiate with the Russians for the return of the Fushun coalmine to Chinese ownership. His six-man team travelled to Shenyang by train, accompanied by a Russian officer, Lt General Marle and on arrival in Shenyang they checked into a hotel to wait for a special train to take them on to Fushun. Chang inquired repeatedly, but Marle now told him that there was no train available and that public security in Fushun was so bad that it was dangerous to go there. Finally Marle decided to go to Fushun on his own to find out about the situation, leaving the anxious Chang behind.

On 10 January, Chinese delegates in Changchun telephoned Chang to say that Marle had arrived at Fushun and that he had rung to say that he had arranged everything and was now waiting for Chang. Four days later Chang, accompanied by seven technicians and seven railway policemen, left for Fushun, where the party was met by Russian officials and taken to a mining club. Once there, the railway policemen were immediately disarmed by local public security agents and placed under the guard of Russian troops. At 8 p.m. on 16 January, Russian army officers and local police went to see Chang, telling him the mine could not be transferred and that it would be better if he returned to Shenyang straight away.

At 8.40 p.m. the party was taken to the railway station and put on the same train that had brought them; their Russian army escorts meanwhile boarded a different carriage. When the train arrived at a small station 25 km from Fushun, it was surrounded by Communist troops. They dragged Chang, his technicians and policemen off the train and took them to a gully, where they were stripped and then stabbed to death. Tung Yan-Ping later protested to the Russians, pointing out that the murders had happened near a small station inside a Russian-controlled area and that the victims were under Russian Army escort on the same train.

The agreed time for the Russian Army's total withdrawal from Manchuria had long expired, but the Russians plainly had no intention of going. In February 1946, there were demonstrations by Manchurians in Chongqing demanding that the Russians leave immediately. On 19 February the Russian ambassador, Petrov, told the Chinese foreign minister, Wang Si-Je, that nothing could be settled until the two countries had solved the problem of spoils of war and he also protested about the anti-Russian demonstration. On 22 February a further demonstration took place, with 20,000 Chongqing students stabbing portraits of Stalin, smashing up the sales office of the CCP's *New China Daily* and chanting anti-Russian slogans. Meanwhile students in other cities staged their own anti-Russian demonstrations. The outbursts of anti-Russian feeling were criticised by the Chinese Communist Party.

Malinovsky finally announced that the Russian Army would leave before the end of April, but that due to transport problems he could not give an exact date. Neither could they wait for the Nationalist forces to take over.

Since the Chinese government would not agree to economic cooperation, the Russian Army would leave their area to whatever armed forces were on the spot, which in practice meant the Chinese Communists. Soon after this, the Russian Army often left suddenly, without notifying the Nationalist government representatives, making it difficult for the Nationalist troops to take control promptly. In many cases the Russians simply handed over control secretly to the Chinese Communist troops.

In late January, Tung Yan-Ping informed the Russian authorities that Chinese officials were ready to take over Heilongjiang province. A Russian lieutenant general replied that there were large numbers of illegal armed forces in the province, which the Russian Army was engaged in suppressing and it would therefore be better if the Chinese officials were to wait in Harbin for a further week or ten days. In the event Nationalist officials waited in Harbin for more than a month, only to read in the Changchun newspapers reports of a newly established Communist government in Heilongjiang province.

The outlook for Harbin was not propitious either for the Nationalist government delegates. Nearly 80 per cent of the men in the city's public security bureau were Communists and intelligence obtained by the mayor indicated that there were about 15,000 armed men in plainclothes inside Harbin waiting to help the Communist troops outside to capture the city. The Communists inside Harbin had already chosen a factory in which to detain the Nationalist government staff and they were considering whether to assassinate the police chief.

In Harbin there were some 3,000 policemen loyal to the Nationalists, armed with a total of 900 rifles, each provided with a few dozen bullets. It was not enough to maintain law and order in the city, let alone fight a war. Towards late April, the safety of the Nationalist staff in Harbin was becoming clearly shaky and four aeroplanes were sent to evacuate more than 70 people to Shenyang. Another plane was sent on the morning of 24 April, but by then armed men had sabotaged the runway and had attempted to capture the airport. The Nationalists still trapped in Harbin sent radio messages telling the plane to go away. They later persuaded the retreating Russian Army to take their group, a total of 72 people, into Russian protection and, leaving with the Russians by train, most of them made their way to Vladivostok and from there to Shanghai.

Qiqihar, the capital of Nanjiang province, was another important city in north Manchuria. When the Russians first arrived there, their commander ordered the Manchukuo chief official to hand over power to a Chinese Red Army commander, Yu Ng-Fu. On 16 January 1946 the Nationalist government staff, headed by the newly appointed Nanjiang provincial chairman, Peng Gi-Cheun, arrived in Qiqihar. The Russians, under their KGB officer, Colonel Burjev, immediately sent the Communists out of the city and then ordered the Manchukuo official to meet Peng and his team at the railway station and to hand over power to them. Peng's authority was hardly valid inside Qiqihar. On 10 April and again on the 16th, he cabled Tung Yan-Ping, reporting that although he now had 7,000 security policemen, the 4,000 inside Qiqihar had only 2,000 guns between them, while the rest of the men were outside. They were often being attacked by the Russians who were protecting the Communist troops, helping them to expand and moving them around by train. Nationalist efforts to recruit extra security policemen were constantly being obstructed by the Russians. Meanwhile Chinese Communist troops were now less than ten miles away from Qiqihar and they had already seized two railway stations south of the city. Peng asked Tung to send him some troops by air.

But Peng's telegram was never dispatched. The Russians intended to keep his team in Qiqihar and to prevent them from having any contact with their headquarters in Changchun and Shenyang. The Russians told Peng that both the telephone and the telegraph services had broken down. Peng then sent his own man to question the staff at the telegraph office. He found out that both services were working as normal. Eventually he was forced to send a messenger to hitch a lift on a southbound Russian army truck to Harbin and then travel by train to Changchun in order to deliver his message.

Tung replied that he was unable to support Peng with troops and ammunition by air. Since there was no chance of Peng being able to resist the Communists, he and his team of 21 men were obliged to give up Qiqihar city and on 23 April two Russian army trucks took them to Harbin. By then the Nenjiang River bridge on the main road was under the control of Chinese Communist troops, but because Peng's team were escorted by Russian liaison officers they were allowed through.

After the breakdown of the Sino-Russian talks in early March 1946, the Nationalist government delegation discovered that the Russians in Shenyang were quietly moving around and that some of the Russian troops had now moved into the barracks of the Nationalist security forces in Changchun and Harbin. Tung suspected that the Russians were evacuating and on 8 March he asked to see Malinovsky, only to be told that the marshal was fully occupied and could not see him for another two days. He then asked to see the deputy chief of staff, Lt General Derogenko, but received the unsurprising answer that Derogenko was away on a business trip and that the two Russian liaison officers had both been taken ill. Tung could see that the Russians were leaving Manchuria, but deliberately keeping the Nationalist government in the dark so that the Communists could make pre-emptive manoeuvres.

On 11 March, Derogenko saw Tung at the Russian Far East Army headquarters. He said that the Russian Army would have left Shenyang completely by 15 March and that they did not think it was necessary to inform the Nationalist government delegation formally, since its Chinese staff had already taken control of the local government and police. The Nationalist government team knew they were not in a strong enough position to defend themselves, so they decided to withdraw all staff from the few Manchurian cities which they controlled and to request Russian assistance to move their troops by rail to Changchun and other areas.

It was amidst this tension that the first of two battles took place in Xi-Ping between the Communists and the Nationalist government. The strategically important city of Xi-Ping, half way between Shenyang and Changchun, was the crossing point of two railways; it was a prosperous commercial and industrial city with a large population. The Russian Army finally left Xi-Ping on the night of 13 March and the city was immediately surrounded by Communist troops. On the 15th they launched an attack and by the 17th the city had been totally cut off.

In Changchun, Tung again went to see Derogenko and said that so far the Chinese government had only been able to set up a few local governments in Manchuria; there had not been enough time to build up a strong administration. Under the terms of the Sino-Russian Friendship Treaty, Russia was obliged to protect these Chinese officials. Now the local government officials in Xi-Ping were in danger and Tung urged Derogenko to ensure that the Russians kept their promise. Derogenko replied that they had received no information about fighting in Xi-Ping; all they had heard was that a railway bridge had been destroyed and some rails damaged.

On 20 March, the officials in Xi-Ping managed to send a message to Tung telling him that fighting had ceased and their offices had been destroyed in gunfire, but that most staff were unhurt. There were no trains or engines in Xi-Ping, but they hoped a train could be sent from Changchun to take them away. The following day Tung went to see Derogenko and asked for a Russian liaison officer to be sent to Xi-Ping to help bring out the stranded officials, but Derogenko answered that they could not do so because they understood that the fighting in Xi-Ping was still going on. Worrying about his trapped colleagues, Tung was extremely distressed and, swallowing his pride, he entreated Derogenko to rescue his men. At last the Russian relented, promising to report to Malinovsky and try his best to help.

Tung now sent his assistant, Major General Zhu Sen-Min, to see the Russian deputy managing director of the railway, Lt General Kalgin, to ask for a train to be sent to Xi-Ping. Kalgin refused to comply without Russian Army permission and Zhu kept turning up at the railway office without getting a satisfactory answer. On the morning of 23 March, on yet another visit, he overheard a Russian official shouting down the phone: 'It's Marshal Malinovsky's order. Have you got the special train ready for Xi-Ping? Who is it that dares to delay the Marshal's order?' Kalgin was a lot more friendly this time. He said that for the sake of Sino-Russian friendship, he had decided not to wait for instructions from the Russian Army and instead would shoulder the responsibility himself for sending a train to Xi-Ping to evacuate the Nationalist government staff. Zhu and his colleagues thought that these were typically double-faced Russian tactics, trying to use the railway to cover up their secret military manoeuvres.

The Communist forces in Xi-Ping were ten times bigger than those of the defending Nationalists, whose forces were composed mainly of police and public security guards. In less than three days the fighting was over and Xi-Ping fell under Communist control, until on 20 May, some two months later, it was recaptured by the Nationalist Army.

Meanwhile Changchun in early 1946 was engulfed by the smell of gunpowder. On the eve of the withdrawal of the Nationalist government staff, the Russians installed a Communist chief to run the police force, which was already in Communist hands. When a policeman was murdered on 15 January, pedestrians near the scene were all thoroughly searched and one man carrying a Nationalist Party membership card was accused of being the murderer. Large numbers of plainclothes police started patrolling the streets and the following day posters appeared on walls bearing anti-Nationalist slogans.

At 8 a.m. the following morning the police captain of the Nationalist delegation protection corps, who had previously served Manchukuo but was now loyal to the Nationalist government, reported to Tung that his corps had received an order to attend a lecture in the police department at nine o'clock. He advised Tung to be prepared for trouble and for his party to be ready to defend themselves. By eleven o'clock, water, telephone and electricity had all been cut off. The existing police protection corps was disarmed and replaced with a new Communist police force, whose members restricted people going in or out of the building and the building was surrounded with heavy machineguns trained on it.

At noon a 'public trial' of the assassin was held in the old Da Tung Square, now renamed Stalin Square. The Russian Army had built a tall monument in the centre of the square consisting of a fighter plane perching on top to commemorate the heroic deeds of the Russian air force. The square was now guarded by armed police carrying rifles with fixed bayonets. Tung saw all this while on his way to meet the Russians at their headquarters. He mentioned what he had seen to the Russian commander, who claimed to know nothing about it but said he would send soldiers there at once to disperse the crowd. When Tung informed him about his delegation which was now under siege by the police, the Russian pretended to look surprised; he promised to rectify the situation and report to Malinovsky about it. Late that afternoon, the hostile police guards were replaced by Russian soldiers.

The slimmed down delegation, which contained representatives from central government departments and senior officials from Manchurian cities and provinces, as well as reporters from Peking, Tianjin and Shanghai, numbered more than 400 men in all. Tung announced that for safety all of them would have to stay together and the delegation residence was turned into a barrack-style dormitory. Before dusk fell everyone was inside.

Armed policemen kept Changchun in a tense atmosphere, searching people in the streets and making arrests. The Nationalist government now suspended its plan to fly in troops to Manchuria and on 20 March Tung wrote to both Malinovsky and the railway authorities to inform them that the Chinese government intended to move its army to Changchun by train and he requested Russian assistance. The deputy managing director of the railway, Lt General Kalgin, replied that they did not object to transporting the Chinese Army; there was however a plague in the Shenyang and Xi-Ping areas and in order to prevent the spread of the epidemic the Russian Army had stopped all traffic in the area. In any case there were no trains, coal, or water along the line and furthermore Russian railwaymen had been attacked. As a result it would not be possible to transport the Nationalist government troops to Changchun.

After more arguments, Kalgin finally agreed to provide the trains. On the following day, he submitted new conditions. First, the transport of Chinese troops to Changchun would have to be approved by the Russian Army; secondly, if Chinese troops travelled northwards by train through the plague area, they would be required to stop half way for nine or ten days for quarantine. Only once they were found to be clear of the plague would they be allowed to proceed to Changchun.

Before the evacuation of the Russian Army, Communist troops had already begun to attack outlying areas around Changchun and it was obvious that their actions were the prelude to a Communist offensive against Changchun. Tung pointed out that all these areas were under Russian control and the Russian Army should therefore have done something to stop the fighting. Derogenko replied that they had orders to withdraw and were not prepared to interfere in local infighting. Worrying about the safety of the Nationalist government staff in Manchuria, Tung asked Derogenko to allow his staff to retreat with the Russian Army into Russia, from where they could make their own way back to mainland China. Derogenko replied that he could not understand why the Chinese staff should follow them to Russia. After they withdrew there would be no need to contact each other any more. He would have to seek instructions from Moscow about taking the Chinese with them.

Tung was angry and upset; he felt the Russians wanted all his colleagues dead. In the end, though, the foreign ministry in Chongqing managed to resolve the impasse through negotiations with its Russian counterpart and an agreement was eventually reached allowing the Nationalist people to leave with the Russian Army.

On 1 April, Communist forces struck at the airfield in the suburbs of Changchun, with the intention of preventing Nationalist government reinforcements from arriving by air. The 2,000 security guards at the airfield fought back all night and by dawn the Communist troops had been beaten back. They were still close by, waiting for the Russians to depart.

In the evening of 5 April, Tung threw a farewell party for Malinovsky and his 20 commanders. Shortly before dinner was served, Malinovsky said to Tung: 'I understand very well that you are in a difficult position. Your country has adopted a pro-American policy, yet here you are in Changchun talking friendship with us. These two positions are plainly incongruous and it is very difficult for you to cope. You have my sympathy.' Tung did not have time to reply.

The following morning the Chinese delegates bade farewell to the Russians at the railway station and Malinovsky and Tung spent about an hour strolling together in the station square. Malinovsky spoke amicably. 'Last night,' he said, 'you brought up the subject of a military takeover. Although the dates of our troops' evacuations from different areas have already been arranged and are to be completed before the end of April, if the Chinese Army has any special requests for the Russian Army to leave cities like Changchun or Harbin on a certain date so that your troops can arrive to take over, you can negotiate with Moscow through Chongqing to get a satisfactory answer. It has always been our country's wish to return Manchuria to the Nationalist government army. Our army was to leave on 3 December last year, but your delegation left Changchun suddenly, so we could not go ahead with the transfer and had to delay our departure temporarily while waiting for your army to arrive. This long wait has caused a lot of misunderstanding, which is why we have to leave quickly now. We are worried that your people may mistakenly think we are handing over power everywhere to the Communist troops. There is a mutual need for Sino-Russian cooperation and we certainly don't want to have any more misunderstandings or to part company in discord. I hope your delegation can go to Harbin with us to maintain contact and I will stay there for two weeks where we can discuss everything.'

Derogenko also revealed that after the previous night's dinner they had received instructions from Moscow telling the withdrawing Russian Army to maintain contact with the Nationalist government delegation. Tung found the sudden change of Russian tune perplexing and the following day he flew to Shenyang to seek guidance from Shon Sae-Fei. However, just before their withdrawal from Changchun, the Russian commanders secretly gave a guided tour to the Communist commander of the Manchurian Democratic Union Army. This officer, whose troops had already surrounded Changchun and were ready to attack the city once the Russians were gone, was taken around Changchun in an armoured vehicle looking to all intents and purposes like a Russian Army patrol and he reconnoitred the positions of the Nationalist troops who had been flown in waiting to take over from the Russians.

The Nationalist government, already in a disadvantageous situation in Manchuria, now made matters worse for itself. One day, soon after Shon Sae-Fei had gone to Changchun to hold talks with Malinovsky, 15 horse-drawn carriages packed with senior and middle-ranking officers of the Manchukuo Army called at Shon's office, where they offered their services to the Nationalist government. They were good fighters who had been trained by the Japanese. After conferring with his aides, Shon advised Chongqing to accept them all into the Nationalist Army, but the Nationalist government disagreed, deciding to reject all the officers. The Nationalist army minister, General Chan Chen, turned away the Manchukuo Army simply because there was no provision for them in his budget, at a time when Changchun was occupied by the Russian Army. Soon afterwards, Lt Col Wong, an officer in the Russian army, later known as Commander Chow Bo-Jon, who was in command of the Chinese Communist troops in their attack on Changchun, swiftly and quietly persuaded the resentful Manchukuo Army officers to join him.

The Communist united front policy to attract enemy soldiers used the slogan 'Come to us. You will be given promotion in our army.' The policy was highly successful and almost immediately 15 divisions of the

Manchukuo Army, about 200,000 men in all, went over to the South Manchurian Army of the Communist commander Lin Biao, taking their weapons with them. As a result Lin Biao's military strength was increased with breathtaking speed. These Manchukuo troops later fought under Lin Biao at the beleaguered Changchun, a battle which was to become one of the Nationalist government's first disasters.

From the beginning of April, Communist troops began to push closer to Changchun. On 14 April, Major General Karloff, commander of the Russian Army in Changchun, left the city with his remaining men and senior Nationalist staff went to the railway station to bid him farewell. As soon as the train carrying the Russians had rolled away, the platforms were sprayed with Communist bullets. Panic ensued; public transport in the city was suspended, shops were closed and people hastened home. It was an unequal battle, with about 8,000 Nationalists, mostly public security guards and policemen, pitted against some 40,000 Communist troops equipped with powerful Russian artillery. The defending force was overcome a few days later, in the early hours of 17 April.

In Harbin that same day, Malinovsky complained to Tung that a Russian railway engineer had been shot dead soon after the Russian Army had left Changchun. Why were the Chinese authorities not protecting the Russians? Russian flags and portraits of Stalin were being desecrated. The Americans were well protected everywhere; why was China treating her allies differently?

Tung replied that as soon as the Russian Army had gone, Changchun had descended straight into war. The security guards and policemen were engaged in fighting the much larger and more powerful Communist forces and there was no manpower to spare to protect foreigners. If the Russians and Chinese had handled the transfer of power better and the Nationalist troops had moved in closely on the heels of the Russian withdrawal, then war could perhaps have been avoided.

With the Japanese brought to their knees by the two atomic bombs, the Russians were able to advance into Manchuria without much resistance and in only six days they occupied the whole of Manchuria. From the seventh day onwards, the Russians also began looting. They issued large quantities of worthless currency, with crudely printed notes without serial numbers and this new currency soon began to circulate widely in Manchuria. Everywhere penurious Chinese, as well as Japanese residents were busy selling their belongings; their customers were mainly Russian servicemen who walked away with the hapless people's possessions after paying them with worthless paper. The Nationalist government later tried repeatedly to obtain details of this shady financial business and about the total face value of the currency already in circulation, but they failed to extract an answer from the Russians.

The Russians also appropriated all the money and valuables belonging to ordinary people kept in Manchurian bank vaults, looking on them as yet more spoils of war. No receipts were given and the loot was deposited in the Russian Red Army Bank.

Because of Chiang's refusal to give in to Russian economic blackmail, the Russians disassembled and took away most of the industrial equipment in Manchuria. They removed 65 per cent of the equipment from the power stations, as well as all the important machines from the Shenyang aeroplane factory, from the Yingkuo magnesium factory and from mines, oil refineries and iron and steel furnaces. They removed 50,000 railway carriages and locomotives, leaving behind just 4,000 ramshackle carriages. Trucks and buses were all taken to Russia. Whatever could not be taken away they tried their best to destroy. After they left, the production at China's biggest coal mine, at Fushun, was down to less than five per cent of its former capacity. The destruction of China's biggest steel factory, at Anshan, was particularly thorough; all its buildings were ruined and it cost a fortune just to replace all the broken glass in windows and doors. Production was down to less than one per cent.

The Russians claimed they were taking away Japanese property as war compensation, although they failed to explain how they could obtain compensation by destroying buildings. The Russian Army dug up the entire length of the 181 km Nenjiang–Ningnan Railway and took it away, tracks and all. This railway had been built and paid for by the Chinese government before 1931, the year the Japanese made their first move to invade Manchuria. The railway had later been seized by the Japanese, but it still legally belonged to China.

An investigation team in 1946 came to the conclusion that the Russians had taken away equipment from Manchuria worth US$858m; including damage from sabotage, China's total loss was estimated at US$2 billion.

Lushun and Dalian remained Russian-occupied zones for the next ten years, until 1955.

72

The Peace Talks

Following the Japanese surrender, the Supreme Commander of the Far East Allied Forces, General Macarthur, ordered the Japanese Army in China to surrender only to Nationalist troops belonging to the legitimate Chinese government. In other words the Japanese were not to hand over any land or weapons to the Communist Army. The Americans also lost no time in flying Nationalist troops to big cities such as Shanghai, Peking and Tianjin which had been surrounded by Communist troops during the eight-year war. Without American help, it would have been very difficult for the Nationalist government to take control of these cities. The American fleet meanwhile transported many of Chiang's troops from southwest China to land at Qinhuangdao, south of Shanhaiguan. From there these troops advanced to Shenyang.

At the same time General Hu Jone-Nan, who commanded Chiang's 400,000 well-equipped troops in northwest China, hurriedly dispatched nearly a third of his forces to north China and Manchuria, hoping to increase his influence there. His armies had spent the war years besieging the Communist base of Yan'an area and, unlike other war-weary Chinese troops, they were still in excellent condition, having taken no part at all in the fighting against the Japanese.

In all, Chiang's regular army numbered some two million troops, with a similar number of militiamen and security guards; together they controlled a large part of China and some 300 million Chinese people. The Communists had some one and a quarter million regular troops, plus about 2.6 million militiamen and together these troops controlled an area containing some 100 million people. The Chinese Communist Party was therefore a formidable force and it wanted the right to accept the Japanese surrender in its own areas. Nearly all the railways in north China were now either under the control of or surrounded by Communist troops, who sabotaged many of them to prevent Nationalist troops from moving into north China. At the time of the Japanese surrender most cities in north and east China were still

465

occupied by the Japanese, who were waiting to surrender to the Nationalist government troops, but many of these cities were besieged by Communist forces and fighting continued even during the prolonged civil war peace talks.

In November 1945, several groups of the Communist forces in north China and Manchuria joined together to form the Northeast Democratic United Army, with Lin Biao as commander-in-chief. With Russian blessing they set up their headquarters in Jiamuse, Heilongjiang province. Mao later admitted that this army had been founded initially with only 100,000 men, but after one month its manpower had more than doubled and by February 1946 the army had grown to half a million men. The success of the Communists depended in part on working hard to build up groups of leading party members everywhere, paying special attention to winning over peasants. Political activists lived with the poor peasants, indoctrinating them with Communist political ideas. Taking care to adopt only mild policies, they demanded reductions in rent and interest payments for poor peasants, while allowing the landlords to remain. They obtained pay rises for factory workers, but encouraged industry to grow and still permitted the owners to make profits. They organised elections to establish local governments and secured the support of the people by improving their living standards. This policy presented the Communists in a good light even in Nationalist areas, whereas Chiang relied more on his well-equipped military forces, one third of whom now had American weapons.

Japan finally offered its surrender on 10 August 1945. Within a few hours Zhu De, the commander-in-chief of the Communist forces, swiftly issued orders instructing all Communist commanders to seize the Japanese-controlled areas, which meant seizing Japanese weapons as well. He also sent Chiang a telegram, under Mao's guidance, protesting against Chiang's order that all Communist forces should remain where they were. On 14 August, Chiang replied by inviting Mao to talks in Chongqing and he repeated the same request three times in one week. On 27 August, the American ambassador Patrick Hurley flew to Yan'an as a peace broker together with the Nationalist government representative, Chang Tze-Jone, to offer Mao a safety guarantee. On the following day he flew to Chongqing together with Mao, Chow En-Lai and several other senior Communists. Chiang's untrustworthy reputation made Mao's arrival in Chongqing look like an act of courage and so the Communists had won the first round. If any harm had come to Mao, Chiang would naturally have been the first to be blamed and he therefore assigned his own security unit to protect Mao. Even though no one was genuinely optimistic about these talks, they began without delay.

With the shadow of civil war looming over the country, the Chinese people, worn out by wars, were longing for peace; few wanted to plunge into fratricidal conflict. Both Chiang and the Communists had to try to find a political solution, to show that after all they had peace-loving natures. Besides, the Chinese Communist Party could not count on Stalin's full support, because Stalin, in his attempts to woo Chiang away from America, had advised the communists to avoid civil war and instead seek a compromise with Chiang and disband the Red Army. In addition, Chiang's armies seemed more powerful than the Red Army and even a short spell of peace could give the Communist Party a chance to strengthen its armed forces.

On 18 September, Mao made a speech at a political tea party in which he said the time had come for the peaceful development of the country. Chinese people had to unite and suppress all internal strife. All political parties ought to follow the leadership of the Nationalist government chief commissioner, Chiang Kai-Shek, to accomplish the dream of the late Sun Yat-Sen to build a new, modern China. He finished his speech by yelling, 'Long live Chief Commissioner Chiang Kai-Shek!'

People who knew Mao said that his adulatory outburst was motivated by fear, because that day he had allowed a fellow Communist, Lew Cheng-Gee, to use his car and the car had been shot at. He thought privately that the bullets had been meant for himself and he repeatedly asked his old Nationalist friends: 'Will I return to Yan'an alive?'

When a senior Nationalist invited Mao to dinner at his home, there were about half a dozen guests, all of them like Mao natives of Hunan. One guest, Zuo Shun-San, said that the Chinese people had suffered tremendously during the eight-year war and they badly needed a period of rest. They all hoped that the Communist Party would not continue opposing the Nationalist government; it was better to have peace.

Mao answered that he was avenging the people of Hunan. They had spilt more sweat and blood in the Northern Expedition and in the war with Japan than anyone else, but they had not been rewarded with high positions in the Nationalist government. It was extremely unfair. During his stay in Chongqing Mao repeated the same speech to people from Hunan whenever he had the chance. Mao's listeners saw very well that he was trying to fan regional dissatisfaction against the Nationalist government and did not seem to be interested in preventing a civil war.

The bargaining between the two power-hungry parties went on for 41 days and nights. After endless discussion, either one to one or in groups, an agreement of a sort was hammered out on 10 October 1945, but none of the key issues were really settled. The two parties would talk again about nationalising armies, reforming the government and enforcing control of their territories. On 11 October Mao flew back to Yan'an.

Two days later Chiang gave a secret order to purge the 'Communist bandits' and his army quickly captured 30 Communist-controlled cities. The Communists put up strong resistance, thwarting the Nationalist Army's attempt to advance deep into north China and Manchuria. At the same time the Communist Party organised a campaign in Nationalist areas protesting against civil war. Before the end of 1945 Chiang was under pressure to accept American mediation and a new American peace broker, General G Marshall, appeared on the scene. After four days of discussion between Marshall, Chow En-Lai and the Nationalist government representative, Chang Cheun, a ceasefire plan was agreed, together with a plan for a consultative political conference to be attended by 38 delegates representing all political parties, to be held soon in Chongqing.

73

A Fascinating Negotiator

Mao Tse-Tung's meetings with Chiang in Chongqing were only symbolic peace talks; the hard bargaining was done by the Communist Party's star negotiator, Chow En-Lai and the Nationalist government's propaganda minister, Wang Si-Je.

During his schooldays in Tianjin, Chow had proved to be a very talented actor, something which proved to be a great asset in his diplomatic career. In early 1920, the leaders of the Chinese Youth Party in Paris set up a patriotic association to oppose the Chinese warlords, which accepted people of all political hues. It included Nationalists, Communists, members of the Chinese Youth Party and many others who were not affiliated with any political party. Chow was one of the directors of this association, as well as the underground leader of the European branch of the Chinese Communist Party. The Communists were eager to recruit new blood and their members began to spread Communist propaganda within the association. Gradually friction developed among members, so much so that they often came to blows, using anything at hand – fists, sticks or stones – and producing many bleeding heads. Chow, as the head of the Communist branch, could not be unaware of the fighting beforehand but he did not want to see the patriotic association collapse, so after every scuffle he would do his best to mend the cracks by inviting leading members of either side to drinks, explaining that there had been a misunderstanding and urging both parties to cooperate as they had before. He looked so sincere that people forgot he was in reality the manipulator behind the troubles.

Years later when Chow attended the Chongqing peace talks, he was always accompanied by a couple of Communist delegates. However, he was always the main speaker and often talked for hours non-stop. Only when he went to see Chiang would he go on his own.

Although it had always been Communist policy to be friendly with Russia and hostile to the West, in dealing with the American peace broker Marshall, Chow assumed a completely new approach. He kept all his customary hostility and aggression towards America well hidden and presented his group as a collection of weak, sad people who were being persecuted by the powerful Nationalist fighting machine. During the talks, which continued in all for two years, he won sympathy from Marshall and his aides, who felt that the Nationalist government was too intolerant and demanded that the Nationalist Army should cease hostilities immediately. When the Nationalist troops followed the ceasefire orders, Communist troops would break up and then inch forward at night. If they came across weak parties of Nationalist troops, they would attack and disarm them. Therefore every time there was a truce, it would be followed by further Communist expansion. Half of the credit for these Communist gains should go to Chow.

Chow did not neglect the small parties. The consultative conference initiated by Marshall opened in early 1946 and during the first three months of that year Chow paid visits nearly every evening to two well-known figures from the small parties, Lee Wung and Zuo Shun-San. He would spend an hour claiming he was there to report to them the inside story of the conference, which the two men had not attended. According to Lee Wung, the so-called inside story was in fact Chow's untiring attempt to emphasise that the ruling party lacked sincerity over the peace talks, that the Nationalist government was preparing for civil war and that the Communist Party was losing out everywhere. But Lee Wung felt the Communists were no more sincere than the Nationalists.

To members of the small parties, as well as to Marshall himself, the Nationalist government's insistence that the Communists should relinquish their army before entering talks about political reform seemed sensible, a view which was undoubtedly unhelpful to the Communists, intent as they were on using the peace talks to expand their power.

But Chow did not reject this point directly; instead he said, 'Now the gentlemen from the third parties have suggested nationalising the armies and then democratising politics, a proposal which is supported by all Chinese people and by the Americans. The Communist Party certainly dares not disagree. But we are determined to form a coalition government first and then nationalise the armies afterwards. We want to do it this way not only for the CCP, but also particularly for the political status of you gentlemen, members of the third parties. It is obvious that the third parties nowadays are esteemed by the people as playing an important role because of your abilities and your policies, so the ruling party is forced to invite you in as opposition parties. You hold the balance between the Communist Party and the Nationalist Party and you stoutly support peace. If we hand over our armies first, then what happens if the ruling party, after unifying the armies, backtracks on forming a coalition government? What can you rely on to force the ruling party to democratise politics? I myself feel that the Communists' few tatty guns represent not only the Communists' capital, they also represent the third parties' capital. Please think about it and don't make all of us lose our bargaining chips.'

From that moment onwards, the consultative conference dropped the subject of military affairs; instead it only discussed politics and, later on, the question of drafting a constitution. Military affairs were still in the hands of the three-man units: one American, one Communist and one man from the Nationalist government.

Apart from the convincing argument above, Chow also had other tactics to steer the third parties away from interfering in military affairs. In October 1946, the exhausted and despondent Marshall asked the third parties to help arrange one more meeting with Chow. A third party leader, the celebrated scholar Leung Shu-Ming, argued that the Communist Party and the Nationalist government should stop their fierce fighting in Manchuria first, otherwise there was no point in having peace talks. He and his colleagues drafted a plan for enforcing a truce in Manchuria, according to which the rival armies were to stay inside their designated boundaries. They offered their plan as a suggestion to the three-man units.

Chow's dramatic reaction, in front of Leung Shu-Ming, was to burst into tears. He complained that Leung Shu-Ming was not behaving as a friend. His assistant, the united front specialist Lee Wai-Han, joined in, heaping verbal abuse on another third party figure and the meeting broke up in bitterness. But Chow did not leave without mending fences; before he went back to Yan'an, he invited Leung and his colleagues to dinner and drinks, apologising and thanking them for their hard work. The alcohol helped to wash the bitterness away.

One senior Nationalist who took part in the peace talks later commented that it was fascinating to watch Chow En-Lai's performance at the peace talks. He could change the basis of his argument so adroitly as to be imperceptible. He would make just enough small, nominal concessions to allow the negotiation to continue and only when one studied what he said afterwards did one realise that actually he had not made any concessions on any key issues. If Chow En-Lai was acting, he did it extremely well. He would leave one with the impression that his reaction to every point during the negotiations was truthful and that he was an honest and upright man. If he told a lie about his party line or shifted his ground, he would present it in such a way as to make it impossible for anyone to reproach him for contradicting himself.

The main force among the third parties was the Chinese Democratic League, which had been founded with Communist sponsorship. Two months after its birth, it signed an agreement with the Communist Party, pledging that it would not negotiate with the Nationalist government without consulting the Communist Party first. In return the Communist Party gave the Chinese Democratic League financial assistance to publish its own newspaper, allowed it to set up branches in Communist-controlled areas and offered jobs to its unemployed members. Chow's attentive care showered on the third parties was so flattering that it could not fail to produce heartfelt thanks. Their members, mostly intellectuals, usually had modest incomes, yet there were many political and social gatherings in Chongqing for them to attend. The rich and the powerful had cars, while the poor had to make do with rickshaws, which often overturned due to the bad condition of the roads in this hilly city. Whenever there was such a gathering, Chow would send a jeep to fetch them and he let it be known that his small car was kept especially for his third party friends.

In addition to wooing the third parties, Chow also made Marshall a happy man. He announced at the political consultative conference that the Communist Party acknowledged Chief Commissioner Chiang Kai-Shek's leadership in the eight-year Sino-Japanese War and they would continue to do so in the future. They would always respect the Nationalist Party's status, which had been won in a hard historical struggle. The Communist Party, he said, had not tried to overthrow the Nationalist government since 1936, nor had it fought against the Nationalist Party for national leadership.

The political consultative conference opened on 10 January 1946 and finished on 31 January. On the last day Chow, on behalf of Mao and the Communist Party central committee, thanked Marshall for having been so even-handed and emphasised that the Communist Party was prepared to cooperate with America on local and national affairs. American-style democracy, he proclaimed, would begin in China and China would follow the American way and work hard to promote democracy and science. Especially it would promote agriculture, industrialisation, free enterprise and the development of individualism to build an independent, free and prosperous China. He also hinted that Mao hoped to visit America.

The basic agreement was finally signed on 25 February, Chow solemnly pledging that the Communist Party would abide by the agreement to cut down the size of the Red Army. Three days later, the three-man team left to inspect the north China war zones. When they arrived at Yan'an Marshall was given a warm welcome, Mao proclaiming in a speech that 'all Chinese people should be thankful to General Marshall, General Chang Tze-

Jone and General Chow En-Lai. They have worked loyally and unselfishly for a peaceful, democratic and united China. Let us cheer the long-term Sino-American cooperation, long-term cooperation between the Nationalist Party and the Communist Party and long-term cooperation of all political parties.' The Communists even composed a song to praise Marshall:

> We are singing for you, singing for your loud and clear call
> of peace.
> Your great influence extinguishes the spreading fire of war.
> Oh! General Marshall, the Red Army offers you the highest
> salute.
> We Communists support you!'

No other American has ever been given such a eulogy by the Chinese Communists.

When Mao saw Marshall off at the airport, someone asked when he would go to Nanking. Mao replied that he would go whenever Chairman Chiang asked him to. Marshall was seemingly moved and left Yan'an a happier man.

74

Not a National Hero

Chiang and Mao gave their ceasefire orders simultaneously on 10 January 1946. However, fighting continued to flare up in many places. The civil war in Manchuria was still smouldering and when the wind blew it burst into flame. One catalyst was the conference resolutions which had outlined the composition of the future coalition government. The Nationalist Party was allocated half the seats in the new government's National Commission, while the remainder went to the non-Nationalists and any change of policy would have to be approved by two thirds of the members of the commission. Chiang had long been accustomed to being accountable to no one and could not tolerate having his power curtailed by anyone, least of all the Communists, so he accepted the resolutions only under American pressure.

On 10 February 1946, ten days after the end of the conference, the Chinese Democratic League held a big celebration in Chongqing. Chiang's security agents arrived, marched onto the platform and beat up a number of the society's most renowned members. Chow sent Chiang a protest letter, but Chiang refused to meet him and flew to Shanghai to demonstrate his complete rejection of Chow and the Communist Party.

For a long time Chiang refused to recognise the smaller political parties. When six small parties joined together to form the Chinese Democratic League, they decided that their first step would be to establish themselves outside China, after which they would fight for their legitimate status inside China. The Chinese Democratic League accordingly announced its birth in Hong Kong on 10 October 1941. The Nationalist authorities denied that there was such a party, but four of its founders soon went public in Chongqing to declare their organisation's existence. From then on, under the manipulation of the Communist Party, it became a thorn in Chiang's flesh and by mid-1944 it could boast large numbers of supporters. Two of its members in Kunming, Professors Won Yi-Dor and Lee Kung-Po, published a pamphlet entitled *Freedom Forum*, which was full of statements such as, 'What do we need? First freedom, second freedom and third freedom!'

Businessmen and industrialists echoed the criticism of the Nationalist government's political and economic restrictions and urged the government to implement democratic reforms.

Lee Kung-Po was a well-known patriot. Back in 1936, he had been one of seven leaders arrested and thrown into jail in Shanghai by Chiang for calling for resistance against the Japanese invasion, but when war broke out he was released. He had been beaten up in Chongqing for celebrating the achievement of the political consultative conference and he was now denounced as a pro-Communist activist. On the evening of 11 July 1946, when he and his wife were walking back home in Kunming, he was shot by an assassin; he died in hospital before dawn.

The other author of the pamphlet, Professor Won Yi-Dor, had originally been a stern anti-Communist, but when he was teaching in the Consolidated University in Kunming he had become a pro-Communist and had joined the Democratic League. With the advent of high inflation he could not support his family of seven and had to supplement his income by teaching in a high school and by carving seals at night. Even so, the family was still struggling on the poverty line, while the corrupt Nationalist officials were enjoying the high life. He gradually became more radical and began to attack the government openly. On one occasion he protested at a university seminar: 'We haven't got enough to eat; how can we do research? We are told not to make trouble, but we have to make trouble. There is only one way out – revolution!'

After Lee Kung-Po's assassination, Won Yi-Dor called an urgent meeting of the Democratic League, which decided to publish an open protest letter and form a committee to organise Lee's funeral. He received many threats, but refused to go into hiding. The funeral service was held on 15 July, but for his own safety he was not asked to give the memorial speech. During the service Nationalist security agents began to stir up a commotion and Won Yi-Dor angrily accused the agents of murdering Lee. He said, 'Not only do the murderers dare not admit that they have killed someone, they even try to smear the victim's name by saying that it was the Communists killing a Communist or that it was a crime of passion.' Following his attack on the Nationalist government, he went on to a specially convened press conference, but on his way home he was shot in the head by several men; his son was seriously wounded while trying to shield him. The Communist Party protested strongly to the Nationalist government and demanded the dismissal of the Kunming military chief, the apprehension of the culprits, protection for people who supported the democratic cause, funeral arrangements for the dead, compensation for the families and the proclamation of official mourning. Mao, Zhu De and Chow also sent condolences to the victims' families.

Two outrageous political murders had happened within five days and people all over the country were shocked. Thousands attended memorial services for the two men in Shanghai, Chongqing, Chengdu and other cities, public opinions blaming the Nationalist government for the crimes. In the words of a condolence telegram sent by the Communist Party on 17 July 1946, 'these unprecedented, atrocious, heart-rending and ugly assassinations have broken the dirty political record of world history. The aggression of the Chinese Fascists has now been thoroughly exposed. All their political deceits have been uncovered by the gunfire of the political assassinations in Kunming.'

If the words 'assassinations' and 'Kunming' are replaced by 'slaughter' and 'Tiananmen Square' respectively, this paragraph would be an accurate description of the massacre of 4 June 1989 when the Communist Party mowed down students in Tiananmen Square.

Chiang, who had genuinely known nothing about the two killings beforehand, was furious. He phoned Nanking from his summer retreat at Lu Mountain and pressed for an answer from his military intelligence chief about the reason for these untimely, stupid acts which had incurred such public condemnation. The intelligence chief found out that the man behind the shootings was the military chief in Kunming, Fok Kwei-Chang. Fok knew that Chiang disliked these pro-Communist democrats and had planned to curry favour by killing them, hoping that he would be rewarded with the post of Yunnan provincial chairman. Instead he was summoned to see Chiang to receive a rebuke and the sack. He was ordered to hand over the gunmen, so he named his two junior security officers. Both men were put on trial, confessed their parts in the murders and were sentenced to death. On the day of the execution, roads were cordoned off, two prisoners sentenced to death for other crimes were plied with alcohol and then taken to the firing range, where they were executed and buried immediately. Such substitutions were by no means unique during Nationalist government rule. Fok did not suffer very long; Chiang soon appointed him to another senior post.

In the autumn of 1947, Chiang declared the Chinese Democratic League to be an illegal body, forcing it to close. He made it clear that its members would be dealt with in just the same way as the Communists. From 15 to 25 November 1947 a national conference, rigged by the Nationalist Party and boycotted by all other parties, approved a new constitution for the Republic of China which recognised the Nationalist Party's one-party rule, or more accurately Chiang's one-man rule.

476

While most Chinese people lived in the kind of penury that drove people like Won Yi-Dor to rebel, the officials in Chiang's party, their families, cronies and associates, could rely on the government machine to make easy money without risk, allowing them to live in luxury. In 1939, when inflation started to bite, China's finance ministry suddenly devalued the shaky Chinese currency, the Far Be. The finance minister, Dr H H Kong, his family and coterie used inside information to purchase large quantities of American dollars, gold and silver and borrowed huge sums of Far Be from the banks to invest in advance, knowing very well that their profit would go up several-fold overnight. They could pay back the banks with Far Be which had been drastically devalued.

In 1940 Chiang's old friend Doo Yue-San, the Shanghai gangster boss, was living in Hong Kong. Chiang invited him to move to Chongqing, where he installed his guest in a splendid villa. 'Major General' Doo had many associates in influential government positions and he founded a textile enterprise, in partnership with Kong and T V Soong, with several factories all over China.

At the end of 1944, the Nationalist government's Central Bank was selling Gold Savings Bonds, which were supposedly as safe as gold. Kong decided to raise the price of gold in depreciated Far Be from $20,000 to a new price of $35,000 dollars per tael. Before the new price was announced, the companies controlled by Doo had already bought large quantities of gold and Gold Savings Bonds; even Doo's chauffeur and butler had bought several tens of taels each. Chiang and Kong, both shocked by this, ordered an investigation and discovered that Doo was the man behind the raids. Before long, it was found that an employee of the Central Bank and one departmental head in the finance ministry had been responsible for leaking the information to Doo. The Chongqing authorities assumed that Doo would be summoned to court to answer questions, but the well-connected gangster boss emerged unscathed. The two arrested men were released and the case soon fizzled out.

However, life was not such a safe journey for those outside Chiang's circle. When the Nationalist government in Chongqing tried to develop the transport system in west China, a Highway Department under the Military Commission was made responsible for building a road between Chengdu city in Sichuan province and Sichon city in Sikong province. The Mieo minority in Sikong produced good quality opium which was smuggled into Sichuan by members of a secret society composed of village officials and local army chiefs, who shared out the profits among themselves.

The proposed new highway was a long road and its construction consequently needed help from local people. Project engineers and management staff would often stay in the villages and towns along the road and so got to know the local people and officials. Soon after the completion of the road, local officials and management staff conspired to use the project's trucks to transport large quantities of opium into Sichuan. The 'Chongqing Highway Department' trucks were military vehicles and they drove freely through checkpoints with no questions asked, earning handsome profits for the smugglers.

This opium cartel was soon entangled in a profit-sharing dispute and certain disgruntled people informed the Chongqing government about the opium traffic. Chiang was furious and more than a dozen project workers involved in the illegal trade were arrested, including the director of the Highway Department, Peng Shar-Pou. After more than a month's investigation, the Military Disciplinary Department compiled a detailed report recommending a variety of penalties; some were to be jailed, others were to be sentenced to death. Peng Shar-Pou himself was at the top of the list, but the Military Disciplinary Department found that he had merely failed in his duty to supervise his staff properly; there was no evidence of him taking part in the crime.

Chiang did not bother to read the whole report carefully. He simply used a red pencil to draw a large circle around all the names of the accused and wrote alongside 'Shoot them all'. The director of the Military Disciplinary Department, Ho Sher-Jue, was a kind man, but he dared not point out to Chiang that Peng Shar-Pou was not guilty of drug smuggling and did not deserve to be shot. Instead he delayed carrying out the execution, hoping that he could find a way to help. He found the Jiangxi provincial chairman, General Shon Sae-Fei, who had come to Chongqing to report to Chiang about business in his province. Ho Sher-Jue asked Shon to plead with Chiang for Peng Shar-Pou's life and Shon succeeded in saving all the accused from facing the firing squad.

When the war ended, Chinese people in Japanese-occupied areas were thrilled at first to see the Chinese government coming back, but their joy was short-lived. Nationalist army officers, security agents and other officials were extraordinarily keen to trace collaborators and their property, operations which provided a great pretext for extortion. Many honest but wealthy businessmen were arrested by 'Chongqing men' and accused of being collaborators and only freed after paying vast sums of money. Houses and businesses were condemned as enemy property and confiscated, often on flimsy pretexts and their owners made to understand that they could only retrieve their property by paying a king's ransom. After one important collaborator, Chow Fu-Hai, was imprisoned, his wife was arrested three times. Each time she faced threats of extortion and only after she attempted suicide was she left alone. The home of a medical doctor had been taken over by the Japanese during the occupation; after the war Nationalist army officers took over the house and refused to return it to the doctor unless he handed over 300 taels of gold, equivalent to 25 lbs. Factories were closed down in the same way, causing thousands of workers to lose their livelihoods.

Nationalist servicemen driving around in Jeeps went into the homes of 'collaborators' to loot the contents, taking away bicycles, watches, phonographs, furniture and anything valuable. Among the political, military, cultural and economic collaborators who were caught was the chauffeur of the arch-collaborator, Wang Jing-Wei, who at that time was running a small restaurant in Nanking. 'Chongqing men' were looking for five 'tze' trophies: *fontze*, *chirtze*, *gintze*, *peltze*, *leutze*, or in other words houses, cars, gold, American money and women.

At this time the revenue of the Nationalist government only represented 37 per cent of its total expenditure; most of the shortfall was made up by printing money. Rural areas had been withering under years of war demands for taxes, manpower, food crops and animals. By 1946, vast expanses of agricultural land lay abandoned. In China's rice basket, Hunan province, nearly 40 per cent of agricultural land was derelict. Tax demands, on the other hand, went up with no respite and the countryside could neither provide industrial raw materials nor consume industrial products.

Many of China's heavy industries were in Manchuria and most were occupied and then destroyed by the Russians. Most of north China, meanwhile, was under the control of the Communists, who spared no effort to make life difficult in Nationalist-controlled areas. Railways were sabotaged, mining areas were attacked and seized and supplies of fuel and agricultural produce were cut off. In areas previously occupied by the Japanese, many factories were closed down by the 'Chongqing men', raw materials were stolen and machines rusted away. Some textile mills stopped work because there was no cotton, fewer than half of the factories in Sichuan province and fewer than one third of the factories in Shanghai were still working.

Doo Yue-San, Chiang's good friend, went back to Shanghai immediately after the war, where he enjoyed the high status of being a special friend of Chiang. When a collaborator, Wong Tao, appeared on the Nationalist government's wanted list, he paid Doo 500 taels of gold to have his name deleted.

During this period Doo and another friend of Chiang's, Dai Yu-Lone, visited their erstwhile friend, the collaborator Chow Fu-Hai, in jail to discuss fixing the exchange rate between the Nationalist currency, the Far Be and the money issued by the Japanese that was circulating in Japanese-occupied areas. Chow Fu-Hai suggested $20 of occupied area money to one dollar of Far Be, the maximum rate to be not more than 50 to 1 in order to keep prices stable. The Nationalist finance ministry, however, fixed the exchange rate at 200 to 1. People in the once-occupied areas fought to get rid of their depreciated money by buying any goods available; as a result prices rocketed and there was enormous resentment at the exploitative policy of the Nationalist government.

The Nationalist government's economic policy had a disastrous effect. The new finance minister, Yu Hon-Jeun, decided that the public was getting too high a rate of interest and he decided to confiscate 20 per cent of the Gold Savings Bonds already sold to the public, which his predecessor Dr H H Kong had encouraged people to buy only six months before. People who lost money were, not surprisingly, very angry. T V Soong, who by then in effect held the job of prime minister, permitted the free import of luxury goods taxed at 50 per cent, with foreign currency provided by the government and soon foreign consumer goods flooded the market. Businesses controlled by powerful people like Dr H H Kong and T V Soong could always obtain foreign currency at the cheap official rate, while most industries were unable to obtain foreign currency at all to purchase essential raw materials, machinery and spare parts. In early 1946 foreign currency began to run short and the import of luxury goods was banned. At the end of the war the Nationalist treasury had US$2 billion in reserve and it later took over enemy property worth a total of US$1 billion. By February 1947, only US$100 million was left, as most of the original sum had found its way into the pockets of powerful people. In the space of one year or so, the exchange rate between the American dollar and the Far Be changed from 1:20 to 1:18,000; the Far Be kept plummeting, while the price of everything else kept shooting up.

In 1948, the Nationalist government issued a new currency, the 'gold dollar note', to replace the old Far Be. The exchange rate between the American dollar and the gold dollar note was fixed at 1:4. It became illegal to hold gold, silver or foreign currency, all of which had to be handed in to the national banks in exchange for gold dollar notes and anyone who disobeyed the decree would be severely punished. People also had to register any foreign property and all prices were compulsorily fixed at the level on 19 August.

In order to avoid price controls, farmers were no longer moving food crops into the cities. Panic-stricken people rushed to buy food and hoarding in Shanghai in particular was extreme. One of the big speculators turned out to be none other than Doo's butler, who owned a large rice shop, in addition to a substantial warehouse and three houses in the French concession which he rented in order to hoard rice. In January 1948, on the eve of the Chinese New Year, crowds of people went to his shop to buy rice, only to find it closed. The crowds were increasing steadily and demanding angrily that the rice shop be opened for business. People became angry when there was no reply and the front door of the shop was soon broken down to reveal sacks of rice piled up to the ceiling. People began helping themselves to the rice, cutting open some of the sacks. Rice began to pour out, causing the sacks above to tumble down and in the ensuing melee several people were crushed or trodden to death.

Looting for rice was increasing rapidly in both Shanghai and Nanking and in Peking flour and rice were difficult to find. Sometimes prices went up two or three-fold on the same day. Power stations were short of both fuel and money; they could only supply electricity to a few districts and every night users had to wait for their turn. Often electricity would come on between nine and half past nine in the evening when there was a curfew in the city, to stall Communist infiltration.

Shortages soon led to hoarding and speculation. Army officials would often collect their unit's wages from the Nanking government and use the money to buy gold, reaping a big profit after a month. By the time they eventually paid their men, the value of the money had dropped dramatically, sometimes by more than half. A major's monthly salary might be barely enough to buy ten packets of cigarettes.

Trying to stamp out the rampant speculation, in August 1948 Chiang appointed economic controllers for Shanghai, Tianjin and Canton to rein in the profiteers. His own son, Chiang Ging-Kuo, the 'crown prince', was appointed deputy controller responsible for cleaning up Shanghai, China's financial centre. Chiang Ging-Kuo proclaimed that he would only hit out at the tigers and would not swat the flies. Among his first catches were the secretary of the finance ministry who was leaking information to a businessman in order to speculate on the stock market and an anti-smuggling official guilty of extortion. The culprits were put on trial and some were sentenced to death. A total of 64 big businessmen were thrown into jail, including Doo's eldest son, Doo Wei-Ping, nicknamed 'Doo Tiger'.

Doo promptly sent his men out on a secret investigation, which discovered that the powerful Yangtze Company was hoarding large quantities of goods. He openly disclosed the information at a public meeting, saying that his son was only a small fish and the economic controller ought to be fair to everybody. Chiang Ging-Kuo, put on the spot in front of large numbers of people, had to send his men to search the Yangtze Company at once. It transpired that Doo's information was correct and the Yangtze Company's boss, Kong Lin-Han, was arrested.

His decision to arrest the boss of the Yangtze Company landed him in an awkward position, which was to spell the beginning of the end for his anti-corruption campaign. Kong Lin-Han was the son of Dr H H Kong and Madame Soong Oi-Ling and was therefore related to the Chiang family. With powerful relatives and plenty of inside information, he was a very successful businessman. His mother was not amused to hear that her son had been arrested and thrown into jail and she did not hesitate to make her displeasure clear to her younger sister, the first lady, Soong Mei-Ling. Meanwhile, Chiang was in Peking discussing the defence of north China with his generals. After receiving an urgent telephone call from his wife he immediately flew back to Nanking, to the dismay of his generals, who were galled to see that Chiang apparently saw his family commitments as more important than the defence of north China.

Kong Lin-Han was quietly spirited out of jail and sent to Hong Kong; the Yangtze Company had got away lightly. Doo's son was also released without charge. Chiang Ging-Kuo's position now became untenable and on 4 November, three months after taking on the job of economic controller, he handed in his resignation.

Within three months, on 11 November 1948, the ill-conceived new economic policy was abolished. The value of the gold dollar note depreciated quickly; its rate of exchange to the US dollar, originally fixed at four to one, was now 30 to one. As a result, law-abiding citizens who had handed over their gold, silver and foreign currency in exchange for gold dollar notes found that they had lost their savings and many people went bankrupt. Nanking was beginning to sink into a state of anarchy. In the face of possible financial meltdown, the Nationalist government relented and announced that people would be permitted to buy one tael of gold each from the national banks, but only in the mornings. Armed police and the military police employed people to queue for them before dawn, but they would open fire to settle disputes over positions in the queue.

One year later the Nationalist government issued another new currency, the silver dollar note, to replace the collapsed gold dollar notes, but it was no more successful than its predecessor, ending up as waste paper in the vicious hyper-inflation. When freezing weather arrived in Shanghai,

China's most affluent city, one bitter night in 1948, 99 corpses, most of them homeless children, were collected the following morning; all had died of hypothermia.

After the end of the war with Japan, Chiang, keen to show the world that he was a generous and noble man, decided on his own to waive demands for compensation. It was a gesture that the long-suffering Chinese people could ill afford. The Communist Party maintained an economic policy of self-sufficiency, encouraging the growth of production and only importing necessities. Prices as a result stayed fairly stable in the Communist areas. However, the Communists printed large quantities of counterfeit money to spend in Nationalist areas, as well as buying up and taking away large quantities of rice to exacerbate unrest and misery.

The economist Professor Ma Yan-Choo, head of Chongqing University's Commercial College, was fiercely critical of the Nationalist government's handling of the economy. On one occasion in 1939, he invited the finance minister, Dr H H Kong, to address an economic institute, using the occasion to ask Kong all manner of awkward questions. What, for example, was the intention behind his ministry's sudden devaluation of the Far Be, which had caused serious financial chaos and which had become a justification for profiteering at the expense of ordinary people and the nation? The audience applauded Ma's courageous questions and the highly embarrassed minister appeared to have lost his tongue. The awkward impasse was only resolved by a ten-minute break, during which Kong made an excuse and fled.

After receiving a report about this unfortunate encounter, Chiang summoned Yip Yuan-Lone, the chancellor of Chongqing University and said to him bluntly: 'You were really confused, how could you make Ma the head of a college? Do you know that he attacked Kong, the finance minister? Any criticism of Kong is an attack on me.' Chiang ordered Yip Yuan-Lone to return, bringing Ma with him. When Ma was told that Chiang wanted to see him, he said: 'I am not going, unless he sends his military police for me.' Later on, Chiang tried to buy off Ma by offering him the job of deputy finance minister, but Ma firmly refused.

Ma continued to berate the corrupt hierarchy in his public speeches, openly calling Chiang a hero only of his clan, not a hero of the nation. On 8 December 1940 he was arrested and sent to jail. In August 1942, the pressure of public opinion, together with appeals by some Americans for his release, finally forced the Nationalists to let him out of jail, but for the next two years he remained under house arrest. In 1944 he was at last allowed to go back to teaching; his principles and behaviour had not changed.

483

75

Chiang Kai-Shek Goes On and On

In spring 1946, Chiang held a meeting with his senior military staff. They were all confident that there would be no difficulty in defeating the Communists completely, since the Nationalist army was so much better equipped than the Communist army. The chief of staff, General Chan Chen, told reporters on 18 October that it would take five months at most to solve the Communist problem. With such an optimistic forecast, Chiang was determined to continue with the civil war.

It was United States policy to urge the Chinese government to form a coalition government and embark on a peaceful and democratic process of reform and the American government tried hard to prevent China from plunging into civil war. In the summer of 1946, Chiang retreated to his summer resort at Lu Mountain with the intention of making it more difficult for the peace broker, General Marshall, to have easy access to him, but between July and September Marshall visited him there eight times, without achieving any progress. Meanwhile the civil war rumbled on. In August 1946 the American government banned the sale of arms to the Nationalist government; the ban was to last for ten months, making things difficult for Chiang's armed forces. He had no wish, however, to give way. On 1 December, General Marshall emphatically pointed out to Chiang the economic and military crises faced by the Nationalist government and urged Chiang that the only way to solve the Communist problem was by political compromise. Chiang replied that the Communists could be defeated within eight to ten months and because the countryside was the backbone of the Chinese economy, there was no danger of an economic collapse. On 29 January 1947 the Americans finally admitted defeat and formally withdrew from mediation between the two warring parties.

In February 1947 the Nationalist government ordered all Communist representatives and their staff in Chongqing, Shanghai and Nanking to leave before 5 March. The *New China Daily*, the only Communist newspaper in the Nationalist area, was compelled to close down.

While the Nationalist government saw American policy as being biased in favour of the Communists, the Communist honeymoon with Marshall was also swiftly over, the Communists accusing the American government of not being even-handed and of contributing to the Communist setback in Manchuria. The Communist *Liberation Daily* published an editorial on 5 June 1946 arguing that America should immediately stop promoting civil war in China and another, two days later, urging people to 'Stand opposed to American assistance in killing the Manchurian people'. They had evidently forgotten that less than a year before they themselves had received precious help from Russia in Manchuria, which had hardly been designed to promote peace. The Communist Party itself never held back from slaughtering Chinese people in Manchuria or elsewhere, as witnessed by their flattening of the Manchurian city of Xi-Ping and their six-month siege of Changchun city in 1948, during which more than 100,000 Manchurian people starved to death. Nevertheless, while the Communists were denouncing America, their junior partners, the Chinese Democratic League, were organising large anti-American demonstrations, boycotting American goods and demanding that American forces should leave China.

The Communist Party now renamed its army the Chinese People's Liberation Army, or PLA. The party worked hard to organise militias and partisans, while their land policy altered from simply forcing landlords to reduce rent and interest to actually confiscating land and redistributing it to poor peasants. It was a policy which won them the wholehearted support of countless peasants and which had the additional advantage of providing the army with an inexhaustible supply of soldiers.

Chiang was still determined that his armed forces should be commanded only by the cadets of the Whampoa Military Academy. He thought, with himself as headmaster and the commanders as his students, the army would always be a reliable powerbase for him. On examining his army rosters one day, towards the end of the war with Japan, he found there were still more than 100 divisions not commanded by Whampoa officers. Why, he groaned, were there still so many of them, after eight years of fighting?

In early 1946 the armed forces minister General Chan Chen, Chiang's favourite general, disbanded all guerrilla forces and those armies whose loyalty was doubtful. The ordinary soldiers were transferred to other units, but the sacked officers, some of them badly wounded, found that they had suddenly lost their livelihoods. One disabled officer became a beggar and carried a placard explaining how he had been wounded. The government found this embarrassing and forbade him to beg and in due course his body was found in a Nanking river. Before long, the government succumbed to public criticism and put all the officers in a training camp, promising to find them jobs afterwards. But when the training came to an end in March 1947, there were no jobs available.

Among these officers was Lt General Chee Ze, an overseas Chinese who had donated his personal fortune to Sun Yat-Sen's cause and had subsequently fought in the Northern Expedition and the Sino-Japanese War. Now he was penniless and in April his wife committed suicide by jumping into a river. Another officer, a major general who suffered from tuberculosis and could not feed his family, killed himself by taking an overdose of sleeping pills.

On 5 May, a large party of dismissed officers and their families went to Sun Yat-Sen's resting place in Nanking, where an officer made a speech condemning the ruling clique for their unequal treatment of insiders and outsiders. Many of the officers had fought for years under Sun Yat-Sen, only to find that they were now being kicked aside. There were shouts of 'Down with the corrupt officials'. The protest was duly reported in the newspapers and the Nationalist government told Chan Chen to find a way to calm down the uproar.

Many of the aggrieved officers decided instead to join the Communist army. Chan Chen was warned that by his actions he was simply increasing the strength of the Communists, but his only reply was: 'Good! If they go over to the Communists, we can get rid of them all in one go.'

The consequence of sectarianism could be very serious for the nation. When, during the ensuing civil war, an army corps commanded by a non-Whampoa officer, Wong Bor-Tow, was under heavy attack, a Whampoa commander nearby, commanding 300,000 troops, firmly refused to help and as a result Wong Bor-Tow's 100,000 troops were crushed by the Communists.

In early 1947, the Nationalists were doing well in the civil war. Although the Communists had inflicted damage on the Nationalists in the west and south of Shandong province, they had lost out in the provinces of Suiyuan and Shanxi and in the north of Jiangsu. Chow En-Lai now asked for a truce so that the two parties could begin discussions on a new government, but Chiang, enjoying the upper hand for the moment, rejected the request, despite growing signs of popular rebellion against renewed warfare, including serious riots in Sichuan, Gansu and Sikong in protest against heavy taxes and military conscription.

In March 1947, 150,000 Nationalist soldiers advanced towards the Communist base of Yan'an. The leading unit, the 90th Division, under the command of General Chen Woo, made slow progress because the

Communists had set booby traps with home-made mines, particularly in the village of Gold Pot Bay, where mines lay everywhere in houses and dwelling caves, making the troops extremely nervous. After fierce fighting, on 18 March the 90th Division approached Yan'an, expecting to enter the city on the following day. The commander-in-chief, General Hu Jone-Nan (who also commanded Chiang's own elite First Division) announced that the first unit to enter Yan'an would be awarded ten million Far Be dollars. Chan Woo knew that his division was in front and there was only sporadic gunfire from the direction of the other units. He therefore felt confident that the prize money was as good as in his troops' pockets.

Late at night, Chan Woo received an order directing his division to another target on the outskirts of Yan'an; they would therefore not be the first to enter the city after all. Instead Hu Jone-Nan's own 1st Division, known as 'the best in the world', which had fallen behind and had not done much fighting, was now given the chance to overtake the 90th Division. Chan Woo could only obey orders, but he was bitter about this unfair treatment by the high command, believing it would not be good for army morale. The following day at noon, soldiers of the 1st Division caught up with the 90th Division on a narrow country path; they told the troops of the 90th Division to get out of the way, saying they had orders to enter Yan'an.

As the Communists had already left Yan'an, the 1st Division captured the city with little resistance. Chiang was overjoyed that his troops had retaken the Communist base after 13 years. His joy was short-lived. Hu Jone-Nan did not know where the main Communist force had gone. During the following month he was defeated three times by the Communist army and less than eighteen months later the Nationalist troops were forced out of Yan'an again.

Following America's abandonment of the role of peace broker, two small political parties stepped in to attempt to perform this impossible job, with no more success. At the end of 1947 the Nationalist government gave up peace talks completely, instead plunging into a full-scale war. On 28 June, the Nationalist government issued a warrant for Mao's arrest.

The summer of 1947 was the turning point of the civil war. Mao's usual tactic was to assemble a large army supported by local armed forces to surround and eliminate the smaller and weaker Nationalist troops. Later on the People's Liberation Army started to assault the big cities. The Communists adopted an all-out offensive strategy, hoping for a decisive defeat of the Nationalists. The Nationalist Army tried to hold onto cities, using them as bases from which to mount attacks, but the Communists were successful at sabotaging railways and roads, not only in Manchuria but also in north and central China, thereby effectively isolating the Nationalist-controlled cities. After surrounding a city, the Communist forces would dig trenches around it, rendering the Nationalist government's motorised fighting and transport units immobile. Supplies of ammunition and food would soon be cut off.

Communist forces also broke open dykes to create flooding. Around October in 1945 they sabotaged dykes along the Yellow River in Henan province, the Grand Canal in Jiangsu and Shandong provinces and the Wing Ding and Tze Ya rivers in Hebei province. It was an effective strategy. As well as delaying the movements of the Nationalist Army, the flooding also produced huge numbers of refugees; furthermore there were ever-increasing numbers of unemployed workers, many of them coming from factories and mines destroyed by the Communists. These vast numbers of people soon became a serious social problem, putting enormous pressure on the government's already inadequate relief services and many joined the army as a way to make a living. This helped the Communists, whose army as a result expanded enormously, enabling its commanders to compensate for their usually weaker firepower by using massed human waves to overwhelm the enemy; the Nationalist government on the other hand soon felt the pinch of a shortage of manpower.

In September 1948, General Chan Yi, the future foreign minister of Communist China, led his army in a successful attack on Jinan, Shandong province. More than 20,000 Nationalist soldiers surrendered without a fight and Chan Yi succeeded in capturing the provincial chairman of Shandong and his army of 60,000 men.

Amid all these troubles the Nationalist Party began to organise a National Congress to approve the constitution and elect a president, for Chiang still craved the title of President of the Republic of China. Two small political parties produced their own draft of a constitution, which suggested a four-year term for a president. Other provisions included a limit of two terms for the president; an Administrative Council, equivalent to a cabinet, would be answerable to a Legislative Council; and there would be nine grand justices, whose remit would be to interpret the constitution.

Chiang appointed a small committee of Nationalists to draft a constitution. They did so within a week and presented the new constitution for debate by the Nationalists. It was an argumentative meeting. Some of the 80 or so members present complained that the constitution destroyed the basis for one-party rule. Chiang's more fervent supporters wanted the president to enjoy an unlimited term in office, while others who disapproved of Chiang refused to allow future presidents to retain power indefinitely.

There were many other points of contention, such as whether there was a need for a standing committee and for the grand justices; the size of the future congress; and how to share out the quotas of members among different groups and parties. The meeting broke up without agreement.

There were more troubles to come. The American ambassador, John Leighton Stuart, let Chiang know that the American government preferred to see Dr Hu Shi elected as president. Such a move was hardly surprising. When Stuart's predecessor, Patrick Hurley, had come to the end of his posting, Chiang had thrown a farewell party for him. Hurley, however, took the opportunity to denounce the Nationalist party in no uncertain terms, inveighing against the government as being incompetent and corrupt. The senior Nationalist officials present were left silent and confounded, while Chiang was seething with anger.

In November 1947 an election was held of delegates to the National Congress. It was at times a farcical affair. There were power struggles between factions inside the Nationalist Party and between the Nationalist Party and its junior arm, the Youth League, in spite of both organisations supporting the same man, Chiang and following the same political doctrine. Senior members from different factions freely announced election rules to suit their own vested interests, creating widespread confusion. The Nationalist authorities would announce that all the candidates had to be nominated by the central committee, otherwise the result would be deemed invalid and yet a second announcement would declare that there was no restriction on nominations.

When it became clear that most winners belonged to members of the Nationalist Party, some of the losers from the smaller parties went on hunger strike. A group of them mounted a demonstration carrying a coffin, while others moved into the Home Affairs Department and refused to leave. Others sent statements to the press announcing their intention of committing suicide. When the Nationalist Party yielded to pressure and tried to coerce some of its own members into giving up their seats, internal war threatened.

Before the second meeting of the newly elected Congress, Chiang chaired a meeting of the party to discuss the nomination of a presidential candidate. He said that any president had to meet a number of requirements: he should be a civilian, an academic and a figure of international standing. Lastly, he did not necessarily have to be a member of the Nationalist Party.

After Chiang's speech the meeting was adjourned until the afternoon. When it resumed, Chiang was absent and the meeting was chaired by General Ho Ying-Yeen. It looked to many as if Stuart had won the day and Chiang was now ready to give way. The person who fitted all four conditions mentioned by Chiang was obviously Dr Hu Shi, not Chiang himself. Accordingly, many of the delegates heaped praise on Chiang, emphasising that he had worked hard and had made a great contribution to the country and that he should be given a temporary rest. Instead they nominated Hu Shi and a few other senior party officials as presidential candidates. Dr H H Kong and a dozen or so of Chiang's confidantes sat silently in the front row, with stony faces.

The following morning Chiang stormed furiously into the meeting, hurling abuse at the men who had nominated Dr Hu Shi. He reminded the meeting of his own great achievements, ending his rant by saying: 'I want to complete what Sun Yat-Sen left unfinished and to be responsible for seeing through the country's revolution. Who else could be better qualified to be the president of China than me?' Those in the front row started applauding and the rest duly joined in. Chiang had played a sly trick; now he knew who was opposed to him.

In 1944, Chiang wrote in his diary: 'As long as I am alive and well, there is a future for China.' After nearly two decades of treating both law and public opinion with contempt, he could still not see that he had driven the people to despair. With an overwhelming conviction of his own greatness, he would never agree to stand down.

On 21 July 1947, the American government sent General Albert C Wedemeyer to China on a fact-finding tour. When he left on 24 August, Chiang duly held a farewell party for him. History repeated itself; Wedemeyer read a statement to the Nationalist government's senior officials and commanders denouncing Chiang's insensitive, corrupt and incompetent government and arguing that China needed a different, more popular, leader to unite the country.

In early 1948, as the general election drew near, it was clear to everyone that Chiang wanted the presidency for himself and that the job was not open to genuine competition. Six ambitious people instead set their sights on the sinecure of the vice-presidency, among them General Lee Jone-Yan, a leading liberal figure who was highly thought of by the Americans. When Lee asked for Chiang's blessing to stand, Chiang expressed no opinion. Secretly he regarded Lee as just an outsider from the Guangxi provincial army. But as Chiang did not categorically object to him standing for the post, Lee plunged into his campaign. Six months later, on 3 April, less than three weeks before voting, Chiang summoned Lee to his residence and told him that the party's central committee, whose job it was to nominate candidates for both president and vice president, had now decided that the vice presidency should go to Sun Kor. He asked Lee, in the interests of the government, to withdraw from the race, but Lee replied that Chiang had left it too late; he could not stop now.

Rumours were rife, some claiming that Lee's ultimate aim was to usurp Chiang's presidency. On 19 April, the 13th meeting of the National Congress, Chiang was duly elected president, with 2,430 votes. Jue Jing, who played the role of handmaiden in the election, got 269 votes. Thirty-five votes were deemed invalid, some of them had Chiang's name crossed out and some of the votes had been cast for the late Sun Yat-Sen.

On 23 and 24 April, the National Congress proceeded to elect the vice president. After two rounds of voting, Lee was far ahead of the rest. Sun Kor was second and Ching Cham third; none of the candidates had received more than half the total number of votes. Chiang tried frantically to stop Lee. He handed out large sums of money in an attempt to encourage delegates to vote for Sun Kor and he told Ching Cham to withdraw and transfer all his votes to Sun, promising Ching that he would be compensated for his expenses. Ching turned him down. On the evening of 24 April, Lee and Ching announced that because delegates were unable to vote freely due to certain pressures, they had both decided to withdraw from the contest for the vice presidency. At this, their supporters decided to abandon the election. Sun announced with embarrassment that he would withdraw from the contest as well and as a result the National Congress meeting on the following day collapsed. Chiang now had a crisis on his hands. He succeeded in persuading the three men into standing for the vice presidency again and he even promised to lend Lee his support, although in fact his group was still working flat out to ensure Sun's election. After two more ballots, Lee was finally elected as vice president with a slim majority.

Chiang resented an outsider coming close to the centre of power. The election result had revealed that his 20-year dictatorship was weakening inexorably.

The Nanking election melodrama dragged on from mid-1947 into 1948, during which time the Nationalists suffered increasing setbacks not just in Manchuria, but also in north, northwest and central China. In September 1948 the half-million-strong army of the Communist commander Lin Biao launched a major offensive in Manchuria. The Nationalist Army was by now divided into three areas, Shenyang, Changchun and Jinzhou and was still holding on to 12 isolated cities. They were attempting to hold the Communist Army here and stop them advancing into north China.

The Communists now concentrated their efforts on taking Jinzhou city in the east of Liaoning province; once it was taken they would be able to cut off traffic between Manchuria and north China, so that the Nationalist

Army could neither retreat nor be reinforced. The fighting was also getting hazardous in Shenyang and Chiang flew there three times to assess the situation. Old habits die hard and Chiang's insider army received air-dropped supplies of food and ammunition, while his outsider army received nothing except a flattering letter from him calling the commanding officer 'brother' and urging him to fight on. His behaviour did not inspire goodwill or loyalty; two outsider divisions in Jinzhou and one outsider army in Changchun chose to defect to the Communists. Others surrendered or were captured and on 2 November Shenyang fell. In 52 days the Communists had succeeded in defeating the 470,000 men of the Nationalist Army, 30,000 of whom were evacuated by sea. The Communists were now able to seize Manchuria, together with a large quantity of American weapons. They had also obtained useful experience in how to attack big cities and how to organise a large-scale war. The American embassy estimated that during the four battles in Jinzhou, Jinan, Changchun and Shenyang, the Nationalist Army had lost 230,000 rifles, of which 100,000 were American-made. The Communists called this operation the Liao-Shen Campaign.

The campaign was followed immediately by a major Communist offensive in central China, stretching from the east coast through the provinces of Jiangsu, Anhui, Henan and Shandong. By now the Communist forces had grown to more than three million men, while the Nationalists had been reduced to 2.9 million men.

Chiang was a careful man; as soon as Lee had been confirmed as vice president, he promptly dismissed Lee's long-term ally, General Bai Shon-Shi, from his post of defence minister and sent him away from Nanking to Wuhan, in Hubei province, to set up a military headquarters. Bai, an able and experienced general, was now the commander-in-chief responsible for the southwest battlefields of the central China war zone, while the northeast battlefields of the central China war zone had their headquarters in Xuzhou, in Jiangsu province. Bai argued that there should be a single headquarters for central China, putting all the armed forces under one command rather than having them split into two battle zones. Chiang, however, flatly rejected the idea.

Chiang, taking personal charge of the Nationalist Army, now went to Manchuria to direct the fighting, only to lose three motorised regiments in a disastrous campaign. On his return to Nanking on 30 October 1948 he called an urgent military meeting to discuss amalgamating the two central China battle zones, summoning Bai from Wuhan to Nanking and putting the whole operation under his command. General Liu Jee, meanwhile, was appointed commander-in-chief of the northeast battlefields of the central

China war zone. His appointment was greeted with dismay in the Nationalist Party. Many people said that Xuzhou city, site of Liu Jee's headquarters, was the main gate leading to the Nationalist capital, Nanking and it should be guarded by a tiger, or if not a tiger at least by a guard dog. Now that the job had gone to a pig, the capital was bound to fall.

A PLA commander in south Shandong distributed leaflets boasting that the previous year they had driven away Chiang's mediocre chief of staff, Koo Jue-Tong. This year the man in charge in Xuzhou was the well-known stupid pig, Liu. If the Communist Army wanted a good life, they should advance fearlessly into Xuzhou and kill the pig.

Liu had a reputation for making stupid mistakes, but even so he had been given the job of guarding the wartime capital of Chongqing during the Sino-Japanese War. Madame Soong Mei-Ling had told her husband that many people were unhappy about Liu's appointment, worried that he was not up to the job, but Chiang replied: 'He may not be able to do a good job, but no one could be more compliant.' During Liu's tenure of office guarding Chongqing, several thousand people suffocated in air raid shelters on two separate occasions. After this disaster he was to be put on trial in a special military court, but having managed to embezzle some army money he successfully bribed his way out of trouble.

A few years later, Liu was appointed commander-in-chief in charge of the northeast batttlefields of central China. Bai found out that Liu had deployed his army in one straight line with Xuzhou in the middle, but there was no time to redeploy the troops. Bai was worried that Chiang was setting up a trap and trying to lay the blame for any failure on him, so he steadfastly refused to take the job of defending the whole of central China.

The war in Manchuria ended on 2 November and four days later the war in central China began. A total of 600,000 regular Communist soldiers, in addition to more than two million militiamen and labourers, took the offensive against the Nationalists, employing their by now well-honed tactic of picking off the Nationalist armies one by one. Soon one 220,000-strong Nationalist army found itself besieged east of Xuzhou and by 22 November it had been defeated. Several times Chiang transferred troops from Bai's battle zone in an attempt to relieve the siege near Xuzhou, but Bai was unwilling to comply. The strained relationship between Bai and Chiang was near breaking point and Bai even threatened to resign. At this point more than 20,000 Nationalist soldiers to the east of Xuzhou defected, having barely put up a fight and several thousand soldiers to the west and south of Xuzhou surrendered, with many more captured or killed. Chiang later admitted that whenever a Nationalist division or army found itself surrounded by Communist troops, the troops were usually defeated within a few hours, or at the most within a day.

The battle for the northeast of central China was over in 65 days. Chiang's government had now lost all of central and east China north of the Yangtze River and Nanking itself was under serious threat. This campaign, which the Communists called the Huai-Hai Campaign, led to almost half a million Nationalist casualties. The battleground had seen many large-scale battles during the civil wars and the Sino-Japanese War, but the most devastating event of all had been that of 9 June 1938, when Chiang had blown up the Yellow River dykes in an attempt to halt the Japanese advance. The Japanese had suffered limited damage and their thrust was no more than slightly delayed. The Yellow River flooding however had brought horrific and lasting hardship to the region, as huge areas of agricultural land, as well as rivers, had been ruined by the ten billion tons of Yellow River sediment that had been deposited in the Huai River basin. This disaster had been followed in 1942 by a great famine in which five million people died of starvation. The Huai-Hai Campaign of 1948 was largely fought in the 54,000 sq km area that had been inundated by Chiang and it was hardly surprising that, when the Communist Army called for volunteers to dig trenches, tend casualties and transport war materials and food supplies, millions of peasants willingly came forward to help.

Meanwhile, 600,000 Nationalist troops in north China under the command of General Fu Jor-Yi converged near Peking, Tianjin, Zhangjiakou and Tonggu, with a view to either escaping by sea or moving inland to Suiyuan province. However, as soon as fighting ceased in Manchuria the main Communist force of 800,000 men advanced quickly into north China in order to join up with the smaller local Communist forces, with a view to preventing the Nationalist troops from fleeing. They succeeded in cutting off their enemy's retreat routes and captured a number of cities into the bargain. The consequence was that Fu Jor-Yi and his 250,000 men in Peking found themselves under siege.

The Communists' extensive and efficient network of underground agents in Nationalist areas was now working hard to persuade Nationalist commanders to defect with their troops to the Communists. The tactic was to send either family members or close friends who were Communist sympathisers to visit their targets. Now the Communists set to work on Fu Jor-Yi through his daughter. Fu was uncertain as to the best course of action and he decided to seek the opinion of General Deng Bo-Shan.

Chiang had recently put his presidential plane, the Cloud Chaser, at Fu's disposal. Now the Cloud Chaser was sent to pick up Deng Bo-Shan and bring him to the beleaguered Nationalists in Peking. Deng was a friend of Fu, but he had also visited Yan'an three times in the past and was on good terms with the leading Communists. When he received Fu's invitation, he realised that it was a cry for help. In Peking the two men had a lengthy discussion about China's present troubles and about their discontent with Chiang's dictatorial rule. Deng pointed out, incidentally, that if China's historical treasures in Peking were to be destroyed by gunfire Fu would be blamed forever. On 31 January 1949, with Deng acting as go-between, Peking changed hands peacefully. Fu's change of allegiance was soon to be followed by other senior Nationalist commanders.

Fu had transferred many of his better trained troops from Tianjin to Peking, leaving Tianjin to be defended by two armies and one incomplete division commanded by Chan Chen-Jet against a Communist force twice as strong. In order to clear visual obstructions and build bunkers, Chan's soldiers knocked down large numbers of houses, leaving thousands of people homeless. One commander was ordered to destroy his military position and then withdraw, but he misunderstood the order and destroyed the village as well; as a result more than a thousand houses went up in smoke. Understandably, the people of Tianjin wanted to see the back of the Nationalist troops. The Communist commanders sent a message demanding that the defenders should lay down their arms and hand over the city peacefully. The senior Nationalist officers held a meeting to discuss how to react to the Communist ultimatum, but none of them were prepared to advocate surrender in public, worried that Chiang's secret agents might be among them, so any indiscretion might put their own lives at risk. Chan himself was determined to fight on, but he was eventually captured by the Communists.

Fu, as a senior former Nationalist general, was given a privileged status by the Communists. Once, when he was visiting his ex-colleagues in a labour camp, Chan Chen-Jet gave his old boss an icy reception. Chan later explained in anger that while Fu was negotiating a secret deal with the Communists, Fu had told Chan to fight on with fortitude and with no thought of surrender. Now Fu was treated as an honoured defector, while Chan himself was in a labour camp for war criminals.

Tianjin fell after 29 hours of bitter fighting, at a cost of 130,000 Nationalist casualties; a further 50,000 Nationalist troops in Tonggu port had managed to escape by sea. The Peking-Tianjin Campaign finally ended on 31 January 1949. Over the course of the campaign the Nationalist Army had suffered some 520,000 casualties. In all, the three major campaigns of the civil war, the Liao-Shen, Huai-Hai and Peking-Tianjin campaigns, had lasted 142 days and had led to some 1.5 million Nationalist casualties. The American embassy estimated that in the last four months of 1948 alone, the Nationalist Army lost as many as one million men and 400,000 rifles. More often than not Nationalist troops had found themselves besieged in isolated cities, unable to obtain reinforcements.

The Chinese Communist Party had signed an agreement with the Russian government on 20 May 1947, giving away a number of privileges in exchange for Russian military aid. In December 1948 the CCP signed a second agreement giving the Russians further privileges on mining in China, as well as rights to station Russian troops in Manchuria and Xinjiang, with a promise that the Chinese Communist Army would support Russia in a future European war or a possible third world war. In return the Russian government promised to train and equip 11 Chinese Red Army divisions. After this deal was struck, one third of all the weapons given to Russia by the American government during the Second World War were transferred to Manchuria and so Lin Biao received large quantities of up-to-date tanks and artillery.

Chiang's grand delusion was crumbling before his eyes. He pleaded repeatedly for more American support, but without success. On 28 November 1948 Mei-Ling flew to America to make an appeal at the highest level for American military assistance and American dollars to prop up her husband's regime. President Truman and his Secretary of State, General Marshall, turned her down; they regarded the Nationalist government's position as unredeemable.

In late December, Bai cabled Chiang to say that they did not have the morale or the resources to fight any more and they no longer had the people's support. Many of the Nationalist troops were inadequately fed and clothed, even in the depths of winter. Some officers recalled that soon after the Japanese surrender, the Manchurian people welcomed the Nationalist Army with open arms and would voluntarily come forward to offer help. But by the time the army started its retreat from Manchuria, it was very difficult to find a local willing to act as guide.

On New Year's Day 1949, Chiang announced that he was willing to resume peace talks with the Communist Party. Now the Communists were winning, however, and they were in no mood to talk. A few days earlier, on 25 December 1948, Mao had announced that Chiang and around 40 of his men had been found to be war criminals. The Communists, he said, were determined to exterminate all the Nationalist reactionaries and to drive the invading influence of the American imperialists out of China.

On 8 January 1949, the Nanking foreign ministry asked the

governments of America, Britain, France and Russia to help arrange peace talks. All of them refused. The American ambassador, J Leighton Stuart, said privately that peace talks could only start once Chiang had gone. On 19 January, Chiang summoned his few trusted subordinates to tell them that he had decided to resign. He said he could either ask Lee, the vice president, to initiate talks with the Communists, leaving after the peace deal was made, or he would go immediately, leaving Lee to deal with everything.

All were silent, not expressing any opinion, so Chiang asked them one by one what they thought of his suggestions. No one begged him to stay. One man said that the matter should have been discussed in the central standing committee. Chiang was piqued at the want of loyal support. 'There is no need for discussion,' he said; 'I have not been brought down by the Communist Party, I have been brought down by the Nationalist Party. I don't want to walk into the party central office again.' When Chiang's words leaked out, people altered them to, 'The Nationalist Party was not brought down by the Communists; it was brought down by Chiang Kai-Shek.'

On 21 January 1949, Chiang 'retired', claiming that from now on he would have nothing to do with the government or the armed forces. It was the third time he had played such a trick. Every time he had secretly retained control over the government, angling to arrange a return. Now he remained president of the Nationalist Party and he kept himself busy with inspection tours to the southeast coastal areas and to Canton, Chongqing, Kunming and Chengdu, to deploy troops and plan the defence of southwest China. He personally supervised the battle in Shanghai, where he was soundly defeated.

While keeping the armed forces firmly under his control, Chiang now moved the air force, together with his government's reserves of gold, silver, foreign currency and much of its military equipment, to Taiwan. He also instructed his military intelligence chief, Mao Yan-Fon, to keep the intelligence service under his own control. Mao Yan-Fon accordingly set up a phoney military security bureau filled with a small number of staff to fool Lee Jone-Yan, but without any operational capability or files to help the new acting boss. Lee was placed in an impotent position, holding the hot potato that Chiang had dropped into his hands, while all the resources were out of his reach. But when he asked Chiang to hand over real power and go abroad, Chiang refused.

On 22 January, Lee took office as acting president to lay the foundations for peace talks. He announced seven new measures, including the revoking of martial law which had been imposed nationwide; the dissolution of the special courts for political prisoners; the release of all political prisoners; and the abolition of censorship. On 1 April a peace delegation consisting of senior Nationalists was sent to Peking.

Meanwhile, the PLA soon arrived on the north bank of the Yangtze River, in sight of Nanking and on 5 February, in the face of this new threat, the Nationalist capital moved south to Canton. Lee and other Nationalists had hoped that the PLA would stop on the north bank of the Yangtze River, so that China could be divided into two parts, a Communist north and a Nationalist south. But the Communists made clear that they were determined to liberate the whole of China and they now submitted conditions for the resumption of peace talks, including the punishment of war criminals and the abolition of the Nationalist constitution. Furthermore, the Communists would take over all the reactionary Nationalist troops and would confiscate all bureaucrats' property. Land reforms were to be implemented and there was to be a new democratic coalition government excluding all reactionary elements.

The Communists were seeking the complete destruction of the Nationalist Party. They now demanded that the peace agreement should be signed by 20 April. Although Lee was willing to accept all the humiliating terms, the hawks inside the Nationalist Party resented the Communists' high-handed manner. On 20 April the Nationalist Party formally rejected the Communists' terms and two days later the Nationalist government sent a plane to Peking to bring its delegates back home. By then, the delegates had already succumbed to Chow En-Lai's united front work, they opted to stay in Peking, thereby abandoning the Nationalist government. On 21 April, the PLA crossed the Yangtze River to seize the rest of China.

The acting president, Lee, arrived in Hong Kong on 20 November and announced that he would soon have to go to America for medical treatment. Chiang sent officials to persuade his scapegoat to stay on, but to no avail. On 5 January 1950, Lee left for America.

Chiang flew to his Taiwan refuge on 10 December 1949. His resumption of power was arranged in early December, when representatives of the Nationalist Party 'appealed' to him to retake the reins. He accepted the 'request' at once and directed the great retreat to Taiwan at the end of December. Only people with unblemished records of loyalty were allowed to accompany him to his safe haven. Those who had once flirted with the Communists, even if they had then served the Nationalist government loyally for 20 or 30 years, were told to remain in mainland China to conduct guerrilla warfare and to wait for the Nationalist government's eventual return. The truth was that Chiang was prepared to feed these vulnerable people to the wolves.

Chiang went on to rule Taiwan like an emperor. He was repeatedly re-elected as president until he finally died in office in 1975 at the age of 89, when power passed to his only natural son, Chiang Ging-Kuo.

Some Nationalists laid the blame for the fiasco in mainland China on the lack of sufficient military support from America, forgetting that during the Huai-Hai Campaign, when the Nationalist Army had suffered a humiliating defeat and the tide had been turned against them, the Communist Army had been much smaller than the Nationalists and its weapons had been far inferior.

Most people in the Nationalist-controlled areas regarded the Communists as a kind of myth; after years of blockades enforced by Chiang's army they knew virtually nothing about the Marxists; but what people did recognise only too well was the Nationalist government's autocracy, incompetence and corruption. Some people said that the Communists had not won the civil war; it was Chiang who had lost it. The simple truth was that Chiang's government had lost the support of the people.

The Chinese people had been abducted by the winners of a military duel and forced to begin a journey into the unknown.

76

The Eyebrows

In July 1947, the Nationalist government had declared the Democratic League to be an illegal organisation; it was therefore disbanded and its chairman and propaganda chief was placed under house arrest in a Shanghai hospital. To escape Nationalist persecution, many Communists and members of small political parties left the Nationalist areas and went into exile in Hong Kong. In addition to the Democratic League, the other parties included the Nationalist Party Revolutionary Committee (a splinter group from Chiang's party), the Chinese Democracy Promotion Party and the Chinese Peasants and Workers Democratic Party and so on; in total there were eight small fringe parties. The Communist Party united front workers had a very busy time in Hong Kong.

The Democratic League established its headquarters in Hong Kong, with branches in Malaya, Indonesia, Burma and London. It now switched from being a 'neutral' party to being a firm supporter of the Communists. Its secretary general, Chow Chin-Min, was in reality an undercover Communist and so were the leaders or secretary generals of every one of the eight small parties. All had been deliberately placed inside the 'third parties' in order to manipulate them to benefit the CCP. Some Communists, particularly the secretary generals of these small parties, kept their CCP membership a secret even to their closest friends; some would take the secret with them to their graves. While the Communist cells were working quietly and secretly inside the small parties, the Communist Party could maintain a tolerant and respectable image; after all, it was allowing eight other political parties to exist, which was one up on Russia.

On 1 May 1948, with the Nationalists facing defeat, the Communist Party made a public appeal to all democratic parties in China, as well as all national institutions and all leading members of society, inviting them to travel north to the 'liberated' area to hold a political consultative conference where they could discuss the formation of a democratic coalition government. The Communist appeal received an enthusiastic response from the small democratic parties in Hong Kong.

The Communist Party cadres in Hong Kong attended to nearly everything, from organising the trip northwards and paying travelling fares, to providing financial help to the families left behind by the prospective delegates, who were to travel to Shijiazhuang in Hebei province where the Communist Party central office had set up its temporary home. These supporters of democracy were given a warm welcome by the very senior Communist officials such as Zhu De, Chow En-Lai and Mao. The guests were housed in the best hotels and Chow En-Lai even found time in his busy schedule to visit them. A couple of months later, eager to please and to be seen to be considerate, the Communists chartered a ship to bring the delegates' families from Hong Kong to Peking. The Communist Party, by now ostensibly a political broad church, assembled 134 people representing not just the CCP itself but also other small parties, the PLA, civilian organisations, industrialists, representatives from cultural circles, minorities and overseas Chinese, to prepare the foundation for the forthcoming Chinese People's Political Consultative Conference, whose function was to give birth to the People's Republic of China. This preliminary conference was designed to impress on the Chinese people and on the outside world that the new government of China enjoyed overwhelming popular support. From 21 to 30 September 1949, the conference approved the new coalition government, a draft constitution, a national flag, anthem and emblem; it also elected Mao as chairman, as well as six vice-chairmen and members of the central committee of the new government. On the following day, 1 October 1949, Mao announced to a packed audience in Tiananmen Square that the People's Republic of China had been born.

The party now announced the creation of the long-awaited coalition government. The jobs of prime minister and foreign minister went to Chow En-Lai. There were four deputy prime ministers, two of whom were non-Communists and a number of the non-Communists were given ministerial positions in some of the 31 ministries. However, it did not take very long for the non-Communists to discover the government's cardinal rule. When the minister was a non-Communist and the deputy a Communist, the real power would be in the deputy minister's hands; when the minister was a Communist and the deputy a non-Communist, the deputy minister's influence was even more insignificant. No department was run by non-Communists only.

When the 'coalition' government went through a reorganisation in October 1954, the number of deputy prime ministers was increased to 12, all of them Communists. The two non-Communist deputy prime ministers were banished to lowly positions as two of the 16 deputy chief commissioners of the National People's Congress. Mao's three non-Communist deputy chairmen met the same fate and at the same time most ministries dropped their non-Communist ministers and deputy ministers.

The Communists quietly and methodically began to adopt the one-party rule which they had loudly denounced as disgraceful and unacceptable when the Nationalists had been in power. People from the small democratic parties now gained themselves a sobriquet, 'the eyebrows', denoting things which have no practical function or are useless but without which a person would look unsightly. And so in Communist China everyone knew that the term 'the party' meant the Communist Party only. The ornamental small parties became so insignificant that they were never taken seriously.

The National People's Congress (NPC), which came into existence in 1954, was nominally the highest authority in China, in contrast to the Chinese People's Political Consultative Conference (CPPCC) which was only set up for consultation. However, even though these two organisations had different names, in reality there was very little difference between them. Both were created and controlled by the Communist Party and they were definitely 'eyebrow' organisations.

All congressmen were theoretically chosen through a democratic process. In reality, they were not elected; many of them were picked behind the scenes by the party central committee and allocated to the provinces, which then submitted these names plus some local names as their provincial congressmen. Some of them had absolutely nothing to do with the province they represented, yet no one could argue with the CCP central committee. There were times when some people did not know that they themselves had been chosen as congressmen. Only when they were told to board a train or plane bound for the National People's Congress conference in Peking did they discover that they had been selected to represent a certain province. Since the whole business was fixed at a high level, often local people, local party cadres and even provincial party officials did not know the names or identities of their own congressmen. People were never asked their opinions, let alone allowed to vote. This peculiar phenomenon was known as 'democratic centralism', a term which had the brain-teasing definition of 'centralism on the basis of democracy and democracy under centralised guidance'.

The office of congressman or member of the Congress standing committee was not a full-time job. It was an honorary position and the members were only required to attend occasional conferences. The motions presented by the government were all party decisions and the Congress's job was simply to rubber-stamp them.

As a rule, elections at all levels in Communist China offered no alternative candidates; only the party-backed candidates were legitimate and so their election was a foregone conclusion. When a man in Sinhui county, in Guangdong province, stood as a candidate during an election, his ambition landed him in court and he was sent to jail for plotting to usurp the leadership. On another occasion, the sole candidate was a powerful Communist who stood on the platform to count the votes personally. With an uninterrupted view of those who did or did not raise their hands to vote for him, it was hardly surprising that he won unanimous support. More than once impatient Communist officials announced the election results before the counting was finished; they simply did away with the pretence.

Sometimes election could be downright hazardous. In April 1969, during the Cultural Revolution, 1,512 Communist delegates attended the Ninth Party Congress. It was assumed that these loyal people could be counted on to cast secret votes to elect Mao as party chairman. However, something shocking happened; one person voted against Mao. The authorities concluded that a vicious counter-revolutionary had infiltrated the party and a special action unit was formed at once, headed by the intelligence chief, Kang Sheng and the public security minister, Sher Fu-Jee, to hunt down the dangerous criminal. They checked all delegates' handwriting and urged everyone to denounce any suspect. The ferocious investigation sent a chill down every voter's spine.

The prime suspect was the foreign minister, Marshal Chan Yi, who was on the verge of being purged because Mao had accused him of being a persistent rightist. The special action unit quickly found Chan's voting paper, which together with several other questionable people's voting slips had been marked by a small number printed on the back, a surreptitious ruse employed by the party congress secretariat. However, Chan had been careful; he had voted for Mao and signed his own name in the bottom corner. All his fellow suspects had voted for Mao as well. The intensive search went on for more than ten days until the congress broke up, but the hunters had still not been able to identify the culprit.

In 1954 the first National People's Congress produced a new constitution for Communist China, which stipulated that the Congress, or its standing committees on different levels – national, provincial, city or county – had the authority to elect, appoint or dismiss leading government officials on the same level. This was one of a long string of democratic rights written into the constitution which could be enjoyed by the lucky Chinese. In reality, many of the party cadres, especially those on lower levels, firmly believed that the party was the ultimate authority and so the congress had to obey the party. When some congressmen exercised their right to examine appointments of local government officials and voice a different opinion, party bosses on the same level often flew into a rage, accusing the congressmen of ignoring the leadership of the party and acting as a rival to the party. They compelled the congressmen to discuss the issues again until they had got their own way. Sometimes party bosses did not bother to consult the congress before publishing government appointments or dismissals. When one local congress demanded an explanation and cautioned party cadres, a county party official refused to believe the constitution document laid before his eyes.

The central committee was uneasy about the image of the party being placed above the constitution. In 1976, after the end of the Cultural Revolution, a circular was sent to all party branches reminding the cadres that it was true that the National People's Congress was written into the constitution as the highest authority in the land, although it was also true that the congress was controlled by the Communist Party. The congress had been given the role of electing the national leadership in front of the Chinese people and the world in order to demonstrate Communist China's socialist democracy and if local party cadres did not follow the same line, they were undermining the party.

At the end of the circular, the central committee advised their local cadres that, after official appointments had been rubber-stamped by the local congress, they should not bluntly announce that the officials had been appointed by the party; instead they should use phrases such as 'the party agrees to the appointments.'

The cadres' insistence on putting the party above the constitution was simply following long-standing Chinese tradition. For several thousand years, power had changed hands only as a result of violence and the victors had always felt they were entitled to throw their weight around unrestrainedly. Democracy was an alien concept which had come to China only towards the end of the 19th century and which was at first learned by the small number of Chinese intellectuals. The Communist Party was led by a small group of dedicated and educated Marxists, but their massive following was drawn from the peasantry. The peasants were taught simple and selective political doctrines by their leaders, who by and large resembled the traditional peasant rebels of bygone days. Mao, who came from a well-off peasant family, seems to have been keener on studying the Chinese classics which related to the subterfuges and power struggles of the old imperial courts rather than Marxist and Leninist revolutionary writings.

Nevertheless the Communist Party insisted that Western democracy was all a fraud and that only the Communists gave the people true democracy and made them masters of their own country.

After the Communists had won power, China was in fact divided up into vast numbers of fiefdoms, big and small, all of them awarded to Communists irrespective of their ability. Clerks, illiterate bodyguards and soldiers could become heads of a junior court or a public security bureau and so on, ruling over a vast population. China consequently had party bosses in powerful positions who had never even heard of the constitution and refused to take it seriously.

While the National Party Congress, officially the highest authority in China, in reality carried practically no weight at all in the Communist Party, the position of the People's Political Consultative Conference was even feebler. Many well-known people who had gravitated to the United Front were sent to these two national institutions. Chow En-Lai's able assistant, Lee Wai-Han, was appointed Minister for United Front Work, with the job of overseeing them and keeping them on their best behaviour. He kept all their personal files and held sway over their livelihoods. When the Political Consultative Conference was in session, its chairman was always a non-Communist, but nobody dared open their mouths before Lee arrived. At one gathering in Peking in 1955 Lee was ill, but he had not informed the conference beforehand that he could not be present and the conference was delayed for three hours.

Lee's good fortune was at its peak between 1956 and 1961, when he was on the central committee of the Communist Party and was much praised by Mao. When the Cultural Revolution began in the mid-60s, all the democratic parties received an ultimatum from the Red Guards ordering them to dissolve themselves. Many United Front members who had once worked tirelessly to support the Communist Party met tragic fates. The Department of United Front Work was closed down and its current minister, deputy minister and Lee were all condemned as members of a 'black gang', taken to violent struggle meetings and put on trial.

The meetings of the Political Consultative Conference came to a halt during the Cultural Revolution, but were revived after the ten-year political storm. Members of the conference had neither financial reward nor political influence. Their chances of ever being allowed to make a proper speech were slim and if they ever voiced criticism on the rostrum, their words would never be reported. Yet it was a job that gave people a certain standing in society and so the party shovelled its spent political forces into the conference. Retired deputy prime ministers, ministers, ambassadors and

505

senior army officers were made one of the two dozen or so deputy chairmen, one of the unlimited number of members or else a member of the conference's standing committee. It provided an activity to brighten up their boring old age.

The People's Political Consultative Conference and the National People's Congress were both handy tools at the party's disposal. They could, for example, carry out negotiations with foreign governments, forging diplomatic relations with countries with which the Chinese government was unwilling to enter direct talks. In the early 80s, for example, the Political Consultative Conference invited the Japanese prime minister to make a speech. Members of the conference's standing committee only learned of the speech from the newspapers afterward and demanded an explanation as to why they hadn't been informed so that they could attend the meeting. The conference secretariat replied that it had in fact been arranged by the foreign ministry, which had decided not to notify the conference members out of concern for their age and frailty and the audience had instead been made up of students from a foreign language college. The Japanese prime minister was quite surprised to see that members of the conference were so young, all of them in their late teens or early 20s. The old people of the Political Consultative Conference were not pleased about being treated in such an offhand manner, but they had to learn the hard lesson that the day when the party had cared about their feelings and their reactions was long gone.

Mao wrote that: 'All criticisms and suggestions exchanged between the Communist Party and other democratic parties must comply with six conditions laid down by the CCP.' These conditions were in fact an expansive dragnet to catch dissidents, making criticism of the party or of any Communist very dangerous. On the other hand there was absolutely no chance for the democratic parties to lay down conditions to prevent paranoid attacks by the CCP.

77

The Socialist Big Brother

The day after the Communist Chinese government came into existence it was recognised by Russia. Two months later, on 16 December 1949, Mao led a delegation to Moscow to take part in the celebrations for Stalin's 70th birthday. Communist cadres in China were required to join in the birthday celebrations and assembly halls were decorated for feasts, in which partygoers bowed to the north to wish the great man a long life, before sitting down to eat the traditional Chinese longevity noodles.

In Moscow Stalin was waiting to meet Mao in his Kremlin drawing room; he did not bother to greet Mao at the doorway, let alone at the railway station. Officials explained that Stalin never greeted or saw off his guests, but some people remembered how during the Second World War Stalin had welcomed the Japanese foreign minister at a railway station. Mao, who had travelled thousands of miles to pay his respects, was obviously less important than a Japanese foreign minister in Stalin's eyes. However, Stalin now recognised Mao's status and promised to lend him support; in other words he would have no more dealings with Chiang.

On 14 February 1950, Chow En-Lai and the Russian foreign minister andrei Vyshinsky, signed a new friendship treaty to confirm the political and military alliance between the two countries. A second agreement provided a $300 million loan to China at one per cent annual interest, which was to be used to purchase military equipment, mostly Russian, to be paid back within ten years. The Russians also agreed to hand over to China free of charge the Russian barracks in Peking and all Japanese properties which they had seized in Manchuria. A third agreement concerned the transfer to China of the Changchun Railway and the Russian military bases in Lushun and Dalian, to take place from the end of 1952. Mao later commented that obtaining aid from Russia was more difficult than prying a piece of raw meat out of a tiger's mouth.

The gift to China of all the Japanese property the Russians had seized in Manchuria was on the face of it very generous, but in reality the Russians had already stripped them of almost all moveable assets; they had even appropriated the good furniture from the homes of Japanese army officers. So the Chinese only received empty, badly sabotaged buildings and in order to restart production in Manchuria China had to buy new machinery from Russia. One thing was certain; the Russians were not going to return the goods they had looted. In the case of the Changchun railway, the Russians offered China a half share of its ownership, ignoring the fact that they had already sold the railway to Japan and received payment. When the Russians entered Manchuria, they immediately looked upon themselves as the owners of the railway again.

The return of Lushun and Dalian was delayed for three years because of the Korean War. In autumn 1954 a Russian delegation headed by Khrushchev visited China to celebrate Communist China's fifth anniversary. The two governments held talks about specific arrangements for the evacuation of the Russian Army, the Chinese asking the Russians to leave behind their military hardware. Khrushchev replied that Russia had not yet recovered from the world war and so could not afford to give away military hardware, but if the Chinese government was prepared to pay for it, then Russia was willing to help. The Chinese agreed to pay, thinking they would get a good deal from their socialist big brother.

Beginning in February 1955, the Chinese troops who were to take over the Russian military bases in Lushun and Dalian also accepted military goods which the Russians passed over to them, without thinking to check on the prices; the goods included guns, tanks, aeroplanes, warships, vehicles and so on, most of them well-worn veterans of the Second World War. When the bill came, it turned out that many had been charged for as new. Some items, such as old oil barrels, were in fact materials which the Russians had received free from America as lend-lease supplies, but all were charged at high prices. The total, which came to $400 million, shocked the Chinese leadership, but it was too late to argue. This new debt came on top of the $1.3 billion which China owed Russia for the Korean War. With simmering but well-disguised anger, on 26 May 1955 the party leadership organised an amicable, comradely send-off for the Russian Army. Communist dogma insisted that all noble qualities belonged to the proletariat, to socialists and Communists, while all the despicable vices were ingrained in the blood of their class enemy. It would be self-defeating to admit that there was no such thing as a selfless socialist big brother.

The not so selfless behaviour also appeared when Chow En-Lai visited the Russian Army in Lushun military base, accompanied by the Russian ambassador. The ambassador expressed his wish to build a

508

monument in China to commemorate the Russian soldiers killed in the 1904 Russo-Japanese war, in which the two countries had used China as their battleground to fight for the domination of Manchuria. Chow sternly rejected the request and told the ambassador to study Lenin's unequivocal comment on Tsarist Russia's policy of greed and brutality in Manchuria.

The Chinese Communist Party did not want to risk falling out with Russia during this uncertain period and for a long time it refused to make public the underhand treatment the party had received from Russia. Throughout most of the 1950s, the Chinese people were bombarded with propaganda about the selfless aid given by their Russian big brother and about the party's unyielding foreign policy of 'falling to one side', or in other words falling into Russian arms. Chinese people could get into serious trouble if they showed disrespect to Russia. One of the unfortunate offenders in this regard was the writer Shiu Jeun.

After the Japanese surrender a large number of Communists made their way to Manchuria and Shiu Jeun was sent there by Yan'an to run a periodical in Harbin. His joy at returning home after 14 years soon changed to shock when he found that life under Russian occupation was even worse than under the Japanese occupation. Reacting with fury, he began to lambast the Russians in his periodical, most famously in his article 'An eye for an eye', in the 53rd edition, in which he urged children to pelt the Russians with stones. In his editorial for the 59th edition, he discussed the different varieties of imperialism, among which he included Red imperialism. Before long he found himself overwhelmed by diatribes from Communist cultural watchdogs and was sent to an open coal mine in Fushun to do hard labour reform for five years, from spring 1949 to 1954. After his release from the labour camp, he wrote a novel, *The May Coal Mine*, published with financial assistance from friends, which was based on his harsh experiences in the mines. The book soon got him into trouble again; he was accused of being full of the rotten ideas of an outright villain, a frenetic individualist and anarchist. He was purged again and for a long time vanished without trace.

78

Counter-Revolutionaries Large and Small

Compared with Chiang, Mao was a very lucky man. He inherited a country free from both unruly warlords and menacing foreign encroachment, except for the two Russian military bases in Lushun and Dalian. His army soon controlled every corner of mainland China, winning the Communists absolute power.

In March 1950, six months after Communist China was born, the Chinese people saw the first of the Communist Party's political lynching storms, the Suppression of Counter-Revolutionary Elements Campaign. Such violent, fanatical and nationwide campaigns soon became a way of life.

This particular campaign professed to have five targets: bandits, powerful bullies, Nationalist agents, leading figures of reactionary religious sects and important members of the Nationalist Party with its Youth League. In reality, the campaign's main purpose was to kill large numbers of unarmed Nationalists.

Mao personally directed the operation. Following the practices of Lenin and Stalin, he began to use terror tactics to strengthen Communist rule. In early 1952 he sent a telegram to officials in Guangdong province instructing them to kill several thousand important counter-revolutionaries, because this was the way to destroy the enemy spirit. On 25 February, he wrote a circular in the name of the central committee to leading party officials throughout China, complaining that except for the big Manchurian cities, none of the country's major cities were carrying out the Suppression of Counter-Revolutionary Elements Campaign seriously on a large scale and he ordered officials to proceed without delay. Peking, Tianjin, Qingdao, Shanghai, Nanking, Canton, Hankow, Chongqing and other provincial capitals were all bound to contain reactionary organisations and Communist officials must begin surveillance immediately and find, arrest and kill proven reactionaries in large numbers within a few months.

Within ten days the authorities in Peking responded to Mao's guidance and carried out the city's first wave of mass executions; on 5 March, 199 reactionaries were shot. Other cities, counties, villages and towns quickly followed suit, each group trying to outdo the others to demonstrate their revolutionary zeal.

To speed things up, Mao delegated powers of arrest and execution to the cadres on the bottom rung of the government ladder and so many of the officials now holding powers of life and death were uneducated and demobbed soldiers who had proved their loyalty to the party in battle. If village cadres wished to kill someone, they did not have to go through the formality of a trial; instead all they had to do was to fill in one execution application form. On one occasion, an ex-soldier turned district party secretary was seen sitting on a chair with a stack of execution application forms from local villages on his lap. He pulled out three forms as a sample and glanced over them. Then he turned the forms over one by one quickly and put a tick on each of them, after which a clerk counted them; there were 160 forms. In a matter of a few minutes, 160 people had been condemned to death.

In no time at all the large-scale summary arrests had filled up all the prisons and temporary jails were set up in villages, counties and districts. In some counties the number of jails multiplied tenfold, but prisoners were always tightly packed, so much so that many were forced to sleep sitting or standing up.

The more Nationalist agents were arrested, the more there were still at large, or so the Communists believed. Sometimes underground Communists and partisans would be arrested by mistake and executed. Often tens of thousands of people would be collected together to watch a public show trial. A group of prisoners would be brought to the meeting and lined up, bound, in front of the platform, while Communist officials read out their crimes and death sentences. The audience was encouraged to hurl abuse and insults at the condemned people as a means of showing their support for the Communist authorities. Most of the condemned were Nationalist army officers, civil servants or party workers who were charged with crimes such as oppressing the people, suppressing student movements or fighting the Communists in the civil war. Communist China had no political prisoners, only counter-revolutionaries and reactionaries. Usually prisoners would have placards on their backs bearing their names and crimes. They would be loaded onto open trucks and paraded through the city, often accompanied by brass band music to the execution ground.

This was the fate that befell a middle-ranking Nationalist official, Yel Bo-Yeu, who in 1948 was director of the education department in

Guangdong province. In 1950 Yel Bo-Yeu decided to go over to the Communists and he and his wife returned to the mainland from Hong Kong. In Canton they were given a formal welcome by the Guangdong branch of the Political Consultative Conference. Soon afterwards he was sent to a Communist indoctrination institution, the Southern University, which had five departments: economy, administration, culture and education, research and workers. He was enrolled in the research department, whose 'students' were nearly all professors educated in Britain and America, or senior Nationalist government officials from the cultural affairs department. The president of the Southern University was Yip Jan-Ying, the Communist chief of Canton city and Guangdong province.

For the first two months the students' work was only 'confession', which meant recounting their life stories from the age of eight onwards, giving details about what they had done, where they had lived, the names of their schools and offices and so on. For each period of their lives they had to name one or two witnesses. Every morning all the students had to attend a political session, in which they were told to confess unreservedly, discard their burden of worries and join the revolution. It did not matter how serious their crimes were; if they confessed now, they would not be penalised for their past misdeeds; if they did not they would have to face the consequences.

Believing what they were told, the students would report everything about their past. After two months, the confession course was wound up. The next course was 'struggle meetings', which as a rule sucked dry people's time, energy and humanity. Every day and night there were small group meetings, medium-sized group meetings, departmental meetings and university meetings, all pressing people to analyse and condemn deeply and thoroughly their own evil past and their old attitudes, ideas, behaviour, sins and crimes.

One day all the students were summoned to a university struggle meeting. The man in trouble was Yel Bo-Yeu, who was condemned as an active cultural operative who had been sent back to mainland China by the Nationalist Party. He was said to have used his position to suppress people during Nationalist rule and now it was the turn of the people to take action against him. When the meeting was finished Yel was put into a prison transport van and taken away to a secret location. The shocked 'university students' now felt as if they were sitting on a carpet of needles, worrying where their own confessions would lead them.

When the raging Suppression of Counter-Revolutionary Elements Campaign in Canton conducted its very first group execution, around 120 condemned people were loaded onto 20 open trucks and paraded through the city, after which they were taken to the Liu Fa Bridge execution range and shot. Yel was on the first truck, wearing a tall dunce's hat with the characters 'Active cultural operative Yel Bo-Yeu' written on it. After he was shot the Yel family home was expropriated.

Many people trusted the Communist promise of leniency, just as Yel had done and made public confessions of their Nationalist past which were later used as evidence for their convictions. The promised clemency did not exclude them from being shot.

In early 1957, the party invited the masses to speak out frankly to give their opinions and any grievances relating to the party; again it loudly promised no retribution to anyone who complained. Yel's widow Young Sheu-Shan, a secondary school headmistress, wept at a meeting saying her husband had been wronged and shot for a non-existent crime. Six months later the party responded with the Anti-Rightist Campaign. Young Sheu-Shan was accused of having a serious problem in her thinking and of trying to overturn her husband's conviction. She was branded an anti-party, anti-people and anti-socialism element, or, in short, an arch-rightist. She was forced to kneel down and crawl at the school struggle meetings; she was slapped and insulted. Eventually she was sent to serve a long sentence in a labour camp.

In Woo Hu city, Anhui province, one of the victims was a former Nationalist official, Gow Tet-Jeun, who was well respected by the local people for his integrity and courage in upholding the law. He was also sympathetic enough to help out many underground Communists. When the huge Communist army was preparing to cross the Yangtze River in the 1949 civil war, Gow had managed to persuade the Nationalist 20th Army chief, Young Gown-Chai, to abandon the defence line along the river bank in order to spare Woo Hu city from the calamity of war, thereby enabling the Communist troops to cross the river swiftly and smoothly. In return the Communists promised not to turn on the Nationalist troops. After the Communists had crossed the river, they broke their promise and went on to slaughter the men of the 20th Army. Distraught, Young killed his whole family and then himself. Gow blamed himself for the tragedy and buried Young in the coffin he had kept for himself. Because of this atonement, the party executed Gow in the Suppression of Counter-Revolutionary Elements Campaign and 300 people who had jointly pledged their support for Gow's good conduct were also either jailed or killed as counter-revolutionaries. Later, in the 80s, the Anhui province party secretary, Chang Kai-Fan, said repeatedly that the party should not have killed Gow, but the party refused to consider Gow's rehabilitation.

Large numbers of Nationalists were killed in the campaign, most of whom had not committed any crimes that deserved the death penalty; they were killed anyway in order to create an atmosphere of terror so as to frighten off any possible resistance. Every village was obliged to take part in the campaign before the inception of land reform and the village killings were even more horrific than the killings during land reform (see next chapter). In the larger villages it was quite common for several dozen people to be executed in one day. According to a report from Cheujiang county, in Guangdong province, a total of 2,969 people were arrested, of whom 731 were put to death immediately, 1,425 were jailed, 165 were let out on bail and the rest were kept under detention. In Nanyang county, in Henan province, more than 1,100 reactionaries were shot in 1950. In Jarjiang county, Sichuan province, there were 954 cases of counter-revolutionaries among a population of less than 170,000. Eighty per cent of the arrests were made without first obtaining approval from any legal authority, while the remaining 20 per cent of approved cases often contained many trumped-up charges. In one small village in Jiangsu province which contained about 200 families, in all more than 40 people were put to death, some of whom were condemned simply for being members of a counter-revolutionary's family.

In a central committee directive, Mao laid down the rule that 'some immediate family members of people who were put through struggle meetings, locked up or killed in the Land Reform Campaign, the Suppression of Counter-Revolutionary Elements Campaign and other socialist reform operations ... should be sent to a labour reform camp.' Communist China's official policy, in other words, was to punish the families of victims.

In 1980 many county archives were at last published, revealing the county's achievements in the Suppression of Counter-Revolutionary Elements Campaign. Nearly every one of the 3,000 or so counties in China had dealt with several hundred counter-revolutionary cases. A confidential document compiled by the judiciary department in late 1952 contained a report on the Suppression of Counter-Revolutionary Elements Campaign which gave the total number of executed people in the whole of China, but when the report was released the seven-figure number had been blacked out. However, when the Communist authorities talked about the achievements of the campaign, they claimed to have liquidated more than two million political bandits or remnants of the Nationalist Party; most of these people would have been shot soon after their arrest. The figure of two million did not include the Communist Army's exploits in the wake of its victorious advance of 1949 during the civil war. Wherever the PLA troops went, they arrested and killed vast numbers of Nationalists from the military, civil and education services immediately. Some people estimated that by the end of 1952 at least five million such people had been killed by the Communists.

The title of the Suppression of Counter-Revolutionary Elements Campaign made it very clear that the targets of the suppression were people, the counter-revolutionaries themselves and not simply counter-revolutionary activity. In fact most of the victims were no longer politically active; however, because they had once served the old regime all were condemned as historical counter-revolutionaries, even Nationalist soldiers who had fought in the Sino-Japanese War. Many had actually defected from the Nationalist government during the civil war to join the Communist army, but were later expelled from the PLA and jailed. It was only in May 1980 that the Communist Party admitted, at least partially, the way it had treated the Nationalist defectors. They were liquidated after the Communists had already won power, not while they were still fighting for it. In addition to the large numbers executed, many more counter-revolutionaries were sent to prisons, labour camps or put under public surveillance and many of those sent to prisons or labour camps died.

According to one Communist official who had once worked in a labour reform department in Xinjiang province, as many as 700,000 counter-revolutionaries from Sichuan province alone were sentenced to serve more than seven years in the labour reform camps of Xinjiang. Most of them were poor and 'middle' peasants (the Chinese Communist system divides peasants into four grades: poor peasants, middle peasants – who were slightly better off than poor peasants – rich peasants and landlords). By early August 1979, nearly 330,000 people from Hunan province had been rehabilitated, which meant that 95.5 per cent of those convicted had been wrongly condemned as landlords, rich peasants, counter-revolutionaries or bad elements.

In April 1954, Mao announced at a central committee meeting that 'in order to suppress counter-revolutionaries, a total of two to three million people were put under public surveillance, jailed or killed.' At a State Council meeting in February 1957, he announced that 'between 1950 and 1952, 700,000 people were killed. In the following three years, fewer than 80,000 were killed.' After giving these sanitised figures, he insisted that there had been nothing wrong with the Suppression of Counter-Revolutionary Elements Campaign and he refused to re-examine any case.

Although millions of middle- to low-ranking Nationalists met with wholesale extirpation, their high-ranking bosses were treated differently. The senior Nationalists who were captured were mostly army generals, with a small number of generals in the security service and civil servants from provincial chairman upwards, as well as the ex-emperor Pu Yi, his younger brother and his important Manchukuo courtiers. All of these men were detained in war criminal reform camps. The most important of these camps, with more than 100 inmates, was in Peking. The erstwhile commanders-in-chief and commanders of army corps in the camps had all fought and killed Communists; they all had copious amounts of Communist blood on their hands. Among them was General Tan Dow-Shen, who had fought in the Huai-Hai campaign, where he had given orders to use poison gas against Communist troops; because the Communists had not been issued with gas masks, their casualties were enormous. For this poison gas attack, Tan Dow-Shen and some of his colleagues were sentenced to death, but the sentence was suspended. The security chiefs who had specialised in catching Communist agents and killing many of them, did not even get death sentences.

The war criminals were made to do manual work such as farming, cooking and carpentry. At the same time they were infused with extra strong doses of Communist indoctrination and group therapy, in which they criticised each other and themselves. They would often be taken out to visit some of the glorious achievements of Communist China, such as the grand new Yangtze River bridge and the fully working and expanded factories in Manchuria, which had been thoroughly devastated by the Russians after the Sino-Japanese War. Particularly impressive was the motor car factory city in Changchun, where the sight of Chinese-made motor cars gave the Nationalist prisoners a pleasant feeling of pride. They also visited schools and shops, where the cadres in charge would make speeches about their progress and success, urging the prisoner-visitors to learn unremittingly from the selfless working class and to try hard to reform themselves, so that one day they too might be able to make some contribution to the motherland.

These top-grade prisoners were never tortured, or even verbally abused. Their errors were dealt with leniently by their prison governors, who would just talk to the wrongdoers patiently and point out that they came from a reactionary class, so it was only natural that they would harbour hostility toward the new society. They were reminded again and again of the contrast between the old society and the new.

These war criminals knew they were well treated; even their food was better than most Chinese people could provide for themselves and their lives were certainly not in danger. Chow En-Lai even found time to visit some of them for old time's sake, because many had been Whampoa cadets and Chow still remembered them from when he had been director of the department of politics at the Whampoa Military Academy. The Communist General Chan Guan also visited prisoners who were old friends from the Whampoa Military Academy, even taking them out of the prison for meals. Lin Biao never came to see his former Whampoa friends. He obviously preferred to have no contact with them.

The soft policy was undoubtedly a success, so much so that even the staunchest Nationalists were persuaded to support the Communist government. After ten years, the first group of reformed war criminals, including General Doo Yu-Ming from the Peking camp and ex-Emperor Pu Yi from the Fushun camp, were granted an amnesty. The newly rehabilitated citizens were given jobs, usually working for the national archives department and later on were promoted to become members of the Political Consultative Conference. These important old foes, patiently and carefully cultivated by the Communists, were then paraded before the world to show that the Chinese Communist regime included a huge sweep of humanity and certainly did not kill its enemies.

Royal foreign visitors were usually interested in meeting Pu Yi in order to see how it was that an ex-emperor was willing to become a commoner and even to support the Communist regime. Others were more interested in meeting senior army officers, particularly Doo Yu-Ming, who had commanded nearly a million Nationalist troops in Manchuria during the civil war and who had been exceedingly loyal to Chiang. Earl Mountbatten, who had known Doo in the Burma war, found him a changed man and asked why he was now supporting the Communists. Doo replied to such questions by saying that because he was Chinese and dearly loved his country, he would support anyone who was good for China. The reformed war criminals were often also used by the Communists to make broadcasts urging their old friends and colleagues now on the other side of the Taiwan Strait to return to the bosom of their forgiving motherland.

The party's double standards paid handsomely for a while. Unfortunately the new life for the rehabilitated Nationalists was not to last. When the Cultural Revolution began several years later, nearly all of them were liquidated; many were thrown into jail or beaten to death. Those who were seriously wounded were taken home to die, because the party preferred to deny medical care to the class enemy. Once the Communists had extracted whatever useful services the prisoners of war could give, there was no reason to continue the soft treatment they had once enjoyed.

Two Ways of Land Reform

Before the end of the bloodbath of the Suppression of Counter-Revolutionary Elements Campaign, another bloodletting campaign had already begun racing ahead. This was the Land Reform Campaign of 1950 to 1952, the Communist Party's centrepiece policy. Mao was adamantly opposed to the idea of the middle and poor peasants receiving free gifts from the Communist Party and peaceful land reform was therefore banned. He wanted them to be conscious of their own formidable power in crushing the rich peasants and landlords.

Back in 1927 the Communist movement controlled a good part of Hubei and Hunan provinces and poor peasants in these provinces were directed by Mao to torture and kill landlords and burn down their homes. The campaigns were extensive and indiscriminate; there were numerous innocent victims and also some unforeseen problems. During the campaign many officers fighting in the Northern Expedition Army turned against the Communists and village clans also used the opportunity to settle old scores. Although most people condemned this campaign as brutal, Mao alone insisted that the policy was 'very good' and as the years went by his view did not change.

By 1933 Chow En Lai had carried out Moscow's instructions to annihilate landlords in Jiangxi province's Soviet districts. Even some people who owned land smaller than two acres qualified for annihilation, while in the early 50s in north Shaanxi province, people who could afford not to live on chaff were classed as landlords. Many innocent peasants were identified as villains and brought to struggle meetings where they faced trumped-up charges from young people who had been manipulated to act as accusers. The Communist cadres in charge of the meeting would ask the crowd: 'What should we do with this person?' The activists planted among the crowd would yell: 'Kill him!' and the victim would then be shot or beaten to death on the spot. Often it was an unexpected outcome for the young activists, since many of the victims were their friends, neighbours, relations or even fathers or brothers and the activists quickly became village pariahs. Before the Communists won power, these village outcasts could only run away from home and join the Red Army. As the slogan 'root out the landlord class' was put into brutal effect, often the entire families of landlords were slaughtered; even babies were not spared. When the Red Army commander Kung Chor opposed the policy, he was expelled from the party for a year by Chow En-Lai.

In 1990, a group of people recalled the full horrors of the 1947 Communist Land Reform Campaign in the east of Hebei province. On one occasion in the campaign a man was shot but did not die immediately; schoolchildren were then encouraged to dig holes in and cut flesh from the dying man's body with skewers, scissors, knives and nails and to smear mud on his wounds. One over-excited boy even cut off both his ears. The victim had been a poor landless peasant, but the village cadres found out that his grandfather had once employed a pair of helping hands and so his class status was changed overnight and his offence was punishable by death.

When the landlords were all gone, attention was switched to people who had a little more land than the average. In one case, a family of eight or nine had three acres of land. They tilled all their land themselves without employing anyone to help, but they still suffered a similar fate as landlords. One reason for the campaign was that the party needed to find money to support its expanding army.

In 1950 Communist policy and "Mao Tse-Tung Thought" on land reform remained much the same. After the first priority of killing counter-revolutionaries had been accomplished, it was followed by the second priority of purging landlords and their families.

The need to mobilise the support of the poor peasants for the Land Reform Campaign, in accordance with party policy and the "Mao Tse-Tung Thought", made the Communist cadres' jobs arduous. They had to visit all the poor peasants to build up a rapport, then persuade them to recall grievances and to encourage them to hate the landlords and rich peasants. When there was no discord, it was the cadres' responsibility to make peasants find some.

One widely publicised incident in north China involved a peasant who was under pressure to make an accusation against a condemned landlord. The peasant thought about it for a long time and finally said 'He once ate an egg of mine and did not pay me.' This was good enough evidence and the cadres worked out the sum. It was said that the egg could have hatched and the chicken could have laid eggs again. After ten years of such repeated reproduction, the sum had multiplied so much that the landlord had to hand over a large sum of money in compensation.

Some peasants with genuine grudges and others who had been groomed to hate were summoned to village struggle meetings, where the accused were compelled to confess their crimes. One semi-secret Communist newsletter, *Internal Reference*, reported on 2 June 1950 that the cadres in Henan province were too easily convinced by false denunciations and beat people up too readily, killing them or driving them to suicide; furthermore, many of their victims were only middle or poor peasants. As a protest against the beatings in Lan Fong county some villagers refused to go to public meetings, but as punishment the cadres forced them to transport water to fill all the water storage urns in the village.

Some absentee landlords who ran businesses in cities or towns were brought back to the villages to face trial for the crime of owning land. They were forced to kneel down on broken glass or other sharp objects, before being shouted at and forced to endure having excreta, snakes, scorpions and centipedes tipped over them. They were kicked and beaten, often to death, with fists or sticks, as their frightened families looked on. After their land had been expropriated and distributed to the poor peasants, their families were thrown out of their homes with only the clothes they stood up in and their houses and possessions taken over by the poorer villagers.

The land reform dragnet did not spare those landowners who had risked their lives to help the Communists during the Sino-Japanese war. When they were brought before the struggle meetings, the Communists they had once protected could only watch, not daring to object; not even poor peasants were allowed to speak up for any landlord or rich peasant. The policy was that beating these people to death was always correct. During the most violent period, some villages summoned Communist cadres who were the children of landlords but who were now working for the party in other areas. Many had also fought in the Sino-Japanese War and the civil war, but even so they did not escape being beaten to death in their home villages.

Members of the intelligentsia were also organised into joining the land reform cadres in their work in the villages. They were told to test themselves in the class struggle so as to find out whether they could stand firmly on the revolutionary side. Nearly all academics, members of democratic parties, medical doctors and senior cadres, particularly those who had lived in 'white' areas, volunteered to plunge into this real-life education in class struggle. A great many university students spent two years receiving education in villages; the other two years of their university training were taken up by political meetings. As a result, when they graduated they knew next to nothing about the subject they had in theory been studying, but they knew how to stir up a crowd. They also learnt how much violence was permissible and that, no matter how unreasonable or unfair it was, no one was allowed to put in any words on behalf of the victims, which would be regarded as an assault on the revolutionary spirit of the poor peasants. When, very occasionally, party members spoke the truth, trying to give victims a little justice, they were punished and expelled from the party. The more serious waverers would be dispatched to labour camps, teaching them in effect that veracity and falsehood were irrelevant and that only the political dogma counted.

The Chinese people and especially the country's left-wing intellectuals in those days, had been deeply affected by an exciting new ideology. It was an ideology which inspired hope and worship and which promised to bring a free, fair and democratic country. Any disquiet caused by the rough justice and brutality was easily brushed aside; instead people blamed themselves for their ignorance about the importance of class struggle and their inadequate understanding of Mao's great teachings. They felt they were not yet staunch revolutionaries and still had many more political lessons to learn.

Land reform brought cataclysm to rural areas and life was never the same again. Soon both rich peasants and landlords found themselves living in dire poverty; some became beggars, others went mad. Their children were not allowed to go to school, let alone university. Many of these people had owned only a few acres of land and their living standards had been only slightly better than those of the landless poor peasants. Their share of exploitation had certainly been insignificant compared with other sections of society such as merchants, corrupt officials and the really big landlords. Nevertheless they were not spared.

For decades to come these class enemies lived under the strict surveillance of the whole village and when anything untoward happened they were as a rule the first to get the blame. On one occasion in 1963, a group of construction workers showed signs of having been poisoned and their old cook, who had once been a landlord, was accused of poisoning them. He was shot. The authorities used the affair as propaganda to alert the public and to emphasise the existence of long-lasting and implacable class hatred; there were newspaper reports as well as a documentary film about the apparently shocking case. Finally, it came out that the construction workers had actually fallen ill with food poisoning which was not the fault of the old cook at all, but his name was never cleared.

Rapes committed by Communist cadres were not uncommon. If the victim belonged to the family of a landlord or other class enemy, she would be better off swallowing her grief and keeping quiet. If she complained, the authorities would allege that the rape had actually been a devious plot by a class enemy to seduce and corrupt an innocent Communist cadre. In such cases it was the woman who was condemned as the culprit.

During the Land Reform Campaign, the party announced to the poor peasants that once they had destroyed the rich peasants and landlords, the poor would enjoy a blissful socialist life. In 1960, the bodyguard of Marshal Peng De-Huai, the disgraced defence minister, complained about a recent visit to his home village during which he found that the village cadres had been even more ferocious than the landlords and the village autocratic officials in old society ('old society' is the Chinese Communist term for pre-Communist society, while Communist society is officially known as 'new society').

In the process of destroying a whole class of oppressors, a new class of oppressors was born in the shape of the Communist cadres. In 1962 Deng Xiao-Ping recalled remarks made by some disgruntled peasants that in 'old society' each village had had to provide for one Bo Jang, but now they had many more Bo Jangs to deal with. The number of village cadres was estimated to be between 16 and 25 million, which meant each one of them was maintained by 20 to 30 peasants.

The violinist Professor Ma Shi-Chown once wrote about a fact-finding tour he had made in 1965 with a group of colleagues in a rural area near Peking, during which he was shocked to find many village cadres behaving like imperious emperors. One of them specialised in stealing valuables, while another one had raped 60 per cent of the women in the village. No one dared complain because the cadres were party officials and in effect the rulers of the village.

The Land Reform Campaign resulted in many middle peasants being wrongly condemned as landlords for letting out small pieces of land. According to the central committee's instruction, 10 per cent of the peasants had to be purged and so at least 30 million of them were brought to struggle meetings or tortured. At least two million landlords were killed and the survivors and their families had to live with the stigma of class enemy for generations to come, even though some had never owned any land and had earned their living as employees all their lives.

The party, in its attempts to build a planned economy along Russian lines, obliged all peasants to sell their 'surplus' to the state. Prospective yields were assessed by cadres and the peasants were given quotas to fulfil. But with unrealistic assessments made by over-zealous cadres, eager to collect as much 'surplus' food as possible for the state, the peasants were never able to retain enough grain for their own needs. Consequently they remained hungry and prone to ill health. Their situation was made worse because for a long time the authorities maintained artificially low prices for agricultural products.

By 1956 agricultural collectivisation was introduced to China, turning all peasants effectively into farm slaves. In Guangdong province, one of the richest in the country, the peasants worked nearly 14 hours a day every day of the year, yet they still did not have enough to eat. The dream of improving their living standards promised by the Communists looked increasingly inaccessible.

Meanwhile the defeated Nationalist Party in Taiwan pursued a free economy, also conducting land reform but through legislation rather than violence. In 1951 a government decree reduced the rent for agricultural land drastically, which increased tenant farmers' income. The decree also banned landlords from taking back their land or letting it to people other than their existing tenants. Consequently tenant farmers had the right to occupy the land permanently and landlords could only sell their land to their tenant farmers. The government also provided loans to tenant farmers to buy the land they were farming. Farmland owned by the government was also on sale, with priority given to self-employed farmers. The legislation produced a smooth and peaceful transfer of land from landlords to peasants; many landlords were happy to sell off their land in order to release capital, which they then reinvested in industry or commerce. Taiwanese landlords were thus eliminated without a bloodbath; not one landlord was tortured or killed in the island's land reform programme.

Taiwanese peasants were free to farm their land without planning interference from their government and without time-consuming political campaigns. Farm produce was tax-free. When the government tried to encourage peasants to switch to other crops, it would offer subsidies and guarantee purchase prices, but peasants were free to sell their produce to anyone.

Taiwanese peasants became increasingly prosperous following the island's land reform. By 1992, every peasant family owned a modern home with all modern facilities such as television, telephone, motorcycle, van or truck. Many had more than one vehicle, in addition to small farming machines. Every family could afford to go sightseeing in Taiwan or mainland China and 20 per cent of families had holidays abroad. The young farmers belonged to an educated generation. Their average annual income in 1992 was US$ 3,910 per head, while in the year 2000 mainland Chinese peasants were hoping for an average annual income of just US $400 per head.

In the early 1950s, peasants' incomes on either side of the Taiwan Strait were more or less the same, but after four decades under two different systems, the Taiwanese peasants enjoyed incomes over ten times higher than their counterparts on the mainland. The Communist Party's bloody land reform policy brought Chinese peasants neither material benefits nor perhaps, to most of them, peace of mind.

80

The Thought Police

In early 1951, a new film, *The Story of Woo Sheun*, was chosen by a popular film magazine as one of the ten best Chinese films of the year.

Woo Sheun (1839–96) who lived during the late Qing Dynasty, devoted his life to giving poor children an education paid for by the money he made as a beggar. His efforts to help underprivileged children regardless of his own poverty won popular admiration. Nobody, not even the party's many authoritative thinkers, thought there was anything wrong with the film. However, on 20 May 1951, an editorial in the *People's Daily* declared: '*The Story of Woo Sheun* has brought to the fore a fundamental question which is, should we eulogise such ugly behaviour as displaying servility to reactionary feudal rulers? Can we tolerate a film that even uses the failure of the revolutionary peasants' struggle as a background to praise Woo Sheun? To accept and put up with such reactionary propaganda, which belittles the peasants' struggle, Chinese history and the Chinese people, shows what degree of confusion is in the minds of people in cultural circles.'

The *People's Daily* was the party's official mouthpiece and its condemnation of Woo Sheun sent out a shock-wave which stunned the whole of China. The author of the editorial obviously possessed the only properly functioning mind in the whole country. Most people felt threatened, but they did not know that the author was actually Mao himself, who looked on Woo as a despicable reformist, a tool of feudal society. If he had had any vision he would have organised an armed rebellion. Woo's failing was apparently that he had not preached Marxism at a time when no one in China had ever heard of Karl Marx. Woo was a lucky man; he had been dead for a long time.

In the middle of the Land Reform Campaign and the Suppression of Counter-Revolutionary Elements Campaign, Mao set in motion a new campaign of mind reform. Screenings of the 'poisonous' film were all cancelled and the *People's Daily* formally called on all Communists to join in the important new campaign. The newspaper, in cooperation with the

Ministry of Culture, sent a delegation to Woo's home town in Shandong province to make a thorough investigation of his life. The resulting report, with a few alterations by Mao, concluded that Woo had been a bad character, a moneylender and a landlord who had been given special privileges by the reactionary imperial government, using education as an insidious means to serve the reactionary government and the landlord class.

Everyone who had praised Woo's noble qualities was now in big trouble, especially the writer responsible for the film's screenplay, who was accused of having reactionary political tendencies. The director made a public self-criticism which was published in the newspapers and the actor who had played Woo was reprimanded; being a Communist, he should have been more politically class-conscious!

Meanwhile nearly all academics, writers, filmmakers and leading figures in cultural circles were submerged in political study, serious debates and soul-searching self-criticisms, many of which appeared in the newspapers. In an attempt to get through the campaign safely and to have their self-criticisms accepted, most pleaded that they had not yet learnt to think in the correct way, but from now on they would study the party's teachings diligently. It was still a honeymoon period for the intellectuals and the party.

Not long after the storm over *The Story of Woo Sheun*, Mao found that another film, a story about the Qing imperial court, had made a major error as well. He accused the ostensibly patriotic film of being in fact thoroughly treacherous. But even though it had already been shown all over the country, nobody had criticised it so far.

After all these denunciations, a national commission for films was set up, with Mao's wife, Jiang Ching, as a member; now it was she who held ultimate power over China's film production. In 1950, 39 Chinese films were produced; in 1951, there were only 12 and in 1952, under the guidance of the commission, just five story films were produced. The film industry was facing a crisis of confidence.

In December 1985, more than 30 years after the incident, the prominent Communist ideologist Hu Chel-Moo publicly admitted that the furore over *The Story of Woo Sheun* had been 'very one-sided and extreme and it could also be said to have been very brutal... The charges against the film were exaggerated to the point of being incredible and this mistake was aggravated by extending criticism to everyone who approved of Woo Sheun as a man with good intentions and to all other works about Woo Sheun, including cartoon books. This erroneous criticism went on for a very long time.'

Soon after the onslaught on Woo Sheun and the film industry, another cultural storm struck China. In early 1953 Professor Yu Ping-Bor published a work about one of the greatest novels of the Qing Dynasty, *The Dream of the Red Chamber*. Two young people criticised Yu for his failure to point out the anti-feudal elements in the book and their comments were later taken up by Mao. Although he was hard at work on the Three-anti and Five-anti Campaigns (see next chapter), he found time to make use of Yu to give his favourite target, the academics, some hefty blows. On 16 October, he delivered an ominous comment which also mentioned the well-respected scholar and leader of the New Culture Movement, Dr Hu Shi:

> This is the first time that anyone has seriously taken aim at the misguided views of a certain 'authoritative' researcher for the last 30 or so years on *The Dream of the Red Chamber*. It looks as if the fight against Dr Hu Shi's capitalist-inspired influence, which has been poisoning young people in the field of classical literature for more than 30 years, can now get going at last.

Mao regarded the book, which portrayed the lives of four privileged families in imperial China, as a political novel about the exploitation of servants, although few other readers had discerned this. Three days after he signalled the attack, he launched yet another political campaign and the battle triggered by the film about Woo Sheun came back to haunt the intellectuals again.

The brickbats hurled at Yu were increasingly vicious. Some said Yu was speaking up for imperialist theory and culture, while others blamed capitalist intellectuals influenced by Dr Hu Shi who were working together with other capitalists to resist socialist reform on the ideological front. The powerful literary censor Chow Young announced that Yu's literary point of view was not only capitalist but also feudal. Its political aim was to persuade his readers to escape from the revolution. Thus what had begun as purely academic literary research was transformed into a violent political fight. Renowned academics were organised into four groups, all of which worked hard to demolish Dr Hu's arguments relating to philosophy, politics, history and literature, while former colleagues or friends of Hu's were required to make self-criticisms in depth.

On 20 January 1986, during the post-Mao era, the ideological mandarin Hu Shing, head of the College of Social Sciences, openly said that the persecution of Professor Yu had been wrong. Not only had it been emotionally hurtful to Yu Ping-Bor, it had also been detrimental to art and to academic development. In November the same year, an article in the *Kwang Ming Daily*, a national newspaper read by intellectuals, argued that Dr Hu Shi had been a great teacher and his many writings were a great credit to his scholarship. He had made important contributions to education and to the New Culture Movement in China during the 1920s.

What nobody dared to point out was that Mao Tse-Tung had been preposterously wrong again and again.

81

The Three-anti and Five-anti Campaigns

Before the Land Reform Campaign had been completed, another group of people were caught up in the Three-anti and Five-anti Campaigns launched in November 1951.

In the fledgling state of Communist China, all major policies were decided by Mao. Until 1953, he gave the impression that the Communist Party would be prepared to work with capitalists to build a pluralistic economy, because many Chinese businessmen were nationalistic and patriotic. After the Communists came to power, however, few businessmen were prepared to make new investments, while tax evasion, bribery, theft and corruption were rife. The Three-anti and Five-anti Campaigns were designed to solve these problems.

The 'three antis' targeted corruption, waste and bureaucracy among state employees, while the 'five antis' targeted bribery, tax evasion, the theft of national property, cheating on government contracts and theft of state economic intelligence. The targets of this campaign were dishonest businessmen.

Like other Communist campaigns, powers of prosecution, investigation and adjudication were handed over to people at the lowest level, who needed only one qualification: they had to be Communists or their supporters. In the Five-anti Campaign, campaign units were usually divided into two groups, one of which worked on employees in an attempt to stir up hatred against their employers. The workers would be told that they had been badly exploited by their bosses and were urged to find out and report their employers' misdeeds. The other group worked on the employers, coercing them to confess their crimes and in many cases businessmen would be detained and tortured to extract confessions without reliable evidence.

A famous victim of this campaign was Lu Zuo-Fu, once praised by Mao as one of the four unforgettable people in modern Chinese industrial history. Lu came from a poor Sichuan family. In 1925, the young and educated Lu raised enough money to buy a small ship, striving to realise his generation's dream of saving China by building up its own modern industry. By 1949 his shipping company had around 100 ships; many of them plied between Chongqing and Shanghai, but his shipping lanes also stretched out to Southeast Asia. Yet, even though he was the general manager of Sichuan Min San Shipping Company, the second biggest shipping company in China, he lived a simple life among his staff in the company's quarters. He owned neither house nor land and he had no private money stashed away in the banks. At one time he had been an assistant minister for transport in the Nationalist government, but after power changed hands in China he defected to the Communists, arranging for his fleet to sail back from Hong Kong to Communist China and he was accorded very favourable treatment by the Communists. After the end of the Sino-Japanese War he had ordered a number of new ships from Canada. By 1949 his company found itself in debt, with payments still outstanding and the new Communist government lent Lu a large sum of money to tide the company over.

Lu was twice given the honour of sitting next to Mao at banquets and Chow En-Lai even proposed a toast to him. However before long, back at home in Sichuan, he was accused of being an unlawful capitalist and put through cruel struggle sessions. In 1952 he poisoned himself, the overseas edition of the *People's Daily* reporting that he had died following an illness.

More than 30 years after Lu's death his name was posthumously cleared by the Communist authorities. A senior colleague, the head of Lu's economic research department, was also cleared, having spent the last 30 years in a labour camp in Xinjiang province. He was rehabilitated, luckily still alive.

Businessmen all over the country, even rag-and-bone men whose total assets might be nothing more than a tatty bamboo basket carried on the back, were under pressure to admit exploitation of their employees, tax evasion, theft or excessive profits and any admissions were followed by a government demand for a huge fine. Men were even denounced by their own families, who had been convinced by Communist propaganda. Often at struggle meetings children would loudly denounce their fathers for having hands stained with their workers' blood, proclaiming how ashamed they were of being the children of capitalists. Some even assaulted their parents physically. Many businessmen who had been defiant up to that point would collapse in the face of abuse from their own flesh and blood; in despair they would admit any crime of which they were accused.

On one occasion in Canton, a merchant and his wife took their five children up to the top of a high-rise building and tossed them out of a window one by one, before jumping out themselves. Even some Communists were shocked by this incident and they tried to restrain their followers from meting out over-zealous beatings. Many more businessmen took their own lives in Shanghai, China's main commercial city. They were liable for tax evasion right back to Shanghai's beginnings as a commercial city during Emperor Kwan-Hsu's reign. Few businessmen were able to pay tax arrears going back for more than half a century and many decided instead to jump to their deaths.

The then mayor of Shanghai, Marshal Chan Yi, later admitted that at the time there had been more than 1,300 'parachuters' in the city. One thing was clear, they had chosen freefall without a chute as a better way out. Some were heard yelling on their way down: 'You can't harass me now!' People chose not to drown themselves, because if their bodies could not be found, the Communists could accuse them of having fled to Hong Kong and the families they left behind would then be in serious trouble.

While businessmen were subjected to the scrutiny of the Five-anti Campaign, in the Three-anti Campaign most state employees whose jobs involved handling money were under suspicion until they were proved innocent. One sales department buyer, Sheu Ka-Chong, of the Pearl River district People's Daily in Guangdong province, was charged as a major corrupt element. Detained in his office block, he was assaulted at struggle meetings to make him confess. Subjected to daily punching and kicking and believing Mao's promise of clemency, the sum he admitted to embezzling grew day by day. He was worn down by interrogators who rotated through the day and night and he was repeatedly insulted, his home searched and his wife threatened. On one occasion a young colleague found a small empty oatmeal tin at Sheu's home, which he regarded as evidence of theft, whereupon Sheu's corruption figure went up again. Another colleague, on the other hand, did not believe that Sheu was guilty and objected to extracting a confession by beating; instead he suggested looking for reliable and convincing proof. But he received a stiff rebuke from his party boss and kept quiet from then on.

After a year Sheu's confessions came to an end and he now had to pay back all the 'stolen' money. His colleagues were sent to see his wife and urge her to come up with the cash and eventually she managed to borrow enough money from relatives to get her husband released. Sheu now became a handy victim for every purging campaign. During one campaign in 1955, he went to his office one day for a political study meeting but failed to return home; instead he spent two years in prison. When he was eventually released he discovered that his wife had died a lonely death in childbirth.

Any bookkeeper or accountant, or any other worker involved with finance who came from the wrong class background, was regarded as being corrupt and even if no proof was found it was assumed that the culprit had cleverly hidden the loot. In the very early days of the Communist regime a patriotic businessman, Woo Guen-Mai, was given the job of deputy chief in a central government department responsible for helping private enterprises to develop. At the time this was part of Communist policy. When the Three-anti and Five-anti Campaigns began, Woo as a capitalist was a target of the five-anti campaign, while as a deputy chief of a government department he was also a target of the three-anti campaign. The revolutionary zealots accused him of being a capitalist agent stalking a government department, ignoring the fact that he had been formally appointed to the post by the prime minister, Chow En-Lai. At one struggle meeting, Woo was ejected from his office with immediate effect; he was not even allowed to clear his desk and take his private correspondence with him.

The Three-anti and Five-anti Campaigns made many formerly busy scenic spots desolate and many famous restaurants were deserted and found themselves close to bankruptcy. It was eventually disclosed that 95 per cent of the victims in the Three-anti Campaign had been condemned in error.

In Mao's 1945 essay about coalition government, he wrote that China did not have too much capitalism, only too much feudalism and imperialism and for some years thereafter the party looked tolerantly on capitalists. By 1953, socialist reforms of capitalism were introduced, announced in the policy: 'to use, to constrain and to reform the capitalists'. All businesses were obliged to accept the state as a partner and the state was to buy out the capitalists in annual instalments, with a view to complete nationalisation within 15 years. Even Chow En-Lai admitted that the capitalists' assets had been valued on the low side, while some capitalists gave up the right to state payments altogether, because accepting even that small sum of money showed that they were still functioning capitalists, which was something that would bring them more trouble than gain.

One victim of the campaign was an old woman who owned a three-storey house. Having no family to support her, she eked out a living by letting out rooms on two floors. But even she was among the capitalists who needed constraint and reform and she was consequently made to accept the state as a partner in her room-letting business. The state bought her out by paying her just 30 yuans per year.

The 15-year plan to nationalise all private businesses was completed within three years. When it was over, many businessmen saw the writing on the wall; they joined the masses in parading through the streets, to the sound of drums and gongs, to celebrate the take-over of all capitalist assets by the government.

When the Cultural Revolution erupted in 1966, the Red Guards forbade the banks from paying out any more interest to the capitalists; the capitalists dared not take the interest anyway. To build Mao's paradise, the Red Guards banned all private enterprise, even the travelling barbers and knife-sharpeners, hawkers and peasant women trying to sell a few eggs in the markets. All these transactions were denounced as spontaneous capitalism and the Red Guards were committed to eliminating all such vices.

82

Hu Fung's Counter-Revolutionary Cabal

Since the Communist Party was determined to control how and what the nation thought, ideological battle was constantly in the air. The commotion stirred up by *The Story of Woo Sheun* and *The Dream of the Red Chamber* was just a small foretaste for the Chinese people; the case of Hu Fung was a much more serious affair.

Hu Fung came from a poor family in Hubei province. He was attracted to Communism while he was very young and when he was studying in Japan in the 1930s he was arrested for being a member of the Japanese Communist Party and deported after three months in jail. He then went to Shanghai and joined the left-wing writers' association and the Chinese Communist Party. He became very close to Lu Xun, the leader of the left-wing writers. He was on bad terms with Chow Young, the party's literary censor in Shanghai.

When war broke out, Hu moved first to Wuhan, then to Chongqing and finally to Hong Kong. Three months after Hong Kong fell to the Japanese, he escaped to Guilin, from where he returned again to Chongqing. As a result of his lengthy travels across China to evade the Japanese, Hu lost contact with the Communist Party, which consequently no longer recognized his party membership.

When the Communists won power, Chow Young became a powerful party chief in charge of the creative arts. While most people wisely did the party's bidding, Hu stubbornly held on to his own literary views. In early 1953, the *Literary Magazine*, the Communist literary standard bearer, published two articles written by party ideologists which criticised Hu's views as an anti-Marxist literary ideology. The articles were speedily reprinted in the *People's Daily*, but so far the fracas was limited to literary differences.

Hu soon found himself under siege. From September 1953 to January 1954 he was summoned from Shanghai to Peking for a series of self-criticism meetings. Hu was not prepared to take such a battering lying down and with help from sympathetic friends who provided him with materials and ideas he wrote a treatise of 300,000 words defending his literary theories. He objected to the view that literature was an appurtenance of politics and that its main criteria should be political and he objected to the way that literature was being detached from historical truth in order to praise political achievements and virtues. He also objected to the way that writers and artists were being treated as political tools and being used for propaganda purposes. He argued for the importance of subjectivity in artistic works and described his two critics' views on what and how to write as knives embedded in the heads of writers and readers, killing off creative and realistic writing.

On 22 July 1954, Hu requested a meeting with Si Jon-Sheun, the deputy director of the party's Culture and Education Commission, to hand over his treatise; he asked Si to pass it on to the party chairman, Mao, the deputy chairman, Liu Shao-Qi and the prime minister, Chow En-Lai. In an attached letter he wrote humbly that he hoped the central committee would examine his treatise, comment on it and give him instructions which he could follow in reviewing his work.

More than a decade earlier, in 1942, Mao had given a famous speech in Yan'an in which he announced that all creative arts had to serve politics, an idea he had picked up from Stalin. From then on, Chinese communists organised activities year after year to commemorate the deliverance of that divine speech. As far as Mao was concerned his guidance was incontrovertible and conclusive. Hu was the first person who dared to challenge his ruling on the arts systematically, seriously and openly. It was inevitable that Mao would not look kindly on him.

By January 1955, the party's propaganda department reported to the central committee that Hu's literary concepts were hostile to the party and the people, so his influence would have to be purged. A heavy blow came from Hu's old friend Shu Woo, who wrote an article published in the *People's Daily* in mid-April 1955 criticising Hu's literary views. Hoping to save his own neck, Shu Woo voluntarily surrendered all private correspondence between himself and Hu from the 1940s; the letters were published in the *Literary Magazine* and were used by Mao in his campaign against Hu.

When the editor of the *Literary Magazine* drafted a comment to be printed alongside Hu's writings, intended to encourage a torrent of criticism, he used an argument based on Chow En-Lai's notion that this was a problem of views. When Mao saw it, however, he said instantly: 'It's no good. You can't use it. This is not a question of views. It is a counter-revolutionary cabal.' Since Mao had opened his golden mouth to convict Hu as a counter-revolutionary, the only thing the party could do was to collect evidence to incriminate him. No one on earth could now save Hu's political life from the block.

In early May 1955 a special unit was established by the department of propaganda and the ministry of public security to investigate the anti-party activities of Hu's cabal. It was a national operation and the homes of everyone who knew Hu – his colleagues, teachers, students, friends and relatives and even people who had once corresponded with him – were all searched. Words taken out of context from letters and diaries were used as incriminating evidence. It had become a frightening political battle in which everybody had to make clear which side he or she supported. Universities and colleges stopped their normal classes and instead submerged themselves for five or six weeks in studying and debating Hu's failings, while Hu himself, brave and composed, was obliged to make self-criticisms.

The distinguished old writer Bar Gin was told to write an article criticising Hu, but he was unwilling to do so. An irritated and impertinent cadre called on him and pressed him to write something and eventually Bar Gin wrote, 'Lu Xun was deceived by Hu and Hu got a guilty conscience.' People who did not heap sufficiently harsh criticism on Hu were required to undertake further self-examination; otherwise they could sink into the position of covering up for Hu's black cabal. Within a few months, five million booklets of cartoon serials were printed to propagate the battle against Hu; the party spared no money or energy in blackening Hu's name.

Mao decided to publish Hu's self-criticism and letters in the *People's Daily* in three batches beginning on 13 May, staying up all night to write comments on them in the name of the editor. For the second publication on 24 May, he wrote:

> At present, there are still classes and class struggles inside and outside our country. The working class and the masses who are now the rulers of their nation must subjugate all the counter-revolutionary classes, blocs and individuals still resisting revolution, foil their activities to restore the old regime and ban all reactionaries making use of free speech to achieve their counter-reactionary purposes.

> They have been looked at as simple cultural workers and that is wrong. They have already burrowed into our political, military, economic, cultural and educational departments. They are regarded as enthusiastic revolutionaries and that is wrong.

Most of them have serious problems and most of them are imperialist and Nationalist operatives, Trotskyites, reactionary army officers or Communist turncoats. These people form the backbone of a covert reactionary section inside the revolutionary camp, an independent underground kingdom.

When the people representing different classes of exploiters find themselves in unfavourable situations, they often use offensive not defensive tactics to protect themselves in the hope of future advancement. They invent things, openly manufacture rumours, or grab at superficial phenomena to attack the intrinsic value of society, praising some people and attacking others, or else they deliberately raise an issue by means of digression to open a gap and place us in a difficult position. In short, they are persistently searching for ways to deal with us, to get on top of us. We, the revolutionaries, must understand their plots and study their strategies in order to overcome them. We must not be too bookish and treat the complicated class struggle as a simple business.

Hu's case was cited umpteen times in China, especially during the Cultural Revolution, to demonstrate Mao's combative vigilance over class struggle. Such persecution enabled Mao to smother dissenting voices. A dissenter stigmatised as a counter-revolutionary could be silenced forever and so no one dared touch the ideas of a counter-revolutionary any more.

Many famous people published open letters in newspapers condemning Hu; within six weeks the *People's Daily* had printed 200 such letters, all of them calling him a wolf, a deadly enemy, a grey snake, a conspirator, an insidious class enemy and so on. Hu's sinful writings, as exposed in the *People's Daily*, were compiled into a book for which Mao personally wrote the condemning foreword and 7.6 million copies were distributed throughout the country. The Chinese Literary Workers and Artists Association and the Chinese Writers' Union expelled Hu from their ranks and appealed to the attorney general to deal with him in the necessary way. Here 'to deal with' was the artistic term for 'to arrest'. The Communists, who controlled both organisations, used the names of the organisations to urge the party to arrest one of their own members; nobody, though, could afford to treat this common CCP trick as a joke.

Hu was also a member of the National People's Congress. The constitution of Communist China stipulated that congressmen could not be summarily arrested, but on 18 May its standing committee solemnly sanctioned a proposal to arrest Hu, although he had already been seized and thrown into jail two days earlier.

Hu's wife, Mai Ji, had helped him copy his treatise and she was accordingly also jailed for many years. She later recalled how:

> Before we had finished our supper, Liu Bai-Yu came with a few people. Hu was very pleased to see the boss of the Writer's Union and invited them into our home... Hu talked with them in another room, about what I did not know. I sat in the sitting room wondering what was going to happen. After more than an hour, a woman came to talk to me exclusively about the anti-party problem. They started to search our home. More people came in, examining all the books on the bookshelves. Hu and I were kept apart all the time. We did not see each other... When they searched our home they showed me the search warrant... They went on until probably 1 or 2 a.m. Hu appeared from the other room; they were taking him away and forbade us to talk to each other. Hu could only say hello to me and then walked out of the front door, taking nothing with him... Thereafter I did not know his whereabouts for 11 years.

Mao announced that Hu's crime was punishable by death but that his execution would nevertheless be harmful to the party's interests, so Hu managed to escape a death sentence. Mao knew very little about Hu and had simply made up an imaginary past for him, but he did not hesitate to label him 'an imperialist and loyal running dog of Chiang Kai-Shek's Nationalist Party from a very early period', someone who 'had a close connection with the organisations of imperialist and Nationalist agents, had long disguised himself as a revolutionary and had concealed himself among progressive people to work for counter-revolution'.

One of the men who really did know Hu was Chow En-Lai. After Chiang had annihilated the Communist New 4th Army in 1941 and had started to arrest all Communist sympathisers in Chongqing, Chow managed to send these people, including Hu, their travelling fares so that they could flee to Hong Kong. However, before they saw the year out Hong Kong was invaded by the Japanese and it was Chow again who organised their rescue, helping them to escape from Hong Kong. When the tension between Chiang and the Communists in Chongqing lessened, Chow asked Hu to return to Chongqing to run a magazine to fight the Nationalist Party with the power of the pen. Now Hu was in dire trouble, but Chow did not lend his support;

he was not even prepared to stick his neck out when Mao indulged in the absurd fantasies which repeatedly brought the nation to its knees, let alone at a time when Mao was pursuing a personal vendetta.

One week after Hu's arrest, 700 people from the literary and artistic worlds held a meeting to censure him. It was chaired by the communist literary scholar Kwok Mor-Yor, who gave a speech arguing that 'nowadays when our people are concentrating their energy on building our socialist enterprises, we can never tolerate an intellectual like Hu openly wearing a Marxist cloak while organising internal sabotage. We must suppress these incorrigible and deliberate reactionaries more severely than before. So I am all for the suggestion that has been made by many organisations and friends that Hu should be dismissed from all his public posts and that he should be dealt with as a reactionary according to law.'

This diatribe was met by resounding applause, but one member of the audience, Leur Yin, asked to be allowed to speak from the podium. Permission was granted and he began, 'Hu's problem is not political; it is a matter of understanding. We cannot call him a reactionary...' But before he could finish the sentence he was shouted down. He was pushed from the podium and put under house arrest. When the Cultural Revolution came, he was sent to a labour reform camp where he was tortured daily; he died in 1969.

All Hu's correspondence was scrutinised, including letters written before 1949 and every person mentioned in his writings was arrested. Hu had recorded in his diary that he had had dinner several times with the scholar Ho Gan-Tze and other friends. Ho was accordingly accused of having a close relationship with Hu and was locked up before any concrete evidence had been found.

One senior Communist, Peng Bai-San, who was the party's propaganda chief in Shanghai, sensed early on that a political storm was brewing. He urged Hu to write a report about the benefits he had acquired after studying Mao's revered Yan'an speech on the guidelines of art, in order to put himself in a better light. Hu found writing this report very trying, but he succeeded in finishing it and Peng took the report to Peking, where he gave it to the literary censor Chow Young. Chow decided that Hu had not actually made any true self-criticisms, so the report was not good enough for publication.

Peng's friendship with Hu cost him dearly when Mao named him as a member of Hu's counter-revolutionary cabal and he was locked up for eighteen months. Although no criminal evidence was found, he was expelled from the party and banished to his home town. In 1965, when the Cultural

Revolution broke out, he was working as a junior clerk in the library of an agricultural college in Henan province. Competing Red Guard factions made it their business to seek out and torture people who had been condemned; Peng had no chance of eluding their attention and was beaten mercilessly, leading him to kill himself. His downfall then contaminated his family. His eldest brother was branded a bad element and died from starvation in 1960; another brother, a cadre, was expelled from the party, while a sister-in-law was beaten to death.

Professor Jar Ji-Fong of Fu Dan University in Shanghai began his writing career in the 1930s, when his novel was published in Hu's magazine. When Hu was under siege in early 1955, Jar toasted his good health, only to be treated as a central member of Hu's cabal and jailed for ten years without having been sentenced. Another professor, Professor Sher Tao, from the Chinese People's University in Peking, had once looked for some Marxist writings for Hu, offered some opinions about Hu's offending treatise and helped to improve it. This now made him one of Hu's reactionary cabal too. The university president, Woo Yue-Cheng, defended Sher as best he could to the Minister of Public Security, but there was nothing they could do because Sher's arrest had been approved by Mao. He spent 22 years in prison.

Equally unfortunate was Shan Din, the editor of a magazine in Shanghai. Several of Shan's former colleagues were condemned as important elements in Hu's cabal and because he had known these people Shan was also labelled as one of Hu's men, so he was sent to prison as well. In a similar way, the president of Shandong University found himself in trouble. He had previously criticised Mao and although he had had no connection whatsoever with Hu, he too was denounced as one of Hu's cabal. After he had spent ten years in jail, his case finally came up before the courts. He insisted that he was not guilty and was therefore sentenced to serve another three years. He was due to be released in 1968, but by then China was submerged in the Cultural Revolution, so he was kept in prison until he became seriously ill. He was sent home, only to find his whole family living in a single room, with no space for him. Instead he volunteered to go back to prison, where he died.

Many people were condemned as members of Hu's cabal merely for having attended his lectures or read his writings, or because their own writings had been published in his magazine, even though they had never met him. The Minister for Public Security, Lor Rui-Chin, had a very busy time, personally signing arrest warrants for Hu's many friends in Peking, Tianjin, Nanking, Shanghai and Hangzhou and in the provinces of Hubei and Hunan. Official sources alleged that Hu's case involved only 2,000 people, but one senior member of the Writers' Union disclosed that more than 100,000 people had been investigated over Hu's case, with over 10,000 sent to prison.

Hu was kept in solitary confinement, without books or newspapers and told to write a confession every day. To kill time he would compose and recite poetry. In all he was locked up for ten years without having been sentenced. By 1965, evidence to vindicate Mao's assertion that Hu's crime justified a death sentence was still wanting, but the authorities were determined to secure an admission of guilt; Hu was equally determined to avoid confessing to crimes he had not committed, although he knew very well it was the only way to get a lighter sentence.

On 26 November 1965, Hu was taken to a Peking court where he was given a 14-year sentence. Knowing he would have to spend another four years in jail, he said nothing and looked relaxed and unconcerned. He was finally released in 1969 in the middle of the Cultural Revolution, but soon afterwards he was sent back to jail and given a new death sentence. This time Chow En-Lai gave him some help and the death sentence was commuted to life. He was finally released on 15 January 1979, more than two years after Mao's death, even though some senior party officials were still pointing out that he had been convicted by Mao personally and therefore his case could not be overturned.

Hu died on 8 June 1985. His wife insisted on keeping his body in a mortuary, refusing to have him laid to rest because his name had still not been cleared. The party at first was only prepared to confirm that Hu had been a member for 38 years, but on 18 June 1988, the party central office formally announced his rehabilitation and made it clear that his literary ideas could be debated as academic points of view.

Whereas Hu paid for his literary ideas with 24 years' imprisonment, the philosopher Young Shan-Jang paid for his philosophical views with only eight years in jail. Young was the principal of the party's Advanced Indoctrination College and his views were at odds with those of Mao. Mao denounced him as a revisionist at a Politburo meeting and Young was demoted; during the Cultural Revolution he was condemned as a traitor and jailed. After his release in 1975, he was banished to Shaanxi province for three years.

In his old college alone 154 people were implicated and large numbers of people all over the country found themselves in trouble. All newspapers were ordered to draw up lists of articles and letters to the editors which had expressed sympathy with Young's views and report the writers' names, addresses and workplaces. These people in turn brought trouble to their families and associates.

Young himself survived his ordeal. Sixteen years later he recounted a well-known case during the Ming Dynasty which had implicated ten groups of innocent people. In his own case well over ten groups of people had been implicated, many of whom he had never met but who had been purged simply because they agreed with his academic views. After Young's case, the cultural purge rumbled on to crucify the economist Sun Jee-Fong, the historian Gean Ber-Jarn and many more.

83

More Hidden Enemies

At the same time as Hu Fung's case, an internal purge was taking place in the Communist Party, after two senior Communists were accused by Mao of being anti-party counter-revolutionaries. Again, many people were sucked into the resulting purge, most of whom were exonerated decades later, just like Hu. But at the time, these two unrelated events, one inside and one outside the party, brought about a nationwide cataclysm.

After the appearance of Mao's editorial maintaining that there were still large numbers of counter-revolutionaries in hiding all over the country, an aggressive campaign to expose them became unavoidable. Throughout the latter half of 1955 the country was in the grip of the so-called Purge of Reactionary Elements. While the Suppression of Counter-Revolutionary Elements campaign had been aimed at killing obvious enemies, the Purge of Reactionary Elements campaign was aimed at liquidating hidden enemies. On 17 May 1955, at a meeting of party secretaries from 15 provinces, Mao announced his plan for catching counter-revolutionaries. His instruction was to capture 1.5 million counter-revolutionaries in five years; in other words the nation had to find 300,000 hidden reactionaries every year for five years.

Every workplace in the country had to fill up the quota of five per cent arrests. If they could not meet the target, their poor showing simply meant that their revolutionary zeal and alertness were inadequate. The more arrests they made, the better revolutionaries they were. Consequently the hunters everywhere tried very hard to exceed their five per cent quota.

When the campaign was unveiled, the party urged everyone to unmask reactionaries. The unmasked culprits would be arrested at once; they could then wait for the authorities to start investigating. However, there were many other ways to get into trouble. A Nationalist brigadier, Koo Gow-Di, had fought in the Northern Expedition and the Sino-Japanese war and had also worked for some time with Communist secret agents. After the Communists won power, he was well treated initially, but when his Communist contact fell from grace in the purge, he was implicated and sentenced to 14 years' imprisonment in a desolate hard labour camp in Qinghai province. After more than 20 years, he wrote home to Shanghai to say he was still alive and was about to return home. He received a reply from his younger brother telling him that his wife, son and daughter had all gassed themselves nine years earlier; they had left him a short note saying they could not wait for him any longer, but when he was released they hoped he would kill himself too, so that they could all be reunited in heaven.

Another victim was the president of Hu Jiang University in Shanghai, who had once represented the Nationalist government in negotiating a secret trade agreement with Nazi Germany. He too was accused of being a reactionary and was sent to jail for six years without trial. Yet another victim was a medical student in Shanghai who complained that medical science in Russia was not up to the standards of Germany and Japan and so it was unwise to teach only Russian medicine in China. She was condemned as an anti-Russian counter-revolutionary, arrested and jailed.

A Wuhan University student reported how at the height of the Purge of Reactionary Elements campaign, a work unit was sent to their university by the party's Wuhan city committee. In a big assembly the cadres said menacingly that they had background material and evidence against the students, who therefore had only one way out: to confess and plead for clemency. Anyone trying to resist would be given more exacting punishment, so all should atone for their guilt. When the campaign entered its impeachment stage, all students were obliged to produce written reports to confess their guilt and to reveal other people's mistakes. Every day there were struggle meetings and many students preferred to jump out of windows to their deaths.

Over 100 people at a teachers' training university in Manchuria were arrested and investigated as hidden reactionaries; another 100 or so people under suspicion were suspended from their jobs and ordered to write confessions. Meanwhile about half the 3,000 staff of the Manchurian Finance and Economics College were under investigation. A total of 61 teachers were confirmed as hidden reactionaries and bad elements and another 200 'problematic' people were dealt with through struggle meetings.

Mao claimed at the end of 1956 that over four million people had been investigated in the Purge of Reactionary Elements campaign, of whom 160,000 were suspects. Of these 38,000 were confirmed as counter-revolutionaries. There had been no killing, however and only 300 or so had been sent to labour camps; the rest had been given their old jobs back. The verdict of Liu Shao-Qi, deputy chairman of the central committee, was that 'the land reform, the Suppression of Counter-Revolutionary Elements campaign, the Purge of Reactionary Elements campaign, the three-anti and five-anti campaigns and collectivisation ... were all guided by Chairman Mao. They were all successful, necessary and indispensable and only 10 per cent of the verdicts were mistakes.'

84

The Flowers Changed Into Snakes

For the international Communist movement, 1956 was a stormy year. The anti-communist upheavals in Hungary and Poland shocked the Chinese Communist Party. Mao argued that the main problem was within the Communist parties, in that once they became ruling parties, they could all too easily become arrogant and bureaucratic, turning people against them and that was why in the past he had enforced repeated rectification movements in his party.

The troubles that befell the socialist countries in Eastern Europe warned him that it was time for the Chinese Communist Party to have another dose of cleansing tonic. In early spring 1957 he delivered a lecture to nearly 2,000 senior people inside and outside the party, entitled 'How to deal correctly with people's internal contradictions'. He invited outsiders, particularly intellectuals, to help his party's forthcoming rectification movement by making frank comments on and criticisms of party policies. He appeared to be sincere and this unprecedented move came as a great surprise since previous rectification movements had been purely internal affairs; outsiders had played no part in them. It looked as if after eight years of repression, Mao had at last granted his people freedom of speech.

At the beginning, most outsiders were jittery because of their past experiences and refrained from speaking out. The department of united front work invited the democrats and people without any party affiliation to a series of 13 symposia from 8 May to 3 June; industrialists and businessmen were invited to a series of 25 symposia from 15 May to 8 June, while academics also got their share of intensive lobbying. The party was trying very hard to make them talk. The *Kwang Ming Daily*, the Democratic League's national newspaper, was urging people to speak out and any responses were immediately printed. Now, all the party cadres, looking humble and sincere, repeated that they welcomed criticism and guaranteed there would be no retaliation. People from every workplace in the country – factories, schools, colleges, universities, offices, villages, mines and so on

– were all asked to divulge their thoughts openly to help the party. The party insisted that it wanted a lively and free atmosphere, a busy and salubrious scene like a hundred schools of thinkers competing to talk, a hundred flowers blooming simultaneously.

Public suspicion about the party's intentions soon faded away and within six weeks the party found itself sliding under a sea of disapproving opinions. Basking in the new-found freedom of speech and believing that they were helping the party to correct its shortcomings, people not only spoke out in public, but also wrote down their opinions on countless wall posters. Most criticisms mentioned the rampant injustice and lawlessness in the previous campaigns.

At a meeting organised by the department of united front work, a former senior Nationalist official, Wong Shou-Shon, said that on his inspection tours around the country he had seen extremely tragic and unjust cases in the campaigns of Suppression of Counter-Revolutionary Elements and Purge of Reactionary Elements. 'We can do nothing for the dead now, yet there are still hundreds of such people under arrest whose cases have not been solved ... Civilised countries would pay compensation to people who have been wrongly jailed, but a socialist country has done nothing ... How can people have faith? How can the country maintain stability?'

In a similar vein, Ma Je-Min, principal of the Central South China Finance and Economics College and a member of the Democratic League, said: 'In the Purge of Reactionary Elements campaign, people who were merely grumbling were regarded as anti-party elements and anti-party meant counter-revolution. This was a way to kill.' Another member of the Democratic League, Professor Qin Jan of Yunnan University, told a reporter from the *Yunnan Daily*: 'At the beginning of the Purge of Reactionary Elements campaign, it was said there must be reactionaries in the university. When the campaign reached the faculty, it was said there must be reactionaries in the faculties. When it came to individual groups, it was said there must be reactionaries in the groups ... But nobody dared say: "Probably not". The authorities resorted to making groundless accusations and 30 or 40 per cent of people were condemned. Originally the party wanted to kill tigers, but they ended up killing wolves, dogs and cats.'

Among the criticisms most resented by Mao were those from Lor Lone-Gi and Cheng Ber-Jeun, who became China's arch-rightists in the 1957 Anti-Rightists campaign.

Lor Lone-Gi was born in 1896 in Jiangxi province, the very bright son of a schoolteacher. He went to Tsing Hua School, or the Indemnity College, in Peking, in 1913 and was very active in the student movement

547

against the many Chinese warlord governments. In 1921 he left China to study politics at Wisconsin University and later on he studied in Britain under Professor Harold Joseph Laski, where he gained a doctorate in political science. In 1928 he returned to Shanghai to teach politics and modern history at Kwung Hua University, also working as the editor of *New Moon* magazine. At the same time he started his long-running battle against Chiang's dictatorship. Chiang forced Kwung Hua University to sack Lor and detained him in the Public Security Bureau as a Communist suspect – although Lor actually advocated a British- or American-style democracy. He was kept in the bureau for six hours, until he was bailed out by the influential Dr Hu Shi and T V Soong. Lor refused to be cowed even after Chiang's agents made an unsuccessful attempt to shoot him; his anti-Nationalist writings were getting more pointed and he started to become more sympathetic towards the Communists. Chiang now changed his tactics by offering Lor an ambassadorial post if he would stop cooperating with the Communists, but Lor refused.

In August 1946, the American special envoy General G Marshall was acting as the peace broker between the Nationalist government and the Communist Party. He asked Lor, by now a leading figure in the Democratic League, whether it would be possible for the Democratic League to join the Nationalist government; this new government might then contrive to halt the civil war and then invite the Communists to join the government afterwards. If the Democratic League was willing to join the government, Marshall would suggest that Chiang should give the league either more seats or a bigger quota for its members in the new government. Lor regarded the offer as a subterfuge by Chiang to drive a wedge between the Democratic League and the Communist Party and he said to Marshall that China's problems could not be solved without the Communist Party joining the government, while the Communists would not join the government before civil war had ceased. It was a primary principle which the Democratic League insisted on and which could not be altered.

In 1947, the civil war mediation fell through and Chiang ordered all Communist workers to leave their areas before 5 March. The Communists hastily moved out and Lor, representing the Democratic League, formally assumed the role of trustee of Communists properties left behind. Before long Chiang declared the Democratic League illegal and started to arrest democrats and Communists, many of whom fled to Hong Kong. Lor was put under house arrest and was rescued by a defecting Nationalist security officer as he was about to be shipped to Taiwan.

Lor, as one of the deputy chairmen of the Democratic League, was given special treatment by the Communist Party following the civil war. He was made a member of the National People's Congress, the standing committee of the Political Consultative Conference and the State Council and he was also given the post of Minister of Forest Industry. Although he was a childless divorcee living on his own, he was allocated a large and splendid house which had once belonged to a Qing Dynasty prince. The government also provided two bodyguards, a chauffeur, a cook, a secretary and a nurse for him.

Cheng Ber-Jeun was born in Anhui province. He was the same age as Lor and was also one of the deputy chairmen of the Democratic League. In September 1922 he left Shanghai on board a French liner to study philosophy in Germany. On the journey he befriended Zhu De and in Berlin he also met Chow En-Lai. Zhu De joined the Communist Party in Berlin at the end of 1922. Cheng soon followed him; his three younger brothers also became Communists.

Four years later, Cheng graduated from Berlin University. He returned to China to join the Northern Expedition and steadily immersed himself in anti-Chiang activities. Lor and Cheng were the founders of two different democratic parties. As a result of Communist manoeuvring, eight small democratic parties, including the parties founded by Lor and Cheng, merged into the Democratic Parties Alliance, later to become the Democratic League. While in Chongqing both men worked closely, loyally and quietly with Chow En-Lai, who stayed behind the scenes, often leaving the Democratic League to do the bidding of the Communists. And so Cheng also enjoyed the fruits of his loyal service. The Communist government rewarded him handsomely; he was made a member of the State Council and of the standing committee of the National People's Congress, Deputy Chairman of the Political Consultative Conference and minister of Transport.

Cheng proclaimed himself a left-winger within the Democratic League. At one time he occupied the position of secretary-general, making him a member of the ruling clique, while the right-winger Lor was still out in the cold. The resulting power struggle between the two men often led to flaming rows. In early 1950, the friction between the two at the central committee meetings of the Democratic League went on for more than a month and all discussions ended in deadlock. Chow En-Lai tried unsuccessfully to act as mediator and Mao also tried to help smooth things over. At last Cheng and Lor came to a reluctant compromise, but they remained implacable opponents.

When the hundred flowers were decoyed into blooming, the Democratic League central office newspaper, the *Kwang Ming Daily*, published many of their members' speeches and writings supporting the campaign for free speech. Lor spoke at a meeting organised by the party's Department of United Front Work and his speech was printed in the *Kwong Ming Daily* on 23 May 1957.

He suggested creating an independent committee set up jointly by the NPC and the CPPCC. This would have three main benefits. First, it might encourage people to talk to the committee. Intellectuals in other provinces were always keen that their opinions should be heard in Peking and the committee would be a useful way of airing grievances. Secondly, it would be a useful means of rehabilitation Some people imagined that the present campaign would be in three stages: speaking out, suppression and retaliation. People obtained such wrong idea through experience. Many of the previous campaigns had had great achievements, although there were certainly also some mistakes. Usually rehabilitation had taken place after the National People's Congress had forwarded complaints to the local authorities, which in turn had forwarded them to the officials in the respective workplaces whose job it was to deal with the complaints. But it was difficult to correct all the mistakes this way. If a rehabilitation committee was established, it would be separated from the Communist-led bodies which had carried out the Three-anti and Five-anti campaigns and the Purge of Reactionary Elements and a committee led by democrats would be far more beneficial for rehabilitation.

Lor's third point was that any victims could make their complaints directly to a rehabilitation committee, thereby deterring people from carrying out reprisals and victims would also have a means of redress. It would be preferable to have a central committee, which would oversee the local branches. If it was a well-managed body, then everyone would speak one's mind. However, said Lor, this was all just an immature suggestion and he was uncertain whether it would be seen as appropriate.

Lor only gently touched upon a very common Communist practice, which was to send letters of complaint back to the workplaces of the writers and therefore into the hands of the party bosses for whom they worked and against whom they were complaining. More than often this practice landed the complainers in worse trouble; they could be accused of resisting the just punishment of the party and the people, or of refusing to admit their guilt.

The blooming flowers meetings organised by the Minister for United Front Work, Lee Wai-Han, for senior members of the Democratic League went on for several days. Cheng preferred to say nothing, but Lee Wai-Han insisted on getting him to speak and arranged two more meetings for the purpose. Finally, Cheng spoke. 'Nowadays,' he said, 'we design every operation first, followed by collective discussion in the light of scientific knowledge, then we make the decision. Should we not apply the same principles to politics and have a politics design bureau, which would put all the major policies through collective discussion before making a decision?'

On 15 May, Mao quietly ordered his senior colleagues to prepare to hit back at the party's 'detractors'. At the same time Communist officials, encouraged by Mao, kept urging their potential victims to speak out, promising again and again that there would be no retaliation. Mao later described this as his ruse to 'lure the snakes out of their holes', although only a few months earlier, back in February, he had declared that stormy class struggle was now a thing of the past. Now, he was planning another all-consuming, nationwide class struggle. Instead of orchestrating a movement to purify the party, he decided it was more important to track down the party's ubiquitous foes. On 8 June an editorial in the *People's Daily*, with a sound like a thunderclap, formally unveiled the great 'Anti-Rightists' campaign.

Soon tens of thousands of factory workers and peasants, coached, organised and commanded by Communist officials, assembled all over the country to denounce the rightists as enemies of the party and enemies of socialism – even though most of the protestors hardly knew what the rightists had done or what it was all about. On 10 June, another editorial in the *People's Daily* solemnly announced: 'Listen! Now the working class is speaking.'

On 15 October, the CCP central committee issued a directive on the criteria to identify rightists. According to one article, rightists were people who maliciously attacked either the party or other leading organisations, or the leadership of the people's government; they were also people who disparaged working-class cadres, peasant cadres or revolutionary activists. This meant that the government and its staff were all officially protected against any criticism. Everyone in China now found themselves in a precarious position; anyone who was accused by a disgruntled cadre of being critical was doomed. The government would clearly not tolerate any criticism.

The opinions that Lor and Cheng had voiced turned out to be the biggest mistakes of their lives. Mao now opened fire with the party's counter-attack, writing: 'During the Hundred Flowers Blooming Campaign, the Democratic League has behaved especially evilly. Its organisation, plan, guiding principles and strategy are all hostile to Communists, hostile to socialism and hostile to the people. Lor's party and Cheng's party have been particularly salient in this turbulent sea, whose rough waves and black clouds have been stirred up by their alliance.'

Within the Democratic League it was common knowledge that the two men did not get on with each other, so the idea that they had formed a political alliance was just unbelievable. But as the verdict came straight from the golden mouth, no one dared challenge it. Cheng was the first of the two to come under fire. Initially he denied his guilt at the meetings arranged to force him to admit Mao's charge, that he and Lor were formal partners in an anti-party organisation. Cheng, heavily beleaguered, gradually caved in and admitted that he and Lor thought alike, so it could be deemed that they had an alliance of minds.

Under such circumstances, there were often people prepared to make far-fetched but ferocious accusations against the condemned men in order to demonstrate their own unfailing loyalty to the CCP. A Nationalist defector, General Ching Cham, denounced Cheng's 'politics design bureau' as 'intending to usurp the party's ruling power, replacing it with Cheng's own Peasants and Workers Democratic Party so that all political parties, large and small, could rule the country in turn.' Before long Ching Cham's sensational remark 'to rule the country in turn' was attributed to Cheng himself and it was widely publicised in an attempt to prove that he was attempting to grab power. Cheng's own party had just a few thousand members and not a single soldier, whereas the Communist Party had more than 20 million members and five million troops and so Cheng would have had to be crazy to contemplate a power struggle with the Communists; yet as a rightist he had no right to defend himself.

Meanwhile Lor, who had been on a visit to Sri Lanka as a member of a Chinese friendship delegation, flew in to Kunming airport on 2 June. Unaware of what had been happening during the past fortnight, he was stunned to see headlines in the newspapers exhorting people to 'Criticise the Cheng and Lor alliance' and 'Unmask the criminal activity of the Cheng and Lor alliance'. Immediately he phoned Cheng in Peking, shouting down the phone: 'When did I form an alliance against the Communist Party with you? You tell me!'

The following day, back in Peking, Lor confronted Cheng at his home. Given that they had had so many quarrels before, he said, it was ridiculous to suggest that they could be allies, even in theory. A highly charged argument raged for three hours and they parted in a fury.

Lor and Cheng were required to attend numerous meetings morning, afternoon and night, where they were the targets of criticism in which their persecutors tried hard to extract admissions that they had been the leaders of a secret alliance opposed to the Communist Party and to socialism. Cheng replied that since they were both deputy chairmen of the Democratic League they had of course been allies; but this was not good enough for the authorities.

Lor refused to concede the truth of the accusation, writing that although some people thought he and Cheng were part of a political conspiracy and some even speculated on when and where the alliance had been established, it was simply not true. Some rightists in the Democratic League claimed they had received guidance and instructions from the alliance, but the letters they were referring to were in fact official documents issued by the central committee of the Democratic League. Lor and Cheng had never sent out any joint instructions and they never talked to each other on a one-to-one basis about politics or Democratic League affairs; in fact in the last two years they had not once met privately.

In addition to being condemned as a conspirator, Lor's other serious crime was his idea for a rehabilitation committee, which denied the great achievements of the Three-anti and Five-anti Campaigns and the Purge of Reactionary Elements campaign. Those close to Lor were under great pressure to expose his 'dirty deeds'. When trapped in such a situation and unable to find anything to besmirch the accused, many people would make things up to reduce the pressure on themselves. Lor's long-time woman friend, Pu Zee-Shiu, the deputy editor-in-chief of a national newspaper, was caught in such a dilemma. After many sessions of harassing meetings in which she was eventually branded a rightist because of her close relationship with Lor, she made up a story about him and handed over private letters he had written to her.

Newspapers, as well as his persecutors, described Lor as deceitful and obstinate. Mao said that Lor was the progenitor of all rightists and would die resisting surrender. As important rightists, Lor and Cheng were actually treated better than the ordinary rightists. Their salaries were cut, but they were allowed to stay in their big houses. Lor's chauffeur and car were withdrawn and he was dismissed from all his posts, except for his seat on the CPPCC.

Lor now led a lonely life, since most of his friends did not dare keep in touch with him. On 7 December 1965 he died of a heart attack. Because he had been a rightist, it was very difficult to find his ashes a permanent home and as a temporary measure they were kept in a storage room in the crematorium. There they remained until the Cultural Revolution, when they vanished without trace.

Cheng also sank deeper in the Cultural Revolution. Red Guards occupied his house and turned it into their headquarters, while Cheng was kept in solitary confinement for investigation. His daughter in Sichuan province was meanwhile accused of trying to overturn her father's conviction and was sentenced to 20 years in jail. In the spring of 1969 Cheng fell seriously ill, but the hospitals were refusing to treat rightists. Eventually Chow En-Lai intervened, telling the People's Hospital not to discriminate against condemned people; but by the time Cheng was finally admitted, his stomach cancer had already become terminal and he died on 17 June 1969.

The third arch-rightist was Choo An-Ping, who, after attending the London School of Economics in 1935, had taught at a university; he was also a writer and editor. In April 1946, after turning down an invitation to work for the Nationalist government, Choo founded a magazine, *Observation*, whose offices were a tiny room in Shanghai. Many famous and progressive people contributed to the magazine, which attacked the corrupt Nationalist government and advocated democracy and liberty. In two and a half years its circulation increased from 400 to more than 100,000, making it one of the most influential magazines in China.

Choo advocated a British- or American-style political system. During the 1947 civil war, he wrote:

> Frankly speaking, we are now fighting for freedom. Under Nationalist Party rule, the question of freedom is about 'more' or 'less'. If the Communist Party becomes the ruling power, the question of freedom will become 'have' or 'have not'. Although the party is talking loudly now about democracy, its fundamental spirit is in reality hostile to democracy. Judging by its methods of rule, there is no difference between the Communists and the Fascists. Both try to control people's will through strict organisation. Amid China's current political strife, the Communist Party's call for democracy aims only at encouraging people to oppose the Nationalist Party. Yet as far as the Communist Party's true spirit is concerned, it is for autocracy and not democracy.

Choo's *Observation* magazine published many articles written by 'special war correspondents', actually Chow En-Lai's secret agents, who revealed many military secrets of the civil war. Chiang, irritated, closed down *Observation* in December 1948. Choo was in Peking at the time, collecting information about the Peking and Tianjin battles, so he had a lucky escape, but two colleagues in the Shanghai office were arrested by the Nationalist security force. The result was that Choo felt obliged to move closer to the Communist Party.

In November 1949, as soon as the Communists took power, the party's propaganda chiefs wished to revive *Observation*. They asked for instructions from Chow En-Lai, who replied: 'The magazine had many readers, so restart it.' Publication therefore resumed, with Choo once again editor-in-chief. After one year the magazine was renamed *New Observation*. At the same time Choo was appointed as a member of the National People's Congress and given other official posts. He now gave up the position of editor-in-chief, though he still remained a special correspondent. Since he spent time touring around China, his news reports began to appear not only in *New Observation* but also in the *People's Daily* and other important national newspapers.

Choo started off as an opponent of Communism, but he soon fell under the spell of the party's united front work. In 1949, when the democrats were all ensconced in Peking's top hotels, helping to create the new China, Chow En-Lai visited these people and walked into Choo's room for an informal chat. Choo, awe-struck and excited, soon fell for the Communists; he accepted invitations to join two democratic parties which numbered some of his friends among their members.

On 1 April 1957, Choo took on the job of editor-in-chief of the *Kwang Ming Daily*; he freely admitted that he had gained the backing of the CCP for the job. This newspaper, founded by the Democratic League, later came under the control of the Communists. When Mao started his Hundred Flowers Blooming Campaign, the party central committee decided to hand back the *Kwang Ming Daily* to the Democratic League. Choo in his new post lost no time in writing to more than 100 celebrated academics, asking them to write for his newspaper. Within a month, the *Kwang Ming Daily* had held 11 symposia, printed 22 full-page reports and published nearly 130,000 words of summary reports about the symposia, plus a great deal of other news, correspondence and special topics. All the writers expressed discontent with the Communists.

On 1 June, at a meeting in the department of united front work, Choo made a famous, or infamous, speech entitled 'A few opinions for Chairman Mao and Prime Minister Chow En-Lai'. He said:

Ever since the country's liberation, intellectuals have espoused the party ardently and accepted its leadership. Yet the relationship between the party and the masses has not been very good in recent years. It has become a problem which needs urgent adjustment in our country's political life. Where is the crux of this problem? In my opinion, the crux is the idea that 'the party owns the world.' I believe that the fact that the party leads the country does not mean that the party owns the country.

The masses support the party, while not forgetting that they themselves are also the masters of the country. A political party gains political power with the main purpose of fulfilling its ideas or pushing through its policies. To put its policies into effect and to strengthen its own political power, the party needs to keep itself constantly strong and to control key positions in government departments; all these are quite natural. However, in every work unit in the country, no matter how large or small, even in a very small group, a party member is installed as the head. Even the most trivial business can only be carried out after the party cadre has nodded his or her head. Is not this style a bit too much? As regards the major national policies, non-party members are willing to follow the party's lead. This is because of the party's great ideals and correct policies, but this doesn't mean the non-party members do not have their own ideas, pride or sense of duty to their country.

In recent years, there have been many party members whose abilities have not been up to the requirements of their posts; besides failing to do a good job and harming the nation, they also cause discontent and aggravate the tension between the masses and the party. The fault is not in the party members, it is in the party which places unsuitable members in all sorts of positions. Is it because of the notion 'All lands under the sky belong to the emperor' that the party behaves this way, resulting in the present situation where everything belongs to one family?

The problem of thinking that 'the party owns the world' is the ultimate root of all signs of sectarianism and the origin of conflict between the party and non-party members. Nowadays, the conspicuous sectarianism and the discordant relationship between the party and the people are national phenomena. The Communist Party is a party of strong organisation and discipline. Do such countrywide shortcomings have something to do with its central leadership? Lately, many people have complained about junior cadres, but nobody complains about senior members. I want to set an example and ask for guidance from Chairman Mao and Premier Chow. Before liberation, we heard Chairman Mao's suggestion of forming a coalition government with non-party members. Soon after the People's Republic of China was established in 1949, there were three non-party members among the six deputy chairmen of the central government and two non-party members among the four deputy prime ministers. It looked more or less like a coalition government. Later on, after a government reorganisation, there was only one deputy chairman of the People's Republic of China and the non-party member deputy chairmen were all moved away to the National People's Congress standing committee. Furthermore, there are now 12 deputy prime ministers in the State Council, but none of them is a non-party member. Is it the case that not one non-party member can do the job? Or is it that not one non-party member can be trained for the job? From the point of wishing to unite non-party members and the country and caring about internal and international impressions, is it possible to think about such an arrangement a little more?

When there are party members and non-party members there will be conflict and such conflict cannot be totally eliminated. It can be reduced to a minimum, if it is dealt with properly. Non-party members welcome this rectification movement in the party. We all like to contribute our humble knowledge to national affairs. However, in reality, the party is so powerful that the democratic parties' contribution is limited. Therefore the problems of how to reduce the conflict; how to harmonise relations between the party and the masses; how to make the party show more respect to the non-party members' status as masters of the nation; how to be more tolerant; how to rule with virtue, enabling all people in the country – the intelligent, the talented and the masses – to find comfort, have to be considered and solved, mainly by the party.

The above speech and Choo's enthusiasm in publishing criticisms of the party, was a fatal blunder. Under intensive fire, he made self-criticisms in the National People's Congress and on 8 June, after only 70 days in the post, he offered his resignation as editor-in-chief of the *Kwang Ming Daily*. Many of its reporters who had ardently promoted the Hundred Flowers Blooming Campaign and written about criticisms of the party were dismissed as 'arsonists'. They were named and publicly criticised in the press.

Choo's salary was cut and he was sent to work as a shepherd near the Great Wall, until after a time he was allowed to live quietly back at home. When the Red Guards ran amok in China, he again became a target for suppression and he was insulted, beaten up and made to sweep the streets. One day in August 1966, when a group of Red Guards knocked on his front door, he jumped over a back wall and disappeared. This was a period when corpses were appearing daily in the beautiful North Sea Lake in central Peking and in the Kunming Lake in the Summer Palace and no one could be sure whether Choo's body was among them. After a few years it was said that he had drowned himself at sea.

Another well-known rightist in the Democratic League was Cheng Nire-Chih, who was placed on a par with Lor Long-Gi and Cheng Ber-Jeun. Born in 1897 to a poor family in Zhejiang province, Cheng Nire-Chih rose through the ranks to become a senior banker, while at the same time devoting himself to the democracy movement and the anti-Japanese War. In 1936 he was one of the seven patriotic leaders of the Save the Nation Association arrested by Chiang. After his release, he and two other renowned figures founded a party which was eventually absorbed into the Democratic League. In the early stages of the Sino-Japanese War, he was the director of the Nationalist government's Anhui provincial treasury and in this capacity he managed to supply the Communist New 4th Army with monthly funds, as well as training a group of financial staff for the Communist Party. The considerable part he played earned him Mao's thanks.

In 1948, Cheng Nire-Chih was invited by the Communist Party to move from Hong Kong to Peking to help build Communist China and in early 1949 he became one of the three senior advisers to the People's Bank. The country was still in the middle of the civil war and Chiang still held half of China. The Communist Party needed to be seen as democratic and tolerant, so the governor of the People's Bank followed Chow En-Lai's instructions and often sought the opinions of his advisers on major financial affairs, especially on economic problems in Nationalist areas. Later on, the new government rewarded Cheng by making him head of the food ministry.

Cheng was an able and arrogant man, with firm views on everything, particularly on how to run his ministry and many of his democrat colleagues

– ministers, deputy ministers, chiefs and deputy chiefs of bureaux – were obliged to learn their lessons fast. This was how the Communist Party ran its secretive one-party state. Nearly all information, even down to everyday statistics, were treated as confidential material which only party members were allowed to see. Every government department had regular internal information bulletins which non-party members were not entitled to read. Without access to information on policy, the democrat officials were unable to deal with practical problems. They soon resigned themselves to doing nothing, expressing no opinions and leaving everything to the Communists and they were rewarded for their docility with steady promotion.

Cheng's bid for power to run his ministry and his arrogant, indiscreet opinions soon got him into trouble. He even criticised Stalin's famous motto that 'all Communists were made of special material,' bluntly stating that people were all the same; no one was made of special material. He amended the sacred Communist tenet that the 'capitalist class should learn from the working class' by adding that the working class should learn from the capitalist class as well. Just as freely, he said that 'bureaucracy is a more dangerous enemy than capitalism... We should extract the cream from capitalism. After getting rid of the dregs, any experience and knowledge beneficial to management and production should be found and used to serve socialism. Bureaucracy forms part of the useless dregs and, when it is used for a socialist purpose, efficiency is even lower than in modern capitalist enterprises.'

Large numbers of people, including the now repentant central leadership of the Democratic League, contributed articles and speeches lashing out at Cheng, mobilised by Communist cadres. Cheng for his part insisted that his views were correct and refused to admit to being wrong or to make any self-examination. Mao described him as having a granite brain. Cheng's wife and children now 'drew a clear line between themselves and him' – well-worn Communist jargon for anybody abandoning a condemned family member or associate, declaring the victim as the enemy to protect themselves. Only Cheng's youngest son stood by him.

Cheng, by then a septuagenarian, was savagely beaten up during the Cultural Revolution; among his attackers was his ex-bodyguard. His loyal son, meanwhile, was arrested for trying to overturn his father's conviction. Cheng went on hunger strike once, but lived out the rest of his disconsolate life on his own, never seeing any other member of his family again. His rightist stigma, or 'rightist hat', was removed shortly before he died in 1977 and in 1980 his name was formally cleared.

Professor Bi Shou-Tung, later Chairman of the Democratic League, was another of the leading democrats to be ensnared. At the inception of the Hundred Flowers Blooming Campaign, he was thrilled with the prospect of academic freedom. When he had a chance meeting with Mao, he told the chairman that for the intellectuals it seemed like early spring. Mao encouraged Bi to write an article based on it. Bi therefore wrote a piece entitled 'Early Spring', which was printed in newspapers but which was later cited as evidence of his being hostile to the party and to socialism. It was said that since he had indicated that early spring had come after Mao's Hundred Flowers Blooming Campaign, this could only imply that it had been bitter winter before that. The only possible explanation was that he was trying to smear the good name of the party and of socialism.

Lor's rehabilitation committee, Cheng Ber-Jeun's politics design bureau and Choo's idea that 'the party owns the world', were known as the three most notorious rightist ideas. Because the alliance created by Lor Lone-Gi and Cheng Ber-Jeun conducted its operations from the central offices of the Democratic League, it had the organisation, plan, ideology and strategy to pursue its aim. As a result, all the Democratic League branches in provinces and cities were now treated as belonging to the alliance and most of the leading figures in the branches were accused of being junior members of the alliance. In one district in Ningxia province alone, which contained 45 Democratic League branches, as many as 33 leading democrats were purged; as senior members of the alliance they were therefore rightists.

At the very beginning, Mao had said at a high-level meeting that 'many professors are not happy with the system of having a party committee in their workplaces and we could consider abolishing this system.' Cheng Ber-Jeun, who had been in the audience, printed Mao's words in a bulletin for members of the Democratic League. Some of those who had heard the speech, such as the chairman and a handful of deputy chairmen of the Democratic League, were in fact undercover Communists, but no one attempted to correct Cheng's report of Mao's talk. The academic members of the Democratic League in universities read Cheng's bulletin and many of them voiced their support for abolishing the university party committees. When all these people were later rounded up as rightists, they argued that they were being treated unjustly, because the abolition of university party committees had been Mao's idea. Communist cadres retorted that Chairman Mao would never have considered such a measure, so obviously it was Cheng who had deliberately misrepresented Chairman Mao's words. In fact Mao had made a U-turn on this subject, but Cheng became a scapegoat among the university rightists, who blamed him and the Democratic League for getting them into trouble.

The opprobrium of the Democratic League drove many new members to resign, while many old members wanted to keep the league at a distance. Some members returned papers sent to them by the league's central office, saying they preferred not to be contacted in case further harm befell them.

More than two decades later, after Mao's death, nearly all the rightists' names were cleared by the party; only a very small group of arch-rightists were not granted exoneration, among them Lor, Cheng Ber-Jeun and Choo. The party could not afford to rehabilitate everyone; some people, after all, had to remain as rightists to vindicate the anti-rightist campaign. On 24 October 1986, after 30 years, Lor's good name was finally restored. The Democratic League had by now found a new lease of life and had rebuilt itself and its central office held a big assembly to commemorate Lor's 90th birthday. The Minister for United Front Work, Yan Ming-Fu, was the guest speaker; he praised Lor as a patriotic fighter for democracy who had made a distinguished contribution to China.

Out of the eight parties in the Democratic League, the three leading parties were the Nationalist Party Revolutionary Committee, the Association for the Democratic Development of China and the Chinese Democratic Alliance. Members of the Nationalist Party Revolutionary Committee were mostly left-wing Nationalists and army officers who had defected and who were understandably very cautious about criticising the Communists. Members of the Association for the Democratic Development of China represented the capitalists who were still suffering from the after-effects of the five-antis campaign and dared not speak out. Members of the Chinese Democratic Alliance were mostly left-wing intellectuals who had loyally followed and supported the Communist Party under Nationalist rule through thick and thin. Regarding themselves as faithful friends of the party, they felt free to give it some frank advice and they were completely unprepared for the cyclone to follow, which made the intelligentsia and especially academics, the target of the anti-rightist campaign.

The party general secretary of the day, Deng Xiao-Ping, who was in charge of the day-to-day running of this national hurricane, made his party's policy clear. 'The rightists' main centres of operation,' he said, 'are institutions with large numbers of intellectuals, for example higher education institutions, some government offices, the press, publishing and literary circles, the legal and medical professions and science and technology departments.' Consequently wherever there were intellectuals, there were plenty of people adorned with 'rightist hats'.

One of the most fatuous acts committed by Communist fanatics in this period was to bring down the economist Professor Ma Yan-Choo. Born on 24 June 1882, Ma Yan-Choo obtained his doctorate in 1914 at Columbia University and the following year he returned to China to teach at Peking University. During the Sino-Japanese war, he headed the College of Commerce at Chongqing University. Often dressed in a traditional long Chinese gown made of blue cotton and wearing a straw hat, he looked like a humble old man. He had a huge public following because he never flinched from openly criticising the corrupt practices of the Nationalist government. In an attempt to buy him off Chiang offered him a senior government post, but he refused the offer, saying that he would not stop criticising the government. Soon he received a letter enclosing a bullet. One day, after delivering a speech at the Central University, he said he knew there had been security agents among the audience. If they wanted to kill him, they could go ahead; he was not afraid.

Within a month, in December 1940, he was arrested and jailed. The official news claimed that 'he had been sent to the front line to investigate the economy'. As a result of public protests and particularly of pressure from America, he was released from prison in August 1942, but he remained under house arrest until 1944. When the civil war drew to a close, Ma was president of Zhejiang University. Mao and Chow En-Lai invited him to go to Peking, where he was given several honorary official positions and appointed president of the prestigious Peking University.

For a long time, Ma had been concerned about China's huge population. In 1955, he became alarmed by the results of many surveys which he had conducted, showing that the population was increasing by an average of 13,000,000 people every year. He was keen that the government should promote a policy of population control, discouraging couples from having too many children by means of a penalty tax. He wanted to publicise the advantages of late marriage and contraception and to change the traditional Chinese desire for large numbers of male descendants. Maintaining that village life was so dull that peasants had nothing better to do in their spare time except make babies, he suggested enriching cultural life and entertainment in the villages to help lower the birth rate.

When Ma first mentioned population control in the National People's Congress, not everyone was behind him. This was at a time when the Russian government was encouraging its people to breed to make up for the huge numbers the country had lost in the Second World War. To many fanatical supporters of Russia, whatever was good for Russia was also good for China. Ma was very angry when someone said that Russia did not talk about the subject so they could not talk about it either. On 2 March 1957, at a high-level government meeting, Ma emphasised the importance of population control and Mao agreed with him, saying 'Ma has made a very good point; I am his comrade.' At that time Mao was urging people to speak out and so in early July Ma's essay on the subject was published in the *People's Daily* under the title 'New Demography'.

Mao came from peasant stock and for centuries China had relied on manual labour. Mao's 'thoughts' included aphorisms such as 'the more people the better' and 'the more people there are, the easier it is to get a job done.' He wrote in 1949 that 'the huge Chinese population is a very good thing. There is a way to cope with it no matter how many times it expands and that is production. Capitalist economists in the West like Malthus made a preposterous assertion that production of food could not catch up with population growth, but this theory was thoroughly demolished by the Marxists long ago and it has also been disproved by the facts in post-revolution Russia and the liberated areas in China.' Hence it was an insult to suggest that a socialist country, with its superior system, could not cope with population growth. Mao swiftly detected that the 'new demography' was a serious political problem.

On 14 October, an editorial in the *People's Daily* urged, 'Forbid the rightists from making use of the subject of population to execute their political plot'. Although the savage criticism did not name names, it was abundantly clear that Ma was the target; his idea was denounced as hostile to the party and to socialism. Far from being a blooming flower, this was nothing more than poisoned grass, a reprint of the theory of the capitalist Malthus.

When the department of united front work asked Chow En-Lai whether they should have denounced Ma as a rightist, Chow replied: 'No. He is a renowned economist and naming him could provoke an adverse response at home and abroad.' But not everyone in the Communist hierarchy agreed with Chow. Before long Ma was on the receiving end of a nationwide verbal onslaught and newspapers and magazines published more than 160 articles criticising him. The campus of Peking University was plastered with 9,000 wall posters mobilised by the university party committee, accusing him of 'using the pretence of academic research to assault the party and socialism' and of 'attempting to destroy socialism and revive capitalism'. Posters were even stuck on his bed.

Ma defended himself fearlessly, as a result of which he was branded as 'assuming a bad attitude', 'resisting the movement' and 'opposing the masses'. His friends urged him to admit that he was wrong in order to avoid jeopardising his own political privileges, but he decided to fight on. In January 1960, he published an article entitled 'To repeat my request', in which he asked that the Hundred Flowers Blooming Campaign be allowed to continue. The edited draft of his article reached Kang Sheng, a secretary of the party central committee and the national security chief, who commented that Ma had been very ferocious recently and his article 'To repeat my request' was a vitriolic attack. His problems were no longer confined to the academic sphere; instead he was using the name of academia to launch a rightist assault and therefore must be unmasked and censured. Kang Sheng ordered the editor to insert a review above Ma's article stating that the article, like many of his writings, was full of preposterous capitalist ideas which deserved to be censured.

Ma's troubles now appeared to be getting more serious. He was no longer allowed to attend the numerous meetings that convened at Peking University with the sole purpose of denouncing him; his writings were banned from publication and he lost the right to defend himself. A lone fighter confronting an overwhelming and hostile force, Ma would be an octogenarian in a couple of years' time, yet he was as indomitable as ever, adamant that he would have to be an exemplar to his students in fighting for the truth and never surrendering to brute force. He commented, 'If they sack me, I don't mind.' He was now dismissed from all his honorary government posts, except for his seat on the CPPCC and was forced to resign his position as president of Peking University.

Ma was not officially confirmed as a rightist. He belonged to the privileged few known as 'rightists under internal control', living for the next 20 years in humiliation and near isolation, rarely venturing out of his home. On 16 July 1979, after the end of the Mao era, the Minister for United Front Work, Lee Kwai-Mire, called at Ma's home to formally exonerate him from dishonour and confirm that his ideas on family planning and the economy had been right. The following year, the Minister for Higher Education, Chiang Nan-Chane, visited Ma, now aged 98, on his sick bed to hand over an official letter appointing him honorary president of Peking University. Chiang Nan-Chane offered his apologies and congratulations to China's grand old man and Ma's article, 'New Demography', was republished.

There were other academics too, such as the sociologist Professor Woo Gin-Chiu, Professor Chan Da and the academician Luk Yin-Fan, who also called in the early 1950s for urgent measures to control population growth. Like Ma they were all accused of promoting Malthus's doctrine, making up stories about a population crisis and intending to stir up anti-Communist riots similar to those in Hungary. All of them were condemned as rightists.

The 1957 census revealed that China's population was 646.5 million, the figure in the 1964 census was 700 million. While Ma was languishing at home because of his demographic crime, China went on to produce another 600 million people, more than twice the entire population of America. In 1997 the Chinese population was 1.2 billion, with unemployment amounting to 250 million.

To commemorate Mao's 90th birthday in 1983, the CCP made an astonishing attempt to rewrite history, praising his important contribution to Chinese population growth control. The party propagandists claimed that putting Chairman Mao and Professor Ma on opposite sides of the argument did not fit the historical facts, as family planning had always been central to Mao Tse-Tung Thought concerning the demographic problem.

Another distinguished academic who became a victim of this campaign was Wang Jout-Shee. Born on 21 September 1903 in Jiangxi province, Wang Jout-Shee spent eight years at Tsing Hua School in Peking, followed by several years at Wisconsin University, where he gained a doctorate in political science. In August 1928 he went to London University to study under Professor Harold Laski, returning to Shanghai in late 1930 to teach and write fearless articles lambasting Chiang Kai-Shek's regime; sometimes he wrote for the *New Moon* magazine of his old school friend Lor Lone-Gi. Left-wing publishers were having a difficult time because of harassment by Chiang's government, often finding their publications banned or confiscated by the post office. In 1932, Wang Jout-Shee founded his own magazine, *Idea and Critique*, which lasted for just one and a half months, or three editions, before it was closed down by the Nationalist government. He then founded another magazine, *Free Speech*, in the first edition of which, published on 1 February 1933, he accused the Chiang government of giving in to the unsatiable Japanese desire for invading China. He wrote:

> The Japanese invasion has come through Shanhaiguan into China proper. Shanhaiguan has fallen and Ehol province is going to fall. Our front-line soldiers are already fighting the enemy, whose enormous army is pressing near. Our lands are arrogated, our people are killed. The League of Nations is blatantly shielding Japan. Britain and France have already come to a secret understanding with Japan. Why doesn't our government fight? Why doesn't it make up its mind to fight? Why doesn't it make preparation to fight? ...

This government does not send a big army up north to recover lost territories; instead it deploys more than 300,000 troops to lay siege to the Communists. During the battle of Shanghai, the government watched as the lone 19th Route Army fought a bitter battle but would not transfer its army in Jiangxi province to reinforce our Shanghai troops.

The first edition was sold out within four days and had to be reprinted to satisfy demand. But before the year was out, the Chiang government had closed down *Free Speech*, ordering that no university should employ Wang. To make a living, Wang opened up a lawyer's office, but his clients soon came under pressure from the Shanghai branch of the Nationalist Party and he received an intimidating letter.

By 1935 anti-Japanese sentiment was soaring in China and in May 1936 the Save the Nation Association was founded in Shanghai, with Wang as one of its leaders. In November seven of the association's leaders, including Wang, were arrested for endangering the Republic of China and for being suspected Communists and instigators of strikes. Another charge concerned striking Chinese workers in Japanese textile factories in Shanghai and the Save the Nation Association collected donations to buy rice for the strikers.

The seven arrested leaders were thrown into jail in Suzhou city. There was a tumultuous national outcry, but Chiang remained silent. After six months, the Nationalist government staged a public trial, in which the seven men were defended by 27 lawyers from Shanghai. Families and reporters were admitted to the gallery, while a big crowd surrounded the courthouse.

Madame Soong Ching-Ling, widow of the Father of the Nation and 12 celebrated members of the Save the Nation Association, made their way separately and quietly from Shanghai to the trial in Suzhou in order to avoid being intercepted by Chiang's police. Soong Ching-Ling demanded to see the senior judge of the provincial supreme court and told him: 'If it is not a crime to be a patriot, then please release these seven people immediately. If it is a crime to be a patriot, then I and my 12 colleagues should also be punished with the seven accused. I now volunteer to go to prison.'

The judge was in an awkward position; he dared not release the seven accused, but he dared not put Sun Yat-Sen's widow in jail. Meanwhile 16 public figures in the US, including Albert Einstein, jointly sent a telegram to Chiang asking him to set the seven political prisoners free.

The Sino-Japanese War finally broke out on 7 July 1937 and on the 31st Chiang, under internal and international pressure, released the seven patriots. Wang had spent his eight months in jail translating a book by his tutor, Professor Harold Laski. This was not the first time he had been to jail. In 1919, the 16-year-old Wang had been one of the student leaders of the May Fourth Movement in Peking, protesting fiercely against the warlord government which was on the point of selling out Chinese sovereignty to Japan at the Paris peace talks. On that occasion he was arrested and detained for five days.

Wang's woes were frequently caused by his patriotism. On 13 April 1941, the Russian government signed a treaty with Japan undertaking that that it would stay neutral over the Sino-Japanese War and that it would respect the integrity of Manchukuo. The Japanese government happily reciprocated by undertaking that it would respect the integrity of the Republic of Outer Mongolia. To the leaders of the Save the Nation Association in Chongqing, it appeared that Russia was stabbing China in the back. They asked Wang to draft an open letter to Stalin pointing out that the treaty had infringed Chinese sovereignty. He demanded that Stalin should answer two questions; first, whether the Russian government acknowledged that Manchuria was an independent country and secondly, whether the establishment of the People's Republic of Mongolia was in accordance with the Sino-Russian agreement of 1924, in which the Russian government acknowledged that Outer Mongolia was part of Chinese territory and that Russia would respect Chinese sovereignty. The draft of the open letter was edited and approved and the nine senior members of the association appended their signatures.

Many of the leading figures in the Chinese Communist Party followed the line of the Russian Communist Party's official newspaper, *Pravda*, which explained that the Russian treaty with Japan was part of Stalin's strategy to steer the Japanese southwards to prevent Russia from being attacked on two fronts, thereby helping Russia to concentrate her resources in the fight against Nazi Germany and Stalin's strategy was correct. But from the point of view of most Chinese people, the Russian strategy amounted to steering the Japanese into China in order to preserve Russia and the treaty was a betrayal.

For a long time the Chinese Communist Party regarded any criticism of Russia as being anti-Communism, so it took a dim view of the association's open letter. There were rumours that the Nationalist government had bribed Wang to make trouble and that Wang had written the letter in advance and forced his colleagues to add their names to it. After the Communists had won power in China all Wang's friends in the association were given ministerial jobs, but Wang himself was ignored. He remained unemployed until 1951, when the president of Fu Dan University in Shanghai invited him to take up a post there.

In March 1957, Chow En-Lai discovered how Wang had been unfairly treated and invited him for a long and friendly chat in Peking. Wang was delighted to find that the misunderstanding between himself and the party had at last been cleared up. Chow now suggested that Wang should move to Peking and should also consider reviving the Save the Nation Association, which should, he said, never have been dissolved. It was a suggestion which demonstrated the high esteem which Chow now had for Wang, because although the party was prepared to tolerate the long-established democratic parties, no new parties or associations would from now on be allowed.

Sadly, Wang's new-found bliss did not last long, because it was shortly after this meeting that the anti-rightist campaign erupted. On 12 June Wang himself was classed as an arch-rightist and the Communists began to dig out every speech and action, old or recent, which might be used to incriminate him. Wang's most malicious crime was said to be his open letter to Stalin, but the discussions about rebuilding the Save The Nation Association were also said to be another of his insidious schemes, never mind that the suggestion had actually been made by Chow. Comments which Wang had made during the Hundred Flowers Blooming Campaign were also used as evidence against him. For example, he had argued that:

> The current bureaucracy is not a unique phenomenon; it is widespread. It is not new, but it has now reached a sorry state. Generally speaking, the lower the rank of bureaucrat, the more autocratic and illegal the incidents... We can guess at the common pattern of speaking out. The more humble the people affected by bureaucracy, the less they dare to speak out ... In the villages, people are more afraid of speaking their minds, so the quietest and most peaceful places have the most bureaucracy.

These remarks were interpreted as Wang's way of extending the Hundred Flowers Blooming Campaign to villages so as to make trouble for the party. His call for a strengthening of democratic law and order and his remark that democracy was inseparable from the rule of law, made him guilty of desiring American-style law and order rather than Communist-style law and order.

The Shanghai newspapers published critical articles full of false allegations, calling Wang a poisoner who was intent on attacking the party and he was forced to write dozens of lengthy self-examinations, self-criticisms and confessions. At the beginning he received some sympathetic letters, but when the tide turned against him he tore them up to avoid implicating other people, only to be forced to criticise himself for his action.

Wang, a good family man, was under immense pressure as a result of family tragedies. His first wife had died and his daughter, a law graduate, had shown signs of mental illness since 1955. Both his sons, one of whom was a bright language student, were also mentally ill; both became violent and had to be hospitalised. Their medical expenses were a heavy burden on Wang and he was consequently in debt. He visited his sons regularly, but was upset when he saw no signs of improvement in them. His critics alleged that his profound love for his children reflected his insufficient dedication to socialist enterprise. Wang's younger daughter, a physics student, was his only hope, a pearl in his palm; but when she did not denounce him as a rightist enemy, she herself was condemned as a rightist and sent to work in a glass factory. Wang felt profoundly guilty for condemning her to life as an outcast.

Professor Wang, as a condemned rightist, could not be permitted to poison the minds of young people any longer and he was therefore demoted to a junior job working in the university library. His salary was also reduced and he was forced to move out of his apartment, which was reserved for academics, into inferior lodgings. Knowing that he would not be allowed to write books, he instead settled down to making new translations of two of Professor Laski's works. The publishers rejected both books, saying they had no plans to publish works of that sort.

In September 1960, his 'rightist hat' was officially removed, but in practice this made very little difference to his reputation. When the Cultural Revolution broke out in 1966, in the eyes of the radicals he was still a condemned rightist. His name, written upside down on wall posters with a big red cross on it, could be seen everywhere in the streets of Shanghai. He was given a new job cleaning the university lavatories and Red Guards from secondary schools and universities ransacked his home in turn, taking all his manuscripts away as offensive rubbish. Next, more than 20 Red Guards from Fu Dan University kicked open his door at midnight one night, with the intention of occupying his home for the foreseeable future. His second wife was thrown out of the house and banned from returning; instead she went to live in the dormitory of the factory where she worked. As the wife of a counter-revolutionary, she had to work under strict surveillance. Wang himself was tortured at home day and night, as the Red Guards demanded that he confess to his criminal activities. Finally, on 21 November 1966, he was handcuffed and taken to one of Shanghai's detention centres, where he was known only as Number 1416; inmates were forbidden from disclosing their real identities. For the next five years Wang was forgotten by the authorities.

Convicted prisoners were as a rule allowed a family visit once a month, but Wang, in a detention centre waiting to be sentenced, was banned from having family visits to prevent any collusion. Instead, once a month his wife brought him medicine and daily necessities, handing them over to the guards at the front gate to pass on to him. Food and correspondence were banned. Being held incommunicado, neither knew what was happening to the other. Wang's physical and mental health were deteriorating, but for a long time he was given no medical treatment. By the time he was finally sent to hospital in early August 1971, he was already dying. He was handcuffed to his sick bed and the doctors treating him were told to ask no questions, just try to treat the prisoner known as no.1416. Three days after his admission to hospital his liver and kidney failed and he died on 5 August, aged 68. His widow was informed of his death on the following day and the heart-broken widow and daughter rushed to the crematorium, in a vain attempt to catch one last glimpse of him after 5 years.

When Wang was detained, his salary was suspended and his two mentally ill sons, both in their 30s or 40s, were turned out of hospital because the family could not afford to pay for their upkeep. Their stepmother tried to look after them at home, but she had to work in the daytime and was worried that the two stepsons, who were both violent, would get into trouble if they left home. Instead she tied up their feet and let them stay in bed. There was little food or medicine available and within three months both men were dead. Wang's beloved daughter, meanwhile, had been condemned as a rightist. The Red Guards shaved half of her head and paraded her through the streets. Suffering from serious breast cancer as well as incurable grief, she died shortly afterwards.

The family's four dead members were buried on a desolate hillside in Zhejiang province. The ashes of Wang's first wife and elder daughter had been buried in a Shanghai cemetery, but the two women's ashes had been thrown away by Red Guards. Wang was now given a false name on his tombstone, in the hope that this could help him to rest in peace. There were only two mourners in the funeral, Wang's widow and son-in-law.

In December 1978, a memorial service was held in Shanghai in honour of Wang. The condolence speech contained a statement that the party had withdrawn the charges for non-existent crimes laid against Comrade Wang during the Cultural Revolution. He had been wrongly classed as a rightist; the CCP central committee exonerated him completely and restored his good name.

Wang's misfortune had stemmed partly from asking Stalin awkward questions. Until the public split between the Chinese Communist Party and the Russian government in the 1960s, official party policy was that Russia could do no wrong. The economist Chen Jar-Cheu was a member of a Chinese friendship delegation sent to visit Russia in April 1956. The local officials, he later wrote, had entertained them with tea and snacks, but no central government leader, not even a minister, would even meet them. Before they left for home, all the Chinese delegates were told to call at an office to collect their farewell presents, a watch and a Russian dictionary. When handing over the presents, the Russians gave their guests a lecture telling them to study the Russian language.

Whenever a Russian delegation visited China, by contrast, its members would be received everywhere by leaders from both central and local government and wined and dined lavishly. The relationship was hardly on an equal footing, but no one dared complain. The new Communist China relied on Russian backing, so protest was something the party could not afford. In 1949, when Mao went to Moscow to sign the friendship treaty, he agreed to Stalin's uncompromising demand that the Chinese should recognise Outer Mongolian independence. Thereafter, nothing would stop the party from insisting on the need to develop and strengthen Sino-Russian friendship. A clause to that effect was even enshrined in China's constitution.

It was against this background that many Chinese slipped up. One well known case concerned the Yunnan warlord, Lone Yun, who had supported the anti-Japanese movement and had secretly joined the Democratic League. For a considerable time Lor Lone-Gi had been working on Lone Yun to persuade him to cooperate with the party in secret. After the Sino-Japanese War, Lone was forcibly taken to Nanking and given a nominal job by Chiang, who made sure that his freedom of movement was restricted. He managed to escape to Hong Kong, then sent his men back to Yunnan to lobby for the Communists. As a result Yunnan went over to the Communists peacefully without any blood being spilled. As a reward for Lone's cooperation, Mao invited him to Peking and bestowed on him privileges equivalent to those enjoyed by a deputy prime minister.

Lone was opposed to Chinese involvement in the Korean War. He poured out his resentment in the National People's Congress standing committee in 1957, pointing out that Kim Il-Sung had launched his war at Stalin's instigation and with his encouragement, calculating that he could seize South Korea. When the Americans hit back, they nearly pushed Kim

Il-Sung and his men into the Yalu River along the China–Korea border. Stalin did not clear up the mess himself; instead he forced China to fight across the border, although at the time China's priority was to capture Taiwan rather than fighting in Korea.

In the end the three-year Korean War not only cost the Chinese army 330,000 casualties, it also landed the country with heavy war expenses and deep in debt to Russia. The Russians contributed not a single rouble to the war, although they made large profits from selling war materials to China and Kim Il-Sung was not exactly grateful to China either. Lone complained loudly that it was unreasonable that China had to pay for all the Korean War expenses.

Lone also talked about American loans to allies and lend-lease supplies in the Second World War. When the war was over, not all the debts were repaid and some loans were simply written off by America. The Russian loan to China, on the other hand, was to be paid back with interest in ten years. Lone suggested seeking a moratorium, paying back the loan in 20 or 30 years so as to alleviate financial hardship in China. Finally, Lone also put in a complaint over Russian looting in Manchuria at the end of the Second World War. He requested that either China should be compensated or else that the material seized should be returned to China.

Lone's opinions had led him into dangerous territory. Inevitably he was named as a prominent rightist and struggle meetings were soon being held day and night at his home under the watchful eye of the party; they were recorded on films and broadcast in order to inform the public of Lone's patriotic crimes. He was forced to admit that he had trampled on the Chinese policy of 'falling on to one side' and had sabotaged the friendship between China and Russia.

A similar crime was committed by Professor Luk Yin-Chee of the Northeast People's University in Changchun city. Luk Yin-Chee had written an essay about the boundary changes in northeast China between 1858 and 1860, when China was under severe pressure from the Opium War and Tsarist Russia had taken the opportunity to seize an area of Chinese territory bigger than Germany and France combined.

Luk suggested redrawing the border with Russia. He pointed out that the Russian history books tried to cover up the true facts and made simplified and misleading statements about the period. He also pointed out that neither *Chinese Modern History*, written by the Communist historian Fan Wen-Lan, nor *Imperialism and Chinese Politics*, written by the deputy Minister of Propaganda, the theoretician Hu Zhing, mentioned a single word about this boundary change. They dealt with this historical period by creating a blank.

Finally, Luk wrote, 'The Chinese Communist Party always feels free to alter historical facts. New China even has to ignore Tsarist Russia's plunder. Is there such a thing as truth any more?'

The anti-rightist campaign condemned Luk for having a narrow nationalist reactionary view and for making up historical events to launch a savage onslaught against socialist Russia and the Chinese Communist Party.

There were many other people like Luk who gained their rightist hats by showing insufficient respect to Russia. A secondary school headmaster in Canton, for example, once made an insouciant remark to the effect that imported Russian calico was not very good looking. He was accused of being anti-Russian and sent to jail without trial for nine months. Another hapless man simply argued that the Chinese should not be opposed to learning English just because they were anti-American; after all, 70 per cent of international science and technology papers were written in English, with less than 20 per cent written in Russian. An 18-year-old Peking art student got into trouble after visiting Lushun, when he commented to a friend that it was unpleasant to see a Lushun street named after a Russian general; and a Communist official was once indiscreet enough to comment on his return from Moscow that Red Square was smaller than Tiananmen Square.

Yet another rightist was a deputy chief engineer, Ma Cheun, from the Hydroelectric Power Station Design College in Canton, who put up a wall poster saying that:

> Among the more than a dozen so-called specialists sent to us by big brother Russia, only three or four are really qualified specialists; the rest are merely experienced shop floor workers or inexperienced youngsters fresh from university. One such specialist did not even know how to do some engineering calculations. Yet they are treated as experts and they often behave as if they have absolute authority, freely issuing inappropriate instructions and making unjustified criticisms. Their living standards are so pampered that every month they have one weeks' holiday to spend in the nearby hot spring resort ... Is this the price to pay for 'falling on to one side'?

Another rightist, Liu Chen, deputy head of the Central China Engineering College, complained: 'There was a time when the Department of Higher Education stressed learning from Russia 100 per cent without any deviation. So we deny everything from capitalist countries. When the capitalist countries had things that the Russians did not, we then criticised these things with our eyes closed. Now that the Russians have such things as well, we can only try to mitigate our embarrassment.'

Another victim was Wang Li-Ming, a member of the Democratic League who condemned the widespread rapes committed by the Russian army in Manchuria after the Second World War, which was common knowledge to the people in Manchuria. The Chinese Communist Party, anxious to propitiate the Russians, insisted that Wang Li-Ming was manufacturing rumours and smearing the Russians to sabotage the friendship between Russia and China. She too was denounced as a rightist and sent to jail, where she died during the Cultural Revolution.

The subject of Russia was just one of the countless minefields that blew up under Chinese people's feet. At the outset of the campaign, the Democratic League enthusiastically set up a number of groups to help the Communist cause. One of them, the science group, was made up of five academics: Tseng Chiu-Leun, a chemist and deputy minister in the Higher Education Ministry; Hua Lor-Guin, a mathematician; Tong Di-Chow, a biologist; and Chen Wai-Chang, Professor of Dynamics and deputy president of Tsing Hua University; and a left-wing economist, Professor Chen Jar-Cheu. The first four had all been trained in the West and all had distinguished academic qualification.

The five men produced a draft on the subject of the development of science in China, which was intended to be used as an internal reference for the Chinese government's benefit. This draft pointed out that China did not have many scientists and the foundations for the study of science were weak. It recommended that scientists, or at least the more successful ones, should be protected and given sufficient financial and other support to help them continue their work. Scientific projects in universities, research institutions and other related enterprises should be coordinated. China should also develop social sciences. It was wrong to deny the existence of social sciences in capitalist countries, or to maintain there was nothing to learn from them. Furthermore, the Chinese government should undertake more survey and research work, instead of treating government policy and directives as indisputable disciplines.

With regard to training postgraduates, everything was decided by the party-controlled personnel office. Only students with the correct class background and who were regarded as politically reliable were selected; their ability was not even a factor and tutors had no say. Many bright students found themselves sent away, while tutors were often stuck with postgraduates who were not interested in their work or who lacked academic ability.

The science group suggested that academic ability should be considered as important as political quality and that gifted young people should be treated equally. But the five men had been sent marching into an area full of quicksand by the over-complacent Democratic League. After the *Kwang Ming Daily* published the report on 9 June 1957, a nationwide campaign began, denouncing the report as being hostile to the party and to socialism. The critics argued that the proposal to protect scientists implied that the party had not protected them up to now. The proposal to change the official view on the social sciences in capitalist countries meant going backwards and trying to revive capitalist social sciences, which were anti-Russian and anti-Marxist. Finally the report did not mention Marxism or Leninism and it did not show that it supported socialism and the party.

The propaganda minister, Luk Din-Yi, openly excoriated the report at a meeting of the National People's Congress and questioned Tseng Chiu-Leun, a deputy minister for higher education, on why he was hostile to socialism and the party.

The report had been discussed, approved and signed by all five members in the science group, four of whom were first-rate scientists in China. To punish all five might give the impression that the party was lashing out indiscriminately, damaging its prestige and instead three of the five – Hua Lor-Guin, Tong Di-Chow and Chen Jar-Cheu – were allowed to slip through the net and simply cautioned that the report had made serious political mistakes. The three were advised to make a joint statement to be printed in the *Kwang Ming Daily* claiming that they had been made use of by the two rightists, Tseng Chiu-Leun and Chen Wai-Chang. Having been granted a lucky escape, Professor Hua Lor-Guin declared on the podium of the National People's Congress that the two rightists had used the names of the other three members in the Democratic League science group to publish a reprehensible report as a way of assaulting the party.

It was true there was absolutely nothing the three who had escaped punishment could do to save the other two. If the three of them had been foolhardy enough to stick their own necks out and refuse to lie, they would have imperilled not only themselves but also their families, friends and associates. The price to pay was to live with a conscience maimed by a brutal and totalitarian regime.

A democratic writer, Shiu Jeun, wrote: 'In the summer of 1957 when I suffered struggle meetings and saw kind people make vicious attacks and honest people lie through their teeth, despair seized me. After harping on and on about anti-rightists, this land was more silent than ever. Revolutionary people became yes-men.'

Chen Wai-Chang was humiliated through cartoons, wall posters, articles and struggle meetings and was removed from his position as deputy president of Tsing Hua University. He became a university cleaner and road sweeper. Rightists lost their right to speak out and were unable to publish their works. Chen's two books, one about dynamics and the other about applied mathematics, were rejected because of his odious new identity. Typesetting for one of the books had already been completed, but the publisher refused to print it; instead Chen was charged for the expense of typesetting and of destroying the lot.

Chen's downfall sent a shock-wave through the community of Chinese scientists and students abroad. Many of them were planning to go back to China to serve their motherland and some had already arrived in Tokyo or Hong Kong on their way home. When they heard that the patriotic Chen had been deemed a rightist, they stopped in their tracks; many decided to apply instead for American nationality.

In 1980, more than two decades later, Chen and Tseng Chiu-Leun were both rehabilitated, the party now saying that the science group's offensive paper was not in fact hostile to socialism or to the party; it actually contained many good suggestions after all!

When the anti-rightist campaign was in full swing, the effort to belittle the academics, particularly those trained in the West, was extended to their professional qualities. They were often depicted as ignorant and useless; it was said that the level of knowledge of some engineering professors was inferior to that of factory workers. In due course, many professors found themselves kicked out of classrooms and their jobs given to factory workers. A situation soon arose that confounded both the students and their new lecturers.

Another resoundingly notorious rightist, Gor Pei-Chi, surfaced from the Chinese People's University in Peking, an elite institution established to indoctrinate cadres for the Communist regime. Gor Pei-Chi, a physics lecturer, spoke out at a meeting arranged by the university branch of the party in the latter half of May 1957. His speech was edited, taken out of context and published by the *People's Daily* twice, without being checked by Gor beforehand. It was also reprinted in provincial newspapers. The *People's Daily* and the provincial newspapers received huge quantities of letters from readers flinging abuse at Gor. The most inimical remark attributed to him was 'kill the Communists'; this phrase became the strongest evidence against him, even though he repeatedly denied that he had ever said it. He wrote to the *People's Daily* asking for a correction to be published, but he was ignored. After being mauled in a series of struggle meetings, Gor was branded an arch-rightist and later as a historical counter-revolutionary, since he had previously worked for the Nationalist government. It now sounded hardly surprising that he would say 'kill the Communists'. He duly became a household name, vindicating Chairman Mao's admonition that vicious class enemies were still operating within the masses. At the end of 1957 he was arrested, sentenced to life imprisonment and sent to serve his term in Shanxi province.

Gor's wife, Zhu Shiu-Ling, was an associate professor of mathematics at the same university. On 31 May 1957, as Gor was becoming headline news, she was admitted to hospital with serious heart trouble following childbirth. She was discharged in November, still very weak, but by then Gor was detained in his office and was unable to go home. When he was sent to jail in December, his salary was stopped and his sick wife was left to support five children, the eldest a 12-year-old daughter. As the wife of a counter-revolutionary, Zue suffered humiliation and contempt everywhere. Psychological pressure made her health worse and she deteriorated into a chronic invalid, bedridden for six years. She was too ill to teach and her family could not live on her sick pay, so instead two of her children were given away to relatives. She also tried to give away the youngest one, a one-year-old, to a childless couple, but when the prospective adoptive parents found out the infant's father was Gor, they were too frightened to go ahead with the adoption. Zhu's second child, a son, often came home from primary school crying because other children taunted him by calling him 'little rightist' or 'little Gor Pei-Chi'. Her eldest daughter was a very bright student and had once won a prize in a Peking secondary school physics competition. It should have been easy for her to pass the university entrance examination, yet when the time came in 1964, no university would accept her. Obviously, her disgraced father was the cause of her trouble and her younger brother, also a very bright student, could expect the same fate. Zhu believed in her husband's innocence and wanted to wait for him to come home, but after seeing her daughter's intense grief, she was forced to face her five children's bleak future. It upset her tremendously that what she was going to do could deal her husband a terrible blow, but she felt she had no other way out. In an attempt to protect their children, she divorced Gor and the children gave up their father's surname, taking their mother's surname instead. However, the move failed to give her children much protection when the Cultural Revolution broke out. A pair of scrolls were pasted outside her front door bearing the words 'Heroic fathers produce brave men, reactionary fathers produce bastards.' Her son was beaten up badly by Red Guards.

In December 1975, the party decided to show its compassionate face by setting free a group of Nationalist officers. Gor was among them, but he was still wearing, after 18 years, his old 'hat' of a rightist and counter-revolutionary. He wanted to go home to rebuild his marriage, but because his name had not been cleared, Zhu dared not take him back and put their children at risk again. So instead in early 1976 Gor went back to Peking, where he moved into a dilapidated room of eight square metres. Local police and the activists of the residents' association had warned the locals to stay on high alert, reminding them that it was very important not to forget the class struggle when a counter-revolutionary moved in to live among them. When the fearsome ruffian actually appeared, he turned out to be just a decrepit man suffering from cataracts and glaucoma and nearly blind.

After an eye operation in 1979, Gor regained enough sight for him to redouble his efforts to write to and to visit anyone who might be able to help in fighting for his exculpation. Documents were gradually found to verify his claim that he had joined the party in 1938 and had worked as an underground Communist agent in the Nationalist government. His two contacts had been arrested by the Nationalists in 1947 and his connection with the Communist Party was consequently cut off, with the result that his party membership could not be proved from that time. His reported remark, 'kill the Communists', turned out to have been taken out of context. What he had said was 'the Nationalists did bad things, so people overthrew them. If the Communists did bad things, people would kill the Communists as well.' Back in 1957 only the words 'kill the Communists' had been published by the *People's Daily*, to be used as prime counter-revolutionary evidence. In May 1983, Gor was rehabilitated and the party recognised him as having been a member since 1938. When his name was totally cleared, his wife wanted him to return to her and their family, but he refused. He was bitter about being abandoned in the harshest period of his life.

Hundreds of thousands of people in China were forced into Zhu's position of having to choose between their condemned spouse and their children. They could not win either way. Gor was, of course, not the only Communist forsaken by the party. The authoress Ding Ling was another well-known victim. Ding's distinguished writing career began in the 1930s when she spent the war in Yan'an as a loyal Communist. Her novel *Sunshine on the Songchen River* had won the Stalin Literary Award in March 1952. Being a veteran Communist, she held many important posts in literary circles.

Ding had been sliding slowly into trouble since early 1952. To the politically vigilant, it seemed suspicious that she had got away unscathed several times when arrested in the 1920s and she was also suspected of having formed an anti-party cabal in recent years. She was soon under investigation and the first signal came when she was removed from the position of editor-in-chief of the prestigious *Literary Magazine* and given a lesser post. She protested and said that she was innocent, because her personal history had already been cleared by the CCP central office in her Yan'an days; it had accepted she had not betrayed the party during her several arrests and releases by the Nationalist Party. She also argued that the accusation that she had formed an anti-party cabal with Chan Che-Shar was groundless, because Chan had just been released from prison and they had had no contact with each other.

But her problem would just not go away. Both Ding and Chan repeatedly requested another investigation to clear their names and on 6 June 1957 the party mandarins in the Writers' Union announced that Ding and Chan's anti-party cabal had never existed. Sadly for Ding, the following day Mao formally mobilised his counter-attack against rightists. After picking up this sinister signal, the party bosses in the Writers' Union made a quick U-turn and declared at the next meeting that Ding and Chan were in fact part of an anti-party cabal after all and now they all needed to dig deeply into the two culprits' backgrounds to search for crimes. Ding was soon given a rightist's hat.

She was denounced for colluding with other writers to oppose the party's leadership. In January 1958, Mao gave orders to censure again the 'poisonous grass' cultivated in Yan'an by Ding and Wang Shi-Wai, the first author to be killed by the party for his writings. Mao personally wrote the following special review for the *Literary Magazine*:

Strange writings are there for all to enjoy, to analyse the dubious meanings. Many people want to read these 'strange writings'. We have collected them and read them all once again. There are certainly some strange characters; people present themselves as revolutionaries but write counter-revolutionary articles.

Thanks to the hard work of Ding Ling and Wang Shi-Wai, poisonous grasses have turned out to be fertilizer. They have become our people's teachers. They have surely taught our people to understand how our enemies work. The people's blocked noses now get unblocked. The naive and unworldly, the young and old swiftly learn plenty of knowledge of the world.

The party branch of the Writers' Union had earlier sent out letters to encourage people to provide more incriminating hearsay evidence about the already convicted Ding. One young army writer, Xu Kwong-Yel, replied that he wished the party branch in the Writers' Union would remember from past experience that they should avoid applying so much pressure that they created an atmosphere where no one dared express any dissenting opinion. Six months later, when the anti-rightist campaign had gathered momentum, party members were also required to confess their relationship with Ding and Chan and Xu Kwong-Yel paid a heavy price for his remarks. He was also denounced as a rightist and the prime reason was his attempt to overturn the verdicts of Chan and Ding.

Ding was expelled from the party, handcuffed, stripped and searched. For a while she was kept in solitary confinement; her husband was locked up next door, but they were forbidden to talk to or to see each other. Soon they were separated. The 65-year-old novelist vanished into a labour camp for two decades. Her friends were shocked when she emerged after being released in 1978; it was like seeing someone rising from the dead. In August 1984 she was completely rehabilitated.

Another group of Communists who got into trouble were reporters who had written about a certain shop in Harbin. This shop had no shop sign; it had been set up to provide scarce goods at low prices for Communist cadres only. Local party bosses disliked the fact that the reporters were revealing party members' special privileges to the public and they alleged that the true intention of the article was to destroy the party's prestige among the people. Although the article had been published in 1956, well before the Hundred Flowers Blooming Campaign, local party bosses felt the urge to settle an old score. One thousand words in length, the article had involved more than 30 reporters from the *Harbin Daily*, *Heilongjiang Daily* and *Chinese Youths' Newspaper*, the official newspaper of the Chinese Communist Youth League. None of them escaped joining the rank of rightists.

A poet, Liu Sar-Hor, had never made any unfavourable comment on party policy or on society, but he got into trouble through one of his poems in which he wrote about a passionate kiss. This was condemned as rightist behaviour worthy of the capitalist class and Liu was accused of being shameless, lewd and obscene.

The party's rectification movement and anti-rightist campaign presently merged into one and the total number of disgraced Communists and Communist rightists trawled up in this two-year purge amounted to several hundred thousand.

Nearly all the party's campaigns required everybody to get involved, to study, to debate, to hit out and to be educated. There was no room for apolitical onlookers. The Hundred Flowers Blooming Campaign swept all students, particularly students in higher education, into the turmoil. Young people had few vested interests and were prepared to speak out against anything they regarded as unfair and unreasonable. University students' flowers all over the country flourished in the early spring, almost to the point of unrest. Most of them directed their verbal barrage at the party's most sacred treasure, the political system and said plainly that they wanted democracy, freedom and human rights.

Professor Ma Yan-Choo explained:

> In previous years, students have followed the teaching of the party and Russian specialists to study documents and books about Marxism. Some students were woolly-headed, but others studied seriously. These serious students have discovered new truths from Marxist theory, dialectical materialism and the Russian socialist revolution. They have concluded that Marxism and all its 'ologies' are now out of date and the Russian socialist revolution is completely wrong, so they do not believe in these things any more.

> Those students who have a clear idea about the Russian socialist revolution now have the courage to speak out to censure the mistakes in the party-led education department. This has enlightened their woolly-headed peers.

In a similar vein, Professor Shee Mong-Shon of the Chinese People's University, who was a long-time supporter of the party, said: 'The party hopes that the Chinese People's University will function like a beehive. After receiving Marxist indoctrination and guidance from the party, the students will fly away everywhere to sting people. Yet when the bees see something not right in their hive, their temperament changes. They are unwilling to sting people; on the contrary, they sting the beehive owner. The party is surprised... But the party must know that an education without truth and humanity is bound to fail.'

From this beehive, the party's indoctrinating stronghold, flew out the best known student rightist, Lin Shi-Ling. She told a meeting of several thousand students: 'Real socialism should be very democratic, but it is not democratic here. We could call this society socialism built on a foundation of feudalism... We should fight for real socialism.'

Lin was sentenced to 15 years' imprisonment. Her classmate, a demobbed army officer from the Korean War, had been assigned by the party to groom Lin to join the Communist Youth League. When Lin went down as an arch-rightist, this demobbed woman officer was regarded as Lin's nanny and went down with her charge. Her husband, still in the army and his army comrades who had all fought for the party in various wars, were all condemned as rightists implicated by the 'nanny'. Even young people who had written to Lin to express their support after listening to her speech were caught in the anti-rightist dragnet.

In the post-Mao era, the party committee in the Chinese People's University concluded after its re-investigation: 'Lin Shi-Ling made use of the party's rectification movement and openly advocated a fundamental change of our country's political system... She was obsessed with purging a large group of undesirables in the party.' As the years went by she refused to admit that her views had been wrong and so she was one of the very small minority who was not granted rehabilitation.

The party frequently asserted that the intelligentsia were in need of re-education by the peasants and working class and aggrieved feelings among educated people in China were widespread. The deputy president of the Peking Normal University, Fu Jone-Sun, wrote that 'Whenever a political campaign was looming, even if it wasn't called a struggle – it might be called study, mind reform or cleansing – intellectuals would be terrified. They fawn on the rulers and in return get either disdain or a slap in the face. This is unprecedented; I cannot think of any prosperous era which ill-treated intellectuals in this way.' Similarly, Professor Tung Tai-Wor of Zhejiang University said: 'The party not only regards intellectuals as its waiters, it also treats them as criminals who are drubbed in every campaign.'

Some of the intellectuals decided the Communists could not be trusted and were adamant in saying nothing, like the Peking University Professor Poon Kwang-Dan, who had once made self-criticisms 12 times during the movement for mind reform, all of which were rejected as inadequate by party cadres.

Although many people admitted there was no freedom of speech in China, few mentioned that there was also no freedom of declining to speak. This was how Jeang Chan got into trouble. In the early 50s, Jeang Chan worked as an English translator in the Xinhua news agency headquarters in Peking. Quiet and taciturn, he was usually ignored by everybody. When the anti-rightist campaign began, the Xinhua news agency required all its employees to produce wall posters and speak out at meetings to expose both enemies and failings in their own minds. Jeang was like a man without a tongue; he found it very difficult to cope with the changed circumstances. He asked his superior to spare him from speaking at the meetings and if possible even from attending them, as he could usefully spend the time in his office doing more translation work. His boss was incensed, accusing him of resisting the campaign and rejecting his request point blank. The naive Jeang then offered to resign; it never occurred to him that resignation meant rebellion. He was now officially a 'black flag', having committed a monstrous crime and the translation section of the Xinhua news agency ran an extra campaign to pull out the black flag. Suddenly all the wall posters were full of criticisms of Jeang. When the new campaign at last found its way back to the anti-rightist course, Jeang left his workplace to stay with his mother in an area that was declining into a slum.

Communist China had only one employer, the Chinese Communist Party. Anyone who displeased the employer took the risk of being unemployed forever, something that Jeang soon found out. Many years went by before he at long last found a temporary job selling cabbages at a nationalised vegetable stall, earning a starvation wage of seven yuans a month. But he failed to keep the job because he was going deaf and instead he found another job as a road sweeper, with the same pay. Again he failed to keep the job, because he was unable to hear a car horn or a bicycle bell and so was a potential danger to other people and to himself.

After his mother's death, he lived on his own in the slum, unemployed and forgotten by nearly everyone except his sister and her family who tried to help him from time to time. One day he fainted and it was five hours before anyone found him. He never regained consciousness and died a silent and lonely death.

Educated Chinese people had good reason to be terrified by all these campaigns. Mao stressed emphatically in July that there should be no let-up in digging out the rightists. Although the quota laid down by him was five per cent, in reality five per cent was not good enough. The party secretary of Peking University, Jiang Long-Gi, managed a ratio of 6.5 per cent, but this was deemed not good enough and he was removed from the job. His successor pushed the success rate up to ten per cent. There were more than 400 rightists among the staff of Wuhan University. One professor there was going into hospital for treatment when a party official asked him to speak out; he replied that he would do so after he had recovered. When the tide turned, he considered he had had a lucky escape, but the party officials had appraised his possible reaction and decided his opinions would not have been correct and so he was counted a rightist as well.

A young primary school teacher read out to her colleagues an article in the *Kwang Ming Daily*. Later, its writer, a democrat, was condemned as an arch-rightist and as a result the newspaper reciter became a small rightist and spent several years in a labour camp. When she was allowed back to the school, she was not permitted to teach; instead her job was to sweep the floor and clean the lavatories. She was only finally rehabilitated 20 years later.

A Peking University student rightist, Wong Jone-Chi, jumped out of a window in a suicide attempt, but he survived. Although injured, he was still forced to attend struggle meetings. Seething with anger, he openly said that he would stab someone to death. It did not matter that this was only a verbal threat, he was condemned as a rightist killer and shot. He was finally rehabilitated posthumously after 20 years.

Another Peking University student rightist, the 18-year-old Koo Wen-Shan, ran away back home to Hangzhou. He was brought back to Peking and sentenced to five years and after serving his full term was compelled to stay and work in the labour reform farm. Gripped by despair, he escaped across the border into Russia. For him it was out of the frying pan into the fire, as the KGB put him into a sack, took him to Moscow for interrogation and then repatriated him back to China, where he was executed by firing squad.

Some people in Peking University nodded their heads when reading wall posters during the early stage of the Hundred Flowers Blooming Campaign and they became known as the head-nodding rightists. Others shook their heads when reading wall posters during the counter-attack against rightists and these people became known as the head-shaking rightists. On occasion, quiet and reserved people also found themselves condemned as rightists. It was said that these people hated the Communists so much that they were unable to speak and could only grind their teeth. So they became the teeth-grinding rightists.

One particularly unfortunate teeth-grinding rightist was Wong Jee-Jone, a geology graduate who worked for a research institution in Qinghai province. In 1957 he took part in a training course in the Peking Petroleum College and when the course finished in early 1958 he returned to Qinghai. By this time the anti-rightist campaign in Qinghai was over, but the party bosses in his workplace had not managed to fill up their quota, so on his return Wong was summoned to see them and told that he was now a rightist. He protested that he had not uttered one word, neither had he written one wall poster, but his argument fell on deaf ears. The party concluded that he was a typical soundless rightist, anti-party to the core. He was sent to a labour camp, while his girlfriend was implicated and dispatched to work in a village as a rightist.

When there were not enough academics to fill the quotas, standards had to be lowered to catch the less educated. For example, two Communist cadres were assigned the job of taking 20 rightists to a labour camp from a county in Gansu province. One rightist escaped halfway through the journey. When the county party boss heard about the mishap over the phone and that they were therefore now one man short of the quota designated by his superiors, he gave orders to use the other escort-cadre to make up for the shortfall. No amount of protest could save the hapless man, who was left behind in the labour camp with the other rightists.

The party officials kept the quota very much in mind. If work units were unable to find enough rightists, Mao regarded them as right-leaning. He asked: 'Is your unit in a vacuum? Other units have rightists, how come yours has none?' Sometimes leading officials of party branches which could not meet their targets were denounced as rightists because the quota had to be filled up.

There were many others, like the aforementioned escort, who were baffled by their own misfortune. A famous composer, Chan Kor-Cin, was encouraged by senior Communists to bring his family back to mainland China from Hong Kong in 1950. During the Korean War, the party encouraged people to make donations to buy weapons and Chan sold his family jewels to donate one plane, as well as sending his son to fight in Korea. Although he had never said anything offensive about the party, he was branded a rightist for coming back from Hong Kong; he was sent to a labour camp in Anhui province, where he starved to death.

Many people in the legal department complained about widespread unlawful killings and arrests. An adviser to the Supreme Court, Yu Jone-Lok, said: 'This present government does not protect the rights of citizens. Its record is even worse than the feudal dynasties and Chiang Kai-Shek.' The cause of all these problems, said Yu, was either the flouting of the law or the complete absence of any rule of law. Court officials felt free to hand out any sentences they liked. The deputy head of the Peking Judicial Department, Lou Bon-Yan, complained that it was against the law to deal with a case by simply following instructions from the local party committee. It destroyed the court's independent position when conducting a trial. A chorus of complaints repeated that many party cadres in judicial departments knew nothing about the law and were bringing disaster upon the people; that political policies were being used as substitutes for the law; that the country was now ruled by men, not by laws; and that the pervasive and brutal injustice inflicted on people was not the fault of an individual personality, it was the fault of the system.

Even the Minister for Public Security, Lor Rui-Chin, a member of the party central committee, let his guard slip. In a speech in July 1956, he discussed the conditions in labour camps, commenting that 'some cadres in a few labour camps treat their prisoners worse than slave-owners treated their slaves... It is not only against the law, it is sheer inhumanity.' He also reported that some prisoners in labour camps and prisons were not even allowed to drink or sleep, while others were forced to work 20 hours a day. After they died, post-mortems revealed that their intestines were as thin as paper. It was cruel, inhuman and illegal.

However, most of these voices came from lawyers who had been trained in the West. They were simply square pegs in round holes and were labelled rightists for the crimes of anti-party leadership and attempting to run an independent kingdom. In all, 83 rightists, including the Chief Justice of the Supreme Court, were arrested in the Peking city judicial department alone. This amounted to a nine per cent purge.

Party secretaries in every branch on every level were now able to wield their power more freely than ever. When a cadre in the Central Forestry Research Institute raped his servant, his party branch treated the incident as internal and confidential party business. The rapist was put under observation inside the party for one year; he was allowed to keep his job and was sheltered by the party. The same thing happened in Fujian Province Normal University, where the head of the personnel department (a department which was staffed only by trusted Communists), raped teachers and students and ensured their silence through intimidation and bribery. The university party branch turned a blind eye to the scandal and tried to protect the rapist. Party branches in the anti-rightist campaign, as in many other campaigns, replaced the judiciary in handing out jail terms to their victims.

Two thousand years earlier, under the Emperor Qin, all those seen whispering to another person were liable to be executed. They would be beheaded and their corpses displayed in the market to serve as a warning to others. On one occasion in 117 BC, when a Han emperor spotted a minister's lips moving slightly but without producing a sound, the emperor decided that the minister was scolding the monarch in his abdomen and he was beheaded. The rulers of new China out-did even the old emperors by setting down quotas which their spellbound followers scrambled to overfill.

85

The Five Black Categories

The rightists now joined the landlords, rich peasants, counter-revolutionaries and bad elements as social outcasts; these Chinese untouchables were officially known as 'the five black categories'.

The first two groups, landlords and rich peasants, consisted of villagers who had fallen in the Land Reform Campaign. The third group, counter-revolutionaries, was divided into two sub-groups, active counter-revolutionaries and historical counter-revolutionaries. Anyone who had displeased the party in word or deed belonged to the former and this included those who had tried to escape from China or who had once said something favourable about Taiwan. Those who had previously worked for the Nationalist government or Nationalist Party, even if they had since worked for the Communist government, were classed as historical counter-revolutionaries. Most people in the fourth group, the bad elements, were young people such as burglars, street brawlers, speculators, prostitutes or people who had married unofficially. The fifth group, the rightists, were mainly intellectuals snared in the 1957 campaign. The party denounced all members of the 'five categories' as dangerous people, political garbage and reactionaries. They were political lepers whom few dared approach.

Most rightists were dismissed from their jobs and their salaries were stopped. The party branch in their workplaces would decide their sentences and announce them at big meetings which everyone was required to attend. On these occasions, activists would lead the audience in abusing the rightists. Most were sent to labour camps, from which many never left alive. A few were demoted and kept in the same workplaces under public surveillance. Their new jobs would be to make tea, wash floors, sweep roads and clean spittoons and lavatories. Anybody who felt these pariahs were not pulling their weight was free to scold them, hit them or kick them and they were not in any position to argue or resist.

They would be required to attend regular meetings at local public security stations, often three nights a week from 7 p.m. to 10 p.m., to study

Mao's teachings, discuss political documents or talk about their self-reform. They were not allowed to arrive late or leave early and even had to ask for permission if they wanted to answer a call of nature. Twice monthly as a rule, in the middle and at the end of the month, they were required to produce written reports for the local public security station on the subject of their thoughts. Were they keen on their political study? Had they learned something and made progress? Were they still disgruntled about anything? Were there more confessions to make? They had to write about facts, their mental reactions and self-criticism; empty talk was not good enough.

Every week they had to hand over all their mail from family and friends to the local public security station for examination. Nothing could be kept back. They had to report everything about the people they knew: their names, addresses and workplaces. How did they get to know each other? How often did they see each other? What did they talk about when they met?

They were banned from going out after 10 p.m. If they wanted to visit their families, they had first to obtain permission by filling in forms from the committees of residents' associations or local public security stations, writing down where they were going, whom they were going to see, what they were going to talk about and when they would return home. They had to be back before 10 p.m. and they had to report their return before going home. If the intended visit was outside town, the local public security station would have to investigate the application. If it was approved, a permit for going away for three days would be issued. If permission was not granted, then of course they could not go away.

The five black categories were not allowed to attend election meetings or express opinions about the candidates. They were also banned from joining in the festival parades or evening parties on Labour Day (1 May), the birthday of the Chinese Communist Party (1 July), the birthday of the Chinese Communist Army (1 August) and the birthday of Communist China (1 October). Since those celebrating the holidays wanted to relax and have fun, all 'dangerous' people were ordered to stay at home to prevent sabotage.

Applications for registering marriage would often be refused, with rightist applicants being told that they had unclean and criminal minds. They should start by reforming themselves and wait till their hats were removed. Only when they had become human again would they be eligible to register for marriage. However, few people wanted to marry someone belonging to the five black categories. Married couples often ended up getting a divorce if one of them sank into such disgrace. Pressure on members of the party and the Communist Youth League to cut ties with their class enemy relatives would be much more severe, as they would be expelled from the organisations and face struggle meetings themselves. Children had to cut ties with their disgraced parents, so the chances of anyone in the five black categories keeping their family together were bleak.

The 'rightists under internal control' were all important people for whom the party had decided to provide some protection. Even so, few of them could escape unscathed for a long time and most fell heavily during the Cultural Revolution. Peking was a city full of rightists. In early 1958 a number of rightist students from several universities were told to report to a certain office, taking with them their luggage. They were then taken to a public security station to record their fingerprints. Some of them refused to cooperate, protesting that they were not criminals, but were physically restrained by security policemen, handcuffed and forced to leave their fingerprints on file. They were transferred to jail and later sent to the notorious Clear River Labour Reform Farm 100 km east of Peking.

There were about 500 inmates in one of the farm units, most of whom were rightists and the rest were criminals. When nationwide famine set in following Mao's Great Leap Forward, the already poor food rations for prisoners worsened still further. At the end of 1959, the rations at Clear River Farm were cut by more than half, but initially the heavy workload was not reduced. The inmates became very weak and eventually manual work had to stop altogether.

In early spring about 300 younger people from the unit were chosen to work in the fields, most of them students from Peking's colleges and universities. The merciless starvation and exhausting drudgery claimed all of them; every single one perished before the summer. Some very weak inmates who had escaped spring work in the fields managed to survive, hoping that when the famine eased up they could one day return home to Peking. In early 1962, their four-year labour training came to an end, but by then Peking wanted to be a crime- and sin-free city and it would therefore not take back bad elements. All the released rightists were instead retained to work on the farm.

Meanwhile, most of the Peking rightists were loaded on to special trains escorted by armed guards and sent to the labour reform farms near the Sino-Russian border in northeast Manchuria. This vast and desolate virgin land, known as the North Big Barren, could house enormous numbers of prisoners; some friends detained there for decades never ran into each other and were completely unaware of each other's existence. All the clothing of new inmates, including underwear, was marked with the words 'labour reform' written in indelible paint, so any rightist who wanted to run away would do better to go naked. Many intellectuals perished in these camps.

Some rightists were treated with special 'kindness' by not being officially designated as prisoners. They were only there to undertake labour training and had not been given fixed jail terms; this meant they could be held there indefinitely. In reality the line between these people and the prisoners was extremely blurred. All their mail was censored by warders and if any inmate stepped over the cordon line without permission the guards were entitled to open fire.

Exhausting manual work, plus the starvation of the early 1960s, took a heavy toll in China's labour reform camps. In the Ja Ban Kol labour reform farm of Jiuquen city, Gansu province, 1,600 out of 2,000 rightists died around 1960. The death rate of rightists in Shanshui farm, Guangdong province, was 20 per cent. A Shanghai language student recalled that there had been more than 400 people in his labour reform group in Anhui province, only about 20 of whom survived the 1960 famine. Many killed themselves, while others died in accidents when carrying out dangerous work without taking safety precautions.

One of the labour reform laws issued by the State Council in 1954 stated: 'When prisoners have served their full sentences they can voluntarily stay on to work in the labour camp. If they have no home to go back to or no way to find work, the labour reform authorities should arrange work for them when possible in the territories with sparse populations.' It also stipulated that prisoners who had not been satisfactorily reformed would have to stay behind to work in the camp after their release.

Although these people had theoretically had their civil rights restored, their movements were still restricted. They were not allowed to return home without a very good reason. The government explained that these measures had been introduced with the aim of reducing crime in cities. The decision whether someone would be forced to stay after being 'released' was in the hands of the officials in each labour camp, who could therefore freely threaten prisoners in their camps with this prospect – a compulsory but disguised life sentence.

Unlike the Suppression of Counter-Revolutionary Elements campaign, on the whole the anti-rightist campaign did not hand out death sentences; instead the rightists were kept alive as 'negative teachers', a title given to them by Mao. Their wretched existence served as a warning to the Chinese people of the dire consequences of getting on the wrong side of the party. Whether the rightists were treated better than the counter-revolutionaries was a matter of debate. A rightist architecture student from Tsing Hua University survived decades in a labour camp strengthened by a burning wish to clear his name. He was eventually vindicated and allowed to go home. But even though he was free, life had passed him by. He found himself with no youth, no career, no family and no more purpose in life, so he killed himself.

In 1962, some party members appealed for the re-investigation and rehabilitation of rightists and some workplaces even started the ball rolling themselves. Mao plainly declared that there would be no rehabilitation for the 1957 rightists, thereby promptly bringing the tentative approach to justice to an abrupt end.

Mao's antipathy to intellectuals was of long standing. It had begun when he was working as a clerk in the Peking University library under Chang Sun-Fu. Chang had been a co-founder of the Chinese Communist Party back in 1920 when he was a lecturer. He later visited Europe, where he introduced Zhu De, eventually the most senior soldier in the PLA and also Chow En-Lai, to the party. Through his recommendation Chow got a job in the Whampoa Military Academy, from which post he went on to build a highly successful career.

As Mao's boss, Chang criticised his unsightly handwriting and made him copy his work again. Furthermore, the celebrated academics in the university did not have time to listen and to talk to a humble library clerk who spoke with a heavy Hunan accent. Mao felt he was being ignored and slighted and began to complain in his letters about haughty academics. He was not the type to forgive or forget and this sowed the seed of misfortune for a whole generation of educated Chinese.

During the siege of Cheng Ber-Jeun, Chang Sun-Fu said that in his opinion Cheng Ber-Jeun's suggestion of a 'politics design bureau' was not necessarily wrong, a remark which was enough to brand him a rightist. Chow En-Lai was always careful not to antagonise his cunning and vicious boss, so when Chang sank into deep water, Chow felt powerless to help.

The party's sanitised figure for the number of rightists caught between 1957 and 1958 stood at 550,000, but leaked confidential documents suggested that the true figure was 1.02 million; some people estimated the true figure as 1.3 million. There were a large number of people not included in this statistic, such as the special group known as the 'rightists under internal control', which spared some people such as Ma Yan-Choo from unrelenting exposure. Some groups were exempted from being charged as rightists, such as secondary school students, the working class and peasants; disgraced people from these sections were categorised merely as anti-socialist elements or bad elements, but they too had to live out the following 20 or so years in humiliation just like the rightists.

Hu Yel-Bound, the more liberal post-Mao minister of the CCP's

Department of Central Organisation, worked hard, after winning Deng Xiao-Ping's acquiescence, to push through a policy exonerating the innocent rightists. From 1979, after 22 years, more than 99.99 per cent of the rightists were at last rehabilitated; the final score left fewer than 100 people remaining as rightists. The party knew only too well that these people were also innocent, but many were already dead. It tried to pacify the families by admitting that the party needed to keep some people on its list of rightists simply to justify the campaign against them and it appealed to the families to make a sacrifice for the sake of the nation's stability.

There was strong opposition inside the party to the proposal to take the exculpated rightists back into their old work units, for many of the erstwhile persecutors by now occupied senior posts, or sometimes the victims' own positions and the work units could therefore not afford to take them back. Instead party policy was to encourage the former rightists to settle down where they were. To most of the victims this meant staying on in the villages or labour reform farms. Most of them had been deprived of their income for years and were now in dire poverty. Hu Yel-Bound suggested compensating them by paying their arrears in wages, but the financial mandarins pleaded poverty, so the compensation scheme never got off the ground.

More than two decades after the anti-rightist campaign, Lee Wai-Han wrote in his memoirs:

> At that time I was the Minister for United Front Work and was very active in the anti-rightist operation. I have a heavy share of responsibility for that enormous mistake and I am still very sorry for hurting all those comrades and friends unfairly.

> The anti-rightist campaign had one very serious consequence. A huge group of intellectuals, patriots and party cadres were wrongly classed as rightists and as a result they and their families suffered years of injustice and ill treatment. Being unable to contribute their talents fully to develop the country was not only their misfortune, it was also a misfortune for our country. According to statistics, there were a total of 550,000 rightists, many of whom were intellectuals with specialist knowledge and experienced managerial workers in commerce and industry. More than half of these rightists lost their jobs and a large proportion were sent to labour training camps or made to work under surveillance. Many lost their homes and their families were broken up. A small number were kept in

their workplaces and given different jobs. Their talents were not used.

Deng Xiao-Ping, who had been in charge of the anti-rightist campaign, came to a different conclusion. He said the problem with the anti-rightist campaign had been that it had hit out at too many targets, but the campaign itself had been necessary, since it was true that there were capitalist rightists attacking the party.

Over a million educated Chinese were swept away by the anti-rightist hurricane of 1957, leaving behind a few survivors who trod nervously and gingerly afterwards. Yet peace and tranquillity were not theirs for long. In 1958, Mao initiated a new campaign known as 'pulling out white flags' and in 1959 he launched the 'anti-right-leaning campaign'. Many people who had survived the anti-rightist campaign did not manage to slip through the dragnets the second or third time and some eminent and acid anti-rightist shock troops soon found themselves being pulled out mercilessly as members of the evil 'big white flags'. People felled in these two anti-rightist follow-up campaigns numbered at least 100,000; they suffered the same fate as the 1957 rightists two years earlier.

When the Communist movement had been at a low ebb back in the late 1920s, Mao had complained, "The people of China do not have common civil rights. Workers, peasants, even the capitalist supporters of civil rights do not have the rights of free speech and assembly. Joining the Communist Party was a major crime.' At a Communist Party national delegates' conference held in Yan'an in May 1937, Mao had made a speech concentrating on the freedom to fight for human rights and democracy and against one-party rule. He said that without these freedoms there could be no democratic reform of the political system and no mobilisation of the people to join the Sino-Japanese war.

During the Sino-Japanese war, the CCP acted as the standard bearer for human rights and democracy and it often looked as though fighting the Japanese took second place. In the early 1940s, speeches by Mao and other leading party members on these subjects were continually reported in the *Xinhua Daily* and *Liberation Daily*.

In June 1944, Mao told a delegation of foreign reporters in Yan'an that China 'indeed had a shortcoming and it was a very big shortcoming. In one word, it was a deficiency of democracy. Chinese people needed democracy very much.' Democracy, he said, had to involve all aspects of society: politics, the army, the economy, culture, party affairs and international relations. All of these needed democracy. Mao sounded like a champion fighter for democracy through and through. Yet when the army commander Peng De-Huai gave a talk about democracy after reading Mao's recorded speech, Mao wrote angrily to Peng to point out:

> Two months ago you made a speech about the inculcation of democracy, but we felt it was improper. I now list my opinions below:

> Your talk was based on the principles of democracy, freedom, equality and philanthropy instead of current political needs in the Sino-Japanese war. You did not emphasise that democracy is for fighting the Japanese but placed stress upon anti-feudalism. You did not say that the freedoms of speech and publication are for mobilising people's anti-Japanese initiative, striving for and protecting people's political and economic rights, instead you put that down to the principle of freedom of thought. You did not say that freedom of assembly and association are for fighting for victory in the Sino-Japanese War and people's political and economic rights, instead you said they are for promoting the mutual assistance and unity of humanity which would be beneficial to cultural and scientific development. You did not say that collaborators and anyone who sabotages unity for fighting the Japanese ought to be deprived of their freedoms of residence, of movement and of communication, instead you only said, generally speaking, people's freedoms ought not to be subjected to any interference.

Apparently Mao found it useful to attach democracy to fighting the Japanese invasion, to advance his current political needs. Lenin's words 'Dictatorship relies directly on violence and it is a political force subjected to no restraint of any law' became Mao's golden rule. When he finally established himself as China's ruler he issued his own edict on how to rule. 'There are many problems,' he wrote, 'which cannot be solved by relying on laws alone. The laws are dead and rigid writings which nobody is afraid of. When the wall posters are put up, criticisms are poured out by the masses, struggle meetings begin and this is more effective than any law.'

Hence, in the 27 years of Mao's rule, Chinese people lived through a series of violent and nearly non-stop campaigns, all of them instigated and directed by the highest authorities. The party accumulated abundant experience of these campaigns over a long period and promoted them coldly and systematically.

In the 1942 rectification movement in Yan'an, directed by Kang Sheng, the party authorities invited people to reveal their critical opinions of their leaders. 'Be brave!' the party urged, pledging no reprisals. Before long, they hit back violently with struggle meetings and arrests. On a training course in August 1943, Kang Sheng praised the strategy of stirring up the masses, cultivating leading attackers, making surprise ambushes, employing beleaguering tactics, encouraging the majority to strike at the minority and dealing with the condemned one by one. He said: 'Ask people to speak out without fear, encourage wall posters which criticise the leadership, refrain from immediate refutation of the wrong ideas and no instant suppression, in order to keep the people busy and lively.'

Outsiders knew so little about the internal affairs of the CCP that history could repeat itself in the 1957 Anti-Rightists Campaign.

86

The Hairs

Most Chinese intellectuals came from the families of landlords, merchants, civil servants and scholars. In a poor China, very rich families were rare. Proletarian intellectuals simply did not exist, for the peasants and working class were just too poor to pay for their children's education, so Chinese intellectuals were inseparable from the small-capitalist class. The party divided them into left, middle and right in order to isolate the 'anti-revolutionary' right-wingers, win over those in the middle and make use of the left-wing revolutionary sympathisers. The policy was very successful and Chinese intellectuals switched their allegiance in droves and joined the Communist fellow travellers' organisation, the Democratic League. When the Communists emerged as victors at the end of the civil war in 1949, very few intellectuals fled from mainland China. Since the Communists had deliberately kept open the enticing prospect of a coalition government, all the moderates turned left and fell into the arms of the Communists.

Mao now described Chinese intellectuals as leftovers from the old society, or 'hairs' which had attached themselves to five pieces of skin, namely imperialism, feudalism, bureaucratic capitalism, the national-capitalist class and the small producers. In the new China all the old skin had disappeared and Chinese intellectuals now had to attach themselves to pieces of new skin belonging to peasants and the working class.

Mao in fact made it abundantly clear that Chinese intellectuals had no independent value; they only existed as an appurtenance and could certainly not stand shoulder-to-shoulder as equals with peasants and the working class. Official party policy therefore had a long-standing antipathy towards educated Chinese.

In 1983, Luk Din-Yi, a former minister of the Propaganda Department, wrote about the purges of the 30s that 'The founders of Soviet districts in the provinces of Hubei, Henan and Anhui and the educated party members in the Red 4th Army, were nearly all killed.' All were killed by their own party, controlled by the senior party official Chang Kwok-Tao.

By the end of 1942, when the party had settled in Yan'an, there were more purges. The security chief, Kang Sheng, directed a rigorous campaign to re-examine all the cadres, present and past, aiming mainly at the educated, many of whom had risked their lives to sneak through Chiang's blockade in order to join the patriotic movement in Yan'an. The party started talking about digging out secret agents of the Nationalists, imperialists and Japanese. They mounted an 'urgent rescue operation' for people who had 'lost their footing'; these fallen people still consisted mainly of their educated followers. Cadres were summoned to a rendezvous to 'study', a euphemism for confession, struggle meetings, denunciation and arrest.

Kang Sheng would often say that someone looked like an enemy agent and this was enough to put someone through gruelling interrogation, often without any investigation or evidence. Suspects would be forced to confess to connections with enemy organisations and some were beaten to death. Even committed veteran Communists could not always escape such persecution. One Communist, for example, had learned a foreign language from an Italian priest when he was a student in Peking and he found himself accused of being an Italian secret agent. Another cadre, Chan Yuen-Fong, refused to admit that he was an enemy agent and was tied up tightly for 48 hours. When he was untied, his two hands had gone dark purple and his wrists began to turn septic. The rope left visible marks on him for years.

This 'urgent rescue operation' was a fanatic and random witch-hunt. In Yan'an, 170 enemy agents were dug out from among the 200 people at a military communication school; only 20 people did not need to be 'urgently rescued' from among the 500 people of the Northwest Community School, where the number of 'enemy agents' reached 96 per cent. The party branch in Sichuan province was said to be an enemy plant and all its members were caught. There was also a fake branch in Henan province. People were denounced with all sorts of ridiculous evidence. One victim, for example, was asked: 'If you were not involved with enemy agents, how could you travel from Shanghai to Peking by train?' When the liquidators could not find fault with a group of young cadres, the intended victims were branded 'unselfconscious enemy agents'.

The purge eventually extended to secondary schools and primary schools. Large numbers of young girls in a teachers' training school were said to be enemy agents who specialised in laying sex traps, while child agents reported in newspapers were getting younger and younger, from the ages of 12, 11 and ten down to just six. One such young agent's elder sister said: 'You only have to buy him a treat and he will say whatever you tell him to say.'

597

Some 'agents' were executed and many others were driven to suicide. Up to 60 people killed themselves in Yan'an alone. A lot of people were kept under suspicion for decades and many revolutionaries found their élan severely dampened. A senior Communist, Chiang Nan-Chane, who later became president of Tsing Hua University and the Minister for Higher Education, wrote a long report to the party central committee in March 1945, in which he pointed out that most party members were of peasant origin and had a deeply entrenched and harmful attitude of hostility to the intelligentsia. His report was held back by the central committee, which regarded its views as mistaken and Chiang Nan-Chane was reprimanded.

In the 50s Professor Leung Shu-Ming had the misfortune of becoming one of the best known sacrificial lambs used to feed Mao's anti-academic appetite. Leung Shu-Ming was a brilliant scholar, invited to teach at Peking University in his 20s by the then president, Chia Yuan-Pei. Mao was at the time a Peking University library clerk living in the house of Professor Young Chen-Jee, who had been his teacher back in Hunan province. Young's daughter later became Mao's second wife. Mao enjoyed his host's generosity in providing him with a roof and food and in return he did odd jobs for the household, such as going on errands, opening and closing the front door for guests like Leung and Young's other university colleagues and friends.

In the 1920s and 1930s, many patriotic academics were leading reform movements designed to help peasants reinvigorate their devastated villages. Among them was Leung, who established the Village Construction Research College, a utopian attempt to unite politics and education in Shandong province. He was respected and unreservedly supported by the Shandong provincial chairman and warlord Han Foo-Cheu, but his utopia was destroyed by the Japanese invasion and Leung left for Chongqing, where he joined the Democratic League. In late 1941, he was sent to Hong Kong to set up the Democratic League newspaper the *Kwang Ming Daily*, supported covertly by Chow En-Lai. Leung also secretly recruited intellectuals for the Democratic League. In 1946 he became secretary-general of the league and he worked hard as a peace broker between the sabre-rattling Nationalist Party and the Chinese Communist Party.

When the Communists invited a long list of distinguished people to Peking in 1949, Leung was among them and he was made a member of the Political Consultative Conference. In its early stages, the CCP central government often held enlarged conferences, in which leaders from the Democratic League and members of the Political Consultative Conference were invited to discuss national affairs. Leung, as a respected scholar and a prestigious community leader, often attended these meetings.

At one such meeting on 9 September 1953, Chow En-Lai urged Leung to make a speech and Leung agreed. He talked about his own utopian experiment for peasants in the 1930s and his special concern about the wellbeing of peasants and villages, going on to say:

> In recent years, the living standard of the working class in cities has gone up quickly, yet peasant life in villages is still very poor. Villagers everywhere migrate to cities including Peking. But the cities cannot keep them, so they are made to go home and this creates conflict. Some people say 'the present-day working class lives in heaven, while peasants are struggling at the lowest end of the scale. The difference is huge.' Such comment deserves attention. It would be wrong to neglect or overlook the majority of Chinese people, the peasants, in the movement to develop our country, especially as the party relied on peasants in the past to establish itself as the leading party. If the peasants are neglected, people will say that you (the Communists) dislike and abandon them after you have gone to the cities. I hope our government will treat this problem seriously.

Mao was not present at this meeting, but Chow En-Lai reported Leung's speech to him. Mao descended on the meeting the following day to give his reply. He said:

> Some people disagree with our General Guidelines (Mao's policy), regard the peasants' lives as too harsh and demand a better deal for them. These may be compassionate politics from the disciples of Confucius and Mencius. But we must know there are big and small compassionate policies. Looking after peasants is a small policy, developing heavy industry and fighting American imperialists are the big ones. To implement small compassionate policies but not the big policies is to help the Americans.

> Some people are teaching grandmother to suck eggs, as if we, the Communists who have directed peasant movements for decades, still do not understand peasants. What a joke! On the foundation of our present-day regime, the fundamental interests

of the working class and the peasants are one. We will not allow this foundation to be split or sabotaged.

Leung felt he had been wrongly accused of trying to sabotage the union of working class and peasants and of opposing party policy and he wanted Mao to take back his words. Following these clashes, however, Chow and Mao arranged to ambush Leung at a meeting of the Political Consultative Conference. When Leung walked into the conference hall, he suddenly felt strange. There were many more people than usual and a copy of his article 'An exhortation to the CCP', written in 1949 when he was a peace broker trying to avert full-scale civil war, was placed on every seat. Chow was officiating and he broke away from the planned agenda to deliver a long speech examining Leung's reactionary past and describing him as a persistent reactionary, wishing to curry favour with the Nationalist Party for money and a high position. Leung, furious, stood up and said, 'I wanted money and a high position? Ridiculous! Ridiculous! Ridiculous!'

Mao performed a kind of duet with Chow, interrupting Chow's speech to lambaste Leung, saying Leung had never done anything good for the Chinese people, nothing at all. Leung was an ambitious hypocrite, a thorough reactionary, therefore he would never accept Leung's opinion. 'To tell you the truth,' said Mao, 'Chiang Kai-Shek uses guns to kill people, but Leung uses pens to kill people. There are two ways to kill people, one with a gun and the other with a pen. The most ingenious camouflage to kill people yet, with no blood to be seen, is to kill with a pen. You are such a killer! If you openly oppose the General Guidelines and say that more help for agriculture is needed, it could be forgiven as being muddle-headed but with good intention. As it is, you oppose it in secret, therefore it is malicious.'

The following day, on 18 September, Leung spoke out at the conference to deny Mao's and Chow's allegations that he was malicious. Asking that he should be given enough time to speak, since his opponents had spoken at such length the previous day, he said, 'I do hope the party and everybody present here will test me. I also want to test the party and see whether Chairman Mao has the grace to allow me to explain everything, so that Chairman Mao will nod his head afterwards and say 'It was a misunderstanding. You are not malicious after all.' This is the grace I request from Chairman Mao.'

Mao answered immediately, 'I probably don't have the grace you ask for.'

'If you had such grace,' replied Leung, 'I would respect you more. If you don't have it, then I shall lose my respect for you.' He then tried his luck further by testing the party. 'The party has often told us to carry out self-criticism,' he said. 'I want to see whether this is genuine or not. If Chairman Mao has the grace to criticise himself, then I shall respect him more.'

To this Mao replied irritably, 'There are two kinds of criticism; criticising others and criticising oneself. Which one should we apply to you? Criticising ourselves? No. It is to criticise you.'

This was in 1953, when the Chinese people were still mesmerised by an unknown political party which promised to be the country's saviour. The prestige of the party and of Mao himself were at their zenith. Leung's temerity stirred uproar among the audience, most of whom were firmly behind their adored Chairman Mao. People began to shout abuse at Leung.

Leung however refused to leave without presenting his own case and Mao said he could have ten minutes. Leung said that was not enough; he wanted to be treated fairly. The conference then decided to take a vote by a show of hands on whether Leung should be allowed to speak and he was voted down. Forced to back down, he lived an isolated life for the next 20 or so years.

Two years later, in May 1955, the party ran a big campaign to root out the influence of capitalist thinkers whose prominent representative was Dr Hu Shi. All newspapers put Leung's views on politics, philosophy, culture and education under intense fire for six months. He remained silent, which luckily and unexpectedly enabled him to escape the trap of the anti-rightist campaign.

Leung also survived the Cultural Revolution better than most of his intellectual peers. The Red Guards did not forget his impudent offence in 1953; they ransacked his home, piling up all his precious books, paintings, scrolls and old-fashioned costumes in his courtyard and setting fire to the lot. His home was later occupied and used as a Red Guard headquarters, but he was not locked up, nor was he sent to a village to receive re-education from poor and middle peasants.

He was also allowed to keep his seat on the Political Consultative Conference. Near the end of the Cultural Revolution, the ruling clique mobilised people to censure Confucius, but it was actually alluding to Chow En-Lai. Leung was asked to speak out several times in his Political Consultative Conference discussion group, but he refused to say anything. Yet declining to expose one's mind was not tolerated kindly. Under pressure, he tried to talk in a euphemistical way about his high regard for Confucius, which at that time was asking for trouble. Immediately he was accused of 'attempting to poison his group' and of 'defending Confucius, a member of the feudalist and landlord class'. Instead of censuring Confucius, Lueng's group switched over to excoriate him for several months.

Mao was an admirer of the First Emperor Qin, who ruled from 259 to 210 BC and who buried 460 dissenters alive. In 1958, talking about the Suppression of Counter-Revolutionary Elements campaign, Mao said proudly: 'Emperor Qin only buried 460 intellectuals, we have buried 46,000, one hundred times more.' Most landlords and Nationalists killed in that campaign were educated people, so the total figure was certainly higher than 46,000. Mao believed Emperor Qin's undoing was that he did not kill enough people, since two very able intellectuals got away and later helped the founder of the Han Dynasty to overthrow the Qin regime. Once, talking about the emperors of the Han and Ming Dynasties, Mao said, 'The few illiterate and ill-educated founder emperors were better emperors; their intellectual heirs were useless at running the country. Studying too many books could harm people seriously but could not make a good emperor.' Mao was no academic, only a junior teacher training student, therefore he was a good emperor.

In 1939, Mao made a speech to commemorate the May 4th Movement, in which he admitted that the Chinese revolutionary movement had originated from the political awakening of educated young people. This sentence was later deleted from Mao Tse-Tung's collected works, published after the party had won power; for the convenience of his teaching some facts were better erased. In January 1956, Mao said at a State Council conference: 'Intellectuals must surrender to the working class. From certain perspectives, intellectuals are the most ignorant of people. If they don't learn a bitter lesson once, they will not be able to change.'

In March 1962, Chow En-Lai announced at a Canton meeting that 'The description 'capitalist class intellectual' is no longer appropriate. They are now part of the working people.' But the new-found happiness of Chinese intellectuals did not last long. The following year, Mao said that 'Most of our intelligentsia come from old society and from non-working class families. Some of them may have come from the families of working class or peasants, but the education they received before liberation belonged to the capitalist class and their views about the world are essentially capitalistic. So they are still capitalist class intellectuals.'

After this, all intellectuals went back to their old positions as the under-class.

Mao Tse-Tung Thought was later developed to a new height during the Cultural Revolution. It included thoughts such as 'more knowledge means more stupidity' and 'more knowledge means becoming more reactionary.' Mao also said bluntly that he would rather ask for advice about state affairs from illiterate labourers and peasants than from intellectuals.

Brutal purges were part of the CCP tradition and they were always well covered up. Few outsiders ever heard of group after group of educated young people in Yan'an being arrested as enemy agents, or the party killing its own people wholesale by shooting, beheading or burying alive. For a very long time, 99.9 per cent of party members were peasants, many of whom reached very senior positions and they all echoed their supreme leader's deep-seated distrust of and contempt for educated Chinese. Chiang's blockade around the Soviet districts helped to stop information from filtering through to the rest of the country, so life in the 'liberated areas' remained mainly a myth to outsiders.

Little did the Chinese intellectuals know that the Anti-Rightists Campaign was only a warm-up game and their ultimate purgatory was yet to come. This demonstrated how poorly they had understood the Chinese Communists and how ignorant they were of the CCP history. Left-wing intellectuals from 1930 onwards played the part of fellow travellers, entirely ignorant of where the party bandwagon was going when they jumped on it.

87

Fast Track to Communism

While it was struggling for power the CCP promised land reform to the poor and middle peasants and this won it redoubtable support from millions of peasants who were willing to fight and die for the Communist cause. The poor peasants' dreams of owning land came true after the Land Reform Campaign bloodbath.   For the first two or three years, Mao and his fellow party leaders said repeatedly that it would take 20 or 30 years for China to become a socialist country and therefore a free economy would be allowed to stay for some time to come. Mao maintained that when conditions were ready, when the whole nation had thought about it carefully and all agreed to go ahead, then China could move into the new era of socialism in a composed and measured way.

Time, however, was running short for Mao, who was then approaching 60. He could not afford to wait 20 or 30 years if he was to acquire the glory of being the creator of a socialist paradise and by 1953, when China was still battling to recover from the civil and Korean wars, he was already in a hurry to push the country into socialism without bothering to seek consent. He started attacking the right-leaning mistakes of other leading Communists and this was to be the pattern of his nearly 30-year rule. The grovelling politburo was by now silenced and submissive; not one member dared to remind him that he had reneged on his own promises made not so long ago, let alone dare to resist his trampling on resolutions passed by the politburo or the National People's Congress, which was after all supposed to be the highest authority in China.

Mao began to push the 500 million peasants into socialist collectivisation and to extirpate capitalism in the rural economy. Peasants were first ushered into mutual aid units, each containing a handful of families. Then a rapid campaign to form elementary cooperatives was launched in 1953, the party declaring that peasants were free to join or not to join the cooperatives and that they were also free to withdraw from them. Their land, livestock and tools were transferred to the cooperatives as capital investment for which they would be given dividends. Although the peasants disliked the idea of sharing their land, livestock and tools with other people, village cadres heeded the party's directive to herd the peasants into cooperatives. Coercion was widely used to guarantee the success of collectivisation.

Some counties held struggle meetings against rich peasants. The county party secretaries would announce: 'Joining the cooperative means going down the socialist road; refuse to join the cooperative and you will be treated like the rich peasants.' An officer from Mao's security guard unit, Lee Yin-Chel, visited his home village in Onping county, Hebei province, where he found that district cadres had been to his village. They had ordered all villagers to stand in a courtyard and then said: 'Anyone who wants to follow Chiang Kai-Shek can stand on that side to work on his own; those who want to follow Chairman Mao can stand on this side to join the cooperative.' Since no peasant dared follow Chiang to become an enemy of the state, it was hardly surprising that they all volunteered to join the cooperative.

In April 1955, Deng Tze-Qua, the vice premier and minister for the Department of Rural Work, criticised cadres for forcing peasants to join the cooperatives by holding meetings continuously for three days and nights. He also reproached them for their method of compensating peasants for transferring their large animals to the cooperatives; they would be paid in three years, five years, or even 100 years. They were called loans, but in fact the animals would never be returned. Due to poor management, many large animals given to cooperatives died. Peasants unwilling to hand over their smaller animals, such as chickens, pigs or sheep, had to kill them instead. There was no compensation for fruit trees transferred to cooperatives, so resentful peasants chopped them down.

Peasants handed over their precious land deeds to the cooperatives, amid the festive sound of gongs and drums, to celebrate their newly found socialist spirit in making their land collective property. All peasants now became wage-earning employees. Their work was now assessed by the cooperative management and as a result disputes over pay were rife.

Following Russian policy, peasants were required to sell all their surplus produce to the state. Every year the central government set down its food purchase targets which were allocated to all the lower-level government units. After the government had taken its share, whatever was left behind, whether or not it was enough for the peasants to live on, was known as surplus food. If the peasants did not have enough to eat, they had to wait until their own food had nearly run out, then the government would sell back grain to them. Most of the time the state took away too much of the peasants' food and the delay in selling it back could cost lives. In the 1959 to 1961 famine during the Great Leap Forward, by the time food supplies were sold back in Gansu province, more than one million people had already starved to death.

This policy was regarded as a crucial step towards the realisation of socialism. Anyone trying to plead on behalf of the peasants was criticised, sent to struggle sessions and sacked or jailed. In one county of Hunan province alone, more than one thousand peasants and cadres got into trouble for expressing dissatisfaction about compulsory purchase and collectivisation. Once, when a large number of peasants wanted to withdraw from their cooperative, the authorities reclassified some of them as reactionary rich peasants who had slipped through the net. After such people had been purged, no peasants dared leave their cooperatives.

In June 1955, the politburo set a target to increase the 650,000 cooperatives to one million before autumn of the following year. Soon afterwards, Mao decided that the figure should be doubled and he hit out at people who tried to stick to the politburo resolution. Party cadres under pressure examined their own right-leaning, conservative tendencies and accelerated their collectivisation plans. In October Mao's original vision of completing agricultural collectivisation in five years was revised down to three years, but just two months later he declared he would complete it in 1956. He had decided it only needed one year.

In early 1956, all peasants were driven into collectivisation. Many cooperatives were badly managed and the unhappy peasants in them became lazy and indifferent. Unrest emerged in many places; some peasants asked to be allowed to quit their cooperatives and others assaulted their village cooperative cadres.

Production was going down. In 1956, the total number of pigs in Fujian province was 20 per cent down on the previous year and tea production was less than half that of the 1930s. Such phenomena affected the rural economy all over China. Mao was well aware of the peasants' feelings, but he commented to the vice premiers Lee Sen-Nan and Deng Tze-Qua: 'The peasants are inconsistent about socialism. They want freedom, but we want socialism.

In this primitive form of collectivisation, peasants were entitled to dividends from their investments of land, tools and livestock, but Communist dogma regarded that as a form of exploitation; hence Mao called the elementary cooperative a 'semi-socialist cooperative'. He wanted the genuine socialist cooperative and he wanted it quickly. He wrote: 'Most of these are small cooperatives consisting of 20 to 30 families. They have limited land, people and capital and cannot use machines to produce on a large scale; they still constrict the expansion of production power and therefore should not remain too long. They should be combined together.'

Before the peasants could settle down into their elementary cooperatives, many of which had only been in existence for a few months, Mao gave orders to form bigger, advanced cooperatives. This meant the abolition of dividends and that all property would be handed over to the cooperatives without compensation. Many elementary cooperatives which had never once paid out a dividend were now upgraded to advanced cooperatives which simply confiscated the peasants' tools, livestock and land. Peasants had no right to choose whether they wanted to join the new cooperative and many thought this new move too rash. But again their resistance was crushed by the party's determination.

In much bigger cooperatives, the peasants became lazier and more indifferent. Deng Tze-Qua said: 'Some cooperatives did not even realise that they had missed out a whole piece of farmland. Nobody cared when harvested crops piled up on the ground and went rotten.' When there was not enough food at home, one or two members from each family would leave their villages illegally to look for a living in the cities, thus beginning the ever-growing exodus from the villages.

By 1958, although most people were short of food, money and fuel, Mao was convinced that China was ripe to form the foundation stones of Communist society, namely the 'people's communes', where everything would be publicly owned. These people's communes would manage their own industry, agriculture, commerce, education and militia. The way pointed out by Karl Marx and Friedrich Engels would eventually expunge the difference between city and village, joining peasants and working class together. It also would eliminate the difference between mental and physical work after combining education and production together.

Responding to Mao's inspiration, the first people's commune was created in Suiping county, in Henan province, in April 1958. Chan Bor-Da, the party's great theoretician and at one time Mao's political secretary, showed great interest in this landmark of the Communist movement in China. He descended on the commune to conduct an experiment to abolish currency, ordering the local bank to print coupons to facilitate a return to a barter system. He also instructed the chief of Suiping county to expand the people's commune.

On 5 August, the whole county was declared a single people's commune, containing nearly ten thousand families, with the county bosses now becoming the commune bosses. The communal ruling body was divided into departments of industry, agriculture, finance, public security, armed forces, transport, management, public relations and so on.

In early August, Mao set out in his special train for a fact-finding tour. His first stop was Xushui county, Hebei province, where the county party branch had answered Mao and the CCP's call to embark on large numbers of construction projects. Local people had recently spent three months building 17 medium and small reservoirs in nearby hills, with another 173 on the plain to improve irrigation. The 33-year-old party secretary, Chang Kwok-Jone, had done plenty of preparation designed to show off local progress. Most labourers were assembled along either side of the railway line along which Mao was going to travel. The show fields had all been thoroughly weeded and dissidents had all been sent away. Chang Kwok-Jone showed Mao around and talked about his county's plans for creating miracles. Their farmland in a very good year would usually produce 750 catties of wheat per mou or approx. 2.8 tons per acre, but now they planned to produce an average of 2,000 catties per mou. Their potatoes, grown in a heap of soil, like a small hill, would yield more than one million catties per mou and they planned to breed pigs weighing more than 1,000 catties each. They even had two simple and crude furnaces in the middle of a field, which Chang Kwok-Jone claimed could produce 200 catties of steel each.

With so many grand schemes in motion, the county's 110,000-strong workforce was organised like an army, with more than 90 regiments and over 200 battalions. Because they were under the command of a single headquarters, transferring the workforce and sending more hands to an urgent project was made easier. At that moment 40,000 people were busy building reservoirs, digging wells, repairing roads or setting up new factories. Mao was very impressed and he particularly liked the practice of a militarised workforce, an innovation which he wanted introduced to all other communes. He also wished to see all the worker-soldiers armed and if there were not enough guns, every district would have to build an arsenal.

From here Mao went on to visit Henan and Shandong provinces. His conviction in the rightness of the people's commune was being strengthened all the time. He believed that, as well as all the other advantages, it would have the additional benefit that all industrial workers, peasants, merchants, students and soldiers who had been gathered together in a people's commune would be easier to lead.

The people of Xushui county were so excited by Mao's visit that the night after his departure they immediately established their own people's commune and Xushui was soon chosen by the CCP central committee to try out the transition to Communism, the supposedly consummate way of life. More than 100 cadres from central and provincial government went to Xushui county to set up a planning unit with the aim of developing the county two or three years ahead of other areas. The experience obtained here could then be transferred to the rest of the country.

This 1958 plan declared that they were aiming to accomplish socialism in 1959 and enter Communism in 1963, by which time all significant physical labour would be replaced by machines. What they intended to achieve was laid down in their prospectus, of which the main points were:

Industry: The people's commune would build many new and modern factories. Every village would have its own garment factory.

Agriculture: The present area of cultivated land would be doubled and the average yield of grain crops would be 8,000 catties per mou. (At the time in this county the average yield per mou was less than 200 catties and people did not even have enough to eat.) There would also be millions of sheep, chickens, pigs and 20 million fruit trees.

Transport: The county would build a 60 km railway and it would also develop motorways and shipping.

Education: All young people under 30 would reach university level within seven to ten years. The county would set up a university. Every village would set up part-time university courses.

Food would be free for all. Clothing and all the basic daily necessities in limited quantities would be provided free as well.

The people of Xushui were organised into a noisy parade, beating drums and gongs and chanting slogans to show their enthusiasm for the blissful life to come.

Mao believed in the explosion of production. He asked the Xushui county party secretary, Chang Kowk-Jone, what they would do with all the surplus food. Fortunately, Mao's great brain worked out an answer for China's forthcoming massive over-production of food. He suggested growing food on only one third of the agricultural land, growing decorative plants on another third and giving the last third a rest. This brilliant solution was written into the documents produced by a party conference held in Wuhan in December 1958. Some areas couldn't wait any longer and immediately tried out the new instruction. The *People's Daily* hurriedly announced in an editorial that 'such an arrangement would definitely work in future, but there is no hurry to adopt it at the moment'.

The new society's first move was to abolish private ownership; this meant nearly everything now belonged to the people of the county. Private homes could be knocked down at any time by the county leadership who wanted to modernise the villages in order to erase the difference between village and city. Within about two months 33,000 shabby homes had been flattened, but the rebuilding project was hampered by a shortage of money and building materials. This created a serious and lengthy housing problem, with many newly built homes without electricity, water, toilet, drainage or sewers. Peasants were forced to move into these new homes, but many resisted. In some areas, furniture and many other household utensils were all counted as public property and people observed that their personal possessions were now reduced to just one pair of chopsticks and one bowl.

Free provision included medical care, funeral and heating expenses, oil for lamps, cinema, bath, haircuts, matches, clothing, shoes, socks, soap, towels and even sanitary towels. In September wages were abolished and instead people were given allowances of between two and nine yuans a month. At the beginning office canteens supplied free and reasonably good food, in unlimited quantities, to demonstrate the superiority of the new life.

Xushui county's subordinate villages also provided 'free' food. Villagers were required to hand over their food stock to their communal canteens and in one village militiamen thoroughly searched every household for hidden food stocks, even digging up the ground to a depth of three feet to make sure there was no grain in the house. The communal canteens, in effect, cooked the peasants' own food for them and called it a free meal. All Xushui county restaurants were nationalised and fed their customers free of charge. There were however many practical problems and heavy costs, which the authorities soon discovered they could not afford. After three months, the happy eating spree was brought to a stop.

The commune's management was centralised in Xushui county head office, which was soon under great pressure. It had to raise money for all the investment projects, for everyone's wages, or later on their allowances and provide people with their daily necessities free. The promise of two free towels per person meant a supply of 1,440,000 towels, but they managed to hand out only a total of 720,000. The truth was they did not have the money. There were limited free supplies of some articles, but most promises turned out to be empty.

Militarisation was strengthened and the communal militias were given 10,000 guns by the central government. The whole workforce of the county-commune was divided into 99 regiments, 666 companies and 1,998 platoons, all of whom were transferred around with military discipline. With cheap labour at its disposal, despite its capital crisis the commune set up 39 factories in towns and 1,348 small factories in the villages. The problem got worse when the commune set up 11 universities, 84 colleges and many other cultural bodies, ignoring the acute shortage of qualified teaching staff. Most of these ventures collapsed sooner or later.

Xushui county's pioneering experiment brought excitement to the rest of the country. The question of whether all these fantastic figures were feasible never arose, because one famous teaching of Mao Tse-Tung Thought said, 'There may be something that hasn't come to one's mind; there is nothing that cannot be done.'

On 14 June the Chinese people were told of another sparkling Mao Tse-Tung Thought. The future Chinese president Liu Shao-Qi told the National Women's Association conference that Mao had twice spoken about the need to abolish families, regarding this as the way to eliminate private property. By then newspapers were also talking about breaking up the relationship between husband and wife. In the wonderful society of Communism, the opposite sexes would live in segregated dormitories and meet once every Saturday. Children would be publicly owned.

After Stalin's death, Mao aspired to step into his shoes to become the leader of the Communist world. He wanted to show other socialist countries how to transfer to Communism. From March to October, nearly a thousand people from more than 40 countries, socialist as well as capitalist, came to find out about Xushui county's way of life and many more came from all over China to learn from this prototype.

The demise of the Xushui county experiment came within six months. Khrushchev was gloating over this when he said: 'Chinese Communism is to drink clear water soup from a big pot, Russian Communism is to have potato and beef stew.' Still, within a few months many features of the Xushui experiment were imposed on people's communes all over the country. The peasants' reaction was described by Marshal Lor Yung-Wun. 'When the peasants thought that Communism was coming close and nothing would belong to private individuals any more, they slaughtered chickens and sheep everywhere; some households killed eight or nine pigs in one night.'

But this time some local authorities took pre-emptive action. Shanxi province laid down rules that all peasants' livestock, business and transport implements, woods, orchards, houses and land became communal property without compensation on the day they announced the forming of a people's commune. Any peasant who slaughtered livestock or chopped down a tree after that day was committing misappropriation of communal property and had to pay back the price in full. And so peasants lost their property overnight without any escape route. The lands they had acquired through the bloody Land Reform Campaign were taken away from them within five years.

Between 17 and 30 August 1958, the politburo held an expanded meeting in the summer resort of Beidaihe, which included all the party's first secretaries from provinces, cities, autonomous regions and government departments. They passed a resolution endorsing Mao's grand scheme establishing people's communes, each of which could have between 2,000 and more than 20,000 families. In five or six years' time, the current collective ownership would evolve to the superior form when everything in the country would be owned by the whole population. The resolution stated: 'It appears that the realisation of Communism in our country is no longer something in the remote future. We should use the form of people's communes to search assiduously for a special transitional way to Communism.'

The party regarded the peasants' small private plots as capitalist relics which had survived several agricultural reforms but which definitely had no place under Communism. Although these private plots represented less than one sixteenth of the collective land, their harvest was usually several times that of the cooperatives. Ignoring this fact, the party decided that private plots and free village markets must be banned. The task of reorganising all Chinese villages took about two months to complete and by the end of October, all 740,000 agricultural cooperatives had been merged into 26,500 people's communes comprising 127 million families, or 99.1 per cent of the nation's peasant population, an average of 4,756 families, or more than 20,000 people per commune.

88

The Great Leap Forward of Steel

While the economy was undergoing socialist reform, Chow En-Lai and some of his senior colleagues disapproved of rushing ahead; instead they favoured steadier, less risky progress. This was at odds with Mao Tse-Tung Thought.

In November 1957, Communist leaders from all over the world converged upon Moscow to celebrate the 40th anniversary of the Russian Revolution, with the Chinese delegation led by Mao. It was at this juncture that Khrushchev announced to the Communist world that the Russian economy would strive to overtake America through peaceful competition within 15 years. Following big brother Russia's lead, Mao obtained consent from other party leaders in Peking to announce to the same Moscow audience on 18 November that China aimed to overtake Britain in 15 years.

The *People's Daily* published a series of editorials to incite the nation to accelerate Chinese economic progress. On 13 November 1957, an editorial commented, 'Some people suffer the right-leaning, conservative ailment, crawling slowly like snails. They don't understand that after the agricultural cooperative movement, our country is now ready and needs a great leap forward on the production lines. This accords with the law of development. The 1956 achievement fully reflected that the great leap forward is correct. The conservative people cannot understand this, nor can they understand the great creativity of the peasant masses after cooperative reform and so they regard the government's draft development plan as rushing forward. They take the correct leaping forward to mean rushing forward.'

This was the first time the term 'great leap forward' appeared in Chinese public life. Mao liked the term very much and called it a great invention. On 12 December 1957, the *People's Daily* published an editorial amended by Mao himself, heralding his directive 'with all our efforts, fighting to build socialism with great thrift, quantity, quality and speed, particularly with regard to industry and irrigation schemes.' This directive became known as the 'General Guidelines'.

From January 1958 onwards, Mao repeatedly censured Chow's senior officials, criticising their opposition to 'rushing forward'. It sapped the enthusiasm of six hundred million people and made Chow's group only 50 metres away from being rightists. Rushing forward was Marxist, opposition to rushing forward was not Marxist. Mao ruled that from then on there could only be talk about opposition to right-leaning, but no more talk about opposition to rushing forward. At a party conference in Peking in May 1958, Mao demanded that the entire country should 'get rid of superstition and liberate the mind'. The party adopted his policy and severely criticised those people who were opposed to rushing forward.

The man held mainly responsible for the 1956 opposition to rushing forward was the prime minister, Chow, who was forced to make a long and humiliating self-criticism at the conference, emphasising his serious mistake in not recognising the miracles created by the people because of their great liberation of mind. He now whole-heartedly admitted that the party central committee and Chairman Mao were correct. He had already talked to comrade Mao face to face to acknowledge that his own way of thinking could not keep up with comrade Mao and he had to work much harder to study the teachings of Mao Tse-Tung Thought.

Chow spent more than ten days composing his speech of self-criticism. Years later his secretary, Fan Yor-Yu, who had assisted him in preparing the draft, recalled how the heavy-hearted Chow had often looked numb. Staying up very late and leaving long intervals in the middle of dictating, he fumbled arduously for the right words to describe what was in his mind. Fan Yor-Yu took dictation from Chow, polished the draft and added the words, 'I have been through thick and thin, days and nights, with Chairman Mao, but my thoughts cannot keep up with him.' When Chow checked the final draft, he struck out this sentence and said, with tears in his eyes, that as far as his relations with Mao were concerned it might be all right to use the sentence after the rectification period, but not before. He added that it clearly showed that Fan Yor-Yu knew very little about the party's history. Chow gave his speech and he was followed by three other senior officials in charge of economic policy who had also opposed rushing forward, who now made harsh and public self-criticisms.

Having put down resistance inside the party, Mao was in a hurry to push Chinese agriculture and industry into the Great Leap Forward. It was said that industrial achievement was measured by steel production. Britain had produced 220,000 tons of steel in 1870 and nearly 21 million tons in 1957 and the total was expected to reach 36 million tons by 1972. When Communist China was created in 1949, Chinese steel production was

150,000 tons, but by 1957 this had gone up to 5,350,000 tons. The Great Leap Forward set a target of 40–45 million tons for China in 1972. Mao wanted China to concentrate its resources on increasing steel production to overtake Britain. The journey had taken Britain 102 years, but China intended to do it in 23 years.

From January 1958, the Chinese people began to leap forward into an inferno at an increasingly frenetic pace. Brilliant Mao Tse-Tung Thoughts kept coming into Mao's head. In December 1957 he predicted that it would take China 15 years to overtake Britain and 50 years to overtake America. Within six months, the time needed to catch up those two highly industrialised countries started to shrink. In May 1958, he reckoned only seven years were needed to overtake Britain; soon afterwards this was cut to five years and then two years and it would take just ten years, or at the most 15, to catch up America. In the same way, the target for steel production was reviewed ever upwards. In January 1958, the annual target was 6.2 million tons, but in March it was revised to seven million tons. In mid-June it rose to 8.2 million tons and the target for 1962 soared to 60 million tons.

On 17 June, the head of the State Planning and Development Commission, Bo Yi-Ball, reported to the politburo that his forecast for 1958 steel production would reach ten million tons. But Mao wanted 10.7 million tons for 1958, doubling the 1957 production. On 22 June, Mao commented on Bo Yi-Ball's report: 'It won't take seven years, let alone 15 years, to overtake Britain. It need only take two or three years and it is possible to do it in two years. It is mainly about steel. When production reaches 25 million tons in 1959, then we will have overtaken Britain on steel.'

Mao's fever seemed to be contagious, because his Minister for Metallurgy, Wang Hur-Shou, suffered an even higher temperature. He reported on the same day to the CCP central committee: 'The production of steel will be trebled to 30 million tons the following year. Four years later it will be 80 to 90 million tons.' Wang was a career revolutionary, not a metallurgist or an administrator and he did not have to worry about minor problems such as raw materials, electricity, technology, equipment or transport. His job was only to dream up ideas. It had always been the party's view that professionals were irrelevant.

Mao was ready to create a miracle for China and to teach the world. In early September 1958, he said at a State Council meeting that not only could steel production be doubled, it was also possible to try to produce 12 million tons this year and, except a few items like shipbuilding, motor vehicles and electricity, China would overtake Britain next year. A 15-year plan would be largely completed within two years. Who could have expected it? He told the nation to fight for 'getting close to America within five years and overtaking America within seven years'.

On 2 October, he proudly boasted to visiting delegations from six Eastern European Communist countries: 'There were so many foolish people in the world like me or us. All these years we did not know that making steel is the important element. We only realised it this year. If you build up iron and steel works, everything else will follow.'

In August 1958, some people's communes were already competing in announcing fantastically high yield targets called 'satellites'. The steel industry was left behind in this exciting era. So far that year it had only produced 4.5 million tons, two thirds of the way through 1958. Only four months were left for China to fulfil the target assigned by the great leader and they were still six to seven million tons short.

The Beidaihe meeting in August decided that steel production was the top priority for the whole country for the rest of the year and all other businesses had to take second place. The party central committee kept applying high pressure on all local authorities, saying Chairman Mao wanted the food production doubled next year and 10.7 million tons of steel this year and he wouldn't accept one ton short!

Mao wanted the nation mobilised to complete the task. Every area was given a production target. Shanxi province, which had a weak iron and steel industry, was required to produce 680,000 tons of iron and 550,000 tons of steel. A minority autonomous area in Guangxi province, where the iron industry was virtually non-existent, was now told to produce 200,000 tons of cast iron and other areas were given much harder tasks. The existing factories' output could not possibly hit the scheduled national target, so the party drove the whole country to build simple backyard furnaces to complement the proper factories. Several million crude furnaces soon sprang up everywhere.

These makeshift furnaces had all kinds of shapes and sizes. Some were more than ten metres high, others had a capacity of only a little more than one cubic metre. Building bricks were in great demand and there was an acute shortage. People had to use their ingenuity to find building materials and the pavement bricks on both sides of one main shopping street in Peking disappeared overnight. Villages burnt all the long grass from accessible hills and used the ashes to make bricks. Many historical buildings were demolished for the bricks, including the 2,000-year-old Han Gok Gate in Sin On county, Henan province, an important and carefully maintained gateway which guarded the ancient imperial capital of Changon. After a major renovation in 1923, this three-storey building had stood more than 83 metres high. In 1958, the county party secretary decided to use the Han Gok Gate's bricks to build his cottage furnaces; when other people reminded him that it was a historic monument, he retorted that even historic monuments had to give way to the top priority of iron and steel production. So two storeys of the Han Gok Gate were demolished and all the historical relics attached to the building were lost. All over the country people destroyed old city walls, knocked down old pagodas and dug up old graves to get bricks. Mao himself had been in the vanguard of vandalism, when years ago he had given orders to demolish the thousand-year-old Peking city walls.

Many places had no time to build furnaces, so they used old kilns or old bunkers left behind by the Nationalist Party or the Japanese. One village used a large ancient temple as an iron smelting furnace. They sealed up the temple to make it air-tight, but there was too much space and the furnace needed huge quantities of charcoal to keep it going. The end product often had to go back to the furnace a second time.

Millions of Chinese worked day and night looking for coal and iron ore everywhere; in all more than 100,000 small caverns were dug in the search for coal. When there was not enough coke, coal was used instead. When there was not enough coal, charcoal was substituted. China was badly deficient in energy; electricity and gas were not used for these backyard steel works and so everywhere in the country, peasants were sent to chop down trees to make charcoal to use as firewood for the improvised steel works. Even bamboos and fruit trees could not escape the chop. A Peking college party secretary ordered his flock to chop up the students' bunk beds to use as firewood. A village in the now-famous Xushui county had burnt up all its trees, so the local militiamen visited every house pulling carts, carrying axes, hammers or any other tools, led by village cadres, to remove one half of every double door to use as firewood, without bothering to ask for permission. When a county party secretary in Sichuan province refused to strip bare a forest, he was duly sacked. More forests were destroyed in this period than at any other time in Chinese history.

Mao knew there were many who regarded such deforestation as a great waste, but in November at the Zhengzhou conference he denied that it was a waste; he saw it instead as a great saving. As millions of people climbed the hills and mountains, they would find resources and gain experience, so this was an income indeed. No one dared challenge this Mao Tse-Tung Thought.

When there was not enough iron ore, village cadres visited people's kitchens. They would ram a thick iron rod into these people's metal cooking pots and then say, 'Oh! Look! Your cooking pot has a hole, it is no good for cooking any more.' In this way they took away cooking pots, kitchen knives, scissors and bicycles. This would also force the villagers to eat in the communal canteens.

Urban people were asked to donate anything containing metal as raw materials, hence door locks, radiators, window bars, iron doors, office safes and even buckles of trouser belts were taken away to feed the smelting furnaces. People even took away metal parts as iron ore from a power generator in China's biggest hydro-electric station, Fong Moon in northeast China. Its chief engineer, Lee Peng, China's future prime minister, could not see any sense in such behaviour, but dared not speak out. He only talked privately to his boss, the Minister for Electricity, Liu Lan-Ball, who after listening to Lee Peng stayed silent for a long pause, but never stuck his neck out to restrain this conduct. Metal relics big and small from old temples – Buddhas, incense burners, tripods and bells – also found their way into backyard furnaces and then into scrapyards.

Anyone who had iron but declined to hand it over would be disciplined, Mao said and the disciplines would be severe. 'First, caution; second, recording a demerit; third, suspension from one's job; fourth, dismissal; fifth, being put under observation within the party; sixth, expulsion from the party.' He ordered that certain railways which for the time being had no economic value could be ripped up.

Nearly every government office built a brick stove in a courtyard, with a fire burning underneath and a large frying pan sitting on top of the stove filled with scrap metal. This process was called 'frying steel'. Senior Communist officials leading the operation would keep watch beside the frying pan all the time and their eyes turned red due to sleepless nights.

In some areas, students joined in the steel production after school. In Guangdong province, the authorities ordered all universities, colleges, secondary schools and primary schools to close down in mid-December. All secondary school children and teachers were sent to support steel production; often they would sleep under the sky in the hills alongside the peasants and workers from the cities and they would chop down trees to make charcoal. Either over- or under-burning would result in a useless product and the charcoal had to be delivered to the furnaces round the clock. The old and the young were all given supportive jobs, even old women with bound feet had to try their best to do one or two runs each day, otherwise they would not be allowed to eat in the canteen.

The party and central government instructed every district to requisition all transport and vehicles, trains, primitive carts, aeroplanes and ships were all pressed into use as people worked around the clock to deliver materials to the production lines. On average more than 35,000 railway carriages were used daily to support steel production. By the end of 1958, 100 million people, about one sixth of the whole population of China, were plunged into this frenzied task.

The party central committee soon pressed the nation to launch steel 'satellites'. The reported figures for national iron and steel production began to shoot up at an amazing speed. The *People's Daily* announced in mid-October that average steel production in the previous week had increased 85 per cent compared with a fortnight before; at the same time iron production had tripled. The highest daily steel production reached more than 100,000 tons, the highest daily iron production was more than 370,000 tons and the charcoal daily record was more than a million tons. Seemingly, under Mao's guidance, China was creating miracle after miracle.

89

The Agricultural Satellites

The leading agricultural satellite producer, Xushui county, gave sensational news about its high yield rice, claiming to have produced 10,000 catties per mou (approx. 375 tons per acre). Its trial field had had such a heavy crop that photographs showed children standing gleefully on top of densely growing rice plants. The trial field was so crowded that electric fans were used to blow air into the field to help ventilation; fluorescent lamps were shining over it all night long to make up for insufficient sunlight. The cost of maintaining the field was considerable. But cool-headed visitors could see straight away that it was a confidence trick.

From early 1958, the cadres of people's communes were under tremendous pressure. They were liable to be publicly insulted or physically bullied by county party bosses who refused to accept normal, sensible production figures. Most of China's 2,000 county party secretaries wanted high agricultural yield pledges so that they could report the good news to their superiors. These county cadres were forced to apply pressure on communes, for by failing to join the feverish trend, they themselves could face unpleasant consequences. One dissenting county secretary who had resisted dense planting was given the sack.

On 27 January 1985 the *People's Daily* quoted Bo Yi-Ball, a vice premier from the days of the Great Leap Forward, as saying: 'In the latter half of 1958 when Xushui county in Hebei province announced that it was moving to Communism, it launched a big campaign to purge counter-revolutionaries. A quota was handed down from head office to catch bad people and negative elements. The job had to be completed before a certain date and culprits were sent to hard labour camps.' The term 'negative elements' was deliberately vague. Anyone who spoke out at a communal meeting to say that their farming satellite target was an impractical figure would be accused of anti-Great Leap Forward thinking and immediately purged. Some physically weaker people who did not exert themselves to the limit and others who made faintly disapproving noises about the worsening food and housing situation, could all be counted as negative elements and punished by struggle meetings, or even end up in a labour camp.

Countless numbers of people throughout China were arrested for criticising the Great Leap Forward. In Shaanxi province, for instance, a certain Wang Wai-Ming sent more than ten letters to Mao, Chow En-Lai and the National People's Congress standing committee, expressing his disapproval of the Great Leap Forward. His county court convicted him as a counter-revolutionary, using his letters as evidence and he was sentenced to ten years' imprisonment. He then took his case to the district court and had his sentence increased to 20 years. While he was in jail he appealed to the high court in the provincial capital of Xian and the court gave him a further four years. He finally wrote to the Supreme Court, accusing the party leadership of allowing junior staff to abuse civil law and impinge on people's rights, but the response of the Xian authorities was to give him a death sentence, amended by a kind person in the provincial court to a life sentence.

One year later, in 1962, the head of the Supreme Court, Sher Ger-Jai, went to Xian from Peking on an inspection tour. He came across Wang's case and decided to intervene. He said: 'It is stipulated in the constitution that people have freedom of correspondence, so why was it a crime when someone wrote to Chairman Mao and Premier Chow expressing his different opinion about people's communes and the Great Leap Forward?' As a result of this intervention Wang Wai-Ming was set free, one of the luckiest people in the legal history of Communist China.

This was a time when commune cadres wielded untrammelled power over peasants. Tying up and beating peasants was common practice in nearly all villages. The cadres would beat anyone who did not loudly support their talk of satellites and they would beat people to death without a second thought. In early 1961, two senior Communists, Tao Jeug and Wang Yin-Jon, went to Henan province during the famine in an attempt to ameliorate the situation. On 2 February, at a provincial party committee meeting, Wang Yin-Jon acknowledged that 'Because of Ping Si county's 7,320 catties per mou wheat satellite, more than 10,000 people were harshly treated, 7,000 people fled from beatings and more than 300 people were beaten to death. How cruel this business was!'

The party secretary and principal of the party's Advanced Indoctrination College, Young Shan-Jang, provided equally grim evidence, reporting how cadres would strip people naked, treating them like Tibetan slaves except skinning them. The cadres would abuse them and hit them. 'They behaved worse than the Japanese. Why did some cadres dare to act this way? Because they had a righteous excuse they were helping to achieve Communism.'

Mao viewed his cadres' beating of peasants as a small misbehaviour for a good cause. He gave orders not to frighten 'those comrades who have committed only small errors.' He did not want to dampen their revolutionary zeal. With his blessing, party cadres knew they could assault people and even kill them without being penalised and the peasants just had to put up with violent treatment for a good cause.

The political climate was such that exaggeration and lies were spiralling upwards rapidly. In May 1958, the party secretary of Suiping county, China's first people's commune, let his underlings know that he would like to see a wheat satellite in his domain. The village cadres of the people's commune knew their trial field had a very good crop, probably a maximum of 400 catties per mou and they had to find a way to please the boss. To begin with they decided to claim that the size of their 20 mou trial field was 2.9 mous only. All their peasants were summoned to an urgent meeting and made to memorise a set of figures as well as the standard answers about the trial fields.

Reporters from the Xinhua news agency came to supervise the harvest and weigh the crop. The total yield of wheat was over 10,000 catties. It worked out at 3,521 catties per mou. After re-checking, it went up by another 300 catties. This wheat satellite of 3,812 catties per mou made the *People's Daily* news headline on 18 June 1958 and the people's commune received joint congratulations from the central government and the party. Visitors, up to 30,000 of them in a single day, flooded in to see the miracle field.

These agricultural satellites were soon popping up everywhere, getting more and more fantastic and sensational every few days. It was said that the key to this agricultural Great Leap Forward was deep digging and thick planting. The great mentor, Mao, said: 'Deep digging is the important linchpin for increased production. Thick planting needs deep digging. Deep digging enables roots to go deep down and the plants to grow strong and deep digging can also retain water. So work hard and dig deep!'

And so everywhere people learned the merit of deep digging, the deeper the better and the more revolutionary. The record was about four metres. People used their initiative to look for fertilisers, which were becoming very difficult to find. Eggs, milk and peanut butter, nearly unattainable for human consumption, were poured into the trial field. Many peasants' thatched hut homes were knocked down or burnt down to use as fertiliser. Dogs, cats, frogs, fish, caterpillars, sheep and even the precious cattle were killed to make an organic fertiliser soup. The party instructed every commune to have its own trial field.

The cadres of Young Mui commune in Zan Shui county, Guangdong province, chose their best land as a trial site. The first thing they did was to make a big billboard proclaiming in large characters that this was their cadres' high yield trial field and their target was 15,000 catties per mou. They dug one metre deep, which could not be done by a plough. Ten strong young men had to dig it with hoes. The lifeless subsoil was brought to the surface and night soil, cattle dung, lime and compost were poured into the site. Under the local party secretary's supervision, planting of seedlings was carried out strictly following the party central committee's specification, which claimed that a specialist study had concluded that the most scientific way of rice planting was at distances of two inches by one and a half inches.

All the experienced old peasants, cadres and activists were summoned to see how it was done and they were joined by a crowd of curious onlookers. They started chatting and someone said: 'Two inches by one a half inches! It won't work, for sure. There will be no room for the rice plants to grow, let alone setting grains. Without ventilation they might even die from over-heating.'

But the party secretary said: 'You are all too conservative. Be brave! How could instructions from Chairman Mao and the party be wrong? How could Lin county's great experiment be false? They produced 200,000 catties of rice in one mou. We will manage this field scientifically. There is nothing to fear!'

The rice seedlings soon grew up, packed tightly together and weeds sprang up fighting to get the better of the rice plants, yet there was no way to do any weeding because there was no room for a hoe among the plants. The party secretary, getting worried, told his cadres to weed by hand. After a couple of weeks the lush green rice plants looked yellow and weak. The party secretary guessed the problem was insufficient nourishment and gave an order to give them more chemical fertiliser. This only made the yellow colour worse. Several old peasants were invited to a consultation at the scene. Their joint diagnosis was that the field was overcrowded, had too much fertiliser and no ventilation.

Electric fans were installed immediately to blow fresh air into the field around the clock, water pipes were rigged up to spray the plants intermittently and water was also conducted to run over the ground of the trial field. The rescue operation worked, the sick plants recovered and turned green. But when the rice flowers began to set and all the other rice grains in the ordinary fields grew heavier day by day and drooped their heads, the rice plants in the high-yield field were still standing upright and pointing at the sky. After the party secretary and his cadres had checked the special rice spikes and discovered they were all empty husks, the billboard and the high yield field quietly disappeared overnight.

Another trial field in Guangdong province went through a different process. The target of this water rice trial field was 120,000 catties per mou. The peasants started by planting seedlings thinly and later on strong seedlings from other fields were transplanted into the gaps in the field. When they started to flower, rice plants from other fields were also transplanted into the field until the site was solidly packed and soft mud was piled up a foot high all around the edge of the field to keep the plants upright. It needed several hundred labourers to dig up nearly ripe crops from 15 mous to create this one-mou miracle field. Many grains fell off during the move; the disturbed plants could not carry on growing normally and could reduce harvest by up to 10 per cent.

Although people in the communes knew too well about the miracle fields, the party officials from local and central government wanted to believe in these satellites. On 27 August, the *People's Daily* sported a huge headline reading: 'The braver people are, the more the land can yield.' It went on to report that in Shouchang county, Shandong province, very few people aimed at just 5,000 catties per mou any more. The whole county was now aiming for 10,000 catties per mou. An early rice yield in Ma Ching county, Hubei province, was a record 36,956 catties per mou.

Film workers controlled by the party's propaganda department were now hard at work making newsreels and documentaries to report to the nation about the miracles of agriculture and steel production. Mao believed that he had unleashed China's productive power and his subordinate Liu Shao-Qi swallowed all the myths. When Liu's home town in Lin Shan county, Hunan province, sent him copies of the *Lin Shan News Bulletin* carrying the story of a local satellite of 65,000 catties per mou, he believed the incredible news. In late September, when visiting Jiangsu province, Liu asked the locals: 'Can't you do better than 10,000 catties per mou? The conditions here are good. Try to dig deeper, you still can harvest more. Carry on like this and we can grow food crops on only one third of the farmland, trees on another one third and the last third can have a rest.'

Chow En-Lai, on the other hand, succeeded in keeping his sense of reality. The party cadres in his home county in Jiangsu province reported to him that the average yield of its 70,000-mou cotton field was about 20 catties per mou. He replied at once: 'Not bad, not bad'. This was at a time when other cotton growers launched their satellite of 1,000 catties per mou. But

Mao evidently believed the lies. Excited by China's liberated production power, he said he had never really been happy before; only the Great Leap Forward had made him a genuinely happy man. The peasants, meanwhile, were swept along by the party's reforms, yet they rarely had a clear idea about Communism. One county party secretary gave a talk to his villagers about Communism as it had been explained to him by a senior party leader. His explanation was as follows:

'People's thought will rise up to a high level and everybody will be totally unselfish. On the material side, food, clothing, housing and transport will all be free. This means that every day everybody can have one egg, one tael (less than 2 oz) of meat and one tael of oil. People's communes are the bridge to reach this target. All the big cooperation projects and free meals are the preparation for the transition to Communism, which will be realised after three years' hard work.'

The supposed unselfishness of this magical existence was certainly hardly prevalent in the transitional period. The communes' projects often made hundreds or even thousands of people work together in chaos, helping those who were lazy or who preferred to muddle through. Whether they were hard-working or not people were paid the same, so the lazy people's way was soon contagious. The demands for the public reserve fund and community chest, as well as the demands for work on big cooperative projects without pay, did not go down well with the peasants. The wages peasants were supposed to get from the communes were often suspended because of shortage of funds, so there was little incentive to work. Some middle and poor peasants were unhappy about the way things were moving and so became victims of anti-right-leaning struggle meetings; they went through similar ordeals to the rightists.

The climax of the people's communes surged in the autumn and winter of 1958, when 500 million peasants were forced into military-style organisations. Males and females lived in separate barracks, grown-ups and children were separated and meals were provided by canteens. Work in the fields was arranged with military precision, with strict discipline and at high speed. If they were not tending fields, peasants would be sent to build reservoirs or roads, plant trees, clear virgin land, build or work in factories. Peasants were not really soldiers, they resented military discipline and resented being deprived of their family life for long periods.

Apart from local projects, people's communes provided most of the 90 million tough and strong labourers for the steel Great Leap Forward. Some of these prime labourers left their villages in the winter of 1958 and did not return for months. They were organised into militia divisions and took their share of grain with them from their own canteens when they went away.

All everyday farmwork had to be done by the elderly and middle-aged men, women and children who were left behind and harvesting the second crops in late 1958 was overdue. The rice plants fell flat in the fields; when touched, over-ripe grains dropped off and probably 30 per cent of the crop was lost. Winter digging was neglected and pests flourished the following year. Planting out the following year's seedlings was late and the blossom risked running into adverse weather. Seasonal farming, in short, was badly hampered by the Great Leap Forward and life in the villages was under strain. Some people said wryly: 'After the autumn we can eat iron and steel; they are more chewy anyway.'

Shandong province's 1958 autumn sowing area shrank by more than a quarter, while the following summer harvest was reduced by more than a billion catties. From late October 1959 seven million young farmers from Shandong province were steered to irrigation construction and the figure rose to 8,870,000 in early December. Even in the spring of 1960, when the whole province was in the grip of a serious famine, there were still several million young peasants engaged in irrigation projects to the detriment of their seasonal farmwork. In 1959 and 1960, around 50 to 60 million mous of farmland in the province went to waste. The 1960 weather was unfavourable for farming, but it was definitely not the main reason for the year's poor harvest and other provinces were similarly affected.

Village life was being changed beyond recognition. The party put out exhilarating propaganda about communal canteens, claiming they would save time, food, firewood and money. In reality, though, it was just the opposite. Many public canteens were hurriedly built sheds with a few tables and no chairs. Some were dilapidated temples which still had some sort of roof, while others consisted simply of a piece of open ground where people collected their meals through a hole in the wall. These canteens were there to cater for hundreds, or even more than a thousand, people in the villages. Peasants were not pleased that they had to eat standing up or squatting down all the time, even in bad weather. Sometimes the young, the old and the sick found it difficult to make the journey three times a day to the canteens and so a family representative would go to collect their share to eat at home. There were also peasants living far away from the villages. Some had to climb up and down hills, travelling considerable distances three times a day to and from the canteens and latecomers often had to queue for an hour.

The grain which would formerly have been paid to the peasants after the autumn harvest was now handed over to the canteens directly by the communal authorities. Now that everyone was allowed to eat as much as they liked, food consumption and waste increased. When they had cooked their own grain at home, the peasants had always eaten frugally to make sure their food would last until next harvest.

There were many other inconveniences of having to eat in the canteens, such as when someone needed to boil a bowl of herbal medicine. They had no choice but to brew it in the big cooking pot of the communal kitchen, because their own cooking pots had all been taken away.

Peasants had traditionally used their spare time to collect firewood for the year and this had never interfered with their work in the field. The village canteens had firewood collection squads made up of ten or so strong workers, who had no time to work in the fields. Canteens also needed administrators, buyers, bookkeepers and cooks, who were also no longer available to work on the land. If the people running the canteens were less than honest, the situation could get much worse. Mismanagement caused a lot of wastage, including losses during transportation from the fields to the granaries.

The communal canteens also wasted huge amounts of food. By the latter half of 1958, food stocks kept by canteens had all gone and in early 1959 the free meal adventure finally came to an end. Peasants were then left to fend for themselves. When they had handed over their private food stocks, most had secretly kept some food back, but it was now difficult to find firewood for cooking as all trees, fruit trees included, had disappeared into stoves for steel production. Even the long grass was used up after a couple of months, so instead the peasants were reduced to digging up short grass, which they dried under the sun and then used sparingly as fuel. By then they were living on little except watery gruel. Once the porridge had started to boil, they would put out the fire to save fuel, using the heat in the pot to do a little more cooking. Sometimes peasants would walk for several days to distant mountains where firewood was still to be found.

The drastic deforestation caused by the search for firewood destroyed China's ecology on an unprecedented scale. One village in Guangdong province had previously been close to two rivers which had never dried up or flooded. Now both of them dried up, exposing the riverbeds and leaving only a streak of water trickling down from the barren hills, taking away the village's water source, as well as the abundant fish, shrimps and shellfish that had been in the rivers.

Since it was government policy to rid the whole country of all vestiges of capitalism, all village markets, private plots and private livestock were banned. This meant that no one could supplement their diet with chicken, duck, pig or home-grown vegetables. When the food situation was getting worse, even when villagers were allowed to keep animals, they could neither find food to feed them nor firewood to cook the feed. They couldn't even dig up wild vegetables to feed the pigs, because they needed them to supplement their own diet. In the past, supplementary businesses during the lull in the farming season had been quite popular; bamboo products alone could bring in some good money for the villagers. Now, though, the bamboos had all been burnt and supplementary businesses were all banned.

The communes' problems were exacerbated by mismanagement. Untrained and incompetent Communist cadres were suddenly saddled with the responsibility of running a huge organisation averaging 20,000 people.

The Great Leap Forward continued into 1959, with every sign indicating all was not well. The monthly staple food ration for city people per head was cut to around 30 catties (approx. 42lbs) and cooking oil to three taels (four ounces). The non-staple food supply was deteriorating and sometimes days went by without any vegetables appearing for sale. Industrial products were scarce, while quality was worse. Some raw materials usually supplied by peasants were no longer available. Shopkeepers were heard recommending goods to customers by saying that their quality was good because they had been made before the Great Leap Forward. In some areas every family was put on a ration of one box of matches and two taels of kerosene each month. Most villagers therefore lived in darkness at night, since their oil lamps were only used in emergencies.

The disaster inflicted on China by the Great Leap Forward grew increasingly dire as the country became paralysed by famine and economic crisis. By November 1958, peasants had already begun to die from starvation, which the Communist authorities called 'abnormal death'. This happened at a time when Mao was worried about how to dispose of China's mountains of surplus food. In the same month Mao said, at a conference in Wucheng, 'Agriculture is advancing fast. Give it one more year and next year, as far as food is concerned, when the yield reaches 1,500 billion catties, the peasants can have a rest and take a one-year holiday. There will be too much food. We won't be able to eat it all.'

In that year, 1958, almost all the young and strong peasants had left their villages to pursue steel production or other projects and many food crops were simply left to rot in the fields. Huge amounts of cotton wool were blown away, flying like heavy snow in the air. The year had a good cotton crop but no proper harvest. While national food stocks decreased, however, national optimism increased – officially at any rate – because the great helmsman Mao had predicted that China would have too much food.

628

When collections of compulsorily purchased grains ran into difficulty, because the peasants did not have enough to eat, the ruling clique decided that the tension over food supplies was caused by the peasants hiding their food. Mao drafted a paper stating that 'the problems in the people's communes, with the big and small production teams hiding their property and sharing out the food privately among their people, is serious. It is a prevalent problem throughout the country, which needs to be solved immediately.'

A hard-hitting campaign to strike at peasants 'hiding property and sharing out food privately' was therefore put into effect. A typical example of what happened was in Yi Bin city, Sichuan province, which had a population of 160,000 in ithe villages under its control. The city party committee dispatched special work units to its villages and more than 2,500 communal cadres were bound and assaulted to force them to reveal the whereabouts of their hidden food stocks. Similar scenes took place in Guizhou province, where several thousand village cadres were sent to prison. In turn the village cadres pressed the ordinary peasants for food and they were often even more brutal and vicious.

By the early summer of 1959, tens of millions of people were starving. On 14 September, Mao wrote to the standing committee of the National People's Congress announcing that the 'political and economic situation in the country is good.' He blamed any difficulties on right-leaning trouble-makers and so a new campaign was launched against right-leaning thought, right-leaning activities and right-leaning opportunists. Mao was certain that after putting down all these harmful elements, the Great Leap Forward could be carried on smoothly and the present difficulties would be solved.

Under Mao's guidance, the Chinese government persisted in the expansion of the Great Leap Forward. Major investment in heavy industry was increased again and again and more people were drawn into the new projects. China's finances sank deeply into the red. Its economic planning was based on ultra-optimistic figures, counting on an unprecedented bumper harvest. The 1959 grain yield was estimated to be 540 billion catties, while the true figure was only 340 billion catties. The central government promptly increased the compulsory purchase of grain, demanding up to 49 per cent of the exaggerated harvest. Yet peasants needed 70 to 80 per cent of their normal crop simply to live.

The *People's Daily* proclaimed on New Year's Day 1960: 'The party and the Chinese people have found three treasures: the General Guidelines to build socialism, the Great Leap Forward and people's communes. The

Chinese people's new target in the ten years to come is to catch up or overtake Britain in the quantity of major industrial products... people's communes have enabled our peasants to put an end to the starvation, famine and death which used to affect tens of millions of people.'

The party's flagship magazine, *Red Flag*, published a series of articles starting on New Year's Day 1960 extolling 'the great achievements secured under the leadership of comrade Mao and the party central committee on the 1959 agricultural front line. Built on the foundations of the 1958 Great Leap Forward which continues in 1959, the large harvest has made peasants' lives better and better.'

The 1959 food crop in Shunyoung district, Henan province was 3.2 billion catties. The district party committee, led by the first secretary, Lu Shen-Won, boasted of having achieved food production of 6.4 billion catties, although the compulsory purchase quota allocated for Shunyoung district was 960 million catties. To show their enthusiasm in supporting the Great Leap Forward, the Shunyoung district party committee volunteered to hand over 1.4 billion catties, leaving local peasants with barely enough food to last for four months. Some counties were left with no more than three months' food stocks, while many communal canteens ran out of food before the end of 1959. To prevent the truth from leaking out, Lu Shen-Won ordered his subordinate counties to forbid peasants from either cooking their food, fleeing from their villages to live as beggars, or from informing senior officials of their plight. All roads leading to and from these villages were sealed off by militiamen, so the peasants were forced to die at home.

It was common practice that peasants' homes were thoroughly searched one by one and whatever little food was found would be taken away. Those who could not hand over food were punished and countless peasants were subjected to interrogation, often for days at a time. Victims would have their teeth knocked out, their hair pulled out and their bones broken; sometimes they would be stripped naked in cold weather and made to parade in the streets. In one extreme case in Si county, Henan province, the ears of four peasants were cut off and the party secretary of Yinhogi commune, Wangchen county, also in Henan, grabbed a peasant woman's hair and dragged her along the ground until she died. Many peasants were either killed or committed suicide.

Peasants in Wanjiang county, Guangxi province, paid for the Great Leap Forward with untold misery. Their party bosses gave an order to put sealing tape on the peasants' cooking stoves, house by house, in midwinter, so that they could not cook their hidden food, or even use the fire to keep themselves warm. Militiamen were patrolling at night; they would search

630

private houses and arrest people if they saw any light from a fire. Peasants were even afraid to cook the wild vegetation and tree bark which many of them collected for food.

In late 1957, before the Great Leap Forward, the party leadership in Wanjiang county suggested relegating production responsibility to each peasant family or small unit, but for his pains the county party secretary, Wang Din, was promptly denounced as an extreme rightist and two of his three deputies were also condemned, as well as 97 other officials in the county government. All were denounced as rightists and many more were implicated and sent to villages to work as manual labourers under public supervision. After this purge the new county party secretary, Hung Hua, vigorously promoted the Great Leap Forward, proclaiming that his county was aiming to be the world champion.

Accordingly, in late August 1958 the authorities prepared the ground for a trial field. They organised nearly a thousand people – peasants, office workers, schoolchildren and teachers – to dig up the ripe plants from more than a hundred mous of paddy fields and replant them in a 1.1-mou trial field in the Red Flag commune. To help the water rice to stand upright, bamboo strips were used to tie large numbers of plants together half way up the stalk; the bundles were then supported by wooden poles. It took three days, everyone working around the clock. A shed was then built beside this very special field for the command unit cadres who kept watch on the spot day and night. More than a dozen people took care of the non-stop task of blowing air into the field. When it was all finished, the superlative water rice satellite was launched.

On 9 September, 6,000 people from other communes and party bosses of all levels were invited to Wanjiang to witness the harvest of this extraordinary bumper crop. In the mid-morning, 400 people started to harvest the water rice; they put the grain into big bamboo baskets attached to the ends of poles carried over the shoulders. They formed a long procession parading through the main streets, ending up in the courtyard of the county committee office where the grain was weighed and stored. As the transport column paraded through the streets, other groups of peasants, waiting under orders in four different granaries with full baskets of grain, joined the procession to swell the numbers. In the confusion of the weighing operation, some peasants did not empty their baskets of grain onto the storage heap but went to the back of the queue to have their grain weighed again and again.

The operation of harvesting and weighing finished very late at night and it was worked out that the trial field had produced 130,434.14 catties per

631

mou. The county party secretary, Hung Hua, announced the miracle to a meeting attended by the nation's press; it was a sensation which duly appeared in the *People's Daily* on 18 September and in other newspapers as well.

A very small section of the trial field was kept intact for visitors who were pouring into Wanjiang from all directions of the country to see the miracle field. The Vietnamese sent a delegation to Wanjiang hoping to pick up some helpful tips and the Russians tried to get information from overseas Chinese students about the incredible news.

Wanjiang county was now a glorious Red Flag county and Hung became a celebrated hero, the proud possessor of dozens of prize banners. He now wielded formidable power, brooking no dissent in his county domain. Wherever he went in Wanjiang he would instruct the local authorities in advance to ensure that people were standing on either side of the road to greet his arrival. When he went to San Cheun commune on an inspection tour, 11,000 out of the commune's 18,000 people turned up to line the road to greet him. Peasants who lived some distance away had had to make their way to the appointed place at night by torch and many had been waiting by the roadside since 2 a.m.

A teacher, Tan Yue-Hua, from Wanjiang Secondary School, said publicly that 130,000 catties per mou was impractical and the whole farce was bringing shame on Wanjiang county. A county cadre, Chang Len-Yen, said in private that the county party secretary was bragging, only to be sent to a labour reform camp for his pains. Some teachers and students in an agricultural college in Liuzhou city in the same province also questioned the figure of 130,000 catties per mou, but they were denounced as rightists, expelled from the college and banished to villages to do hard labour.

As Wanjiang county inflated its harvest figure, the central government increased its compulsory grain purchase quota accordingly. In 1958, the central government demanded one fifth of Wanjiang's total yield, without knowing that it in fact represented 70 per cent of Wanjiang's total harvest.

When the 1959 campaigns of anti-right-leaning and protecting the Three Red Flags (that is, the Great Leap Forward, the increase in steel production and people's communes) swept through the whole country, the peasants of rural China were accused of hiding away food and plunged into an unrelenting purge. Hung upheld party policy with inexorable determination. At one big production team meeting, 13 hungry and wounded peasants died, but Hung said nonchalantly: 'These people have deserted socialism, so it doesn't matter if some of them die.'

The Wanjiang county authorities transferred local people's food stores and animal fodder from the small local warehouses to the national granaries. They only just met the quota allocated by central government and made it clear that they would not open the granaries even if people were dying of starvation; they would shoot anyone trying to steal food. Many hungry people were indeed shot while attempting to break into the granaries, while others fled to the cities to beg for food. The Wanjiang authorities gave orders to pursue and arrest them and those who were captured were locked in a small, stuffy and crowded room where it was impossible to sit down. In all, some 44 people died under these conditions, while Hung also ordered that if any runaway refused to come back, they could legitimately be beaten to death on the spot.

In March 1959, in the early stages of the famine, one county cadre, Tam Shao-Yoo, wrote under a pseudonym to central government and to the newspapers giving graphic details of the unprecedentedly hard life of local people. His letter was intercepted by the county authorities and the local public security department reprinted the letter so as to trace the handwriting in the Wanjiang county area. They finally tracked down Tan Shao-Yoo and subjected him to a series of struggle meetings. He was sacked and sent to do hard labour in a village 'supervised by the masses'.

To cover up the famine in Wanjiang county, Hung ordered the local post office to impound all letters posted to his superiors and deliver them to the local party committee. 'Why the fuss over a few people's deaths?' he said. 'Life and death are only laws of nature, after all.' Cadres who reported peasants falling ill and dying from famine, or who reported seeing dead bodies on the roadside unburied, were liable to be punished by suspension, dismissal, struggle meetings or labour reform.

But by March 1960, the district party committee, the superior body to which Wanjiang county reported, at last detected large numbers of people dying or dead in Wanjiang and they sent a team there to investigate the problem. The Wanjiang county authorities held several secret meetings preparing to stall the investigation and Hung published a menacing message warning people not to give information to the investigation team, saying: 'Making improper reports is a very serious matter; it is a struggle between the enemy and us.'

When the investigation team arrived, they realised how serious the situation in Wanjiang was. However, when they tried to report back to their superiors, their telephone calls failed to get through and their telegrams were retained and handed over to Hung. Hung was furious, accusing the investigation team of being hostile and hell-bent on looking for trouble. The

633

team was forced to revise the death toll downwards again and again, while Hung claimed that the deaths had been caused by a contagious disease. His deputy, who carried a gun, dared the investigation team to put their signatures on the report.

Eventually the senior party officials of the district descended personally on Wanjiang county and the investigation at last went ahead. Hung, meanwhile, was promoted in January 1960 to work in Liuzhou city. He took up his new position on 5 March, but was promptly demoted once the truth about Wanjiang county came out. He was brought back to Wanjiang to face struggle meetings, expelled from the party, arrested and finally, on 31 October 1963, given a five-year jail sentence; he eventually died in a labour reform camp.

The Wanjiang story was certainly not unique. Another secret report surfaced years later concerning the once-prosperous county of Fengyang, in Anhui province. Just as in Wanjiang, the party cadres in Fengyang county carried out the party policy of creating huge production teams. In one case, 31 villages belonging to Chel San big production team were given just a few hours' notice that they had to merge into six groups in half a day. More than 300 houses were knocked down and 40 people from 14 different families were made to live in just three adjoining rooms. Their front door was locked at night and guarded by militiamen carrying wooden rods and the inhabitants were only allowed out in groups to visit the lavatory. Many people became homeless and more than 100 people left the area. Anyone who resisted the measure was expelled from the party and the Youth League and even found their food withheld. Many villages in the county became uninhabited.

The county officials held a conference to combat the concealing of property, during which many of the lowest-ranking cadres were beaten. The communes, the big and small production teams all held their own lengthy meetings, which went on for more than 40 days, including New Year's Eve, all for the purpose of forcing peasants to hand over their food.

Harvests in the last years of the 1950s decreased, but the county party asserted that production had in fact increased. The 1958 yield was 180 million catties, 13 million catties less than in 1957, although the party's estimate was 400 million catties. Grain production in 1959 was 109 million catties, 70 million catties less than the previous year, in contrast to the party's estimate of 400 million catties. Large compulsory purchases followed the high estimate. After deducting the peasants' needs (food, seeds and so forth), the 1958 surplus was just 11.8 million catties, but the authorities compulsorily purchased 70 million catties. The total output in 1959 was barely enough for the county population to live on, but the authorities compulsorily purchased 59 million catties. The 1959 grain harvest of the San Wang big production team in the Woo Den people's commune was 35,000 catties, but the authorities demanded 58,000 catties. Eventually the team handed over 33,000 catties, leaving themselves with virtually no food.

From the winter of 1959 to the following spring, 15 per cent of the population of Fengyang county died, while a further 3.4 per cent fled the county and 31 per cent fell ill. One in ten people had dropsy. Farming came to a complete halt. When the county party secretary, Zhao Yu-Shoo and the commune's party secretary, Dong An-Chun, asked a village doctor, Wang Shen-Sun why the dropsy could not be cured and whether he was short of medicine, the doctor answered that they were short of food. The doctor was arrested on the spot and put through a struggle meeting. People dared not say that the cause of the 'abnormal deaths' was starvation, so instead they blamed hygiene.

Some desperate people took dead bodies home to eat. A couple even strangled their eight-year-old son and cooked and ate his body. The county party secretary, not wanting the truth exposed, treated such cases as political sabotage, directing the public security department to make secret arrests, intending to imprison the culprits until they died to destroy any evidence. In all there were 63 secret arrests in the county and out of those arrested 33 died in jail. To cover up the tragic situation, some areas stipulated that bodies had to be buried deep so that crops could be planted on top. Crying was not permitted and mourning costumes were banned. One production team forbade the mourning families from wearing the traditional white; instead mourners were told to wear red.

The senior party officials in Fengyang county managed to maintain their own privileged life; they didn't seem to care about the suffering of the people. When someone reported that large numbers had died, he was condemned as a troublemaker. According to one peasant, 'in the autumn of 1959, there was no food at all. People died every day. When Dong An-Chun (the party secretary of Woo Den commune) came to check our work, he told cadres that the current situation was very good. There had been 2,500 people in our team, but now there were just 1,300. We reported to Dong An-Chun that many people were dead, but he said we were playing games. We took him to look at the bodies, but he just said that if people didn't die, the world wouldn't be able to accommodate them all. He also said there were births and there were deaths; how could anyone guarantee one would never die on a certain date?'

The party officials of Fengyang county were among the most fervent supporters of Mao's policy and they had set their sights on achieving a

Communist society within six months. In 1960 the villages had a total population of 330,000, but in all more than 60,000 villagers died to pay for their fabulous satellites. The satellites with 'abnormal deaths' were everywhere. Most surviving peasants were weak and sick. Dropsy, the famine sickness, was widespread in the spring of 1960. Victims generally felt tired, drowsy, dizzy, unsteady and easily out of breath. Many had to support themselves with a walking stick. Their skin was swollen, some could hardly open wide their eyes and had difficulty working with their swollen fingers. They would watch the ripe grain swept away by the wind, or leave it rotting in the fields, for they did not even have the strength to salvage it for food, let alone go out to work in the fields. Peasants' rations were always lower than those of people in the cities. In a rich area such as Guangdong province, some peasants were given 200 catties of grain, including the husk; this meant 15 catties of staple food per head per month for nine months, until the next harvest in June, although under normal circumstances, a growing youth or manual labourer needs at least 45 catties per month. Peasants consequently searched for any non-poisonous wild plants in the distant hills to fill their stomachs, risking unpleasant consequences.

In the old days, in times of famine peasants had often fled to the cities, where the food supply was usually better. Now, under the Communists, people needed written permission to leave their villages, to buy bus or train tickets and to travel. To buy food they needed food coupons, which were only issued by the authorities at their permanent home addresses and peasants were therefore unable to move to the cities. In effect, peasants were tied firmly to their villages. Whereas in the past famines had affected only certain parts of China, the famine resulting from the Great Leap Forward affected the whole nation, including people in the cities.

From 1956 onwards it was central government policy to stop peasants leaving their villages and in March 1959 government policy began to instruct every province and city to repatriate peasants back to their villages. Some peasants fled repeatedly from their villages, only to be sent to labour reform farms.

Food stocks in big cities like Peking, Shanghai and Tianjin were getting very low and the government announced a reduction in rations of grain and cooking oil. In many places people could not buy food without coupons, when using coupons to eat in restaurants meant queuing for an hour or two for a plateful of rice, plus a few strips of vegetables. There was no meat and in Peking cabbage became the staple food. Some, driven by hunger, sneaked into parks at night to pick leaves from the trees, while children often hung around restaurants and stood beside tables where customers were waiting for food. When food was served, some would simply stare, while others would grab the food and stuff it into their mouths. Teachers and students alike were very weak and physical education classes were cancelled. Dropsy started to appear in the cities.

At the height of the great famine, the CCP leadership offered advice on how to look for food substitutes because of the 'temporary food shortage'. They made three recommendations, the first of which was to cultivate globelet algae. The way to do this was to dig a large pool, fill it with water two feet deep and allow algae to grow. The main culture medium was human urine, which enabled the algae to multiply quickly. The authorities claimed that drinking one bowl of this nourishing liquid daily could help prevent dropsy. The second piece of advice was to eat the heart of banana trees and rats; the authorities assured people that rats tasted delicious and eating them would have the added bonus of controlling their numbers. The third piece of advice was to steam rice three times, each time adding more water, which could double the volume of cooked rice. Cooking without washing the rice could also increase the volume of cooked rice by five per cent.

People were not thrilled by these ideas. Some said liquid algae was no good for people who had been starving for two years, while others declined to drink liquid mixed with urine. Many, out of desperation, said that if there was the faintest chance the algae might help they would drink it anyway. As far as rats went, many people were already eating them, but many rats had starved to death themselves and by now they were rare. The triple-steamed rice was just a waste of time and precious firewood; adding more water to rice could not solve the real problem.

In Guangdong province, there was no food for the communal pig farms. Some local party bosses instructed the communes to use a newly invented recipe which was a mixture of human excrement and mud from the bottom of ponds, which they claimed was highly nourishing and would cause the pigs to grow faster. The pigs in one communal farm, however, rejected the reeking diet. Instead, tormented by hunger, they went berserk, screaming and dashing around. After a couple of days, some of the pigs succumbed and ate a little of the new feed, while some stronger pigs performed the incredible feat of jumping over a 6 ft high fence and running away to look for food; they did not get very far, though and were soon recaptured. After more than 40 days, the emaciated pigs looked as if they were on their last legs. One of their keepers had been attacked by hungry pigs that had gouged the flesh from his legs, exposing the bones. From then on, his colleagues had to go into the pens in a group, with firewood or wooden boards tied around their calves, while another group carried wooden rods to protect their workmates who were handling the feed.

It was later observed that the famine struck hardest in the provinces which had set up the biggest satellites. Anhui province, under its left-wing party secretary Tseng Shi-Sain, had launched more satellites than any other province and more people died from starvation than in any other province. Often Anhui soldiers serving in the armed forces would hide and cry when they received letters from home; almost all lost family members in the famine. In some cases villagers, fleeing from starvation, visited their children in the army and were fed by the hosts, despite army officers trying to send them home. They refused to go home to die.

Famine also brought the education revolution in many communes to a halt. Schools were instructed to hold classes only in the mornings and to give no homework. Both teachers and students spent their afternoons and evenings resting; they had no energy to do anything except perhaps grow some vegetables. Even the two afternoon political study sessions were cancelled.

After the 1958 steel fever, 1959 saw tens of millions of the fittest farmers engaged on grand irrigation projects. No one dared to call back their workforce to tend to the fields and thereby risk being accused of sabotaging socialism. One of the well-known irrigation projects was in Gansu province, where the party administrators decided to divert the Yel River from Min county up to the hilly county of Hinyang, hundreds of kilometres away. As with most Great Leap Forward enterprises, there was no proper professional investigation, study or planning. Mao proudly declared: 'A great engineering project of guiding the Yel River up the hills in Gansu province is now in progress; it depends solely on the leadership of the party and on the Communist spirit of the Chinese people.'

Between 1958 and 1961 there were around 100,000 manual labourers in Gansu province, all engaged in building irrigation channels. Starvation and overwork resulted in large numbers of casualties and many runaways were caught and locked up, starved and tortured. Nearly 10,000 people lost their lives during the Yel River project. Like so many other ventures during the Great Leap Forward, it was a complete failure; not one drop of water was brought up the hills.

Thousands of dams, irrigation channels and reservoirs were built in the Great Leap Forward. Some were abandoned during construction for lack of resources, while many others were completely useless and highly damaging to the environment. Several new Yellow River dams helped to silt up the river, raising the riverbed and within three or four years turning 100 million mous of farmland on either bank into lifeless saline earth. After a few years all the dams were blown up, since many reservoirs were either faulty or dangerous. One, in Shangshing county, Henan province, collapsed one midnight while under construction, drowning several thousand workers, the victims of ruling cadres who knew a lot about revolution but nothing about engineering, yet who felt free to direct the construction work. Tragic events such as these were usually hushed up and the public rarely heard about them. In 1961 alone, abandoned projects cost the nation 15 billion yuans.

The Communist Party was suffused by vanity and delusion promoted by Mao. Some cadres would rather let their people starve to death than admit to their superiors that they were short of food. Thus the then party first secretary in Jiangsu province, Jiang Wai-Ching, commented on a party official in Boyin county: 'A bloody bureaucrat! When the provincial government tried to send him some food he turned it down and 40,000 people starved to death.' When famine struck in Gansu province, Chow En-Lai phoned the Gansu provincial officials and asked whether they needed the central government to send them food. One provincial party secretary replied that their peasants were eating as much as they wanted and still had plenty left. However, news of the devastating 'abnormal death' rate in Gansu finally reached Peking and the central government mounted an urgent operation to send food relief. The army was drafted in to help distribute food from house to house, but by then a million people had already starved to death.

There was a period when government granaries were still full while peasants were starving, but the authorities refused to open the granaries. Occasionally, there were cadres who took it on themselves to hand out food stocks from the granaries. One party secretary of a big production team in Wanjiang county, Guangxi province, Chac Yue-Jan, gave away 60,000 catties of grain to dying peasants, only to be punished by expulsion from the party; he later starved to death himself. Another two county officials in Guan county, Sichuan province, tried to keep back food from the granary to help the local communal canteens which had exhausted their stocks; both were criticised in 1964 and sacked.

On 26 January 1960, the CCP central committee produced a paper which reported: 'The current food situation is very good. National food reserves at the end of June 1959 were 34.3 billion catties and by the end of June 1960 there will be 50 billion catties.' In fact, by the end of June 1960 the real figure for national food reserves was only a pitiful quarter of that sum. On 23 March the vice premier, Lee Fu-Chun, delivered a speech to the National People's Congress on the 1960 national economic plan, praising the success of the 1959 Great Leap Forward and saying that compared with 1958, Chinese industrial production growth was 35.3 per cent and agricultural production growth was 16.7 per cent. Riding high on optimism, the Chinese government exported 4,150,000 tons of food in 1959 and 2,650,000 tons in 1960, when the country's peasants were dying by the million.

As the famine crisis deepened, the situation could no longer be covered up. A few months later, in October, the *People's Daily* reported that 'Our agricultural production this year has suffered the worst natural disaster for 100 years. Nine hundred million mous are badly affected and some of the particularly bad ones yield nothing at all.' The authorities began to admit there was a food problem, blaming the famine mainly on two years, later on three years, of major natural disasters.

At the end of 1960, the Hubei provincial chief, Chang Tee-Sher, telephoned the vice premier, Lee Sen-Nan, also from Hubei. Chang Tee-Sher said pleadingly: 'Vice Premier Lee, even if you behead me, you must give me 200 million catties of food; people here simply cannot survive any more.'

After a moment's silence the answer came. 'Even if you behead me, I haven't got the food.'

90

100 Per Cent Human Error

In his memoirs published in the 1980s, Young Shan-Jang, the principal of the Communist Party's advanced indoctrination college, included the following stories from the period of the Great Leap Forward.

In January 1959, I took several comrades with me to Henan province to visit our cadres sent down there [people were sent to work in the lower level setups to gain experience]. I also wanted to find out about their work and study. We arrived at Zhengzhou city, Henan province and stayed in the provincial party guesthouse for a few days. Having heard of my arrival, many old comrades visited me. During conversation they told me some stories of deceit, one of which concerned Mit county, where people did not have enough food. The population was undernourished, dropsy was common and some people had starved to death. The Health Ministry sent officials there to investigate and they found that these allegations were true. I was terribly shocked by what I heard. At that time the Henan province party delegates' conference had just ended and I was given copies of all the bulletins and speeches. I had already told my cadres who had been sent to work and study in four different counties to convene in Dungfung county so that I could listen to their reports. On top of the big pile of papers given to me by the Henan party committee was the speech made by the party secretary of the county I would be visiting the following day. I was so pleased, I read it right away. However, I found it full of colourful sentences, such as: 'Without lying we could not stir up the masses' enthusiasm to work, without lying we could not promote the Great Leap Forward, without lying we would lose face in front of the people' and so on. The conclusion was of course that they had to lie to carry out the Great Leap Forward. I was puzzled and could not understand what it was all about.

The following day the province party committee sent a cadre to accompany me to Dungfung county. I summoned my cadres there to a meeting, inviting them to report to me about their work-study conditions there. They had all spent many years working at grass roots level before and were highly experienced. When I went there, they had been 'studying' there for more than four months and had already formed a clear idea about local conditions. The Henan province party committee cadre who accompanied me on the journey was present at our meeting and my cadres were very keen to talk about unimportant business. I still couldn't quite understand it. However, late at night, my cadres came to see me and told me of the real situation they had seen in the last few months. What they had seen and what was being publicised in newspapers were two completely different things. For example, two comrades had talked about Ching Gwan commune, where they both worked. The mother of the commune director had gone to see her son to ask for some food, but he had none. The mother left crying. If he had grain, he would have given some to his own mother, but he did not have it, so what could he give away? Members of this commune already had no food. The province was reported to have produced 1,000 catties per mou, so how was it they had nothing to eat so soon after the autumn harvest? There was another work-study cadre from the central government's Department of Organisation, who now worked as the county's party secretary. I told my cadres from Peking to report to him about the real situation. They said he knew everything, but there was nothing he could do. He could only let people sun-dry sweet potato canes, grind them into powder to make thin paste to drink to relieve their hunger a little.'

'A commune in Ping See county, Henan province, had launched a wheat satellite of 7,320 catties per mou. This commune's party secretary was invited by the head of a Peking advanced theory study organisation to lecture the scientists in Peking. His speech was later published in a science magazine with the title 'Solving the puzzle of 7,320'. The author invented all kinds of 'bases' and 'theories', presenting the concocted 7,320 as something real. He travelled everywhere to deliver his lecture, bragging about their grand achievement of 7,320 catties of wheat per mou. When I was banished to Tong Guan, Shaanxi province, in 1975, local people said he had also made the same deceitful speech there.'

'A Ching Gwan commune cadre was very adept at cheating. When senior officials came to check their food stocks, she led them to inspect the warehouses at night. They first went in through a front door where they could see a lot of grain. After walking out of the same door and doing a few rounds in the streets, she led them into the same warehouse through the back door, where there was also food in store – in fact it was the same pile of grain stock and furthermore there was a layer of grass at the bottom. One secretary of a big production team attended a Peking model labourers' meeting for the achievement of producing 10,000 catties of sweet corn per mou. Members of his commune said the figure of the yield was a lie, but the secretary said: 'Never mind, let this one pass but be truthful next time'. So he took with him this great success of 10,000 catties of sweet corn per mou to the Peking model labourers' meeting, eventually obtaining the grand title of 'hero worker' and returning home in glory. Another place that had no equipment surprisingly produced 1.3 million tons of steel within 24 hours, which was reported in the *People's Daily*. There were so many such stories one couldn't retell them all in several days. This was the true picture of life in the 1,000 catties per mou national champion province during the era of the Great Leap Forward. Other comrades also told me many more bizarre stories of lying and cheating which they saw with their own eyes. I was terribly shocked.'

Communist policy in the people's communes brought many problems, among which were the community chest and the public reserve fund. The community chest was spent on welfare services such as old people's homes, nurseries, sport and cultural service corps, while the public reserve fund was spent on communal big production teams, factories and business enterprises. Since these projects were vigorously encouraged by the party, the commune authorities felt justified in extracting money freely from the peasants, who found the demands difficult to cope with. Lack of funds and the passive resistance of the peasants soon reduced the welfare services to something existing in name only.

The industrial enterprises of the communes were no more successful than their agricultural adventures. The new factories' first problem was to find a steady supply of raw materials. Their production shrank day by day, with some coming to a complete standstill. During the Great Leap Forward, some 20 million prime labourers were drawn from villages to towns or cities to work in factories. By the end of 1960, the central government started to urge these people to go back to farming in their villages and nearly all the Great Leap Forward factories were closed down.

Industrial enterprises unrelated to people's communes also pursued their own Great Leap Forward. A vice premier, Bo Yi-Ball, described the industrial fanaticism of 1958: 'People freely altered the design and structure of buildings, freely substituted necessary materials and freely breached regulations and rules.' Many newly-built factories collapsed. 50,000 people died in 1958 from industrial accidents.

'Liberated' minds worked diligently to give education a Great Leap Forward, aiming to bring all Chinese people up to higher education standard within 15 years. Textbooks would be rewritten in order to shorten the time of conventional schooling. They thought that a single subject teaching method would be the breakthrough. This meant concentrating on one subject for a period, hence each of the one-year courses such as physics, mathematics, chemistry, languages and so on could be taught in a few weeks or so and therefore the lessons could be cut to half or even one third of the time.

This revolutionary teaching regime overwhelmed schoolchildren with one term's knowledge in just one week, with no time for exercises. These poor young souls did not have a clue about their school work. Universities were regarded as the forefront of the ideology battle between socialists and capitalists, therefore large numbers of students were recruited from working class or peasant backgrounds. It did not matter that some of them had failed five subjects in their secondary school final year.

There were also many Red and Specialist universities set up by communes. These universities took in peasant students, most of whom had not even completed their primary school education, but were now working in the daytime and studying at night. They would graduate from these universities in a couple of years. The first secretary of Guangdong province, Tao Jeug, described the 'universities' as follows: 'a setup with a few militiamen was called a military academy; a setup with a few carpenters was called an industrial college.'

Many counties claimed to have turned all their people literate in just a few months through educational satellites. Any scepticism about such revolutionary ideas would be condemned as the capitalistic resistance of a seriously right-leaning person. After soul-searching and self-criticism, such people could face demotion or dismissal.

The party never admitted that it had bungled the economy, insisting that the economic situation was 'very good', 'getting better and better', or 'generally speaking, good.' For the first 40 or so years not one Communist leader admitted that the Chinese economy was in trouble.

In 1981, a resolution at the party congress laid some of the blame for the calamity of the Great Leap Forward on the Russians and during that period the two countries fell out with each other. Russia unilaterally tore up 343 contracts, abolished 257 joint projects on science and technology, withdrew all 1,390 Russian specialists from China within one month and pressed for loan repayments. The CCP for its part alleged that China had had to send large quantities of food to Russia to pay for the Chinese debt, that Russian betrayal had led to the Chinese famine, damaged China's economy and sent the Great Leap Forward into difficulty. In reality, during 1960 and 1961 China owed Russia about 2 billion yuans. It would have been difficult to blame China's great famine on the Russians, since the Great Leap

Forward had caused a total economic loss of 120 billion yuans. Compared with the self-inflicted wounds, the Russian debt was insignificant.

The party leadership never dared reveal the truth about the Great Leap Forward. Historians had to make use of whatever information was available to appraise the tribulations. It is now clear that the millions of tons of steel produced in the Great Leap Forward was nothing but useless scrap. The 1957 grain yield was 390 billion catties; the 1960 grain yield was 287 billion catties, down 26.4 per cent compared with the previous year. In the same period oil producing crops decreased by 54 per cent, which was below the 1949 level when the Communists had won control of China. Heavy industry was doubled at the expense of light industry, while consumer goods were in short supply and living standards in the country deteriorated.

More people died from famine in the densely populated south than in north China; there were more than a million victims each in the provinces of Sichuan, Anhui, Henan, Hunan, Shandong and Guizhou. Sichuan province, under the left-wing leadership of Lee Jin-Chuen, claimed a vast number of victims even before the other provinces had reached rock bottom. Near the end of 1960, dropsy steadily invaded the cities, affecting more than 10 per cent of the students and teachers in Chongqing's nine universities. Among the fourteen universities in Taiyuan city, Shanxi province, 13.5 per cent of people suffered from dropsy, as did more than 35 per cent of staff in the Shandong provincial treasury department. In China's first people's commune in Suiping county, nearly 4,000 people, or about 10 per cent of the population, died, while the death rate in some of its production teams reached 30 per cent.

Numerous ghost villages emerged where everyone had perished. In Si county, Henan province alone, there were 639 ghost villages and Henan was only one of the many provinces worst affected by the Great Leap Forward famine. The State Council was compelled to consider importing grain from abroad; unwilling to give capitalists and revisionists cause to scoff at his socialist reforms, Mao refused at first, but between 1961 and 1964, ten billion catties of food was imported annually. It certainly helped to solve Mao's problem of how to dispose of China's 'mountains of surplus food.'

During the Great Leap Forward, many provincial authorities, even those in remote and poor provinces like Inner Mongolia, Qinghai and Gansu, competed to squander money on building deluxe villas for Mao. After his death, Deng Xiao-Ping said: 'After 1958, there were houses built everywhere especially for comrade Mao and other central leaders. It created a very bad impression and wasted a lot of money.'

Mao never disagreed with such perks, nor did he ever allow local people to use the villas, which were unoccupied for most of the time. He was very fond of the 'Water Dripping Cave' near his home village and personally told the Hunan provincial party secretary, Chang Ping-Fa, to build him a villa there, complete with its own road. Construction began in late 1960 and was completed in late 1962; Mao stayed there just once.

The members of the CPPCC and the NPC never dared to voice criticisms during the Great Leap Forward, their only business being to concentrate on studying Communist policy and Mao Tse-Tung Thought. China was not without scientists and engineers who should have known better, but 1958 came on the heels of the 1957 anti-rightist campaign, which made sure that rightist intellectuals lost their right to speak. Those who had escaped the dragnet were suffering from severe shell shock and entirely lost their voices.

In 1962 Liu Shao-Qi visited his home village in Hunan province and made a thorough investigation of conditions there. He said afterwards that a stone tablet should have been erected so that the lesson would never be forgotten. When he was back in Peking, he spoke out at a State Council meeting: 'The three-year economic hardship was caused by 30 per cent natural disaster and 70 per cent human error.' This infuriated Mao, who regarded it as one of Liu Shao-Qi's crimes.

In 1956, before Mao's Great Leap Forward, there was a minor famine in Guangxi province. None of the party bureaucrats, at any level, made an effort to ease the peasants' plight and as a result 550 people died. The party central committee and State Council dismissed the provincial party secretary, Chan Marn-Yuan. The *People's Daily* commented on the case, accusing him of being a bureaucrat who was apathetic about people's lives.

A few years later, it was estimated that around 30 to 44 million people had perished in the Great Leap Forward famine. This time the *People's Daily* kept very quiet and showed no indignation about the loss of life. Mao never admitted that his policy had been wrong; instead he blamed the catastrophe on his cadres, claiming that they had not carried out his policy correctly.

Sitting on top of more than 30 million corpses, Mao remained as the party's icon, as infallible as ever.

91

Working Holiday at Lu Mountain

By May 1959, many mandarins and cadres felt unable to conceal their worries about the worsening economic situation from Mao. Mao however wanted to press on with his Great Leap Forward. He was told face-to-face by peasants in his home village that they did not like communal canteens and he knew there were some reckless, left-leaning obstacles to accomplishing his policy. To clear up these obstacles in order to ensure that the Great Leap Forward could proceed smoothly, a politburo meeting, enlarged to include many other senior party officials, was to be held in the summer resort of Lu Mountain. Senior party members from all over the country arrived in late June and early July; it was to be a working holiday for everyone. Mao was in a light-hearted mood and urged everyone to keep their heads.

Discussions were unusually frank, since delegates were obviously feeling uneasy about party policy. The first party secretary of Hubei province, Wang Yin-Chon, gave a stark report about the failures of 1958. The lessons were painful, he said. That spring five million people had been living on just a few taels of food, on congee (a sort of thin gruel). Around 1,500 people were already dead and 150,000 people had dropsy. But telling the truth was not easy, because county party secretaries and worker-heroes lied to one's face. We needed to make a full appraisal, not worrying that we might talk about many mistakes which could harm people's zeal. Wang Yin-Chon spoke bluntly; he was not afraid of being regarded as right-leaning as long as he made everything clear.

Among the senior members was the defence minister, Marshal Peng De-Huai, who had at first decided not to attend the Lu Mountain Conference since he had just returned from a two-month foreign tour. He told his secretary to ask for leave for himself from the party central committee office, but the following day Mao telephoned to say that he would be waiting for Peng at Lu Mountain, so Peng left for the summer resort at once. There was enough recreation in Lu Mountain to entertain all the dignitaries, but Peng never attended these diversions. Declaring himself uncouth, he never appeared at the dancing parties which Mao, Liu Shao-Qi, Zhu De and Chow En-Lai enjoyed. Instead he spent his time attending meetings and reading documents.

The previous year, Peng had travelled extensively in China and visited ten provinces, where the effect of the Great Leap Forward had deeply disturbed him. At an enlarged politburo meeting about three months earlier, he had discussed some of his more worrying discoveries. 'Do not think that I have made out the situation to be more serious than it really is,' he said, 'or that I have exaggerated. Is the Great Leap Forward policy basically wrong? Yes, I think it is wrong. But it is no good to talk in meetings about something being wrong if we don't take action to correct the situation. It could affect not only army training, but also the future and destiny of our country, which is much more serious. When such a time comes, I am afraid people will no longer have faith in Communism.'

Mao, unperturbed, said, 'I think the problems mentioned by some comrades are just minor problems. They are just problems among comrades on lower levels who have not pushed through party policy thoroughly enough. Comrade Peng, you are in charge of the army, so you shouldn't meddle with other business. If you got yourself involved in other businesses, what would other comrades think? Problems of industry, agriculture and economy cannot be dealt with in the way you suggest.'

'I don't mean to interfere,' Peng replied. 'I say this because I sincerely care about your and the party's prestige. I have a duty to speak out.'

Mao grinned and said, 'I know, I know. You are always like that.'

Peng was well-known for being honest and straightforward. In the early days of the Lu Mountain Conference, he spoke bluntly during a group discussion; some of his remarks even directly touched Mao. Peng said that in his opinion it was a little too early to form people's communes; it would be better to have had a trial period for six months or a year. He said that, in his view, the leadership, including Mao himself, were responsible for the crisis of the Great Leap Forward. The party committee collective leadership was being ignored; only Mao's word counted.

Peng's audience was petrified and he was urged to modify his tone. But he did not try to cover up his views even in front of Mao. The minutes of his opinions were sent to Mao surreptitiously by Kor Hin-Shi, whose political acumen soon won him a place in the politburo. Mao stuck to his earlier decision that all the problems had been dealt with and he did not answer Peng's question about 'leadership responsibility'. The conference was soon to close as planned on 15 July and many people had already stopped talking about shortcomings or problems at the conference.

Peng wanted to talk to Mao face to face. He went to Mao's residence, but was turned away by security guards because the chairman had just gone to bed. During the civil war, Peng would often walk unannounced into Mao's bedroom and Mao would always get up at once to discuss the problem. But all that had changed. Driven now by a compelling urge to bring the people's woes to Mao's attention, Peng decided to write to him. His letter, delivered on 14 July, turned out to be a fatal turning point, making Peng the best-known and highest-ranking victim of the Great Leap Forward.

Peng had written a courteous, private letter, but on 16 July Mao ordered that it should be 'printed and distributed to every comrade for reference'. Mao summoned three members of the politburo standing committee, Liu Shao-Qi, Zhu De and Chow En-Lai, to see him and showed them Peng's letter. They remained silent as usual, waiting for Mao to speak. Mao asked disingenuously whether he could make a suggestion. He wanted everyone attending the conference to judge the nature of the letter. The three men had no objection and Mao's suggestion became a resolution. Such meetings were very typical all the way down the party. The boss would present the main theme at the beginning of the meeting and the other members would support the 'suggestion' at the end.

Mao launched a ferocious attack on Peng, accusing him of making mistakes beginning from the Long March in the 1930s and of being a counter-revolutionary, a right-leaning-opportunist. He forced those at the conference to choose between himself and Peng by threatening to lead the peasants to overthrow the government. If the Liberation Army would not follow him he would seek the support of the Red Army, but he thought the Liberation Army would follow him.

Nerves at Lu Mountain were drawn tight by the palpable tension in the air, as the delegates voiced their support for party policy, thereby implicitly condemning Peng's view. The security chief, Kang Sheng, sent Mao a note saying, 'May I be so bold as to suggest no toleration.' He accused Peng of having been a long-standing dissident inside the party.

For the unity of the party, Peng consented to a self-examination. Yet he was worried that his examination would encourage Mao in his mistaken view of the situation, giving rise to terrible consequences. Once Peng's letter had been made public, some people felt that any criticism of the party, or of Mao's policy, was unthinkable, or rather unacceptable. Although there were people who felt the same way as Peng, they preferred to guard their tongues; most people were just watching and guessing what was in Mao's mind.

One man in a delicate position was Chang Won-Tian, once the

general secretary of the party in its Yan'an days. A Russian-educated intellectual, Chang Won-Tian realised that he was no match for Mao, so in practice he surrendered his authority. To show his high regard for Mao, Chang Won-Tian decided to hold all politburo meetings in Mao's residence. Later on, his own political fortunes were eclipsed. When the Communists came to power, he merely became an alternate member of the politburo and a deputy foreign minister.

After the 1956 'anti-rushing forward' dispute, Chang began to have doubts about Mao's guidelines. In the Great Leap Forward, he ordered all steel production inside Foreign Ministry compounds to stop. On 21 July, after Mao had signalled his counter-attack, other delegates at the Lu Mountain Conference began to join in condemning Peng. Chang Won-Tian stuck his neck out at his group meeting and spoke for three hours in support of Peng's views. They must all discuss their faults openly and honestly, said Chang Won-Tian. They had to keep in mind what was practical. Some people ignored economic reality, saying that only politics counted, but such an attitude was simply impractical. They were all deficient in their understanding of many things and should not overthrow the old order recklessly. They should certainly stop bragging recklessly about catching up and overtaking the highly advanced countries in the world.

This bold speech earned Chang the reputation of being the second bluntest person at Lu Mountain after Peng. Peng's reliable assistant, General Wong Kar-Tsung, chief-of-staff of the PLA, was now summoned to Lu Mountain. He arrived on 18 July and found out soon enough that there was heavy pressure to forbid people from talking about faults at the conference. Wong Kar-Tsung had visited districts and garrisons all over China and was well aware of the deepening tragedy of the famine. Yet he thought there were problems in Peng's letter. He certainly would have advised Peng against writing it, but sadly it was too late. At a small group meeting the following day, he said he agreed with Chairman Mao's view that they should acknowledge all the good points and discuss the mistakes. Examination of the mistakes could help China move forwards, not backwards.

All through his tactful speech he did not once mention Peng's letter. On 23 July, Mao made a rancorous speech and although he did not name names everyone understood who was under fire. When the shocking diatribe was over, he dismissed the meeting without bothering to ask the party's other vice chairmen whether they had anything to say.

After the meeting Chow Siu-Chow, Chow Wai and Lee Yui, three senior officials, called on Wong Kar-Tsung to talk about their own assessment of the situation. Chow Siu-Chow commented on Yuan Si-Kai's desire to be emperor back in the 1920, remembering how a newspaper had been started which specialised in urging him to ascend the throne and Yuan Si-Kai certainly liked it. Chow Wai, deputy secretary of Hunan province, thought Mao had kept quiet for several days at the beginning with the intention of exposing everyone's stance. Lee Yui, deputy Minister for Water-Powered Electricity, was agitated, saying that no one person could cover up the sky with one hand. Wong Ka-Tsung kept cool and advised his comrades not to speak in such a way; instead they should try to speak to the chairman. But the chairman was burning with anger, said Lee Yui and they could not talk to him.

At that moment Peng walked into the room and overheard their conversation. He tried to calm them down by saying it was good to clear up some differences of opinion. But he did not stay very long. Chow Siu-Chow visited Peng twice in early July. As the party boss in Hunan province, he told Peng of more than a dozen problems in his domain. 'People want a stable life,' he told Peng; 'The peasants are afraid of change. The system of providing people with material needs ought to have been done on a small scale simply as a form of social security. Overdoing this system contributes to a decrease in production. There are problems of management as well as problems of reward. The communal canteens are a trying business to people and they are wasting money; they should definitely not have been expanded so widely and people should have been allowed to join voluntarily.'

The chance meeting of these four men with Peng was the starting point of their woes. They were summoned to see Mao when the chairman dropped hints that they should abandon their sympathetic views of Peng for their own good. At the 23 July meeting, Mao publicly revealed his reaction to Peng's letter and Chang Won-Tian's opinions. 'Right now,' he said, 'we and the masses are united. Yes, there is a little bit of petit-bourgeois fanaticism, but not very much. They want to establish people's communes and communal canteens and work enthusiastically on big cooperative projects. Can you say this is petit-bourgeois fanaticism? No; these are not petit-bourgeois, they are poor peasants, lower-middle peasants, proletarians and semi-proletarians. Communal canteens are good, we cannot criticise them yet. It was my suggestion to produce 10.7 million tons of steel – or rather it was my determination. Ninety million people turned up for this project. You say that the gain does not compensate for the loss? The next thing is people's communes, which I didn't invent; I merely made the suggestion... Have they failed as well? The comrades attending this conference all say there are gains, they are not complete failures. Is it that most have failed? No.'

651

Talking about the opposition to rushing forward, he said: 'If we give them a 'tall hat' [flattery], this reflects the wavering nature of the capitalist class; or, to put it one grade lower, it is petit-bourgeois fanaticism. Because the nature of 'right' is usually influenced by the capitalist class, under the pressure of the imperialists and capitalists, they turn to the right.'

At a further meeting on 2 August, 147 members of the central committee were present, together with 15 observers. Mao carried on his uncompromising purge, declaring that there was a frenzied attack on the party by right-leaning opportunists. After concentrating on Peng's many problems of non-cooperation with himself in the past, he accused Chang Won-Tian of having a 'relapse of his old illness' and a series of problems. A letter recently written by Mao to Chang was printed and distributed to everyone at the meeting, which began with the words:

'How did it happen that you have sunk into the 'Military Club'? It is really that birds of a feather flock together? You have forgotten all the important Marxist teaching and its wonderful truth, and you have run instead into the 'Military Club'. It is really a precious union of military and civil abilities, complementing each other.'

This was the first time the 'Military Club' had been mentioned. It followed as a matter of course that the Military Club was an anti-party cabal, which had perpetrated a well organised assault on the party. An authoritative verdict on Peng De-Huai and Chang Won-Tian was now announced and there was no chance for them to appeal.

On 12 August, Mao declared: 'It seems right-leaning emotion, right-leaning thought and right-leaning activities exist everywhere in different degrees and are increasing everywhere; in some areas the party is under ferocious attack from right-leaning opportunism.' This denunciation was followed by his order: 'Crush these perverse trends'.

The order was as usual executed at great speed with terrific force all over the country; the purge lasted six months. Mao sanctioned a series of documents for the purge and the *People's Daily* was full of instructive editorials.

By mid-August, the conference passed a resolution against 'the wrongdoings of the anti-party cabal headed by Peng De-Huai' and another resolution for 'protecting the party lines and fighting against right-leaning opportunism'. On 16 August 1959, the Lu Mountain Conference finally closed. Its final communiqué read:

This conference points out with satisfaction that in the first half of this year every section of the national economy continues to leap forward from the level of the 1958 Great Leap Forward. The total value of industrial production has increased 65 per cent compared with the same period last year. Railway transport capacity has increased by 49 per cent. The total yields of wheat, early rice and rape seed have outweighed last year's extra bumper harvest. The retail sale of consumer goods has gone up 23 per cent and market supply has already increased. The conference opines that for this year we should revise the four big targets of steel, coal, food crops and cotton. The new targets are as follows: Steel (product from the improvised furnaces excluded) will increase from last year's 8 million tons to 12 million tons, a 50 per cent increase. Coal will increase from last year's 270 million tons to 350 million tons, a 24 per cent increase and food crops and cotton will increase around ten per cent each from last year's confirmed figures of 500 billion catties and 42 million piculs.

The conference points out that the post-adjustment national economic plan is still leaping forward. The conference also points out that the assaults by imperialists and their running dogs on the General Guidelines, the Great Leap Forward and the people's communes have again disgracefully failed. The conference asks party committee members of all levels to censure determinedly and overcome the right-leaning opportunist thought of some cadres, insist on the supremacy of politics and fully mobilise the masses to complete and exceed the quotas of this year's leaping forward plan.

On 28 August, the Xinhua news agency reported that the 24,000 people's communes had been strengthened and were all developing healthily. On 29 August, the *People's Daily* carried an editorial headed, 'Long live the people's communes!' which was full of success stories from the people's communes and which concluded 'People's communes will never collapse; we have a million reasons to shout out loudly: Long live the people's communes!'

On 1 September, the editorial headline in the *People's Daily* read: 'The theory that "the gain is unable to compensate for the loss" is dead.' The party's leading theoretical magazine, *Red Flag*, also carried an editorial entitled, 'To refute the preposterous talk of national economic proportional imbalance.' Later in the month the editorial headline in the *People's Daily* read: 'Communal canteens have a great future.'

Like all the previous campaigns, the anti-right-leaning campaign involved millions of people. After a period of studying the party resolutions, Mao's many speeches, Peng's letter and Chang's opinions, everyone was expected to join the chorus to rail against the two condemned men. A period of self-examination and denunciation of other people were to follow. The criteria for pinpointing right-leaning opportunists was approved by the CCP central committee on 27 November. The net was cast wide, with millions of people caught for all sorts of diverse reasons; because they had openly disseminated right-leaning talk and attacked the General Guidelines, the Great Leap Forward, or the people's communes; they had actively advocated Peng's 'creeds', publicly defended the 'anti-party cabal' attacking the party central committee and Mao; they had committed mistakes more than once and harboured discontent towards the party. On this occasion they were again using the Great Leap Forward as an excuse to assault the party; or, lastly, they had leaned heavily to the right when executing party lines. Ever since the launch of the Great Leap Forward they had been committing serious right-leaning talk and actions and they refused to be awakened.

Apart from singling out right-leaning opportunists, many different sizes of 'right-leaning opportunist anti-party cabals' were also unearthed. Although the central committee decided not to extend the campaign to factories and villages, such places were affected just the same. In Hunan province around ten per cent of cadres in villages were condemned. In Guangdong province the percentage was higher and struggle meetings somewhat resembled the anti-rightist campaign. In many cases the victim's head was pressed down and there was frequent chanting of 'Down with right-leaning opportunists!' and 'Long live the General Guidelines, the Great Leap Forward and the people's communes!' But it was certainly less vigorous, either because people could see the folly of it, or perhaps they were hungry. The energy just wasn't there.

Many university teacher-communists were caught in this campaign. They were regarded as having grim capitalist thoughts, of flaunting their specialist status and of disobeying or even opposing the party leadership. For this anti-right-leaning campaign, the CCP central committee decided the percentage of wrongdoers needing rigorous attention should be kept under one per cent. In early May 1962, Deng Xiao-Ping discussed the rehabilitation operation needed for this campaign. He estimated around ten million people had been condemned and, as members of their families were bound to be affected the total figure for those felled by this campaign was several tens of millions. Out of the total of 26 million party members, 3.65

million were judged as right-leaning adventurists, who made up one third of the ten million victims. The rest were mostly working-class people and peasants who disapproved of the Great Leap Forward and the people's communes.

Liu Shao-Qi and Deng Xiao-Ping, who in 1962 were in charge of the day-to-day running of the party, tried to salvage China from the mortifying situation by rehabilitating junior cadres and ordinary people together. Ten million people were absolved altogether from their sins. 'Class enemies' were not included in the lucky ten million. Hungry peasants who complained, turned to theft or stole seedlings for food, were branded 'class enemies'. Many of them were sent to jail, beaten to death or driven to suicide.

There were numerous other enemies to keep the party busy, as they found some landlords, rich peasants, counter-revolutionaries, bad elements and rightists who had slipped surprisingly through the many nets, large and small. There were also ever-increasing numbers of 'new-born' enemies and families of counter-revolutionaries who had fled abroad. All these people were duly caught in the new anti-right-leaning campaign. They could not be granted rehabilitation.

Ten million lucky people and their families were given a new lease of life, but Mao found this leniency deeply repugnant. At the outset of the Cultural Revolution, in August 1966, Mao wrote his famous wall poster attacking Liu Shao-Qi and Deng Xiao-Ping and it turned out that one of their crimes had been this mass rehabilitation of 1962.

Peng, whose outspoken comments had sparked the anti-right-leaning campaign, found his own troubles were brewing fast. Visitors urged him to offer his repentance for the sake of party unity, otherwise he would be expelled. Night after night Peng was unable to sleep. Instead he sat in a rattan chair in the courtyard, facing the darkened mountains, wondering what had happened to him. He had only expressed his opinions, after all; how could his words have led to such a grim situation? He thought he had been telling the truth politely and had done nothing wrong, so initially he refused to write any self-examination.

The highest-ranking army officer, Marshal Zhu De, tried very hard to intercede on Peng's behalf, reminding Mao how for several decades Peng had fought the hardest battles and performed the most difficult tasks; the party could surely not expel him. Mao answered that Peng had been plotting to split the party even during the Long March; he was the one who had persuaded Lin Biao to write the letter demanding the transfer of military power from Mao to Peng himself.

Mao never sincerely admitted that he had ever made mistakes and Peng was the only senior man who dared to criticise him openly. When Peng said that the leadership should accept responsibility for the terrible mistakes of the Great Leap Forward, the result was a vindictive explosion from Mao. Party members were confronted with the grave prospect of splitting the party, even though many of them felt Peng was only exercising his legal right. In the end nearly all of them chose to forsake him.

Peng had bluntly pointed out before that democracy in the party's central standing committee was abnormal. Chow Siu-Chow had made similar remarks; he had said: 'The number two big boss (Liu Shao-Qi) finds it inconvenient to talk, the number three big boss (Chow En-Lai) and the army chief Zhu De cannot talk. Chan Yun and Deng Xiao-Peng find it difficult to talk. Chairman Mao always rides roughshod over everyone and there is no other road or U turn.'

Mao understood all these men only too well and he knew very well that he had a 'golden mouth'. In early April 1959, at the seventh session of the Eighth Party Congress, he commented that even Liu Shao-Qi, the man who had fought alongside him for years, did not dare to speak out in front of him. Twenty years after the Lu Mountain Conference, Marshal Yip Jan-Ying recalled how many people, including Liu Shao-Qi and himself, as well as the prime minister, all thought what Peng had said was right. Later on, though, Mao had revealed his displeasure, so they all altered their opinions and joined Mao in censuring Peng.

On 23 July 1959 Mao announced his all-out attack. The next group of sinners to be damned were the members of the so-called Military Club. Now the problem of Peng and Chang was to do with the class struggle. They were immediately banned from going to the residences of Mao, Liu Shao-Qi and other senior members without permission and their cars were forbidden to leave Lu Mountain. Planes in Jiujiang city airport, at the foot of Lu Mountain, were not allowed to take off without the permission of either Mao or Liu Shao-Qi. The culprits were segregated, forbidden from contacting each other and thereafter nobody visited them. Yet Mao was not content with making them prisoners. Never flinching from laying bogus charges and twisting facts, he wanted their reputations irretrievably smeared so they could never make a comeback.

When Chow En-Lai first read Peng's letter, he felt there was nothing vicious. Now he spoke out, saying that the central standing committee had talked to Peng, regarding his letter as a well-planned, well-prepared and well-organised campaign. It had showed hostility to the leadership of the party, to the General Guidelines and to Chairman Mao. Peng was also accused of leading the Military Club.

The deputy party leader, Liu Shao-Qi, did not have the courage or the discernment to stand by Peng and protect the principle of democracy; instead he too denounced Peng's anti-party past and his Military Club activities, saying it was clear that, after the Russian Communist Party's 20th National Congress, there were people in our party, among them Comrade Peng, who were keen to oppose a 'personality cult' in China. When they had held meetings in the West Building, said Liu, on several occasions Peng had suggested that they should not sing *East Is Red*, the song praising Mao in extravagant terms and he had also objected to chanting 'Long live Chairman Mao' (this was a reflection of the chant used to greet emperors in imperial China).

Peng had criticised Stalin's behaviour in his final years, involving the absence of collective leadership. He also pointed out that the chairman did not make self-criticisms, as a result of which, after the 20th Party Congress, many people had been keen to oppose Mao's personality cult. Liu Shao-Qui had thought this was totally wrong, he said; 'in fact, it is the kind of activity that sabotages the party, the proletarian enterprise and the revolutionary spirit of the people.'

At the time Liu Shao-Qi was encouraging people to push Mao's personality cult to new heights. Ten years later Liu, as the President of the People's Republic of China, was himself viciously purged by Mao, who had learnt to make good use of his personality cult and of his fanatical worshippers. Liu had sowed the wind and in due course he was to reap the bitter whirlwind.

Zhu De, kinder than the others, spoke with a more tolerant tone. But before he had finished talking, Mao lifted his leg, scratched his shoe a few times and said: 'Scratch the itchy leg on the outside of the boot'. Zhu De, embarrassed, shut up and remained silent until the meeting ended. Later on he had to make a public self-examination for not condemning Peng harshly enough.

Lin Biao poured out the most virulent slurs against Peng, accusing him of being ambitious, a plotter and a hypocrite. He also suggested that the battle with Peng needed to be raised to a much more serious level. The vilifying labels devised by Lin for Peng stuck firmly and soon became Peng's official description. As soon as Lin arrived at the Lu Mountain Conference, he asked: 'Comrade Peng has just toured around eastern Europe and Russia; what mission did Khrushchev assign to you?'

Peng jumped up and replied: 'I cannot understand one word of any foreign language; you go and ask the interpreter.'

By early 1961, Lin had replaced Peng as the defence minister. To prevent Peng from returning, Lin invented rumours that Peng had plotted with foreign countries during his eastern European tour. This accusation was included in official documents and distributed among senior cadres.

At the time of the Lu Mountain Conference Lin wrote in his diary about his disapproval of the Great Leap Forward, calling it a foolish act based on fantasy. He disapproved too of Mao's latter-day campaign against the revisionists, regarding it as a nasty and ruthless verbal attack which was absolutely wrong. But Lin did not reveal his true feelings; instead he heaped praise on Mao. Such outstanding duplicity won him Mao's favour and he was eventually chosen as Mao's heir-apparent.

The party central committee at the Lu Mountain Conference formally concluded that Peng was a hypocrite, adventurer and plotter, as well as the head of the 'Military Club', an anti-party cabal with Wong Kar-Tsung, Chang Won-Tian and Chow Siu-Chow as members. They were trying to usurp the power of the party, to split the party and to take over the army. Peng was dismissed as defence minister, but for a little while longer he kept the posts of deputy prime minister and politburo member.

The violent purge that followed fell on the armed forces. From 18 August to 12 September, 1,500 army officers above the rank of divisional commander, attended meetings in Peking to censure Peng and Wong Kar-Tsung. They demanded confessions from the condemned men about their activities, their organisation and names of the other members of the 'Military Club'. Peng denied there was such a thing as the 'Military Club'; instead he said, 'If you must have one, then I will form one now. Whoever wants to join the club, apply now and I will write your names down.' He took out pen and paper and signified he was waiting. The soldiers warned him indignantly not to be stubborn. The deputy political commissioner of the air force, Woo Fa-Shan, now shouted that he wanted Peng to repay a blood debt because he had killed a company commander during the Long March. Immediately a colleague rose and protested, 'Nonsense, you are making this up, simply rumour-mongering. Were you there? I was there and I did it. Commander-in-Chief Peng was not present and did not know about this matter.' This colleague was General Jone Wai, chief of staff of the Peking district army. He declared that he would join Peng's Military Club and they could shoot him if they wished.

The meeting descended into turmoil. Two armed guards led by security men were ordered to enter the meeting hall. Jone Wai was handcuffed and dragged away, shouting 'Chairman Mao, don't be hoodwinked by them. They are the real culprits; you have to be vigilant!' It is to the great credit of the party's propaganda department that the image of a noble and innocent Mao was so deeply imprinted in people's minds.

The department of the chief of staff held a meeting on 22 August, which was intended to criticise Peng. The chairman of the meeting, General Wan Yi, put forward the proposal: 'Anyone who disagrees with the opinions of Commander-in-Chief Peng, raise your hand.' No-one raised his hand. Wan Yi then announced: 'It seems there's nothing to criticise. The meeting is now closed.' And immediately after the meeting, Wan Yi was arrested. Two more generals, Hun Sher-Gee, Deng Hua and a number of other officers were censured and ordered to make self-examinations.

On the last day of the military purge gatherings, Mao arrived to the sound of deafening applause. He delivered a powerful message, emphasising the importance of censuring the capitalist military line of Peng and Wong Kar-Tsung and the right-leaning opportunists in the armed forces.

The military commission's enlarged conference, chaired by Lin Biao, now passed a resolution denouncing Peng and Wong as thorough hypocrites, adventurers and plotters. They had conspired for a long time to usurp the army, the party and the country. On this occasion their assault on the party was minutely planned, prepared and organised. It was the inevitable outcome of their growing personal ambition, of foolishness bred by greed. They had rejected the party's exhortation and ignored the party's discipline.

The resolution also decided to launch a campaign to censure the capitalist military line of Peng and Wong and the army's right-leaning opportunism. Within two months, through criticism and struggle sessions, Peng's subordinates and those close to him were purged and around 17,200 army officers, including several full generals, were condemned.

On 20 March 1943, Mao had been elected chairman of the politburo and central secretariat. The politburo also stipulated that Mao had the final say on everything discussed at their meetings. Later, absolute obedience to Mao was enshrined in the Chinese constitution, which meant that disagreement with him amounted to breaking the law.

After spending more than half a century searching for democracy, the Chinese people found themselves being returned to an imperial dynasty by the CCP.

92

Only Our Great General Peng

Peng De-Huai was born in 1898 into a peasant's family in a village in Hunan province. He started his working life at the age of nine tending animals and then worked 14 hours a day in a mine. He later got a better job working only 12 hours a day as an apprentice cobbler and in addition he took other menial jobs working long hours but earning him next to nothing. Before he was in his late teens he joined the army and it was there that he first met revolutionaries and began seriously studying political works. It was, therefore, when serving in the Nationalist army that he was first attracted by Communism.

After Chiang Kai-Shek's suppression of the Shanghai Communists in 1927, Mao Tse-Tung fled to Jinggangshan with his 600 or so men. His two bandit blood-brothers had fewer than 200 men. In May the following year, Zhu De joined Mao in Jinggangshan with 1,600 troops, among whom were the senior commander Kung Chor, the regimental political commissar Chan Yi and the company commander Lin Biao.

Mao received Zhu with mixed feelings. On the one hand he was pleased to have a bigger armed force, better able to resist the Nationalist offensives; on the other hand he was worried there could be a clash with Zhu, whom Mao did not trust. For a long time Mao dared not sleep in the same place two nights running. By December 1928, the brigade commander, Peng and a brother officer, Wong Kung-Leug, defected from the Nationalist army in Ping Jiang and went to Jinggangshan, taking with them nearly a whole brigade and the Nationalist Party offered a big reward for Peng's head.

Mao and Peng came from not only the same county of Xiangtan, in Hunan province, they even came from neighbouring villages. Mao made use of this regional affinity to cultivate a special friendship with Peng. Their combined forces were stronger than Zhu's and Mao could now sleep at ease. Peng had brought him a sense of security.

After the Jinggangshan interlude, Mao and Zhu's Red Army took the offensive in 1928, occupying the surrounding border areas between

Jiangxi and Hunan. Mao was the leader of the local Red Army as well as the local party and local power gradually converged into his hands. The party central committee in Shanghai, as well as some of Mao's local colleagues, were aware of his dictatorial style and were unhappy with it. His followers, they said, only knew about Mao, they did not know about the party.

In September 1928, Mao started an operation to 'wash' the party in his area. This was the earliest model for the internal party purges which made educated people with family background as landlords or rich peasants the main targets. This moderate purge 'washed away' disobedient people, those with undesirable social connections and those who had relatives working for the Nationalist Party. Peasant members of the party were all given membership certificates, but not the educated members, who had to obtain approval from their superiors.

Mao's domination in this area was not yet firmly established. When the leaders of the Red Army and the party organisations in southwest Jiangxi province disagreed with Mao's reorganisation by the end of 1929, citing the central committee as the final authority, Mao denounced the dissidents as opportunists, landlords, rich peasants and agents of the Nationalist Party. In February 1930 he launched a brutal, large-scale purge against the 'AB' (Anti-Bolshevik) group, which lasted two years.

One 'urgent announcement' from the purgers gave very clear instructions. 'The AB group is very sinister, cunning and extreme. Without the cruellest torture, they will never confess. It is necessary to use both hard and soft tactics to interrogate them; study their statements to look for clues and follow them up. The priority is to make them expose the organisation of the AB group in order to extirpate it.'

Suspects were beaten up and burnt all over their bodies, their fingers were broken and some died instantly. When some wives went to see their detained husbands, they too were arrested and tortured as members of the AB group. It was hardly surprising that many people confessed their crimes and implicated their friends and colleagues as AB group members and thousands of culprits were executed. Educated communists from landlord and rich peasant families and anyone who had ever disagreed with Mao, all feared for their lives. Now, Mao had found a way to crush dissent, simply by branding people as the enemy inside the party; he was then justified in eliminating them physically.

In December 1930, in the middle of this purge, mutiny flared up in Fu Tin, the seat of Jiangxi province's Soviet district government, where some Communist troops openly declared that they supported the commanders Zhu De, Peng De-Huai and Wong Kung-Leug and denouncing Mao.

It seemed Zhu had not instigated this rebellion, but he had no intention of supporting Mao either. Mao was now in a somewhat shaky position. Peng immediately made clear that he supported Mao. Zhu had to present a united stance with Peng and so the mutiny was crushed. Mao subsequently accused his opponents of being members of the AB group and more than 10,000 of them were killed. This enabled him to secure controlling power over his Communist army. Again he had been helped and rescued by Peng.

During Chiang's five offensives against Communist bases in the 30s, Peng fought many tough battles to protect Mao and the party central committee. It was Peng who was the commanding officer of the spearhead unit in the First Army Corps during the Long March, breaking through several heavy blockades and seizing important positions to help the main column get through and eventually escape to Yan'an. The most important assistance Peng gave to Mao was at the Zunyi meeting, where he was one of the first to attack the international faction, thereby helping Mao seize power.

Peng spent much of his time fighting against Chiang for the Communist Party's survival. He would speak to Mao on the telephone every day during these battles, worrying deeply about Mao's safety. In those days, Mao wrote the following poem:

High mountains, far-flung roads and deep trenches,
Enemy cavalry are galloping everywhere,
Who dares to stand firm and cross swords with them?
Only our great General Peng.

Peng was quick-tempered, unpresumptuous and unperturbed. Chiang's aeroplanes often dropped leaflets into Communist areas offering large rewards for catching important Communist leaders, including Peng, dead or alive, yet outside his command station there was usually only one sentry and he often walked around town without a bodyguard. As the deputy of Zhu, chief of the Chinese Communist army during the eight-year Sino-Japanese War, Peng spent much of his time in the Tai-Hun Mountains in the southeast of Shanxi province, where the Communist army set up their front-line headquarters. He got to know the penurious hill villages and often spent his own meagre allowance on helping the poverty-stricken peasants, even helping them in person to do manual work.

When he was visiting eastern Europe in early 1959, he phoned Wong Kar-Tsung from Romania to inquire specifically about economic conditions at home. The day after he returned to Peking, he spent a whole morning talking to Wong about the extent of food shortages in different areas. He was extremely concerned about the serious famine in Gansu province and decided to use army transport to help send grain to the worst affected areas as a matter of urgency.

His attendant disclosed that Peng ate very little on his train ride to Lu Mountain. When he asked: 'Why do you eat so little? Is it because of not sleeping well on the train?' Peng in reply pointed at the window and said: 'Just look outside, how can one swallow the food?' Only then did the attendant spot many hungry, haggard-looking people holding onto the station railings, gazing at the train with an expressionless stare. They were obviously refugees from the famine.

Talking about not having enough food in China was to Mao an unbreakable taboo. Many people in the past, touching on this topic when encouraged by the Communists to speak out, had unfailingly landed themselves in trouble. The Communists had always insisted that nobody could starve to death in Communist China, so the party would never admit that people were dying from starvation right under its nose.

Peng's trouble was not just his mentioning that people were starving; another issue concerned the reorganisation of the armed forces. Modelled long ago on the Russian Red Army, the Chinese Communist army also had political workers attached to every unit, whose job it was to indoctrinate and mobilise the fighting forces. As commander-in-chief of the Chinese People's Voluntary Army in the Korean War, Peng had found the old practices inefficient, confusing and time-consuming. Made defence minister after the Korean War, he had tried to reform the armed forces and in 1955 the PLA was formally transformed into the regular army. Officers were given ranks from second lieutenant to marshal, a total of 13 grades, to replace the imprecise titles of platoon level cadres, divisional level cadres and so forth. They were now paid salaries and obeying orders replaced mobilisation by political sermons. This reorganisation was welcomed by all officers and soldiers, making Peng very popular, but the move clashed with Mao's idea of guerrilla warfare and Mao felt Peng was usurping his army. Peng was later accused of attempting to weaken political work inside the armed forces.

Soon after the Lu Mountain Conference purge Peng was dismissed as defence minister and his job was taken by Lin Biao, whose first action was to abolish all military ranks and salaries. The whole army instead went back to the old system dating from the time of guerrilla war, when all servicemen had been provided simply with certain material needs, plus a small allowance.

Mao's other grudge against Peng concerned his eldest son by his second wife, Mao Oun-Ying. When the Korean War broke out in 1950, Mao Oun-Ying wanted to prove his worth and fight in Korea. While Mao was hesitating, his fourth wife, Jiang Ching, who was jealous of the stepson enjoying his father's favour, instantly made encouraging noises, saying that the chairman's son really ought to be leading by example on the front line. Mao was at last persuaded to let his son go. The party propaganda machine, not missing a trick, dutifully reported that Mao had voluntarily sent his son to the Korean battlefield.

Mao Oun-Ying joined the Chinese People's Voluntary Army as a staff officer. Peng was mindful of not putting the young man at risk and kept the young man close to himself in the relative safety of the command headquarters in a disused mine, a one-mile deep cave which could accommodate over a thousand people. Mao Oun-Ying, however, was headstrong and keen to show off his prowess and before long he was killed in an American air raid.

Mao blamed Peng for not reporting his son's death to him promptly. In fact it was the other members of the party central committee who had decided to wait for a less difficult moment to break the news to Mao, hoping to soften some of his pain. Mao's grievance was of course not about the timing of the report, it was about Peng's failure to give his son foolproof protection.

When the Korean War was over, the party propaganda department instructed writers to exalt the Chinese army's heroic adventure in Korea. Writers heaped praise on Peng for repelling the American imperialists even though the Chinese soldiers were only sustained on poor rations and equipped with backward weapons. Ding Ling, the famous woman writer, announced that she would write Peng's biography.

Such gossip found its way to Mao, who decided that this trend could not be allowed to continue. Ding Ling was bourgeois, while Peng had made mistakes in many previous battles. How could he be so impudent as to have a biography? It was preposterous. Since the great leader himself did not yet have a biography, it was outrageous for any other Chinese person to have one. Mao banned Ding Ling from writing Peng's biography.

Soon after, the CCP became the master of China and it was time for the leaders to relax and enjoy life. One of their favourite recreations consisted of dancing parties held in Central South Sea, which was part of the imperial palace complex – now the Red Forbidden City. Many top party leaders lived inside this exclusive, heavily guarded area. Notable people inside and outside the party were often invited to these social gatherings, which was good for united front work.

The PLA had several cultural service troupes full of pretty young female performers, who were often summoned to the leaders' dancing parties in Central South Sea and were often kept there for several days. These cultural service troupes had many performing duties, as well as rehearsals for dancing, singing and drama. When some performers disappeared for days into Central South Sea, it inevitably caused inconvenience to the discharge of their proper duties. Since the summonses were not issued by Mao himself, the director would often find an excuse to turn them down. The staff of the Red Forbidden City who were in charge of looking after the chairman's welfare felt the need to have their own supply of pretty young dancing partners for the leader, so they tried to form a Central South Sea cultural service troupe. Peng asked them wryly if they were selecting imperial concubines.

The Red Forbidden City eventually kept the cultural service troupe which had once served the Chinese People's Voluntary Army during the Korean War, renaming it the Central South Sea Cultural Service Troupe. All of its members, apart from the band, were young girls whose new duties were to dance with the leaders, usually at weekends. Peng was disapproving, on one occasion remarking that he didn't object to the chairman dancing – although he didn't dance himself. But why did they have to have the Central South Sea Cultural Service Troupe and keep young girls in Central South Sea? If people knew about these goings on, they would use the swear-word. These remarks appeared in an article written around 1990 commemorating Peng, breaching the party's sacred principle of keeping the scandals of the hierarchy firmly under wraps and causing great anger in some of the senior leaders of the day.

Peng also commented that, even if the emperors used to keep 3,000 girls in their harems, the Communists should not copy them. Peng thought that the party hierarchy should be the same as when its headquarters were in Yan'an, when families used to enjoy themselves at weekends together.

Mao's personal physician, Dr Zhisui Li, wrote in his memoirs that the purpose of setting up the Central South Sea Cultural Service Troupe was to provide reliable and young dancing partners for Mao. There was a rest room adjoining the dancing hall for Mao's special use only and Mao often danced into that very private room with a young girl. On one occasion a student from a drama school in Peking was invited to a Central South Sea dancing party. When she was summoned there again through her school's party leadership, she steadfastly refused to go, but would not say why. It was hardly surprising that the girl soldiers of the Central South Sea Cultural Service Troupe were unhappy about their new duties. Distressed and tearful, some of them complained to Peng. Consequently, in his role as defence minister, Peng dissolved the Central South Sea Cultural Service Troupe and assigned all the girls to other jobs; many woman soldiers were demobbed, out of Mao's reach. It was a move that could hardly endear Peng to his leader.

It was common knowledge to senior people that Peng was avowedly against a personality cult. When the Chinese Army's cultural service troupe visited Moscow, he gave orders not to sing *The East is Red*, the adulatory song dedicated to Mao, to avoid being regarded by the Russians as encouraging a personality cult. In 1956 at the National Party Congress, Peng proposed to delete Mao Tse-Tung Thought from the party constitution and he persistently opposed the worship of any person. All these incidents were later counted among his anti-Mao crimes.

On his eastern European tour, Peng ran into Khrushchev in the Albanian capital, Tirana. Peng visited Khrushchev one night in the Russian embassy, where he was kept chatting the whole evening. Once back in China, he sent Mao a report about his conversation with Khrushchev. Mao did not believe him and suspected instead that Peng and Khrushchev had formed a conspiracy to spread revisionism within the party. No matter how much Peng explained, he could not produce a witness, since the interpreter, a Russian Chinese, was condemned as a spy. Peng's troubles were snowballing fast. Mao not only accused him of conspiring with the Russians, he also accused him of collaborating with reactionary forces worldwide, including America.

Having lost his job, Peng was also deprived of his housing privilege and he therefore lost his home in the exclusive compound, so at the end of 1959 he moved out of Central South Sea to a western suburb of Peking. In June 1962 he wrote a long letter to the party central committee and Mao, pleading that he did not found an anti-party cabal and protesting that he was not collaborating with any foreign countries. He appealed to Mao and the party central committee to make a special investigation of his case in order to clear his name. Mao responded by accusing Peng of trying to 'overturn the conviction'. Mao's supporters immediately repeated the accusations, refusing to reopen Peng's case.

In the autumn of 1965, Mao decided to give Peng a lower-ranking job in Sichuan province. Peng turned it down, writing to Mao that he would like to be a peasant in a state farm. On 23 September, the day after receiving Peng's letter, Mao telephoned Peng, inviting him to see him in Central South Sea. In an attempt to persuade Peng to go willingly to somewhere far away from Peking in order to isolate his main target, Liu Shao-Qi, Mao appeared cordial and friendly, waiting outside his residence to greet Peng as an old friend. They had not seen each other since the Lu Mountain Conference. Mao laughed heartily and said, 'Maybe truth is on your side. Now it is our strategy to develop inland, to be prepared for war. Most of our investment is in southwest China and that area is very important. It is good for you to go to the southwest. Perhaps you could still command an army in the future to restore your good name.'

Peng replied with a wry smile, 'There may be trouble for me if I go there.' Mao tapped his own chest and said, 'If anyone disagrees, let him come to talk to me.'

Soon Liu Shao-Qi, Deng Xiao-Ping and Peng Zhen arrived. They shook hands with Peng. Chow En-Lai had another engagement, so he could not come. Discussing the Lu Mountain Conference, Mao said: 'I think we should look at old Peng (De-Huai) in two different ways. In the days when we smashed Chiang Kai-Shek's first, second and third blockades, we cooperated with each other very well. Then there were the three fraudulent letters intended to sow discord, sent to Zhu De, Peng and Wong Kung-Leug and Old Peng sent a special messenger to deliver them to us. In the counter-revolutionary mutiny of Fu Tin, they (Peng and his colleagues) held a meeting and made a public statement denouncing the Fu Tin mutiny. He dealt with that business well and he was also determined to fight against Chang Kwok-Tao's attempts to split the party. His achievements at the northwest battlefields of the War of Liberation can't be denied either. So why discredit someone completely when he makes a single mistake?'

Peng was extremely touched by such considerate and broad-minded comments and thanked everyone profusely. However, on 30 November, soon after he arrived in Sichuan to begin his new job, the *People's Daily* published an article, entitled 'A review of the newly compiled historical drama *The Dismissal of Hai Rui*'. One of the party's old tricks to purge someone was to precede the purge by an open attack on a similar historical figure. Ostensibly the article was a review of a drama, but in fact it was a coded criticism of Peng.

Neither Peng nor those close to him understood what was happening. The central leadership had just given Peng a job, therefore they still trusted him, yet within three months the party's mouthpiece, which was under Mao's strict guidance, was making another attack on him. He was clearly still a marked man.

By the end of July 1966, the Cultural Revolution was already beginning to grip the country. Friends advised Peng to leave Chengdu, the capital city of Sichuan province and escape into the countryside, but he refused, preferring to continue working at his post. Before long posters appeared 'uncovering' his plots, claiming that ever since he had arrived in southwest China he had used all his energy to build up a counter-revolutionary headquarters and was plotting a come-back. He was leaving poison everywhere and was collecting ammunition.

Red Guards began to arrive at his home to make trouble and the situation became more unpleasant by the day. On 24 October 1966, Mao accused Peng at a high-level meeting of collaborating with Gow Gon and Yel Shu-Shi to deceive the party. He had apparently organised the 'Hundred Regiment Campaign' during the Sino-Japanese War with the intention of establishing an independent kingdom without discussing the campaign with Mao beforehand.

As well as offending Mao, Peng also made an enemy of Mao's fourth wife, Jiang Ching. At Yan'an, many senior Communists had been opposed to Mao marrying Jiang Ching and among them Peng had been a very forceful objector. After the two were married, whenever Peng went to Mao's home on official business, he never acknowledged Jiang's presence and Jiang was not the forgiving type.

When Jiang became the brightest new political star in the Cultural Revolution, she urged her followers into action by saying: 'You people are so powerful; how come you cannot even get hold of Peng?' As a result, several groups of Peking Red Guards from different colleges were spurred into action, fighting among themselves for the kudos of kidnapping Peng and bringing him back to Peking. When Chow En-Lai heard about the plot, he informed the military authorities in Chengdu and Peking, telling the would-be-kidnappers that they would be responsible for Peng's safety on his journey.

The Peking Red Guards couldn't wait and the struggle against Peng took place on board the Peking-bound train. In barely more than a year, Peng was back in Peking, where he spent the rest of his life in detention or in jail. On 27 December 1966, the train carrying the kidnapped old soldier rolled into Peking railway station, which was filled with the banners of assorted armed factions. Different groups of Red Guards, backed by Lin Biao or Jiang, were quarrelling with each other, all trying to take Peng as their own trophy. The group East Is Red, from the Geological College, won through sheer weight of numbers and succeeded in bearing Peng back to their college. After some difficult negotiations, Peng was finally handed over to the Peking district army and detained in a poorly furnished room.

Red Guards from different colleges and universities now took turns to molest Peng. In the early summer of 1967, the East Is Red group, which represented the Central Cultural Revolution Small Team, controlled by Jiang, began to interrogate Peng, trying to force him to admit collaborating with foreign countries, being hostile to the party and betraying China. Peng was beaten and kicked and ordered to confess his 'black' (that is, underhand) relationship with Liu Shao-Qi, Deng Xiao-Ping and Marshal Hor Lone, his crimes of opposing Mao's military strategy in the Korean War and his complicity in Mao Oun-Ying's death.

On 19 July, at the instigation of Jiang's followers, the Red Guards from Peking Aviation College, a faction by the name of the Red Flag, took Peng to a small struggle meeting in their college, attended by just three or four dozen Red Guards. They tried to make Peng sign a statement pleading guilty and offering total surrender to the proletarian revolutionaries. When Peng refused to be cowed into submission, he was beaten to the ground more than once and left unconscious.

After this meeting, Peng's condition deteriorated markedly. A report stated that ever since the struggle meeting of the 19th, he had eaten and slept very little, lying down to rest as soon as he was back in his room. He had an aching chest and difficulty in breathing and was groaning continuously and he was also unable to spit out phlegm. On the 20th, he reported that his chest pain had been spreading and getting more severe and that he found it painful to get out of bed. A doctor examined Peng and found two of his ribs broken, one on the left and one on the right and both his pulse and his blood pressure had gone up.

A week later, on 26 July, a struggle meeting against Peng, organised jointly by the East Is Red and Red Flag groups and attended by 100,000 people, was held in the sports ground of the Peking Aviation College. Chang Won-Tian was taken there to keep Peng company; both victims were bound and heavy placards placed around their necks. Near the end of the meeting, the two men were forced to walk through the crowd with heads bowed, where they were punched, kicked and spat at by the bloodthirsty mob. Both men collapsed half way through.

Next, the two bound men with their placards were put on a truck and taken into Peking city, where Red Guards made them bend over, then pressed down their heads and twisted back their arms. They were held in this so-called 'jet style' position and paraded through the streets. When this was finally over, the 69-year-old Peng needed two men to support him from the truck back into his room. He lay in bed, hardly able to move his arms or to walk. At another struggle meeting held in the Workers' Sports Ground, also in front of 100,000 people, Peng was knocked to the ground seven times.

Although his ribs were broken, he refused to kneel down and still tried to stand up. After being taken to a series of struggle meetings, Peng's imprisonment was spent on reading, writing 'confessions' and self-examinations, or being interrogated by investigators.

The special team responsible for investigating Peng's case proposed to dismiss him from all his posts inside and outside the party, expel him from the party permanently and sentence him to life imprisonment, with his civil rights proscribed for life. Accordingly, on 3 November 1970, the sentence was approved.

There was tremendous pressure on Peng's wife, Pu Oun-Shiu. On top of his other problems, the extremely serious accusation that he had collaborated with foreign countries was the last straw and she decided to seek a divorce. Pu Oun-Shiu's elder sister, Pu Zee-Shiu, was a well-known rightist; she was the girlfriend of the arch-rightist Lor Lone-Gi. The Pu family was therefore already in serious trouble and Pu Oun-Shiu found it too frightening to have one more label, the wife of a collaborator with foreigners. Nevertheless, divorce did not help her. In the Cultural Revolution, her whole family was purged. Her younger brother's teeth were all knocked out and she was dragged around by Red Guards over small stones under the scorching summer sun without shoes and socks.

She met Peng for the last time in 1967 when both of them were held in the 'jet style' on the platform at yet another struggle meeting, this time at Peking Normal University. Since she was forced to bend down all the time she could only see part of her husband's shoe from the corner of her eye. She later heard that the Tsing Hua University Red Guards had lined up in two long rows, each person brandishing a wooden rod. Peng was forced to walk through this human alley as blows rained down on him.

Although Peng had expressed the wish that he could spend the rest of his life as a peasant, in the event he did not have the good fortune to till the fields; instead he was sent to the exclusive prison of 'Chin City' outside Peking, where many well known people were kept. There was no central heating, even in the freezing winter, so Peng and his fellow inmates had to chop up firewood for themselves.

In spring 1973, Peng, now 75, became seriously ill and he was transferred to No. 301 military hospital, which was under the control of Jiang and her gang. All the windows in Peng's ward were pasted over with three layers of newspaper to make sure that he could not see the sky and the room was so dark that the lights were kept on during the day. The string for fastening his trousers had been taken away. He wanted to write, but was not allowed to have a pen. He wanted to listen to the radio, but his radio was sabotaged. His watch was taken away so that he did not even know the time. His only companions were books. A soldier stood outside, guarding his ward. In late April 1974, Peng's illness was diagnosed as terminal cancer and only then was his niece, a doctor, allowed to visit him. Before long, one side of his body was paralysed and he became bedridden. A middle-aged soldier now sat opposite his bed all the time, watching him, noting down his every movement and his every word. His most fervent wish was to clear his name and from time to time he shouted that he wanted to see Chairman Mao, that he had never opposed Chairman Mao or collaborated with foreign countries. He seemed to blame only Jiang for his predicament and repeated furiously to his warder: 'Listen, you bastard spy! I curse her, I curse Jiang, that daughter of a stinking tart. You write it down.'

Soon he no longer said anything, instead he spent his time tearing his cotton quilt and, by using his teeth and his still movable right arm, he managed to cover the floor every day with cotton strips. A nurse brought him another quilt, which he tore up the same way, although the weather was already cold.

When Peng was close to death, Jiang's Gang of Four finally gave permission for his ex-wife, Pu Oun-Shiu, to sit at his bedside but, terrified of struggle meetings, she refused. On 29 November 1974, the 76-year-old Peng died a lonely death, with no family or friends at his bedside. His desperate wish to see Mao, Chow En-Lai or Zhu De was not granted.

Over a decade later, in post-Mao China, enormous numbers of people purged in the Cultural Revolution, some dead but some still alive, were at last declared not guilty and had their good names restored. Peng, luckily, was among them. A memorial service was arranged for him and the party leadership inquired about his ashes, but they could not be found. However, many years earlier, the wife of a Sichuan provincial chief, Lee Da-Tsang, had visited Peking and told Pu Oun-Shiu to remember that if Commander-in-Chief Peng were ever rehabilitated, his cremated remains were to be found in the Sichuan party committee office.

The party central office therefore sent an urgent telegram to Sichuan province and his secretary and bodyguard were ordered to take his ashes to Peking. The two men were surprised to hear that Peng's ashes were in Sichuan and nobody knew where they might be. After a search, they found a simple wooden box bearing the writing: 'Wang Cheun, 30 years old, native of Changdu city'. The two men took one look at the box, started crying and refused to take it. This man was surely not their old boss. But staff in the office said, 'You have to understand, if Commander-in-Chief Peng's name had been written on it, who would have dared to keep it?'

A scheduled commercial flight for Peking was kept waiting until two glum-faced men boarded the plane, one of whom was clutching a wooden box. Peng was finally on his way to a place where he could rest under his own name in everlasting peace.

93

Lee Yui's Notebooks

One book which gave accurate first-hand information about the 46-day Lu Mountain Conference was first published in 1988, for the party's internal consumption only. It was written by Lee Yui, a government minister who during 1958–59 had acted as Mao's secretary, taking detailed notes of all his speeches and conversations at the Lu Mountain Conference. Lee Yui's notebooks had been confiscated in the Cultural Revolution but were eventually rediscovered among the Red Guards' archives. The book contained no accusations, only records and so was different from other writings. Lee Yui made it very clear that the Great Leap Forward and the people's communes were launched by Mao, whose aim it was to run the economy himself. Lee recorded how on one occasion in 1958, Mao had banged the table and said, 'Why is it that only Chan Yun can take charge of the economy? Why can't I run it?' Lee also recorded Mao's admission that he had been the inventor of the Great Leap Forward.

Since the summer of 1958, the foolishness and absurdity of the Great Leap Forward had already been obvious to most party members. Chow Siu-Chow reported that 50,000 cottage furnaces had been built in Hunan province in 1958, but 20,000 of them were actually never lit. Chow En-Lai felt truly uneasy about steel production during the Great Leap Forward and before he went up to Lu Mountain on 19 May he sent a three-man team (his own secretary, the minister of the party propaganda department, Luk Din-Yi and an industrial specialist) to investigate the situation along the Tianjin–Pukou railway all the way down to Shanghai. He later received a report about the shocking waste of the cottage steel industry. When there was no proper equipment to convert coal into coke, heaps of coal were burnt on open ground. Only a small portion in the centre could be used as coke, while most of the coal was burnt off for nothing. Many furnaces were built with ordinary bricks instead of fire bricks and therefore could not reach the necessary high temperatures. The iron produced by cottage furnaces contained too much sulphur and was therefore useless, yet this iron was included in the production figures.

Many people, like the Shanghai mayor and party secretary Kor Chin-Shi, lied about their steel projects. Kor Chin-Shi pledged that Shanghai would produce ten million tons of steel annually by 1962. Chow En-Lai's team did their calculations and found that Shanghai could not even cope with transporting the raw materials needed, not to mention the many other problems. In those days party stalwarts insisted that people should not count the cost and anyone who dared mention the problems would get a severe reprimand from their bosses.

The Great Leap Forward proceeded with the claim that China would achieve Communism ahead of Russia. Even though many senior Communists knew the situation was dire, they would not risk speaking the truth and thereby offending Mao. A lot of people were brainwashed idolaters, some were unashamedly obsequious and among them the Mayor of Shanghai, Kor Chin-Shi, won the first prize. He said: 'We must believe in Chairman Mao to the point of superstition; obey Chairman Mao to the degree of following him blindly.'

The discreet Chow En-Lai, whom Peng once called to his face 'a crafty old scoundrel' tried to stay out of trouble. He told Peng to learn to be compliant, saying that he had offended his superiors. On 26 July, Chow made a long speech affirming that Mao's Great Leap Forward was unquestionably right and that they should not have looked only at the financial side. They had to appreciate the political benefits too and it was worthwhile to subsidise the campaign with several billion yuans. Yet Chow could not conceal his worry about how to reach the targets and he urged everyone to work hard to keep the economy going. Finally he mentioned some trivial news: the current year's steel production had to be reduced by some 3.02 million tons.

Liu Shao-Qi, in his 17 August speech, declared that the Lu Mountain Conference had been a great victory for the party. Some people wrongly condemned the Great Leap Forward and the people's communes as mistakes, but this was contrary to the truth. It was a normal revolutionary phenomenon to make mistakes. The most important part of Liu's speech praised Mao as the best leader, better even, perhaps, than Marx and Lenin. Liu proudly announced that he had always wanted to promote a personality cult and comrade Mao's authority in China.

Many people joined in to make concerted attacks, accusing Peng of being a hypocrite, a devious schemer attempting to besmirch Mao's good name and assault the General Guidelines so as to usurp Mao's leadership.

Consequently all party members had to join in urgently to protect Chairman Mao, the central leadership and the General Guidelines. The senior Communists had indulged in party politics and thereby let the nation down.

Members of the 'Military Club' were similarly condemned; Peng, Chang Won-Tian and Wong Kar-Tsung all admitted their 'guilt' against their will, for the good of the party. They were accustomed to obedience and accepted it as their duty.

Before Mao left Lu Mountain on 19 August, he wrote to his aides saying he intended to defy the attack, traducement and doubts regarding the people's communes from foes at home and abroad, from people who did not understand the truth. He gave an order to collect information from peoples' communes all over China for a book devoted to the success of the people's communes. The job had to be completed within three months and he would write a foreword for the book.

The book, entitled *Long Live People's Communes*, was later compiled by the Xinhua news agency. The People's Publishing Company finished its print run before the end of 1960, but by then the communal canteens had already closed down for lack of food. The people's communes were dropping dead in droves and the surviving ones were all terminally ill, as their inhabitants were literally starving to death by the million. *Long Live People's Communes* was quietly dropped; it was a costly still-birth.

Lee Yui was punished for his dissenting views and for speaking his mind at the Lu Mountain meetings and was forced to serve 20 years in a hard labour camp. He joined many of Mao's private secretaries who also ended up in labour camps, prisons or killed themselves. After the Cultural Revolution, in the autumn of 1980, he was rehabilitated. The party leadership encouraged him to write down his experiences as a witness of the important Lu Mountain Conference. His book was banned in the early 90s as party members became increasingly corrupt following China's open-door policy. A backlash surfaced in the form of Mao-worshippers who remembered the Mao era when nearly everyone was poor and most people dared not make money illegally.

94

The Silent Exit from the Great Leap Forward

Copies of Peng's letter were distributed as negative teaching material to senior party members, but ordinary cadres did not have the chance to read it, let alone the public. Many ordinary people held views similar to Peng's after their experiences of villages. Surely it was difficult to claim they were influenced by him. But no matter how mild the disapproval, the critics were all condemned as right-leaning adventurers from rich peasant or other well-off families and they were therefore speaking for the capitalist class. A campaign to silence them was soon underway.

These village visitors, from all walks of life and from many different class backgrounds, were all purged. The party caught a vast number of culprits from all sections of society, only later realising that they had cast the net too wide. Trying to minimise the damage, the leadership decided to expunge all the individuals' dossiers gleaned from the anti-right-leaning campaign. A separate decree made it clear that Marshal Peng was not included in the pardon, because he was ambitious and intended to be dictatorial, so he was therefore different from the rest.

The consequence of the 1959 Lu Mountain Conference appeared with astounding speed. The great famine arrived in 1960 and 1961. It was later revealed that confidential telegrams giving details of the famine were pouring continuously into the offices of Liu Shao-Qi and Chow En-Lai, but Mao never once mentioned this criminal outcome of the Great Leap Forward to any of his close aides – though his penchant for liquidating people was put on hold for a while.

It was later discovered that during the Great Leap Forward, many important national policies, leading to serious consequences, had been signed by Mao without having been debated by the central committee or investigated by specialists. The people's communes were launched with no regulations, no plans, no preparations and no trial projects. The party central committee simply forwarded Mao's personal orders, which were often capricious and contradictory. By now Mao treated the politburo as his

676

underling. The famine unavoidably swelled the ranks of dissidents and sowed the seeds of the Cultural Revolution, when Mao embarked on a 10-year reign of terror to eliminate his political foes.

Before long peasants began dividing the communal land secretly among themselves, so that many areas remained only nominally people's communes. In fact when the authorities had originally swept the peasants into people's communes, some village cadres had secretly allowed their villagers to keep private plots, the produce from which saved many lives.

Not every cadre was willing to compromise party policy. More typical was Pung, a county party secretary from near Tongshan city, who came from peasant stock. Pung had been a militia man during the Sino-Japanese War. He was an extremely loyal party member, who enforced all his leaders' instructions meticulously. When the party decided to root out spontaneous capitalism, Pung organised meetings in his subordinate villages, instructing the peasants to destroy private plots. Whenever he was driven through villages and saw children watering their vegetables, he would stop and chase the children away.

The peasants were naturally unwilling to give up their small private plots. After attending a series of meetings in the villages, Pung's deputy and the county public security chief reported to him about the popular mood and suggested revising the drastic operation. Instead, the two cadres were accused of protecting the 'capitalist way' and severely criticised. Under heavy pressure they kept quiet.

Pung personally supervised the destruction of all private vegetable plots. A peasant in one of the villages had a wife who was in hospital and he had great difficulty in finding the money to pay her medical expenses. He also had a toddler and a blind mother and the family depended on the income from their private vegetable plot. He kowtowed to Pung, begging him not to ruin his vegetables. Finally he pulled out a knife and said: 'Cut me up first before you chop up my vegetables.' Pung was unmoved and ordered his men to get on with the job. The distraught peasant cut his own throat on the spot, to the distress of the villagers. Everyone in the village went to his funeral. On their next visit to the village, Pung's deputy and the public security chief were surrounded by angry villagers; they tried hard to find an explanation. They visited the bereaved family, but could only listen to the blind old woman wailing. The village party secretary also moaned that he too could not go on living any more, because he couldn't face the dead man's family.

The county party secretary, Pung, had of course done nothing wrong; he was only executing party policy and in due course he received promotion. The aggrieved family was given government compensation, but there was nothing else the government could do; after all the man had killed himself.

On 23 February 1962, the central committee, now run by Liu Shao-Qi and Deng Xiao-Ping, issued formal instructions to alter the basic unit of the people's communes from big production teams to small production teams, permitting peasants to keep small private plots and small-scale family businesses. The party also made it clear that people should be paid according to their work, which meant no more Communist egalitarianism or prolonged voluntary labour. Peasants could now legally sell their private produce in the free markets which had been banned from 1958 but which had been revived in 1960. This helped to restart the devastated rural economy and the villagers now returned to the cooperative stage of 1957. There was no chance the party would publicly admit that it had made a terrible mistake, so the name 'people's commune' was retained, maintaining the pretence that the system was still alive.

Although the party formally allowed free markets to return to the villages, it gave no instructions as to where they would stand in the cities. As a result there was confusion in all the big and medium-sized cities, some of which allowed free markets to return, while others steadfastly retained the ban. Several economists made a joint statement in April 1962 at the Political Consultative Conference, pointing out that although the country as a whole should aim to produce enough food, not every people's commune should treat food production as a priority, otherwise industrial raw materials would be sacrificed. They disagreed with the official view that industries should acquire their raw materials locally and produce for local consumption, regarding this idea as untenable since light industries in big cities like Shanghai and Tianjin would not be able to obtain all their raw materials locally. Lastly, they suggested opening up cities for farming produce markets, so as to stimulate production and trade. Three years later they were condemned as being 'anti-socialism' and accused of trying to sabotage the socialist economy.

When the grave results of Mao's economic policy became evident in 1959, some attempt was made to restrain his disastrous influence. On 27 April 1959, Liu Shao-Qi was elected as the President of the People's Republic of China by the first session of the Second National People's Congress. He replaced Mao as head of the government, while Mao remained as Chairman of the Communist Party. To cover up this mild political coup, the party was at pains to explain to the Chinese people that Chairman Mao was still leading the country, but he needed to devote more time to develop important policies and theories. He had therefore given away the onerous administrative work to Liu.

To show that everything was fine, in October 1960 the party arranged for Mao to go on an inspection tour. Following this, an urgent decree about rural work practices was announced to protect Mao and the party, in a desperate attempt to escape responsibility for the economic calamity. The decree contained sentences such as: 'cadres everywhere have not carried out the party central leadership's policy correctly. Chairman Mao has made a special inspection tour to Kunming, Changsha and other areas and has discovered that some cadres strung peasants up and beat them.'

Mao retreated from the stage, leaving Liu Shao-Qi and Deng Xiao-Ping to clear up the mess he had left behind. The two men loosened the iron grip of some of the more extreme left-wing policies, edging towards causing the Great Leap Forward and the people's communes to die a quiet death. Staring at the fact that nearly all peasants wanted to divide the land and that production was much higher when they were farmed as family units, Deng announced in early July 1962 that the party central leadership was considering legalising the division of land among peasant families. On the industrial front they freed the professionals and technicians from the domination of party bureaucrats and in 1963 the economy at last began to show signs of recovery.

When Mao found out about the policy U-turn, he asked furiously, 'Which emperor made these decisions?'

95

Socialist Education

The official face-saving term for the biggest famine in human history was 'the three difficult years'. It was obviously hard for the party to ignore completely the 30 to 44 million corpses produced by its criminal policy. At the 7000 people's big conference in Peking from 11 January to 7 February 1962, even Mao felt obliged to say that the central leadership had had shortcomings and had made mistakes and he himself was primarily responsible. It was an extraordinarily equivocal self-criticism, containing only one short sentence, but many other senior members followed him to make public self-examinations.

However, the conference made clear that the Three Red Flags (Great Leap Forward, great steel production, people's communes) could not be neglected and the Lu Mountain case could not be overturned. This meant Mao's policy and authority remained untouchable. Even though by then the Three Red Flags had already been thoroughly shredded, no one was brave enough to point out the facts.

In the latter half of 1962, peasants began to sell sweet potatoes, yams, sweetcorn and green vegetables, as well as small quantities of pork, a few chickens and ducks in the markets, but there was no fruit except the fast-growing bananas, because nearly all fruit trees had been chopped down and burnt as firewood for producing steel. It would take years for most trees to bear fruit again.

Many urban people could now fill their stomachs perhaps two-thirds full, but they still devoted all their spare time to looking for food and growing their own vegetables. Poor peasants lived on three meals of porridge a day, sometimes supplemented by yams, sweet potatoes and vegetables, while the better-off peasants could afford to have three or four meals of cooked dried rice each week. Often a few months before the summer or autumn harvests, peasants would run out of food again. They then had to rely on a sideline as a source of extra income, or else on wild vegetation gathered in the woods.

On 1 August 1962, Mao wrote: 'The party has executed a series of correct measures in the villages and the economy in more than 90 per cent of people's communes in the country has already achieved a healthy development. Less than 10 per cent of the workers in these areas work in family units and all these people have already changed direction. Such a demand only reflects the desire of backward peasants.'

As the food supply was improving, Mao returned to centre stage. In early August 1962 at a meeting in Beidaihe he declared that dividing land among peasant families meant rejecting socialism and going backwards down the capitalist road. It was class struggle. Mao regarded this issue as the touchstone for true Marxists and he was angry with senior colleagues who dissented, such as the vice premier and Minister for Rural Work, Deng Tze-Qua, who had always advocated allowing each peasant family to work as an independent unit on their own land. Reality had unfailingly demonstrated that this produced the strongest incentive for peasants to increase production.

One of the straying Marxists, Mao's deputy Liu Shao-Qi, promptly made a graceful U-turn as soon as Mao's stance became clear and began to lecture on the importance of a collective economy. In September 1962, at the tenth session of the Eighth Party Congress in Peking, Liu attacked Deng Tze-Qua's ideas. Mao also severely criticised Deng Tze-Qua, claiming that his Rural Work Department had not done one good thing in ten years, as he had always taken the stance of capitalist democratism. He had made the mistake of dissolving large numbers of agricultural cooperatives earlier, promoting lone workers or family units and opposing building up a collective economy.

The party resolution ordered village cadres to compulsorily take back land which had recently been allocated to each peasant family and from now on until Mao's death peasants again returned to working as socialist serfs.

On 9 October 1962, Deng Tze-Qua's Rural Work Department was abolished and his agricultural policy was denounced. In 1965 he was dismissed as vice premier, before being persecuted mercilessly in the Cultural Revolution and banished in 1969 to Guangxi province. Without showing an ounce of repentance, he commented that Chinese peasants were realists and the day would come when China would adopt the family unit system again. Deng Tze-Qua died in 1972, through lack of proper medical care, but he was vindicated in 1980 when Deng Xiao-Ping eventually dissolved the people's communes and resumed the land division policy he had abandoned nearly 20 years earlier.

Mao had kept comparatively quiet about the class struggle in the 'three difficult years', when people were only interested in looking for food. As soon as the people's hunger lessened he felt it was time for class struggle again.

On 26 September 1962, the last day of the tenth session of the Eighth Party Congress, in addition to inveighing against Deng Tze-Qua, Mao admonished the nation never to forget the class struggle. When the Communists were facing annihilation in the 1930s, they had coined a slogan, 'Chinese people don't fight other Chinese.' It was a slogan that touched the nation's heart and won the Communists a lot of sympathy. But now the gullible Chinese people were being told that they had to fight their fellow Chinese every day, every month, every year for ten thousand years.

In October 1962, the Hunan province party committee reported that 25,000 production teams had broken up in 1961 and 1962. The people who supported the division of land into family units included landlords, rich, middle and poor peasants, plus a small number of party cadres. Anhui province made a similar report, where 60,000 production teams were involved. Mao was alarmed, pointing out there was a fierce class struggle going on in China. Landlords and rich peasants were sabotaging the collective economy, attacking poor and middle peasants to usurp their leadership and trying to restore the old feudal rule. Embezzlers, speculators and sinners inside official institutions and the collective economy were collaborating with landlords and rich peasants to do evil.

The party central committee accepted Mao's assertion and decided the nation needed a new purge, which duly began in early 1963. The peasants' resistance to collectivisation was channelled into a class struggle and the class enemy was to blame. Mao said: 'This revolutionary campaign is the biggest struggle since the Land Reform campaign. For more than ten years we have not had anything so inclusive, extensive and thorough. This time the campaign deals with people inside and outside the party, from top to bottom.' He also said: 'We did it in 1952 and again in 1957, but only in urban organisations, universities and colleges. This time we have to make a good job of socialist education in the countryside, spending at least three or four years on it. Let all the demons show up. It would not be sufficient if just half of them appear, because they could still shrink back into their hideouts.'

This 'socialist education' campaign was also known as 'the four cleansings'. It was designed as a detailed examination of people's politics, their attitudes, their finances and their relations with the party. According to Mao, around one third of the power was still in the hands of the enemy or enemy sympathisers. 'We have worked for 15 years,' he said, 'and have now got two thirds of the country. But still a branch party secretary can be bought off with a few packets of cigarettes, not to mention by marrying a daughter off to him.'

In the cities, the four cleansings concentrated upon vetting people's financial integrity, defining their class status and searching for any enemies who passed themselves off as revolutionaries. Lengthy political study sessions, criticisms, self-criticisms and struggle meetings returned to dominate people's lives. Since the disgraced Marshal Peng had held many important positions in northwest China, Shaanxi province was regarded as the centre of his anti-party cabal and naturally was badly contaminated. Consequently socialist education in the province was more left-leaning and more heavy-handed than anywhere else. In 1964, Shaanxi province arrested 6,470 people and detained another 5,000 and in all 3,200 people were expelled from the party. Many middle-ranking government officials were arbitrarily detained while under investigation.

Beatings and illegal detention were much worse at lower levels. Nine university students in Xian city committed suicide when students were made to carry out self-criticism on their revisionist thinking. Some secondary and primary schools searched for and criticised little landlords, little rich peasants and little capitalists, to establish a predominance of poor and middle peasants. In some cases children were driven to run away or even kill themselves.

The literature of Shaanxi province came under strict scrutiny. Nearly all the works on the achievements of local Communist heroes were regarded as dubious material and all documents and literary writings about local or national Communist leaders or martyrs were banned, except those about Mao. The four cleansings fiercely attacked the non-collective rural economy. Some leaders bowed to severe pressure and made self-criticisms on the subject; the deputy chairman and vice premier, Chan Yun, wrote several times to Mao pledging to agree to Mao's line, but forgiveness was not granted. When the Cultural Revolution came, Chan lost his job.

Deng Xiao-Ping, the CCP general secretary and vice premier, came under suspicion because of his infamous theory of cats. Deng had said that 'the good cat is the one that can catch rats; it doesn't matter whether it is white or black.' This meant he supported the more productive system of family units, which became one of his major mistakes. He was purged by Mao twice.

Many regional party leaders also fell down over this issue, among them Hu Kai-Ming, a courageous and open-minded official in Hebei province. Hu was an economics graduate who had been a student leader in the 1936 Xian coup. In 1959 he volunteered to take up a junior position as

683

a city party secretary for Zhangjiakou, a very poor district where ten per cent of the communes were short of food. With bitter winter closing in, many peasants still did not have a single adequately warm garment. Zhangjiakou was vast and sparsely populated and village houses were often as much as two or three kilometres apart. When communal canteens were set up, the villagers had a hard life. Every day they wasted hours making trips to the canteens instead of working on their land. Food rations were meagre; some people ate more than their fair share and this became the source of a lot of friction. People were so despondent they often lost any inclination to work.

Hu brought this problem to the attention of the provincial party committee and asked the authorities to consider closing down the communal canteens. The answer was uncompromising. 'Communal canteens are the strongholds of socialism; Zhangjiakou cannot do without them. Communal canteens can only be improved or upgraded, not suspended or closed down.'

Hu made a personal survey of communal canteens and found that people did not like eating in them. So he risked his neck to close them down in his region. In May 1961, the party formally decided to leave the decision to peasants on whether they wanted to keep their communal canteens. So the canteens began to close down quickly; by this time most communal canteens in Zhangjiakou had already closed down long since.

The 2.8 million people of Zhangjiakou spent the 'three difficult years' in a state of untold misery. In 1961, many peasants sold their clothes and tools to buy expensive grain; some left home to beg for food, while others resorted to selling their children. Although the sowing season was nearly over, large areas of farmland were still abandoned. Hu, extremely worried, tried to find a way to alleviate the peasants' plight and give them an incentive to work on the land.

In the people's communes everyone was paid the same, in order to teach peasants the noble proletarian quality of unselfishness. Wages were calculated from the income of the whole commune and later on from the income of the big production team. Whether they were hardworking or lazy, people were treated the same.

Hu once met a group of peasant women, one of whom talked about a big, strong mule that had died earlier that year. Everyone was laughing, rushing to the scene and waiting to share out the meat. Hu asked why and was told that they were in a big production team, so there was not enough to go round – evidently no one really cared about public property. Hu asked whether, if their earnings were calculated from the income of their small production team, they would be happy when their livestock died. The

684

women, fighting to get a word in, told him that it would be rather as if their own animal had died; they would certainly be in tears.

Another story came from grumbling office workers who in the busiest farming seasons were sent to villages to help the peasants. While these urban cadres acquired sore backs and aching limbs from their hard work in the fields, the peasants, led by their production team leaders, went to town for sightseeing and shows.

Hu also heard about a small group of peasants who produced better vegetables than any of the other production teams. He went to find out the truth and saw with his own eyes some unusually well-grown vegetables and learnt that a small number of people had joined the group of their own free will, sharing all the income directly from their group's production. They started work early, finished work late and were more careful. Before this new arrangement, their vegetables had grown badly, just like all the other vegetable production teams. Yet they were afraid of telling the truth in case they were accused of going down the capitalist road.

After a careful study of peasants' problems, Hu could see perfectly well that when the reward did not match the contribution, any incentive for work was eroded. This meant that egalitarianism did not work. He felt it was better to reform the policy thoroughly and return the responsibility of production to each family.

Hu wrote to Mao in 1962 appealing for a policy rethink which allowed peasants to work as family units. This clashed directly with one of Mao's 'red flags', the people's communes. Mao was as determined as ever to obliterate peasant family units, but many peasants and cadres at grass-roots level did their best to keep the family unit system going in secret.

Mao openly named Hu as one of the wrongdoers and from then on Hu was a target of continuous and intensive criticism. In 1964, he and his two senior officials in Zhangjiakou were condemned as an anti-party cabal, which was later broadened to include three more men. Nearly 10,000 people in Zhangjiakou suspected of having contaminated minds were put through an examination and 14-day training programme. Countless other people were implicated in this case.

When the Cultural Revolution arrived, Hu's fate went from bad to worse. He later recalled: 'When I was taken under guard to face many struggle meetings in the Zhangjiakou communes in 1969, people sometimes gave me bowls of cabbage and buried at the bottom I would find pork and bean curd, things rarely seen in those days. At dead of night, cadres and village friends sneaked in to see me and console me, telling me to have faith in history to make a fair judgement on who was right and who was wrong.'

Hu was lucky enough to see history make its judgement; he was rehabilitated after Mao's death.

Numerous ordinary people were purged by the 'four cleansings' for supporting the peasants in their attempts to work as family units. There were, for example, two young teachers in Jiangsu province, New Wai-Sen and Choi Fu-Min, who wrote to Mao many times in 1961 and 1962, appealing to the leadership to adopt the family unit system nationally. Both were arrested in early 1963; after spending three years in jail under investigation and interrogation, both were convicted of being active counter-revolutionaries and sentenced to ten and five years in prison respectively. Under political pressure, New Wai-Sen's girlfriend married someone else. His brother was also implicated and, after receiving a stern warning from the party he was compelled to leave the armed forces.

The party could see that many village cadres were now going down the capitalist road; they pointed out that people in the past had always sympathised with rural cadres in big and small production teams, because they were all poor and middle peasants, the desirable class background and had given meritorious service during the Land Reform campaign. They were hardworking Communists who had never complained and people therefore forgave them even when they went down the capitalist road. On the other hand, people were irritated by the lawless behaviour of landlords and rich peasants, particularly the rich middle peasants who had made a lot of money in recent years. Popular sympathy for the wrong-thinking cadres therefore had to be stamped on. The targets of the 'four cleansings', the cadres, would spread rumours saying 'the ordinary people will be liquidated first, the cadres later.' But this time it would be different; it would be the cadres first, the ordinary people later.

The central leadership gave instructions on how to run the campaign. Mao said, 'Brave elements can be used for a while. When we began fighting, we relied on villains who were not afraid of death. There was a time when the army wanted to be rid of villains, but I disagreed.' And so villains were used to pursue the socialist education campaign, for they knew how to extort confessions.

The party had led the poor and middle peasants to seize power and property in the villages and made them rural China's rulers. Now the party treated all such people – for example, team leaders, book-keepers and warehousemen of big and small production teams – as prime suspects, even before any evidence had been collected.

In 1964, Mao repeated the same message endlessly: 'The lesson of class struggle is compulsory. All university staff and students should work for the four cleansings in the villages, leaving no one behind... They must also join the class struggle starting from this winter or next spring for five months. Only this way can the intelligentsia learn revolution.'

However, not only university students and staff were sent to cleanse the villages. One hot summer night in 1964, nearly all the communist elite in Peking, including members of the politburo and all the marshals, were summoned to a meeting at which Liu Shao-Qi and Chow En-Lai appeared on the podium. Liu made a short speech telling his audience not to hang around in Peking. They should all go to the villages for a spell to join the four cleansings campaign, as they had to understand the situation and discover new problems. He finished abruptly by saying: 'Anyone who doesn't want to go to the villages will be kicked out there.'

Liu's wife, Wang Quon-Mei, after spending some time in a rural area, had just written a report in which she described many peasant cadres as corrupt and accused them of embezzling public money. Following Liu's speech, Chow advised the audience to join her campaign; he also advised them to invite Wang to give their departments a lecture about her experience in the villages.

On 16 August 1964 Liu wrote to Mao suggesting he should send an overwhelming force to the counties, where they could work under the guidance of provincial party bosses to clean up the cadres at local level. Mao approved of the idea and so from the second half of 1964 groups known as 'big army corps' were sent out to counties all over China. A group of 10,000-strong liquidators arrived in one county to strike at the rotten local cadres and the number of victims increased enormously.

Many liquidator teams, or 'work units' – formed by city people such as teachers, students, blue-collar workers and city cadres – were billeted on the poor peasants. Just as in the Land Reform campaign, people from the work units were required to eat, live and work in the villages with their destitute hosts so as to cultivate trust and solidarity in order to collect information on suspects and build up momentum for the campaign.

Mao had pointed out that the class enemy was behind most of the troubles, so the first mission of socialist education was to stoke up the fires of class hatred. Many people from the wrong class background now found themselves caught. On one occasion, when a work unit arrived at the Stonebridge Commune in Chongqing city, Sichuan province and started to search for class enemies, they discovered a production team leader, Liu Mou-Shing, who had occasionally employed helping hands before the advent of Communist China. Furthermore, his wife had been looking after an old cow, which had just died. His class status as a result of these shocking findings was revised to that of rich peasant, he was accused of sabotaging the production and ordered to write a confession and his fellow villagers were compelled to denounce him. In the end he drowned himself.

Another victim was a certain Wang Ma-Som, who had come back from Hong Kong to the Pool Inn Commune in Jinjiang county, Fujian province. He was now denounced as a robber and a suspected enemy agent, because he was a frequent visitor to Hong Kong and, worse, had a camera and tape recorder. The work unit, however, could not find convincing proof of his crimes. When the higher authorities started to criticise the right-leaning tendency of the campaign, he was quickly labelled a 'bad element' and convicted of being a counter-revolutionary, he was sent to a labour camp for 12 years and eight months. Most cases such as these were decided informally by a small group of people with no legal training.

A landlord, Liu Won-Choi, from the richest family in Dayi county, Sichuan province, became particularly notorious in the socialist education campaign, although he was dead. Depicted by the authorities as a vicious bully who had stopped at nothing in exploiting his tenant farmers, his family home became a centre for national class struggle education at the peak of the propaganda thrust. Every day streams of visitors would arrive at the house, where they were shown a water dungeon in the compound where he locked up peasants who were unable to pay their rent. A female peasant, Lun Yuet-Ying, who had suffered these brutal ordeals, made a whole series of class education speeches everywhere, recalling with emotion the terrible experiences she had endured in the water dungeon. Sculptors created a set of sensational clay figures portraying the fiendish man demanding money with violence.

Liu Won-Choi's ignominy was lifted in the early 90s. His former employees and tenants came forward to testify that he had actually been a kind and compassionate man. Whenever there was a bad harvest he would reduce his rents and some old peasants even said that if it had not been for Liu's charity, they would have starved to death long ago. The story of his water dungeon was also a fantasy; in reality it had been simply used to hide his opium. and had never been filled with water.

As part of their compulsory socialist education, peasants were obliged to attend meetings every night, at which they were urged to report to the work units about their production team cadres' economic crimes, corrupt lifestyle, as well as any instances of their sheltering the class enemy, bullying poor and middle peasants or supporting a private-enterprise economy. Any guilty cadres were taken to struggle meetings in their production teams and any peasants who showed no interest in the sessions were courting trouble.

Many production teams in inland China were very poor and consequently little in the way of public funds passed through their cadres' hands. In the arid county of Zhang Yer, nearly every family lived in extreme poverty. Whenever there was a sunny day, people all sat under the walls sunbathing. Old people went topless and children under 12 or 13 were completely naked because they had no clothes. When the local work units reported to their superiors that the local cadres were clean, they were rebuked for right leaning. Struggle meetings usually succeeded in extracting confessions from at least some victims; figures for money and grain they had embezzled increased daily, often rising to fantastic sums. Those who admitted their guilt but could not repay the stolen goods were beaten and in woo Jiang commune more than a dozen cadres died.

Whenever a cadre who was not a party member was found to be innocent, the higher authorities would deem this conclusion unsafe. When important party officials were reported to have committed serious crimes, the authorities usually would not believe these accusations. There was a case, involving one local party boss who armed himself with a gun and turned up at a villager's wedding night. He kicked the bridegroom out of the room and raped the bride. In another case, a husband protested when his wife was raped by a party boss; the husband was then hung up and beaten. Many lawless senior communal cadres were cleared. Ordinary people could only conclude that party cadres in high positions were protected and the true targets of this campaign were the cadres at grass-roots level, with non-party member cadres as the prime targets. In Fong county, south Shaanxi province, every commune made ordinary peasants the targets of the campaign and some production teams forced every family to pay compensation. Any income they made from selling firewood, vegetables, chicken eggs or even working as child-minders was condemned as the fruits of exploitation and they were forced to pay compensation.

This radical left-leaning policy seriously impeded Shaanxi province's recovery from the Great Leap Forward. All private businesses and markets in rural areas were denounced as 'capitalist tails' and closed down. The liberal Communist leader Hu Yel-Bound learned that in Lan Tan county near Xian city, a big production team's 400 families were raising only 25 pigs. Meanwhile in Chang Oun county, Shaanxi province, 76 per cent of the party secretaries of big production teams were sacked. The cash compensation demanded by the campaign authorities from the three counties – Chang Oun, Yan'an and Xi Shen – stood at 8.13 million yuans. This meant an average reparation of 183 yuans per village cadre, while at the time the average annual income of the destitute people of Shaanxi was only 122 yuans. In the course of the campaign 430 people in these three counties committed suicide.

As long as the campaign lasted, any potentially 'unclean' village cadres were frightened suspects waiting to be sentenced; all were therefore careful and assiduous at work, hoping to offset some of their punishment by merit. When many of them were eventually exonerated from serious corruption charges, their sense of grievance and resentment exploded, particularly in the case of those who had been abused and beaten for long periods. Many began to work less hard, counting the days until they could leave their cadre jobs.

This time most victims of the campaign were middle and poor peasant cadres, the very people the party relied on to keep them in power. There were 26,500 people's communes in the country and the average population in each commune was more than 20,000. If each commune had 300 to 500 victims, this meant between 8 and 13 million people were condemned, though the true figure could well have been even higher.

In January 1965, another directive produced under Mao's guidance instructed the work units of the four cleansings to implement a 'supplementary democracy lesson'. The intended targets this time were those landlords and rich peasants who had slipped through the net or whose previous struggle meetings had been insufficiently ferocious. Now the work units were told to put them through extra struggle meetings as part of the four cleansings campaign.

96

Lee Yuen-Hok, Lan Ping and Jiang Ching

Mao's fourth wife, Lee Yuen-Hok, was born in 1914 in Zhu city, Shandong province, the daughter of an irascible carpenter nicknamed 'the local wolf'. Lee Yuen-Hok behaved badly in school; after quarrelling with and spitting at her teacher, she left school in 1922. She then enrolled in a drama school in Jinan city at the age of 15 and the following year married a school friend. After a few months she left her husband to work as a librarian in Shandong University in Qingdao city. Her new lover, a Communist student called Wong Jin, renamed her Lan Ping and in 1933 she joined the Communist Party.

In July 1933 the Communist underground network in Qingdao was destroyed and Wong Jin was arrested. Lan Ping fled to Shanghai and lost contact with the party. She began to mix with Trotskyites and was arrested in October 1934. In December she made a written statement rejecting the Communist Party and soon afterwards she was released on bail. After Mao's death, the party published her criminal record, which included details of her fraternisation with the Nationalist prison guards.

In the spring of 1935, she started to make a living as an actress working for film and drama companies. Neither a great beauty nor a great acting talent, she never secured any important roles. In April 1936 she married a scriptwriter, but walked out on him after little more than a month – in between her three marriages she had a whole range of casual partners.

When the Sino-Japanese War broke out on 7 July 1937, Lan abandoned Zheng Min, a drama director who was her latest lover and made her way through Xian to Yan'an. Arriving there in August, she met Kang Sheng, an old friend from Shandong province who was now the party security chief. Lan concealed her treachery in Shanghai prison and was recommended by Kang Sheng to work in Lu Xun Art College. She rejoined the party and soon found a new bedmate, Xu Yi-Sin, a senior administrator at the Lu Xun Art College.

At that time, Mao's marriage to his third wife, Hor Tze-Jan, was going through a bad patch, since Hor resented Mao's constant interest in other women. Brought up in a small backwater town, Hor was not well educated and held somewhat strait-laced views. When Mao and the American writer Anna L Strong had a friendly embrace after an interview, Hor was furious because she thought such a thing should only happen between husband and wife, so she went up to the American woman and slapped her in the face. Mao promptly hit his wife and a big fight followed.

In early 1938, the pregnant Hor left for medical treatment in Russia out of pique and Kang and his wife quickly got hold of Lan and installed her in Mao's house. He had once said: 'To achieve a good relationship in Chinese society, to keep a firm footing and be successful, one has to have regard for two factors. The first is teaching, building up the relationship between teacher and disciple; the second is match-making, making good deals between men and women. These two factors not only gain you goodwill, they can even become the foundations for long-term friendship and grace.'

Mao's staff were mostly country folk who were not very good at running a house, so his residence and office were often messy. Lan was glib and knew how to behave herself. She soon made a favourable impression, putting Mao's home and office in good order. She later admitted that every step of the whole process to catch Mao had been made under the guidance of Kang and his wife.

Mao and Lan were soon living together and after three months Mao announced that he wanted to marry her. Wang Si-Yin, a cadre in the Central College for Party Members, knew about Lan's past. He wrote to the titular general secretary, Chang Won-Tian, several times saying that Mao should not marry a woman such as Lan. Chang went to see Mao, but as soon as he opened his mouth Mao made his displeasure obvious and Chang dared not produce Wang Si-Yin's letters. He and his wife were not invited to Mao and Lan's wedding. Wang Si-Yin later became the chief official of Shanxi province and in the early stages of the Cultural Revolution Kang sent his men to Shanxi to beat him to death.

In November 1938 Mao formally announced that he would wed the 21-year-old Lan and he gave her a new name, 'Jiang Ching'. Most party members disapproved of the marriage, sympathising with Hor, who had gone through the hardship of the Long March and was very much one of them. They regarded Jiang Ching as a social-climbing bed-hopper with a dubious past and disreputable moral standards. The fiercest objectors were Chang Won-Tian and Peng De-Huai; they earned the fierce enmity of Jiang, who eventually made sure their final downfalls were as bitter as possible.

The only person who supported the union was the smooth and clever Chow En-Lai, who could see that Mao was already deeply infatuated with Jiang.

To find a way out of this public discontent, Zu De acted as mediator. He told Mao that they could get married, but said that Jiang should not be allowed to hold any important job or to have access to the party's confidential papers; she should not be allowed to use the party's name to pursue any activity in public or to interfere with the party affairs.

These terms were acknowledged by Mao and the politburo and for more than 20 years Jiang had nothing to do with politics. Her most senior position was as a middle-ranking official in the art world and she was fairly isolated from leading Communist circles in Yan'an. However, she was still able to pursue pleasure. From April 1949 to spring 1956 she sought medical treatment in Russia four times. As well as staying in hospitals and convalescent homes, she stayed in Stalin's villa in a Moscow suburb, where her entourage included medical staff, security guards, cooks, chauffeurs, a private secretary and interpreters. She enjoyed watching American and European films, with her own personal interpreter on hand to explain to her what was happening. She also amused herself with games, dancing and photography and on occasion had Chinese fruit and vegetables flown to Russia especially for her.

When back in China she spent her time in city resorts around the country, or in her various luxury villas which all had to be decorated, rebuilt or extended to her specific taste. It was all a long way from her humble days in Shanghai.

Yu Yor-Moo, wife of the vice premier Chan Yun, knew Jiang well from their days in Yan'an. In spring 1962 she visited Shanghai with her husband and discovered that Jiang had three extravagant villas in the city. In 1970, Yu Yor-Moo was thrown into a labour reform farm, yet she still openly berated Jiang as a parasite and the party's biggest exploiter, who luxuriated in the high life.

In 1949, Jiang became interested in photography and was fond of flaunting her photographic flair. As Red royalty, she could not move around freely outside her exclusive compound; she was also pernickety and suspicious when she went into the world of the ordinary people, hence her photos were mostly of flowers, birds, fish and scenery. She would send professional photographers to choose the scenery, set up equipment and watch the weather, often for days. A special telephone hot line was installed for her and when the best conditions occurred she would be informed immediately. She would turn up to press the button and her attendants would deal with everything else.

Towards the end of 1972, Chow En-Lai suggested decorating the state guest houses with Chinese arts and crafts, which had been out of favour during the Cultural Revolution. The proposal was approved by the politburo and so Chinese arts and crafts showed signs of coming back to life. Del Yu Tai state guest house, the No. 18 building inside Central South Sea, consisted of prestigious accommodation used for receiving foreign heads of state. Its bare walls were redecorated with a dozen or so Chinese paintings, all of them the works of accomplished painters. In October 1973 Jiang condemned one of these paintings, featuring a handsome cock crowing at dawn, as a 'black painting'. She insisted that the painting's true intention was to insinuate that the capitalist black arts had been treated badly. On 17 March 1974 she organised her own private 'black paintings' exhibition, sending an invitation to Chow En-Lai for the show.

Before the state visits of two Third World presidents to China in early November 1974, Jiang summoned the Del Yu Tai guest house workers to a meeting, where she criticised the paintings as capitalist in style and said that they must go. But what, asked the workers, were they to do with the empty walls? Jiang agreed they had to have decoration of some sort. Fortunately she had taken some photos of flowers and she would have these enlarged and framed to replace the unacceptable paintings.

Before long her photos were accordingly hung up in the Del Yu Tai guest house. After three days, all of them suddenly disappeared and the Chinese paintings were back on display in their old positions. The security guards, frightened out of their wits, quietly found out what had happened. Mao at the time was touring south China, but he kept his eye on what was happening in the Del Yu Tai guest house. He phoned Jiang in a rage. 'What right do you have to take down the Chinese paintings in the state guest house and hang up your own photos instead? Bloody arrogance! Take them down, take them all down!' A few days afterwards, Jiang's pretended calmness gave way to hysterical anger. In a fury she ran into a courtyard with a big pile of her enlarged photographs, which had cost more than a thousand yuans and set them on fire.

In the post-Mao era, the Chinese government Planning Commission disclosed that all Jiang's photographic equipment and materials had been imported goods paid for out of government funds. On one occasion in 1972 she had ordered the purchase of 60,000 metres of Eastman Kodak colour film from Hong Kong.

Jiang's relations with other people were often strained. She was in the habit of giving other people new names without bothering to ask their permission. According to many she was 'the woman no one likes yet no one

694

dares to offend'. One of her bodyguards, Lee Len-Cheng, recalled how he and his colleagues often had to play poker with her. On one occasion Lee put down an incorrect card, much to Jiang's rage. She threw away her cards and ordered Lee to stand outside in the cold as punishment. He was advised to apologise to her but refused, saying, 'What is there to apologise for? It was only a mistake in a poker game.' He stood there until Jiang finally woke up from her nap and released him. Lee complained to his superior officer, Lee Yin-Chel, who did not like Jiang either, having also had a big row with her over poker.

Another of Jiang's bodyguards, Big Chow, had worked for her for many years. Once, for some trivial reason, Jiang had condemned him as a counter-revolutionary. His superior knew what Jiang was like, so he quietly sent Big Chow away. A few months later, Jiang ran into Big Chow inside Central South Sea and insisted that he should come to work for her again. Big Chow put up a fierce resistance, but his superior officer worked very hard to make the 'counter-revolutionary' return to Jiang.

When Jiang was not sleeping well, Dr Xu Tao prescribed sleeping pills for her, upon which she made a terrific scene, claiming that people who let her take sleeping pills were all counter-revolutionaries trying to poison her. She sacked Dr Xu, leading Mao to say to her angrily, 'Xu is my doctor. What right do you have to sack him?'

There were countless unpleasant incidents stirred up by Jiang. Mao once said to her, 'You cannot get on with anyone and you make enemies everywhere.' He once commented to an aide, 'Jiang Ching has a tongue like a knife and she is hurting people all the time. After I am gone, people will fix her death.'

In 1949, after Peking had been peacefully handed over to the Communists, a group of well-known writers and artists had formed a national association and more than 800 people were invited to its first conference in July to prepare a congratulatory address to celebrate the forthcoming creation of the People's Republic of China. Anyone who had made any impression in the art world and who showed no overt anti-Communist sentiments was invited; their elite status was therefore implicitly acknowledged by the new regime. In reality the association was under the direct control of the CCP Central Propaganda Department. Yet Jiang was not invited. She was in fact snubbed by those in cultural circles. When the Cultural Revolution came, the Culture Department and the Central Propaganda Department were among the first to be smashed by her.

It was an uphill struggle for Jiang to get herself into the limelight and the only field in which she could claim to know anything was the world of the performing arts. Having failed to achieve fame on the stage, she would instead try to make herself known as a political censor. In 1950, *The Secret Story of the Qing Palace*, a film produced by a left-wing film company in Hong Kong, was shown in China. Mainland newspapers on the whole gave it good reviews. It praised Emperor Kwang-Hsu's efforts to seek political reform, while also showing the killing and arson carried out by some of the Boxer extremists. Jiang found political errors in the film and she started insisting that it was reactionary and should be banned. But the film industry authorities and the Party Central Propaganda Department disagreed with her, arguing that it was patriotic and defending it against her barrage of verbal attacks. She sought support from Mao, who was now hard at work putting his new empire in order and did not have time to support her. Only in 1954, when he denounced the research papers of the novel *The Dream of the Red Chamber*, did he mention the film in a letter to the party central committee, writing that 'some people say that '*The Secret Story of the Qing Palace* is a patriotic film, but really it is a film of betrayal. After it was shown all over the country, nobody criticised it.'

And so, after years of being snubbed, Jiang finally came to fame. In 1951 she won a big battle over another film, *The Story of Woo Sheun*. Using Mao's wry argument, Jiang concluded that the beggar educationist, Woo Sheun, was begging for pity from landlords while training immoral helpers for the enemy. Woo Sheun was a bad man; he should have joined the contemporary peasant uprising to overthrow the feudal landlord class.

She collected articles in newspapers which praised Woo Sheun's noble behaviour, presenting all the offensive material to Mao and urging him repeatedly to chastise the 'black gangs'. Mao agreed it was time to purify people's minds and on 20 May a critical essay about Woo Sheun, written by Mao, was published in the *People's Daily*. *The Story of Woo Sheun* was banned and Woo Sheun's 25,000 outspoken admirers were denounced.

Jiang longed to present herself as the standard-bearer of literature and the arts, now that she had successfully demonstrated her political acumen and her potential to raise a cultural storm. Still, she was kept away from any senior position until 1964, on the eve of the Cultural Revolution, when at last her name appeared among the delegates from Shandong province to the National People's Congress. Wang Quon-Mei, the educated and graceful wife of Liu Shao-Qi, was now enjoying praise for her well-received village experience report. Furthermore, not long before, as the wife of the Chinese president, Wang had accompanied Liu on a state visit to Indonesia and this put her in the international spotlight. Mao felt his envious wife could do better.

97

The Breakthrough

In 1956 the term 'Mao Tse-Tung Thought' was deleted from the new party constitution, with Mao's approval and in 1959 Liu Shao-Qi took over the job of President of the People's Republic of China. These changes were seen as signs that Mao's economic policy was failing, his prestige was going down and his power was diminishing. The catastrophe caused by the Great Leap Forward and the people's communes was now gradually turned around, through the efforts of Liu Shao-Qi and Deng Xiao-Ping. By 1964 the economy had revived and Liu's prestige soared within the party. As Mao frequently stayed away from the centre of power in Peking, his influence on policy-making decreased. He felt Liu was challenging his supreme position and he needed to take power back into his own hands.

In the spring of 1965, while Mao was in Changsha city, in Hunan province, he sent for Guan Fung (a literary cadre man) and several others and told them that he wanted their opinions about the nine essays which he was preparing to publish as part of the fifth volume of his selected works. They had all been written in the late 30s, when the Communists were fighting Wang Ming's left- and right-leaning policies and they contained criticisms of many leading comrades, made to clarify Communist policy. 'When we understand the past,' he said, 'we can understand the present and the future more clearly too. There are revisionists inside the party even now, who want to follow in Khrushchev's footsteps and make trouble in China. Could you stop them making trouble? No. They are determined to restore their rule and they have to be fought.'

Guan Fung was puzzled that Mao had not sent for him through central government channels in Peking, instead of contacting him through the Peking office of the Shanghai newspaper the *Wen Hui Daily*. Guan found Mao using some very sharp language to criticise a 'Hu Fu' in his essays; he did not understand the significance of the writings, but he sensed bitter fighting was looming within the party. He did not know then that 'Hu Fu' had been the pseudonym that Liu Shao-Qi had once used.

During the second half of 1964 and through 1965, Mao worked very hard to plan mayhem for the ruling clique inside the party, who he claimed had gone the capitalist way. Looking for a breakthrough to bring the party into a state of fratricidal war, he had considered using either the four cleansings campaign or his unpublished articles.

Mao's political private secretary from his Yan'an days, Chan Bor-Da, said later that from October 1964, when Khrushchev was toppled by Brezhnev, Mao was worried about his own position. He harboured an intense dislike of the leading clique headed by Liu's faction, yet he could not find a good excuse to rid himself of them. The entire population of China was busily engaged at the time in studying Mao's books and he was preparing to publish the fifth volume of his selective works, as well as considering whether to include several articles written long before which criticised Liu, mainly over his mistakes of right-leaning opportunism. According to Chan, Mao had said to him, 'Hurl a few bombs to demonstrate that I am not the same as the emperors. Liu and I are fellow travellers and we are not comrades with the same idea.'

Chan recalled that he had dropped hints to Liu that he should make the necessary self-examination in front of Mao. When Liu heard about Mao's intention of publishing the articles, he asked him to refrain, arguing that it would be harmful to the unity of the party, because Mao had also criticised several other leading comrades by name, including comrade Chow En-Lai. It was in other words very clear in Mao's mind, although no one else was aware of the fact, that no matter from where he launched the attack, it had to lead to the ultimate target, which was Liu. Mao finally found the breakthrough he was looking for in the story of Hai Rui.

As early as April 1959, Mao had mentioned the story of the courageous Hai Rui in his speech to the seventh session of the party's Eighth National Congress. He began by commenting wryly that there seemed to be a tendency to avoid criticising his shortcomings and he went on to say that he had once sent a biography of Hai Rui, who lived during the Ming dynasty, to comrade Peng De-Huai. Hai Rui had been very direct and had written an extremely blunt memorandum to the Emperor Kai Tsing, who had indulged in Taoist magic to search for an elixir and who had done no work during his 40 years on the throne. The emperor had read the memorandum then thrown it to the floor in a fit of pique. He had then picked it up to have another look and thrown it to the floor again, then picked it up once more and thought that actually Hai Rui was after all a good man. Yet he had Hai Rui arrested and, full of hatred, he decided to have him executed.

However, the emperor died, whereupon a jailer congratulated Hai

Rui, telling him that at long last he was going to be freed. Hai Rui thought the jailer was joking, so he ate a huge quantity of meat and rice, thinking he was going to be decapitated. The jailer assured him that he was not going to be killed, for the emperor had died and at this Hai Rui had begun to cry, bringing up all his food. 'But,' Mao concluded, 'our comrades do not have Hai Rui's courage.' Mao also mentioned three letters which Lee Yui, one of his private secretaries, had written to him, commending Lee Yui for giving him just the bones and no meat. He would have liked, he said, to have had some meat to eat as well, but he was still very grateful for Lee's valuable help.

That evening, Lee met Mao's private secretary, Tien Jar-Ying and his former private secretary, Hu Chel-Moo. They had all found Mao's outburst puzzling. Tien wondered whether Mao had taken too many sleeping pills the night before. In his speech he had appeared to be encouraging people to learn from Hai Rui, to be brave and tell the truth; Communist cadres should not do worse than a truthful Ming dynasty official. Hu said that Hai Rui had been mentioned by Mao more than once, although in reality Mao would prefer not to see Hai Rui appear anywhere. Both Tien and Lee thought that Hu was the one who understood Mao best.

Chinese emperors had demanded absolute obedience and worship and giving an emperor a dressing-down would have been unthinkable. Here Mao was publicly praising Hai Rui and inviting historians to study his actions. The deputy minister of the Central Propaganda Department, Chow Young, went to Shanghai to encourage people to write about Hai Rui and produce dramas based on this historical marvel. In this puzzling atmosphere, the distinguished historian Woo Han, who specialised in Ming Dynasty history, gave his considered opinion. Woo was a professor at Tsing Hua University, a deputy mayor of Peking and an undercover Communist; he was also one of the deputy chairmen of the Democratic League. He had once said that in his opinion the League should obey the United Front Work Department. He was a loyal Communist to the point where he believed firmly that all democratic parties should obey the Communist Party.

Woo now wrote an article entitled 'Hai Rui scolded the Emperor', which was published on 16 June 1959. Later on, when he produced an essay commenting on Hai Rui, he was careful enough to ask the party's authoritative theorist, Hu Chel-Moo, to vet it before publication. Following this, the famous Peking opera singer Ma Lan-Leung visited Woo and asked him to write a script about Hai Rui for his Peking opera. Woo knew very little about Peking opera and even less about writing a drama script, but he

699

did not want to disappoint Ma, so he did his best. With some professional help, he produced a script entitled *Hai Rui's Dismissal*, which was performed with Ma playing the role of Hai Rui.

Jiang, at this period, did not have a formal job and she spent a lot of her time watching traditional Peking operas, including some which were banned or rarely performed. After watching Woo's *Hai Rui's Dismissal* in July 1962, she insisted the drama was alluding to reality, trying to help overturn a convicted case. Jiang talked to four ministers and deputy ministers in the Central Propaganda Department and Culture Department, saying that Woo's Peking opera had serious political problems and should be banned. Her suggestion was rejected, but she then pointed out to a deputy minister of the Culture Department, Chi Yan-Min, that there were too many politically incorrect dramas being staged. The Culture Department should pay attention to them.

In the wake of this skirmish, many plays and operas were criticised or banned. In August 1963, all the left-wing films produced in Hong Kong were banned. Jiang herself, who naturally had an incorruptible mind, carried on importing large quantities of capitalist films for herself.

In early 1964, Jiang asked whether Kang Sheng could recommend a good writer with a reliable political background. Her plan was to strike at academic works first and gradually drag the disputes over to the political arena. She told Kang clearly that she saw a possible fight as the means of bringing about a big political storm. The writer would have to be prepared to be sacked, to serve a prison sentence, or even to die, without exposing the people in the background, although when the situation changed then of course they would speak out. The writer must therefore have excellent political consciousness, because the fight would be brutal.

With the assistance of Kor Chin-Shi, the Mayor of Shanghai and Chang Chun-Chel, a Shanghai party boss, Jiang found her writer, Yel Won-Yuan, in Shanghai in 1965 and he was accordingly put to work on savaging Woo's drama. Jiang explained to Kang that Yel's article would have to be published under an individual's name to test the water, to lure snakes out of their holes and to fan up a fire-storm. They needed to go deeper step by step, to reorganise the forces and theoretical warriors of their own class in this fight and also to examine party cadres' consciousness and power.

Kang knew very well that it was actually Mao who was speaking through Jiang's mouth. The secret planning was mainly done in Shanghai's Peking opera house, with Yel having to rewrite his draft nine times. Each time Chang Chun-Chel hid the draft in a film cassette and flew to Peking with it on the pretence of working on a drama or studying the tape to improve the music and Mao amended the draft 9 times. They kept this a secret for seven or eight months, even from Chow En-Lai.

After Yel's tenth attempt, Mao was finally satisfied and the final draft of 'A review of the new historical drama *Hai Rui's Dismissal*' appeared in Shanghai's *Wen Hui Daily* on 10 November 1965. In it, Yel censured Woo openly, sending a shock-wave through academic and cultural circles. People in central government offices and the Peking party committee, with a sense of foreboding, tried to guess the background of the article.

The Mayor of Peking, Peng Zhen, was not pleased that Yel had lambasted his deputy without notifying him in advance. He had seen the opera, he said and it was not all that pernicious. Leading officials in the Central Propaganda Department and the Xinhua news agency felt that Yel's article, accusing Woo's drama of trying to overturn a conviction and arguing that peasants should work their own plots, was just too far-fetched. Over the next two weeks none of the Peking newspapers reprinted Yel's article. Mao, then in Shanghai, was incensed and decided to publish Yel's article as a booklet for sale nationwide. On 24 November China's flagship bookshop, the Xinhua bookshop in Shanghai, was ordered to send telegrams urgently to Xinhua bookshops all over the country to ask how many copies of the booklet they would order. The Peking Xinhua bookshop was instructed by the city party committee to express no opinion. Under pressure it was finally forced to order the booklets on the 29th, but it refused to sell them. Shanghai, dominated by Jiang and Chang Chun-Chel, was locked in a stalemate with Peking. Finally Chow En-Lai was brought in to break the impasse and Peng Zhen was compelled to permit publication of Yel's article. Most people treated the whole affair as a purely academic argument; only the review in the PLA newspaper declared Woo's drama to be a poisonous weed which was hostile to the party and to socialism. Most Peking newspapers stressed that it had to be a fair debate.

Meanwhile Mao was issuing regular broadsides, arguing that the prime evil of *Hai Rui's Dismissal* had been to do with dismissal. Emperor Kia Tsing, he said, had dismissed Hai Rui; they had dismissed Peng De-Huai in 1959 and so Peng De-Huai was also Hai Rui. In other words, Woo was trying to overturn Peng De-Huai's conviction. In fact Woo was neither related to Peng De-Huai nor a friend. Peng Zhen was irritated by the insinuation of links between the two men, telling Mao that they had made investigations and found no connection between them.

This attack on Professor Woo followed sustained assaults on a number of celebrated scholars, among them the economist Sun Jee-Fong, the director of the Economic Research Institute. From 1962 onwards, nearly all Sun's views on cost, profit, bonus, management and similar subjects were criticised, although at first the critics did not name him in person.

Sun Jee-Fong strongly disapproved of the way the Chinese economy was managed, with matters such as costs and efficiency completely ignored. He was particularly disturbed by the appalling waste of the Great Leap Forward and of the people's commune canteens. Many of his colleagues thought the same but kept silent, but Sun Jee-Fong was determined to speak out. He wrote to the central authorities to suggest abolishing communal canteens and also for 'the restoration of the good name of profit'. By autumn 1964, he was condemned as an arch-revisionist who supported profit and self-rule for all business and industrial enterprises. His Economic Research Institute was suspended and its entire staff sent to villages to work for the four cleansings campaign. A work unit moved into his Institute and he was put through more than 40 purge meetings. Eventually he and many of his colleagues were charged with forming an anti-party alliance and in autumn 1965 he was sacked and sent to a labour reform camp. On 4 April 1968 he was transferred to the Chin City prison, where he was held incommunicado, unable to write, read newspapers or see anyone except his jailers and interrogators. Often he was interrogated at midnight, forced to confess his own crimes and report other people's crimes. After eight years he was released, but warned to behave himself. In 1976, Jiang mentioned Sun Jee-Fong in a speech, saying that he was attempting once more to overturn his conviction. He was only finally rehabilitated by the party central committee in 1979 after Mao's death.

Another cultural victim was Professor Gean Bor-Jarn, a famous historian and deputy president of Peking University, who was criticised publicly in December 1965, one month after the publication of Yel's bellicose article. On 24 March 1966, the *People's Daily* and the magazine *Red Flag* published an article simultaneously, entitled 'Comrade Gean Bor-Jarn's historical views need to be censured', which dissected Gean's academic essays published between 1962 and 1964, taking words out of context and concluding that he was a representative of capitalist historians who were trying to oppose the Marxist historical point of view.

Gean, for example, had said: 'Do not idealise the leaders of peasant wars'. This showed that he was twisting and smearing the ideal of peasant revolution. He had urged that historical influences by individuals should be given their due, which showed that he was eulogising the emperors, their generals and ministers. He had always repeated, in discussing major uprisings, that the feudal rulers had had to make concessions to the peasants in order to restore order, which amounted to publicising the idea that concessions by the ruling class had pushed forward historical development. Such arguments were included in the list of Gean's six major crimes in a belligerent article written by Jiang's writers.

On 3 June 1966, following the formal launch of the Cultural Revolution, an editorial in the *People's Daily* gave Gean more condemnatory tags, such as 'the royalist in historical circles', 'the reactionary academic authority of the capitalist class', 'the major rightist who slipped through the net', 'the anti-Communist veteran' and 'Chiang Kai-Shek's henchman'.

Gean was also censured by his university colleagues and students. Even Mao did not forget him. On 18 August 1966, the first time Mao inspected the Red Guards in Tiananmen Square, a girl Red Guard was awarded the glory of meeting Mao on the city wall. Mao said to her: 'Little girl, have your people criticised Gean Bor-Jarn? People like him have studied many books, yet the more they study, the more reactionary they become. But a capitalist academic like him is still useful to our people; he can sweep the floor and clean toilets.'

Within a week, Red Guards went to Peking University to ransack Gean's home and destroy his books and paintings. In the autumn of 1968 Gean and his wife were evicted from their home and detained in a dark room where Gean was subjected to session after session of struggle meetings organised by Red Guards, many of them schoolchildren.

Soon after this Mao commented at a meeting that it made sense for China to retain intellectuals from the old society such as Gean. They could still be of some use because we were able to find out about the emperors, kings, ministers and generals from the professor. When this casual comment reached Peking University, Gean was released from his isolated detention cell and in November he and his wife were allowed to move back into their university quarters. Four days later, he was put through a gruelling interrogation by a special investigation unit set up by Jiang's team. By then Liu Shao-Qi had been condemned as a collaborator for his role in helping the Nationalists during the 1935–36 negotiations between the two parties about their second period of cooperation; Gean had helped in ensuring that negotiations went smoothly.

A fortnight later, in December 1968, a special investigator reported that Gean had been a key figure in the case of an enemy agent and he was ordered to confess his crime. He nodded several times and said: 'Yes, yes, I am the key figure. I will definitely confess.' But that evening, he and his wife took overdoses of sleeping pills and both died.

Young Shan-Jang, a philosopher, member of the party central committee and head of the party's Advanced Training College, also joined the victims of the cultural purge. He was horrified by the sheer mindless behaviour of the Great Leap Forward and in a lecture he commented that in some places it had been 'one per cent realism and 99 per cent romanticism,' a remark which soon caught the attention of Kang Sheng, the chief of the thought police. Young's college party committee was made to criticise him for eight months, but failed to change his views. In July 1964 he was publicly impugned in the *People's Daily* and soon afterwards he was condemned as a traitor, collaborator and counter-revolutionary revisionist. On 18 May 1967 the 71-year-old was sent to jail for eight years on Kang's orders, followed by three years' exile to Shaanxi province. He was finally exonerated by the party after Mao's death, on 4 September 1980.

As with so many other distinguished academics who fell into disgrace, Professor Woo Han, the author of *Hai Rui's Dismissal*, was regarded as yet another of the deviant characters who lurked in cultural circles. In early 1966 a five-man team was set up by the politburo to draw up a formula for a national discussion about the direction of culture. It consisted of Luk Din-Yi, the vice premier and head of the party's Central Propaganda Department and the State Council's Culture Department; Chow Young, deputy head of the Central Propaganda Department; Woo Lun-Cee, director of the *People's Daily* and the Xinhua news agency; Kang Sheng; and Peng Zhen, who acted as chairman. The team held a meeting on 3 February 1966, most members agreeing with Peng that Woo's problem was an academic affair and that his critics should not have over-reacted.

The following day Peng wrote, in an article known as 'February Conspectus', that people should 'persist in seeking facts, insisting on the principle that everyone is equal before the truth. One should win people over by reason rather than behaving like an autocratic warlord, crushing others by brute force.' Kang raised a lone dissenting voice, insisting that Woo's problem was political, because it was connected with the political background of the Lu Mountain Conference.

On 8 February, the five-man team reported their discussions to Mao in Wuhan, in Hubei province. Again Mao insisted that the prime evil of Woo's *Hai Rui's Dismissal* was to do with dismissal and that it was connected with the Lu Mountain Conference and Peng De-Huai's right-leaning opportunism. Twice Mao asked Peng whether he considered that Woo was hostile to the party and to socialism, but Peng did not give him a direct answer. Mao made it quite clear that Woo had insinuated that he had sacked Peng De-Huai. By now he had done as he had intended all along; he had covertly dragged a cultural problem over to a political battle.

At a politburo standing committee meeting between 17 and 20

March, Mao talked about the problem of censoring academic work. He argued that the policy of accepting all intellectuals after the liberation had had both advantages and disadvantages. The intellectuals now held the real power in academic circles; the further the revolution advanced, the more they resisted it and the more it was exposing their hostility to the party and to socialism. People like Woo and Gean were Communists, but they were also anti-Communists, actually they were Nationalists. This problem was still very much misunderstood and many critics had not yet begun censuring academics. However, people everywhere had to pay attention to schools, newspapers, publications and publishing companies and find out who was really in control.

Mao said that China needed a Cultural Revolution in literature, history, philosophy, law and economics, all of which required stern criticism to discover to what extent they were genuinely imbued with Marxism and Leninism. He went on to condemn Peng's February Conspectus as muddling up the divisions between classes and confusing right with wrong and if the Peking party committee and Central Propaganda Department continued to shelter bad eggs, they would have to be disbanded.

Hai Rui's Dismissal was written under Mao's instigation. Although at the time several other dramas about Hai Rui were being performed in other cities, Mao picked on Woo only, because he knew that the Mayor of Peking and the Peking party boss, Peng Zhen, would try to shield Woo, who was Deputy Mayor. When Woo and other leading cultural figures in Peking had been brought down, Peng could then be easily implicated. This would lead all the way to Liu Shao-Qi, since Peng belonged to Liu's camp. Using millions of Chinese people as dupes in his personal power struggle, Mao picked Woo's drama to start his fight, artfully naming it the 'Cultural Revolution'.

Woo was sent to prison, while his wife was locked up in a small bathroom in a labour reform camp until she was paralysed and dying; only then were their young children allowed to take her home, where she died the following day. Seven months later, in 1969, Woo's children were informed that their father had died that morning. He had wanted to see them before he died, but the prison authorities didn't know the children's address. Woo's 15-year-old daughter, deeply hurt by the family tragedy, had a nervous breakdown and after several miserable years she also died.

After Mao's death Gean and Woo, together with many others, were at last rehabilitated. The official term to describe endings such as these was 'They died in difficulty.'

In mid-April, an enlarged politburo meeting was held in Hangzhou, the scenic city near Jiang's command headquarters in Shanghai. Mao said that the air in Peking was too depressing; he didn't want to live there and would rather stay in Shanghai. Peng Zhen went to the meeting at Hangzhou. On arrival he requested a 20-minute audience with Mao, but Mao refused to see him; this meant he was in big trouble. All conference delegates were staying together in the Silun Hotel, but when they went for walks after their meals, no one would walk with or talk to Peng. Occasionally some old colleague or friend found themselves unable to avoid having a few words with him, but they would only talk about the weather. Nobody would dare talk about the business that really mattered.

At the meeting, Mao accused the Peking party committee of being a misguided and close-knit organisation, impermeable to even the smallest drop of water and he maintained that Peng had concealed his true nature for the past 30 years. Peng's associates in Peking were very nervous, because everybody knew that the trouble was only just beginning. On 1 May, Labour Day, Peng failed to appear at the celebrations and on 7 May an alternate member of the politburo, Lee Sher-Fung, was appointed to replace Peng as the first secretary of the party organisation in Peking. The second secretary was also replaced.

When it was known that Mao had savaged Peng's February Conspectus, Liu Shao-Qi told a group of senior colleagues, including Lee Sher-Fung, that Peng had been opposed to him for a long time and that he had frequently told Mao that Peng was hard to control. Peng, said Liu, had often bragged that he had rendered outstanding services, when in fact he was not all that able. Little did the audience know that Liu himself would soon run into trouble.

In mid-May another enlarged politburo meeting was held in Peking. Mao was still away and so Liu chaired the meeting. The first session opened on 11 May. Lee Sher-Fung recalled that Liu looked uneasy and was obviously under pressure. Liu sympathised with Peng; he thought that Peng had made mistakes, but he surely did not deserve to be treated in this way. The air at the meeting was tense. The purgers had made ample preparation in advance. Peng had no right to defend himself and so was isolated from the very beginning. Whenever he opened his mouth, he was promptly rebuked by Kang Sheng and Chan Bor-Da. Liu said to Peng, 'Even now you are still talking tough, but I saw through your inflated individualism some time ago. Why do you hold Chairman Mao's banner so high in order to deceive us? You are a two-faced person feigning compliance; you are the revisionist in the party's central authority.' Kang looked complacent, while Chow En-Lai, careful as ever, did not speak.

On 16 May the meeting voted for the central committee's circular, which had been prepared beforehand. Known as the 5.16 circular, it had been written under Mao's supervision, with a good part of it written by Mao himself. It condemned the February Conspectus as being hostile to the authority of the party, hostile to Mao's policy of Cultural Revolution, hostile to the implementation of socialist revolution and to the left-wing proletariat. It gave a serious warning:

'The representatives of the capitalist class who have passed themselves off as revolutionaries in the party, government, armed forces and cultural circles are in reality a group of counter-revolutionary revisionists. When the time is ripe, they will grab political power and replace proletarian dictatorship with capitalist dictatorship. Some of these people have already been detected by us, others have not yet been discovered. Some are still trusted by us and are being groomed as our successors. Such people, like Khrushchev, are sleeping beside us. Party committees at all levels must pay full attention to this.'

The 5.16 circular disbanded the five-man team led by Peng. The three men most closely involved in producing the February Conspectus were Peng and two deputy ministers of the Central Propaganda Department, Yel Jin and Shee Li-Quen. Peng went to jail; after his release in 1975 he was banished to Shaanxi province. Shee Li-Quen also went to prison, while Yel Jin hanged himself.

A new organisation known as the Central Cultural Revolution Small Team was now formed, with Chan Bor-Da as team leader, Jiang as first deputy team leader and Kang as adviser. Mao issued instructions, which stated: 'The Small Team works under the politburo standing committee and its job is to lead the Cultural Revolution directly.'

Mao's wife, Jiang, was the de facto boss of the small team. Placed above the State Council and directly under the politburo standing committee, which by then was filled with yes-men, this small team was in effect above the government and the party. Mao had made Jiang the second most powerful person in the country.

While plotting for the big internal fight, Mao's main concern was the loyalty of the armed forces and he spent a good deal of time in secret talks. In late 1965 and early 1966, while in Wuhan and Hangzhou, he twice summoned the military chief of the Wuhan area, Chan Jai-Dow and said to him: 'There could be revisionists in the central authority. Who would you listen to, me or somebody else? You have denounced Lor Rui-Chin [the chief of staff of the PLA], but there are more Lor Rui-Chins in even higher positions, all wishing me to resign, damning me as Khrushchev damned

Stalin, forcing me to resign like Brezhnev replacing Khrushchev. All these are possible; don't think that I am making this up. You all have to prepare for this. What are you going to do when such a thing happens?'

Chan Jai-Dow answered without hesitation: 'Chairman, keep your mind at ease. I stand firmly on your side, determinedly fighting all the revisionists to the very end. I only support you, no one else. Someone has mentioned this to me already.' Mao was naturally very pleased with the general for giving him the reply he wanted.

On 30 May 1966, Liu Shao-Qi, Chow En-Lai and Deng Xiao-Ping, all sailing with the Cultural Revolution wind, wrote to Mao with details of their plan to send a provisional work unit, led by Chan Bor-Da, leader of the Central Cultural Revolution Small Team, into the offices of the *People's Daily*. Chan would take control of the newspaper and direct the news broadcasts of the Xinhua news agency, radio and TV. Mao approved the plan the same day.

On 31 May, Chan's team accordingly moved into the *People's Daily*, sacking the chief, Woo Lun-Cee. Chan immediately started work on the landmark editorial for the following day, 1 June 1966, officially unveiling the Cultural Revolution with the following bellicose message:

'Within a few months, many millions of workers, peasants, soldiers, revolutionary cadres and members of the intelligentsia have responded to the party central and Chairman Mao's fighting call and armed themselves with the weapon of Mao Tse-Tung Thought to sweep away the goblins and demons who have occupied our culture and minds. The fight is like a hurricane, swift and fierce, breaking the mental chains of the exploiting class which have been fettering them for so long. All the so-called specialists of the capitalist class, scholars and teachers, will be smashed and their imposing manner sent crumbling to the ground.'

The editorial stressed that the fundamental problem of revolution was political power, without which the people would lose everything. The reality was that in order to recapture his own absolute political power, Mao was plunging the nation into an anarchic ten-year reign of terror.

98

The First Marxist Wall Poster

What better place to detonate the Cultural Revolution than a university, where the natural urge of young people to rebel and reform the world could be easily stirred up to make trouble? On 14 May 1966 Tso Ye-Oul, Kang Sheng's wife, arrived at Peking University with a five-person investigation unit, ostensibly to find out the situation regarding the censuring of academics. Her real purpose was to collect material for bringing down Peking city's party committee. Tso had a number of meetings with Professor Chan Shou-Yi, a member of the Peking University party committee, in which she maintained that the university's performance on censuring academics was insufficiently rigorous. She tried to coax Chan Shou-Yi to denounce the Peking University party secretary, Luk Ping and the leadership of the Peking city party committee, which had a separate department to direct the affairs of universities.

Chan Shou-Yi would not denounce the university authorities and Tso instead turned to a group of young teachers. On 17 May, she summoned the philosophy faculty party secretary, Nep Yuan-Tze, to a guest house near Peking University. After listening to Nep's report about what was going on in the university, she told her to study Mao's 5.16 circular carefully and then to write wall posters.

On 25 May, a wall poster signed by Nep and six young colleagues appeared outside the university canteen denouncing the university party bosses, accusing them of sabotaging the Cultural Revolution; the knife was pointing straight at the Peking city party committee's university department as well. The wall poster ended with three slogans: 'Protect the party central leadership', 'Protect Mao Tse-Tung Thought' and 'Protect proletarian dictatorship'.

The 1957 anti-rightist campaign had taught that Communists were sacrosanct and above criticism and therefore an open denunciation of the university party bosses naturally caused an enormous shock. Most people played safe by sticking to the line taken by the university party committee and therefore when the committee called for a counter-attack, a multitude of wall posters appeared denouncing Nep and her colleagues as plotters, law-breakers and traitors to the party.

Kang Sheng realised Nep was under siege and sent a copy of her wall poster to Mao in Hangzhou, without consulting the politburo. On 1 June, Mao ordered all radio stations in China to broadcast Nep's article in full, calling it the first Marxist wall poster. Although Mao was not in Peking, through Kang he manipulated every move of the Cultural Revolution. On 2 June the new management of the *People's Daily* published Nep's article in full, with the headline 'Seven Peking University comrades have exposed a big conspiracy.' The editorial on the same day, written with the guidance of Chan Bor-Da, appeared under the headline 'Cheers for a Peking University wall poster'. It claimed that the Peking University party committee was not made up of true Communists; it was in fact an anti-party bloc. The *People's Daily* asked all revolutionaries to 'accept the party central leadership, headed by Chairman Mao, unconditionally'. It exhorted the Chinese people to 'fight staunchly against the black gang, which is opposed to Chairman Mao, opposed to Mao Tse-Tung Thought and opposed to the instructions of Chairman Mao and the party central authority. These people must be destroyed, no matter what banners they carry, how high their positions or how senior their qualifications.'

Mao's mouthpiece sent out the messages that Mao's wishes and Mao Tse-Tung Thought, were above both the law and the party and therefore it was perfectly acceptable to trample on the constitution to destroy anyone who disagreed with him. Two months later, on 5 August 1966, Mao wrote in a wall poster about the two articles above: 'The nation's first Marxist Leninist wall poster and the *People's Daily* editorial were very well written; please read them once more!'

The editorial was reprinted by local newspapers all over the country and within a few days had attracted millions of letters and cables in support of Nep and her colleagues. Tens of thousands of people from every corner of Peking thronged round Peking University to offer their support, Nep suddenly became a heroine and Peking University as a consequence became the centre of the Cultural Revolution.

Before long the same process had taken place in a total of 55 colleges and universities, as well as some secondary schools in Peking; campuses were deluged with wall posters denouncing their own party chiefs and deputies, who found themselves dragged to struggle meetings. Classes were disrupted, much to the joy of some students. Class struggle was the order of the day and it quickly spread to other parts of the country.

This was exactly what Mao wanted. One month later he commented approvingly when promoting Nep's wall poster of 1 June, arguing that its writers had the responsibility of pursuing the Cultural Revolution and Mao himself and his group depended on them, the revolutionary students and teachers.

On 9 June, as the student unrest grew, a group of senior party officials – Liu Shao-Qi, Chow En-Lai, Deng Xiao-Ping, Kang Sheng, Chan Bor-Da and Tao Jeug – flew to Hangzhou to ask Mao to return to Peking to deal with the crisis. Mao refused and the group left without getting any clear instructions. Liu worried that the country might easily drift into chaos and that Mao would pin the blame on him. Back in Peking the politburo decided, at a tense meeting, to follow the precedent of sending out work units to control the situation. Liu informed Mao in Hangzhou of their decision and Mao concurred. Accordingly, Chow En-Lai arranged to transfer more than 10,000 people from the armed forces to Peking, where they were sent into colleges, universities and government offices as work units, taking over the administration from the displaced officials.

In fact the newly appointed Peking party committee under its new head, Lee Sher-Fung, had already started just a few days earlier (on the 5th), sending work units into education institutions in an attempt to stop the unrest spilling onto the streets. The work units under Liu's instruction set upon the rebels who were attacking their party chiefs. Within three weeks, by the end of June, nearly 10,000 students had been condemned as rightists, while several thousand teachers in just 24 higher education institutions had been condemned as counter-revolutionaries.

But the rebellious Peking University teachers and students did not succumb easily; instead they successfully encouraged resistance outside the university. The conflict between the rebels and the work units was increasing steadily and some institutions drove their work units away. Tension was increased on 16 June by an editorial in the *People's Daily* commenting on the downfall of the president of Nanking University, Qang Ya-Ming and the reorganisation of the Communist Youth League and Peking party committee. The editorial opined that 'this group has a peculiar logic; anyone who exposes them and attacks their black gangs is condemned as being hostile to the party and to the central authorities.'

The party's powerful mouthpiece pointed out the delicate reality that the 'black gangs' were actually made up of people who had been appointed by the party and who had worked as party chiefs for years. This message sent the students' antipathy to the work units soaring. They began to ignore the work units and instead intensified their struggles against the black gangs.

On 18 June, the rebellious students at Peking University seized more than 60 university party officials, including the chief, Luk Ping and took these black gang members to struggle meetings with their faces painted black and their clothes torn. At the meetings buckets of paste were poured over their heads and posters were stuck on their bodies. They were adorned with tall dunce-hats, made to kneel down, kicked, punched, dragged by their hair and paraded around.

The work unit at Peking University considered that the young rebels' conduct had gone too far and the struggle meetings were broken up with the support of Liu and the Peking party committee. Liu revealed the 18 June incident in Peking university in a bulletin distributed throughout the country, in which he cautioned the public not to be unnecessarily vicious when dealing with party officials.

Liu failed to understand what was in Mao's mind. Even in mid-July he still regarded the campaign as an attempt to eliminate bureaucracy and he thought it would probably all be over by the end of July. One month earlier he had told the new first secretary of the Peking party, Lee Sher-Fung, that he would like his wife, Wang Quon-Mei, to join Tsing Hua University's work unit, because she could learn from the work, improve herself and speak out for the campaign. Lee agreed and said he would arrange for her to go there soon and on 19 June Wang went to Tsing Hua University. In Mao's view she paved the way for Jiang to move from the background to the front of the stage.

In mid-July, the party central committee held a meeting chaired by Liu, at which a vigorous debate took place on some of the measures implemented during the Cultural Revolution. Many committee members supported the decision of Liu and Deng Xiao-Ping to send in work units. On 18 July, the last session of the meeting, Jiang appeared but said nothing and as the meeting was about to break up she left without a word. Lee suspected that something was going wrong.

On the same day, Mao's special train suddenly arrived back in Peking. Liu heard the news and went to see him immediately. There were several cars parked outside Mao's residence and lights in the building were fully on. It looked as if Mao was receiving guests, but Liu was turned away by the guards, who said Mao was tired and had gone to bed.

Jiang and Chan Bor-Da told Mao that the turmoil at Peking University on 18 June was an example of revolutionary action; the work unit restraining the action was suppressing revolution. Mao agreed with them and when he met Liu and other senior figures the next day, Mao bluntly said that it was wrong to send out work units. Some universities and schools had suppressed their student movements, but only the warlords would do such a thing; woe betide anyone who quelled a student movement. Liu had reservations about disbanding the work units, believing that there was no other way to enforce the party's leading role.

The following week, Mao hit out in a number of high-level meetings, accusing the Peking party chief, Lee Sher-Fung, of almost putting out the flame of the Cultural Revolution. 'What are you trying to do?' he asked. 'You decided to give the students leave to pursue revolution, but when the masses rose up you crushed them. What are you thinking?'

'If mistakes were made in higher education,' Liu replied, 'yes, I am mainly responsible. Other comrades have no responsibility for them.'

'Work units are bad for the Cultural Revolution,' said Mao bitingly. 'They hinder the movement. They can neither criticise nor reform. Disband them all!'

Mao used the Central Cultural Revolution Small Team to foment the students' opposition to the work units and ultimately their opposition to Liu. On 22 and 23 July, Jiang and Chan Bor-Da went to Peking University on the pretence of investigating the Cultural Revolution. There they declared support for those who had been chastised by the work units, Jiang declaring that they were the true revolutionaries. She also sent a message of support for a student ringleader who had been locked up by Tsing Hua University's work unit.

On 24 July, Mao made a speech to the politburo standing committee and the Central Cultural Revolution Small Team, full of praise for the latter. Meanwhile Jiang, Chan Bor-Da and Kang, in a frenzy of activity, organised huge meetings on the 25th and 26th at Peking University, both of which were attended by some 10,000 people. On the 27th they went to a meeting at Peking Normal University, at which Kang declared that Chairman Mao had not sent out a single work unit. Chan denounced the work units as obstructing the students' Cultural Revolution and urged that they be disbanded. Jiang appeared to be the most revolutionary of them all. She made a long speech at Peking University, excited to the point of losing her self-control. She poured out stories of family quarrels, disclosing that she was on bad terms with her stepdaughter-in-law. This provided both amusement and bewilderment for the audience.

With Mao's backing, the Central Cultural Revolution Small Team was winning the battle and on 28 July all work units were finally disbanded. All teachers and students who had been convicted as rightists or counter-revolutionaries by the work units were all 'liberated' and on 29 July Liu Shao-Qi, Chow En-Lai and Deng Xiao-Ping were compelled to make self-examinations at a big meeting in the Great Hall of the People, admitting their error in sending out the work units.

From 1 to 11 August, Mao chaired the 11th session of the eighth meeting of the Communist Party central committee. On 4 August he severely criticised Liu, accusing him of being capricious. He had ordered students to suspend their lessons for six months in order to join the revolution, yet when they had begun the work he had denounced them. It was at best a problem of direction, or at worst a policy mistake and it was anti-Marxist. 'Demons and devils,' said Mao, 'are here at this meeting.'

Liu again admitted that he had been responsible for sending out the work units. He had made a mistake, he said and he was not afraid of being sacked. There were five things of which he was not frightened: he was not frightened of being beheaded, of going to jail, of being expelled from the party and he was certainly not frightened of being sacked. He was also not afraid of his wife divorcing him. Everyone had to be prepared for such things.

On the following day, 5 August, Mao put up his own wall poster inside the compound of Central South Sea, bearing the title 'Firing at the command headquarters... my wall poster'. It ran:

The first Marxist-Leninist wall poster of the nation and the editorial of the *People's Daily* were so well written! Comrades, please read them once more. Yet in the following 50 days or more, certain leading comrades from central and local government went the opposite way, adopting the stance of the reactionary capitalist class and practising for the dictatorship of the capitalist class. They struck down the heroic Cultural Revolution of the proletariat, turning right and wrong upside down, confusing black with white, besieging revolutionaries, suppressing different opinions and implementing white terror. They are pleased with themselves at strengthening the capitalist class and destroying the will of the proletariat. How evil they are! Take the right-leaning in 1962 and the incorrect tendency of 1964, when the danger came from the far right, yet looked as if it was from the left; doesn't that make one think hard?

After accusing Liu of being guilty on the issue of the work units, Mao's wall poster claimed that there was another illegal headquarters and that Liu was its evil commander; he tried to make Liu admit that all his life he had been an incorrigible right-leaning opportunist with devious motives.

Mao was tightening the noose inch by inch; his tactic now was to group old sins and new sins together.

The new Peking party chief, Lee Sher-Fung, was also under pressure to examine his mistakes. He later recalled an occasion when Mao had questioned him persistently about Liu's doings, dropping hints in an attempt to make him denounce Liu and Deng Xiao-Ping. Mao had told Lee that, up until 22 August, Liu had still failed to understand the problems exposed in Mao's wall poster. He had claimed to have no hidden motives in pursuing his incorrect policy; he had claimed it was simply a case of misunderstanding and that he had certainly never undertaken any surreptitious activity. But he himself, Mao said, had simply wanted Liu to make self-criticisms relating to some of his past mistakes, but Liu's self-consciousness was not up to it.

Liu was only following the party's established practice of sending out work units, as in the Land Reform and Four Cleansings campaigns. It was therefore a thunderclap to him when he was felled by Mao on this issue, particularly as when Mao was in Hangzhou he had agreed to Liu's proposal to send out work units. In November Liu told friends that, following the central committee meeting, he wanted to play no further part in the Cultural Revolution. Why, he asked, was he still in so much trouble? His wife, Wang Quon-Mei, said that Mao was quite satisfied with Liu's self-examination. Liu worked very hard every day from dawn to dusk and wanted with all his heart to do a good job. Yes, he had made mistakes, she admitted, but it was at a time when Chairman Mao was not directing national affairs and Liu had had to make important decisions.

Liu must have thought that, since he was still President of the People's Republic of China and a member of the politburo standing committee, Mao would be unable to deal him a deadly blow. He and his wife were both totally unaware of and unprepared for, the forthcoming inferno.

99

The Red Guards (1)

The wall poster produced by Nep Yuan-Tze and her colleagues at Peking University on 25 May 1966 whipped up enthusiasm among the students, encouraging them to imitate and even outdo the Peking University rebels. Meanwhile, the campus of the neighbouring Tsing Hua University contained a subsidiary secondary school and a primary school mainly for the children of the university staff. Since the two universities were so close together, any trouble that broke out in one was bound to spread quickly to the other.

On 29 May 1966, several students of Tsing Hua Secondary School had a heated discussion in a small pavilion in the nearby Summer Palace, where they decided to form their own secret organisation. One student suggested that the group should call themselves the Red Guards. Under this group's influence many other secondary school students now formed their own secret Red Guard organisations, naming themselves Red Guards, Red Flag, East Wind and other similar names. They all took vows repeating their determination to protect Red political power, with the support of Chairman Mao. It was their unavoidable duty to liberate the whole human race and all their actions were directed by Mao Tse-Tung Thought. They were determined to shed their last drop of blood to protect the party and the great leader.

On 24 June 1966, the Tsing Hua Secondary School Red Guards put up wall posters propagating Mao's instructions to rebel and pledging themselves to smash up the old world completely. Liu, still in charge of the Cultural Revolution, maintained that the mission of the secondary schools in the Cultural Revolution was largely to vet their staff and all the secondary school teachers in Peking were herded together in their own schools to make self-examinations and confess their misdeeds. With their teachers fully occupied, the students could run wild, getting in the way of Liu's work units whose members regarded the Red Guards as 'underground organisations illegally inciting people and pursuing counter-revolutionary activities'.

Many Red Guard groups were forced to break up, but they tried to fight back. The Tsing Hua Secondary School Red Guards wrote to Mao to seek support and on 1 August Mao replied, giving them his unequivocal backing, thereby transforming the young rebels overnight into anti-work unit heroes. The Tsing Hua Secondary School Red Guards immediately made public Mao's letter. Realising that they would have Mao's blessing, gangs of Red Guards swiftly emerged all over China and as a result all lessons in secondary schools and universities ceased. The students spent several years playing their part in the Cultural Revolution and they never returned to their studies.

Mao felt that in this power struggle he could not rely on either the party or the Youth League, whose first secretary, Hu Yel-Bound, was known as 'little Liu Shao-Qi'. Mao could not rely on the working class either. At an earlier period Liu had been chairman of the National General Trades Union and Liu's successor, Liu Lin-Yi, was not known to be a Mao admirer. So instead Mao chose the more impressionable young students, telling them to 'bring down the people in power' and repeating that 'it is reasonable to rebel.' Mao's henchmen, headed by his wife Jiang, were there to guide and steer the young hotheads to crush his opponents.

In 1964 and 1965, on the eve of the Cultural Revolution, Mao told his nephew, 'Schools should allow students to rebel. Go back there to lead the rebellion.' In May 1966 he announced that 'the education system needs to be revolutionised. The phenomenon of our schools being ruled by capitalist intellectuals must not continue.' Such talk was in effect a mobilisation order and young students duly rose to the bait.

The Red Guards had grown up under the Communist regime and were spoon-fed with the Communist dogma that 'the sky is immense, the earth is immense, but neither of them is as immense as the party's loving kindness. Your father is dear to you, your mother is dear to you, but neither is as dear to you as Chairman Mao'. Now these young people were out to enforce Mao Tse-Tung Thought and to protect their dear leader. They tried hard to look like warriors, dressing themselves in old army uniforms of a faded yellowish colour, which were often too large for them. A leather belt was an important part of their dress code, for it could be readily used as a weapon, especially the metal buckle end, to whip the class enemy. To show they were manly and tough, they liked to use foul language and swear. Groups of Red Guards roamed around on 'confiscated' – in other words stolen – bicycles like wolf packs swooping upon their prey.

As a result of the prevalent brainwashing and suppression of information, many Chinese, especially young people, knew virtually nothing about the outside world, but they did know a lot about class hatred and class struggle. They knew there were five red categories – the offspring of the working class, poor or middle peasants, martyrs, poor city people and revolutionary cadres who had joined the party before 1945. These people were considered to have a good lineage and were therefore 'red and superior'. Those whose parents had joined the party after 1945 belonged to the second class and those whose parents belonged to the five black categories – landlords, rich peasants, counter-revolutionaries, bad elements and rightists – were called children of bitches. Only children who were red and superior were allowed to join the Red Guards.

On 1 July, the anniversary of the Communist Party's foundation, the Red Guards of Tsing Hua Secondary School and the Red Guards of Peking University's subsidiary secondary school held a party for the students from both schools, at which the elite were separated by a cordon from their inferiors, children with a good lineage in front and children of bitches at the back. Even in nursery schools for three to five-year-olds, the children of rightists were spat at and called 'little rightists' and when there were only one or two such children in the class, they would usually sit in a corner because no other children would play with them.

From June 1966, students were encouraged to purge black gangs in their schools – teachers, that is, who were supposedly hostile to the party, to socialism and to Mao Tse-Tung Thought. The prime targets were usually university presidents and school head teachers. The purge soon developed from plain verbal abuse into violence and relations between teachers and students swiftly changed. Students now called their teachers by all kinds of rude and insulting names. Teachers could not answer back, hit back or even beg for mercy; they had absolutely no protection. This was a time when revolutionaries were perfectly free to beat up supposed class enemies with impunity. If the victim hit back, this would be condemned as class revenge or counter-revolutionary aggression.

Many teachers were tortured. Teachers with the wrong class background were naturally to be condemned, but even good and experienced teachers were often condemned as capitalist, reactionary academic authorities. When teachers had criticised or disciplined their students, the students wanted revenge. Good-looking teachers would elicit envy, while ugly teachers would cause displeasure. All were beaten by their students. For example, the head teacher of Peking Normal University's subsidiary secondary school, Gow Yun, was forced to stand in the scorching sun while his students pressed a roll of drawing pins into his forehead and poured boiling water on him. Pupils from Peking's primary schools whipped their female teachers, shaved half of their heads and compelled them to drink urine or to eat drawing pins or faeces. The oldest of these children was just 13.

The Red Guards in effect took charge of all education premises, which they often used to carry out beatings. Although second-class children were not allowed to join the Red Guards, they were allowed to take part in beating people. Usually the most ferocious acts were committed by secondary school students in big cities such as Peking, Shanghai, Nanking and Guangzhou, where there were large numbers of children who were red and superior. Sometimes students were forced to beat their parents. In Peking a young boy was forced to beat his father who was eventually beaten to death; not long afterwards the son had a mental breakdown and showed no sign of recovery after 30 years.

If someone was unable to cope with the gory scene of a class struggle, help could be arranged. Cowardly youngsters might be taken to see the mutilated body of a person who had committed suicide by lying across a railway line. With this salutary lesson, they should be better equipped to cope with struggle meetings.

On 28 July, Jiang told a meeting that although they didn't advocate beating people, neither did they object to it. When good people beat up bad people, she said, it served them right. When bad people beat up good people, it made the good people glorious and when good people beat up good people, it was a misunderstanding, but still the two groups would get to know each other through fighting. Often, when the Red Guards assaulted people or ransacked homes, a member of Jiang's central Cultural Revolution team would mingle with the crowd dressed as a student and spur on the attack. As millions were being terrorised by these 'warriors', Mao commented, 'the more chaotic the better'.

The first teacher to die from beating by Red Guards was a 50-year-old deputy headmistress, Ben Jone-Yun, who had taught for 17 years in a secondary girls' school, a subsidiary school of Peking Normal University with 1,600 students. On 4 August, two other well-known Peking secondary school students assaulted and tortured their own head teachers. This news quickly sent other schools into the same fever and students of Peking Normal University's secondary girls' school started their own attacks.

Another deputy head teacher, Hu Jee-Tao, recalled her ordeal in an article written in 1986: 'In the afternoon of 4 August, several of us leading cadres were 'studying' together in the office. Suddenly seven or eight students ran into the room yelling: 'Black gang! Don't move!' Some of them carried wooden rods, others had whips. They beat us up badly... In the evening my husband saw my weals and asked "How come your school is in such disorder?" I said "The work unit has gone. Nobody is in charge of the school. There is nothing we can do".'

Ben Jone-Yun was among the wounded teachers. When she returned home she told her family that the students could beat a party member, a teacher, to death, just like beating a dog to death. Even so, the following morning, on 5 August, she could not avoid going back to her school as usual. That afternoon, some fourth-year students initiated the beating of members of a black gang. Five senior teachers, including Ben Jone-Yun and Hu Jee-Tao, had black paint poured over them and placards hung around their necks. After being paraded around with dunces' caps, they were forced to remain in a kneeling position or to carry heavy loads. Boiling water was poured over them and they were beaten with rods studded with nails. After three hours or so of torture, Ben lost consciousness in front of the entrance to a students' dormitory and all four other teachers were seriously wounded. Although there was a hospital just across the road, it was two hours before Ben was finally taken there; she was dead on arrival.

The news of the first teacher to die from beating by students was reported to the party leaders, but no action was taken to stop the violence. Within a week, on 11 August, Red Guards at a teachers' training college in Jiangxi province had paraded and tortured 140 teachers and other staff under the baking sun. Four people died.

On 22 August, a Public Security Ministry report was approved by the party central committee and made public. It included an instruction to the effect that 'Using police to suppress the revolutionary students' movement is strictly forbidden.' Three days later, the Xinhua news agency produced a detailed report about the 'little warriors' who had begun a general attack on all the old ideas, old culture, old customs and old habits of the exploiters' class in Peking, Shanghai, Hangzhou, Wuhan, Changsha, Jinan, Nanchang, Zhengzhou, Hefei, Nanking, Fuzhou, Harbin, Changchun, Shenyang, Chengdu, Nanning, Xining, Hohhot, Wulumuqi... in fact virtually all provincial capitals. The report also claimed that the Red Guards' actions enjoyed enthusiastic support from the great masses of the working class and the poor, low and middle peasants. Having received official sanction for mob rule, the violence of the schoolchildren intensified. In Peking's West City precinct, seven secondary school head teachers were beaten to death in August alone.

In Peking the secondary school Red Guards amounted to as many as 20 per cent of all schoolchildren in the city. They soon formed their own picket teams and set up their own torture chambers, labour reform camps and jails in their own schools. The first picket team in Peking was in West City;

many of its members belonged to the 6th Secondary School, a few hundred metres from Tiananmen Square. Here the picket team made a music classroom at the back of the school into a prison, where they forced their prisoners to kneel on cinders or to have a boiling water bath. They burnt their prisoners' hair or cut their buttocks. Some pickets wrote slogans on the walls in their prisoners' blood; 'Long Live Red terror!'

This particular prison was well used; nine teachers found themselves locked up in it for more than three months. Soon teachers were no longer the only targets; schoolchildren with either dissenting views or with the wrong class backgrounds were also taken to struggle meetings and detained. Among them was a 19-year-old sixth-form student, Wang Kwong-Hua, who was the son of a small property owner and therefore a member of the capitalist class. He had also made the mistake of disagreeing with the theory of blood lineage. On 27 September he was seized and thrown into his school prison, where he was tortured badly; he died the following night. Another victim was a retired caretaker, the 80-year-old Xu Pei-Tian, who had worked at the school all his life. He too was condemned as scum, beaten, given a bath in boiling water and then strangled. A property owner, Ho Han-Ching, living near the school was also taken to the prison and beaten to death. In addition to those who died, nearly 30 people were seriously disabled by their torture in this prison.

On 4 August 1966, Red Guards from among the second-year students of Peking Normal University's secondary girls' school decided to purge their classmates who came from 'bad family backgrounds'. Slogans such as 'Down with the children of bitches' were scrawled on classroom walls. There were 40 girls in the class, 10 of whom were Red Guards and thus entitled to sit on chairs, while 20 girls who were not good enough to join the Red Guards but not the children of bitches sat on the floor. The ten children of bitches were made to stand in front of the class and a long rope was used to wrap round their necks to link them together. They were beaten and pressed to confess their own reactionary thoughts and their parents' crimes.

At Peking's No.1 Secondary School 300 students were kept in its school labour reform camp, where the penal system was similar to that of the 6th Secondary School. One prison was in a secondary school attached to the Central College of Fine Arts in Peking. A survivor from this prison, Chang Long-Long, wrote years later about his grim experience. The prison here was on the third floor of the grey school building and prisoners were often taken down to the interrogation rooms and torture chambers in the basement. When Chang Long-Long entered one of these rooms for the first time, he

721

was shocked to find the layout rather professional. Several strong lamps shone in his face and he was greeted by a group of students waiting for him coldly and quietly, fiddling with torture weapons. The smiling leader sitting behind a desk in the dark was the gentle Zhao, his classmate and good friend for the past five years. They used whips, nails and metal rods on their victims and blood would often splash onto their white shirts. They felt no guilt, certain that justice and truth were on their side, enthusiastically singing the praises of one of their colleagues: 'He was really smashing! He kicked the teacher Liu Shun right in his face!'

Before punching Chang Long-Long, one schoolmate said loudly: 'I have never beaten anyone before, but now out of revolutionary indignation and for the people and the motherland...' Chang Long-Long was knocked to the ground. Another teacher, Chang Shu-De, had been in jail several days and was badly injured when Chang Long-Long joined him on the third floor. One day Chang Shu-De was taken to the basement again and never returned. People said he had killed himself there. Another teacher, Jin Tze-Lin, came to take Chang Shu-De's place. After returning from an interrogation, he smashed the glass in the window with his head and tried to jump out. Several student guards dragged him back inside and gave him a fierce beating in front of Chang Long-Long. Another teacher jumped out of a window but did not die, only succeeding in breaking both his legs. One surviving prisoner had a damaged eardrum, while another one had cigarette burns on his cheeks.

After two decades, some erstwhile school jailers became troubled by their consciences. The governor of the school jail, Zhao, sought forgiveness from Chang Long-Long. Zhao said he had been under pressure and was anxious to prove that he was on the right side; he was only a front man. The chief plotters, including people from the Public Security Bureau, had stayed in the background.

Beatings were carried out by groups of Red Guards. Because people were beaten to death by the crowd, no individuals were held to be responsible and no questions were asked afterwards, therefore the Red Guards had nothing to fear. According to figures given by the *Peking Daily* on 20 December 1980, a total of 1,772 people were beaten to death in August and September 1966 in Peking alone and this figure did not include those who had tried to escape being tortured by killing themselves.

Some teachers who did not belong to the 'ruling clique' were allowed to leave the labour reform camps at the end of 1966. But teachers with questionable backgrounds and those who had been beaten to death were forgotten for years. Twelve years later, in the summer of 1978, the *Peking*

Daily reported that some counties and districts had held exoneration meetings or memorial services for the dead teachers. Some bereaved families demanded punishment for the culprits, only to be told that the time for prosecutions had already passed.

On 18 May 1966 Mao's official heir, Lin Biao suggested for the first time the destruction of 'old thinking, old culture, old customs and old habits' and his words were echoed in an editorial in the *People's Daily* on 1 June. On 18 August, when Mao was inspecting Red Guards in Tiananmen Square, Lin again called for the 'little warriors' to take instant action. Red Guards quickly set off to destroy the 'four old things', starting with changing the names of everything. Everything from shops, streets, factories and schools to people and communes were all given new revolutionary names.

On the morning of 19 August, the streets of Peking began to swarm with nearly 300,000 Red Guards, all of them singing a song entitled *Revolutionary Rebellion*, with words taken from Mao's quotation. The Red Guards put up posters proclaiming that they were smashing up the old world and building a new one. There were street assemblies and inflammatory speeches. The road sign of the main thoroughfare, Chang An Avenue, was covered by a sheet of paper bearing the new name, East Is Red Highroad, while Tung An Market became East Wind Market, because it was a revolutionary idea that the east wind overwhelmed the west wind. Peking Union Medical College was renamed Anti-Imperialism Hospital and Tung Yan Hospital was instead named Workers, Peasants and Soldiers Hospital. Tsing Hua Secondary School's new name was Red Guards Fighting School.

On 24 August, 400,000 Red Guards congregated near the Russian embassy chanting slogans such as 'Down with Brezhnev' and 'Down with the Russian Revisionists'. The road where the embassy stood was given a new name, Anti-Revisionism Road and the Peking No.2 Secondary Girls' School, on the same road, became the Anti-Revisionism Road Secondary School.

On the evening of 19 August, a large group of overbearing Red Guards from three secondary schools marched into a famous Peking Duck restaurant, Cheun-Jui-De. They made the restaurant workers break up their sign, which had hung there for more than 70 years and replaced it with a wooden board bearing a new name, Peking Duck Restaurant. The Red Guards then went through every room in the restaurant, tearing to pieces all the scrolls of Chinese paintings and calligraphy, as well as any traditional artifacts they found, including screens, lanterns, flower pots and records of Chinese operas. Instead the restaurant was compelled to buy 100 portraits of Mao and plaster them all over the walls. Ten Red Guards were left behind to live in the restaurant, to act as security workers and to promote Mao Tse-Tung Thought.

On 22 August, the actions of the Peking Red Guards were broadcast to the nation by radio and the following day all major newspapers in the country put the story on their front pages. The *People's Daily* carried two editorials on the same day, headed 'Workers, peasants and soldiers must give the revolutionary students staunch support' and 'Very Good work!' The Red Guards' wanton destruction was highly praised by the party's propaganda machine and it quickly engulfed the whole country.

The Red Guards believed that red and left indicated progress and revolution, so they altered China's traffic rules to force people to walk and vehicles to drive on the left and to make red traffic lights signify 'go' and green traffic lights signify 'stop'. Red Guards would frequently stand alongside the traffic police and railway police and force them to order traffic to move on when the lights turned red, succeeding in causing large numbers of traffic accidents. Eventually Chow En-Lai had a word with the Red Guards, explaining that the old signals were standard all over the world and that red lights were better able to alert people. Promising to consider changing the colours in future, he managed to stop the chaos.

At the instigation of the central leadership of the Cultural Revolution, the Red Guards decided to change the entire country to the revolutionary colour. They forced people everywhere, in villages, towns and cities, to paint all their buildings red, with yellow or white slogans eulogising Mao and his sayings. The interiors also had to be mainly red. China soon became a red ocean in which nearly all buildings looked the same, a state of affairs which caused great inconvenience. On 30 December 1966, the Communist Party central committee and the State Council issued a circular forbidding the practice, accusing it of sabotaging the Cultural Revolution and within a few days the red ocean disappeared.

Fishing, a popular recreation in Peking, was condemned as an 'old habit' and the Red Guards beat up anglers and broke their fishing rods. Soon they also turned their attention to people's appearance, singling out 'five cuts' – long hair, pigtails, permed hair, jeans and pretty skirts – for their disapproval. Women as well as men were warned to cut their hair short. The Red Guards set up stations outside the entrances of schools, colleges and government offices for 'destroying old things and establishing new things'. Equipped with a few chairs and a desk, these places would offer an intimidating haircut service and anyone going in or out of the building would be forced to adopt a revolutionary hairstyle on the spot.

In Lone Moon county, in Guangdong province, Red Guards put up a wall poster in every hairdressing salon in the town declaring that 'having a shampoo after a haircut is a corrupt and pleasure-seeking practice, typical of the capitalist class and should be banned. You are ordered to give up this practice immediately.' The Red Guards threatened to hurl stones at the mirrors if any salon refused to obey. To avoid trouble the salons gave in, but cadre and worker customers were fiercely opposed to the ban, arguing that they spent more than ten hours a day working and studying Mao Tse-Tung Thought; they had no time to wash their own hair, unlike the young devils from the schools who apparently had nothing better to do all day long than to wander around aimlessly. The customers put up their own wall posters, signed with the names of Red Guards, saying that 'giving a customer a shampoo is to serve people better and accords with the patriotic and hygienic movement.' After citing some of Mao's sayings to strengthen their argument, they ordered the salons to 'restore the service at once, or be responsible for the consequences.' Hairdressing salons in Peking were given orders to ban all manicures and massages, while dental departments in hospitals abandoned the practice of cleaning patients' teeth. All these actions were aimed at rooting out capitalist decadence.

The Red Guards also took it on themselves to direct Chinese people's attire. Clothes of European or traditional Chinese style would be torn up or cut into strips. Some Red Guards from Peking's 6th Secondary School one day spotted a teenage girl wearing a floral pattern skirt. They dragged her into their school, beating her and asked indignantly, 'Is this a proletarian dress?' The school caretaker said a few words in a vain attempt to help the girl out of her trouble, so he was also beaten severely. The Red Guards' questions were often not easy to answer. On one occasion a group of Red Guards whipped a foreign language student, demanding to know why, being a Chinese, she was studying a foreign language. Footwear did not escape the critical censorship of the Red Guards. People who were found wearing high heels were forced to throw away their shoes and walk barefoot, while the fronts of leather shoes would be chopped off if they were pointed.

On 23 August, a group of university Red Guards in Peking went to the Summer Palace in the western suburbs to break up old statues and other relics of the old world. The same thing happened in many other well-known temples and parks, with Mao's portrait replacing all the defaced scrolls.

Confucius had stipulated the Chinese code of conduct for three thousand years, but now that China had Mao, there was no more room for Confucius in Chinese history. So on 9 November, 200 Red Guards from Peking Normal University travelled with an army of rebels to Qufu, Confucius's home town in Shandong province and announced they had been sent by the Central Cultural Revolution Small Team to destroy everything to do with Confucius. The Confucius temple and palace in Qufu had been designated as a protected cultural heritage of national importance by the State Council in 1961 and the local authorities – the Shandong province party committee, the Qufu county party committee and the Confucius temple management – tried to stop the Red Guards from destroying the historical relics. But the Peking Red Guards, supported by Red Guards from local schools, held a public meeting attended by 10,000 people at which they agreed to send a letter of protest to the State Council. They then began to destroy the site. They gouged out the eyes of Confucius's statue in the temple, dug a hole in the position of his heart and stuck posters all over the statue calling Confucius the number one rogue. They then toppled the statue, loaded it onto a truck and paraded it through the town, before breaking it up and setting it alight. In addition to destroying Confucius's tombstone and levelling his grave, they also dug up a coffin belonging to one of his descendants and exposed the corpse. They defaced all the tablets, statues and carvings on the site and set fire to its buildings and cultural relics.

The Peking Red Guards stayed in Qufu county for about a month, during which they destroyed 6,618 cultural relics, burnt 900 scrolls of paintings, calligraphers' writings and 2,700 ancient books, more than 1,000 of which were rare and valuable. More than 1,000 historic stone tablets were damaged, including more than 70 grade one objects designated as being of national cultural importance.

Such wanton destruction took place everywhere. Some of the losses were in the Ming Dynasty valley of kings near Peking. This site contained 13 mausoleums and one of the underground palaces, Ding Mausoleum, now attracts a huge number of tourists. On 24 August 1966, Red Guards arrived in the valley. They began by smearing the large sign reading 'Ding Mausoleum' with paint. They proceeded to drag the corpses of Emperor Wan-Li and his two empresses out of the mausoleum, piling all the portraits and other burial articles they could find around the corpses. Amid yells of 'Down with the headman of the landlord class', they hurled rocks at the three corpses, reducing them to fragments and then set fire to the pile. After the Cultural Revolution, the authorities made three replicas of the big coffins to replace the originals.

The Red Guards tried their best to control the minds of the Chinese people. They regarded all books, whether Chinese or foreign, ancient or modern, particularly any book concerning Chinese history, as feudal, capitalist and revisionist poison. There was a ban on reading books, except for Mao's selected works and the Little Red Book of his quotations, the 'fragrant flowers' which the Chinese people were coerced into reading. Although the works of Karl Marx and Friedrich Engels had not yet been declared harmful, people were cautioned by the deputy chairman, Lin Biao, that the era of Marx and Engels was far too remote for China and that the Chinese people should instead spend 90 per cent of their time reading Chairman Mao's works. Under Mao's instigation, all books found by the Red Guards were torn up or burnt. If there was not enough time for complete destruction, brick walls were built to seal up complete libraries. Not even the humble libraries in secondary schools escaped and it was not until years later, when the Cultural Revolution was finally over, that libraries were allowed to reopen.

Cemeteries were not excluded from the Cultural Revolution either. Many graves belonging to 'reactionary' people and their families and any graves which looked in any way feudal, capitalist or revisionist were vandalised. Several graves belonging to distinguished literary masters were destroyed in this way and any tombstone in Peking's Eight Treasure Hill public cemetery with the word 'Mister' inscribed on it was damaged, because this was regarded as a special term used only by the capitalist class. Three such graves in the cemetery were dug open and the remains smashed, eight tombstones were destroyed and 45 others were badly damaged and thrown away. The images on 64 tombstones were broken and a total of 120 graves vandalised, nearly a quarter of the graves in the cemetery.

Another victim was Woo Sheun, the Qing Dynasty beggar educationalist, who was buried in Shandong province. On 27 August, a group of teachers and Red Guards from local secondary schools destroyed Woo Sheun's grave and dug up his corpse. After parading it through town they held a meeting where the corpse was put on public trial. It was later broken up and burnt. Also destroyed was the grave of Hai Rui, the Ming dynasty official who had dared to criticise his emperor and who was buried on the island of Hainan. After the Red Guards had destroyed Hai Rui's grave, they tortured and killed the old caretaker.

Also destroyed was the grave of Zee Kor-Fa, the Ming Dynasty hero famous for his last stand against the Manchurian conquerors in Yangzhou city, Jiangsu province. The temple containing his shrine was left in ruins by the Red Guards, but was repaired after the Cultural Revolution. A similar fate overtook the grave of the Soong Dynasty hero Yue Fei, who had defended his country against foreign invasion and who was buried near the scenic West Lake in Hangzhou. Yue Fei's grave was classed as an important item of cultural heritage and had been placed under special protection by the State

Council, but this did not stop the Red Guards from wrecking the grave. It was finally repaired in 1979.

On 29 August, 1,000 revolutionary teachers and students in Canton assembled at the Yellow Flower Mound, the collective burial place of 72 comrades of Sun Yat-Sen who had given their lives to overthrow the monarchy in an attempt to turn China into a democracy. The revolutionaries denounced the Statue of Liberty erected on top of the monument as evidence of imperialist and capitalist poison. They claimed that the 'So-called liberty, equality and universal love are merely fig leaves used by the capitalist class for covering their shameful deeds. In the old society, working people only had the liberty of being oppressed and exploited. We are the masters of the country now and we will not give the capitalists and revisionists any liberty. We will bury the old world completely, create a new world and make sure the proletarian enterprise lasts forever.'

After the Statue of Liberty had been convicted of these heinous crimes, the revolutionaries attacked the statue with hammers, amid resounding applause and shouting of 'Long live Chairman Mao!' and 'Long live the proletarian Cultural Revolution!' Similar scenes took place in war cemeteries all over the country, where the graves of soldiers who had died fighting in the Sino-Japanese War were also vandalised by Red Guards.

With China's historical relics, arts and crafts facing annihilation, a small number of brave people tried to rescue what they could. The calligraphy of the brilliant Soong Dynasty poet Soo Tung-Ball was exquisitely carved on 126 stone tablets set into a garden wall near the city of Wuhan. Before the unavoidable visit from the Red Guards, the caretakers whitewashed the stone tablets and wrote some of Mao's sayings on them in red paint. When the Red Guards arrived with their big hammers, they were dumbfounded. One of them accused the caretakers of playing devious tricks and pretending to be revolutionaries. He swung his hammer round to strike at a tablet, but the hammer landed on the character 'Mao' of 'Chairman Mao'. Immediately someone in the group screamed, 'Grab the counter-revolutionary! Protect Chairman Mao with our lives!'

The hammer-swinging warrior was promptly denounced as a 'counter-revolutionary criminal caught in action'; he was bound and forced to undergo a struggle meeting on the spot. He was severely beaten, then sent to a public security bureau where he was sentenced to ten years' hard labour.

The calligraphy of Soo Tung-Ball survived the attention of the Red Guards, but the famous stone carvings at the Lone Moon Caves in Luoyang, Henan province, were not so lucky. Many of its small statues of Buddha were decapitated. In Anhui province, the Red Guards destroyed large numbers of beautifully carved and gilded wood panels featuring ancient Chinese figures which had decorated the village houses. A few panels were saved because their owners had had the foresight to cover them with posters of Mao's sayings. Everything to do with Mao, of course, was sacrosanct.

The frenzy of 'destroying the four old things' quickly reached the minorities. The poor and middle peasants from a commune in the suburbs of Wulumuqi city, Xinjiang province, marched into the city, banging drums and gongs, yelling slogans and carrying placards offering the Red Guards their support. One small production team near Kunming city, Yunnan province, gave their village a new name: Revolution New Village and all 64 families in the village's small production team bought new portraits of Mao and posters of his sayings to decorate their homes. Tibetan peasants from six villages near Lhasa city sent 280 people to the city to support the Red Guards. The huge Jarsalebu monastery in Xigaze city had been designated back in 1960 as an important national cultural heritage under the protection of the State Council, but this did not stop the Red Guards from ravaging the site, destroying pagodas and manuscripts, statues of Buddha, five tombs of Panchen Lamas and the temples which housed their shrines. Inner Mongolia abolished its age-old annual festival to commemorate Genghis Khan.

Ransacking private homes was an important part of the campaign to destroy the four old things. Groups of Red Guards would barge into homes, shouting and swearing; they would order everyone outside and place guards on all the doors. Based on information provided by the local public security force, they would seize those 'runaway landlords', 'women of the landlords', or 'rightists who have slipped through the net'. They would force their prey to kneel, then whip, punch and kick them and demand to know where the black gang hid the title deeds for their land and their secret ledger. There would be further beatings if they did not get a satisfactory answer.

The Red Guards would take away virtually everything in the house, including clothes, beds, bedding, furniture and valuables, all of which would be stacked up on a waiting truck outside the house. They would trample on children's toys for fun, smear sesame paste on walls, pour oil, soya sauce, vinegar, salt and sugar everywhere and dig holes in an attempt to find any title deeds, secret ledgers, guns or ammunition. Any household goods they planned to leave behind they would smash up. Red Guards from other schools might visit the same families too and some houses were ransacked more than 20 times.

According to incomplete statistics, Peking managed to salvage 117 tons of metal cultural relics from copper refineries, more than 3,200,000 tons of information and reference books from paper mills, 185,000 scrolls and paintings, 2,357,000 old pictorial books and 538,000 mixed cultural artifacts from several collection centres which housed the confiscated material. Out of the 6,834 ancient cultural heritage sites listed by the first Peking city survey in 1958, as many as 4,922 were destroyed, most of them ruined in August and September 1966.

The Peking Red Guards would order the families of their victims to return to their home villages, despite the fact that many had never even been to these villages and public security police would soon appear to deliver ultimatums telling the families to leave the city. During August and September, 85,198 people in Peking were sent back to the villages and 33,695 homes in Peking were ransacked. Between 23 August and 8 September, 84,222 homes were ransacked in Shanghai and 64,056 in Suzhou city.

While residents of Peking were being arbitrarily banished, thousands of Red Guards congregated to guard the main entrance to the railway station. When the evicted people arrived to catch their trains, looking pallid and carrying their sparse possessions, the young rebels would find themselves overwhelmed by class hatred and would use their leather belts to give the 'black gangs' a good beating. Some of the five black elements regarded as having serious problems were escorted into the station by Red Guards through underground passages lined on both sides with other Red Guards carrying whips. The 'bad eggs' would emerge bloody and bruised.

In late August, the Minister of Public Security, Sher Fu-Jee, gave a speech to the staff of the Peking Public Security Bureau, telling them not to feel restricted by past regulations, whether of the national government or of the public security organisation. 'I don't advocate the masses beating people to death,' he said, 'but when the masses hate the bad people and we fail to dissuade them from beating those people, then don't try to stop them.' He emphasised that the Public Security Police should support the Red Guards and supply them with information about the five black categories. At a meeting attended by the public security chiefs from the provinces of Gansu, Shaanxi, Hubei and many of the country's major cities, Sher Fu-Jee said that they should not be too concerned if the Red Guards beat people to death. 'We should not operate by normal rules and regard such acts as criminal… If you detain or arrest the attackers you will be making a mistake.' On 26 August, Sher Fu-Jee's speech was circulated to all offices of the Public Security Bureau and the bureau in Dacin county, near Peking, immediately provided the local Red Guards with information on black elements in the area. By then, incited by the party propaganda machine, Red Guards were emerging everywhere in China and nearly every group was a law unto itself.

On 27 August, peasant Red Guards from 48 big production teams belonging to 13 communes in Dacin county sprang into action to rid the Chinese Communist paradise of class enemies. They went to the village of Dasinzhung and, in the space of three days, killed a total of 325 landlords, rich peasants and their families, either hacking them to death or burying them alive in an old well. The oldest was 80, the youngest was just 38 days old. Twenty-two families were completely wiped out. The Red Guards sent letters or telegrams to family members living elsewhere, asking them to return home but failing to tell them that their families had been killed and that they were actually being summoned to their deaths. On 1 September, the Peking city party secretary, Mar Li, went to Dacin county and managed to stop the wholesale slaughter.

The many different groups of Red Guards of Dacin county renamed their county 'Red Flag county'. Each group began to issue handbills in enormous numbers, all headed 'Urgent orders'. One group ordered all businesses to move from the cities to the villages, on the grounds that most people in cities were evil, while others called for the uprooting of Roman Catholicism.

The Red Guards of Dacin county descended on the nearby labour reform farm and demanded to know who were the worst demons and devils among all the inmates. It was all too clear that those locked up in the cells answered best to this description and accordingly the Red Guards opened the cells and gave all the inmates a severe beating. One man was locked up simply because he refused to make a self-criticism.

Sher Fu-Jee's instructions were loyally obeyed everywhere. The public security police would tip off the local Red Guards, leading to a frenzy of beatings and torture. Many secondary schools and universities would organise regular meetings as a means of purging anyone from the five black categories among the local residents. At one secondary school affiliated to the University of Agriculture, as many as 130 teachers and students from the wrong class were beaten in a single meeting on 26 August.

The Dasinzhung massacre was lauded as the 'revolutionary act' of the Dacin county Red Guards and before long many 'supreme courts' of the poor, low and middle peasants sprang up in the suburbs of Peking and in Guangxi and Hunan provinces. These 'courts' sentenced countless political prisoners and their families to death, to be killed by a wide variety of hideously cruel means.

One year later, one of the most anarchic regions in the country was Mao's home province, Hunan. A certain primary school teacher, the 52-year-old Chow Cheun, lived in Yuanshankou, a subsidiary village in Dow county.

731

Chow Cheun's husband had lent 100 yuans, a considerable sum at the time, to Tong Shin-Hou, the party secretary of a big production team. When Tong became head of the village's 'supreme court', the first group of people he targeted were Chow's family, in order to avoid having to repay the loan. On 26 August 1967, Chow's entire family of five, together with another 20 people from 'bad family backgrounds' were taken by 'court' order to a mountain, where they were beaten around the head with iron rods and thrown unconscious into a deep hole. When Chow came round she found that her husband, their three children and one other woman who had landed on top of the dead bodies were still alive, but her husband and the other woman had already gone mad. After screaming for several days, the two mad people died; one after another her three children also died, but miraculously she clung to life and seven days later she was at last found and rescued. Tong, the culprit, was finally punished many years later, in 1985, by expulsion from the party.

Dow county spent 88,234 yuans and gave 421,095 catties of food as rewards to executioners. One man sent to carry out executions reported back to his 'supreme court' after killing 19 people, but the 'court' leader told him that it was difficult to work out the reward for 19 executions, so he should go back and kill one more person to make a total of 20.

In Dow county, in the 66 days between 13 August and 17 October 1967 a total of 4,193 people were killed, with a further 326 driven to suicide. The killings involved 36 communes and 1,590 production teams, with a total of 2,778 families. The victims included Communists, members of the Communist Youth League, poor, low and middle peasants, government cadres and demobbed soldiers. In all, more than 10,000 people were killed in Dow county alone during the whole of the Cultural Revolution, but the Dow county killing spree fanned the fever in ten neighbouring counties too.

The killers were put on trial in the 1980s, but the courts usually sympathised with them on the grounds that the crimes had been committed in a unique historical period under the influence of extreme left-wing attitudes and if the defendants showed a good attitude by admitting their guilt they were treated leniently. The result was that many murderers were simply expelled from the party.

These extreme left-wing attitudes were strenuously promoted as the Cultural Revolution was unveiled on 1 June 1966. The new management of the *People's Daily* promptly launched a campaign to glorify Mao's thoughts and from the following day the paper carried Mao's sayings daily as front-page headlines.

On 4 June, the *People's Daily* carried an editorial headed 'The new victory of Mao Tse-Tung Thought' and on 6 June both the *People's Daily* and the PLA newspaper published front-page articles with enormous headlines reading, 'Raise high the great red flag of Mao Tse-Tung Thought, carry on the proletarian Cultural Revolution to the end'. On the following day both newspapers carried an editorial headed, 'Mao Tse-Tung Thought is the telescope and microscope of our revolutionary enterprise,' claiming that 'Chairman Mao is the red sun in our hearts, Mao Tse-Tung Thought is our lifeline. Whoever is hostile to Mao Tse-Tung Thought, no matter when or whatever 'authority' he is, we, the whole party and the whole nation, must attack him.' All Chinese newspapers and magazines informed people regularly that 'Mao Tse-Tung Thought is the communal wealth of revolutionary people,' or that 'Mao Tse-Tung Thought is the lighthouse of revolutionary people in the world.' There were reports too about people in other countries longing to read Mao's writings and of foreigners heaping lavish praise on him.

There were reports too about the enlightened thoughts of Chinese soldiers after they had studied Mao's works. One soldier said that 'Chairman Mao's books are not gold, they are more precious than gold. They are not steel, they are stronger than steel,' while another said that 'Every sentence in Chairman Mao's books is both a war drum and the truth.' On 26 July, an editorial in the *People's Daily*, headed 'Following Chairman Mao forward in high wind and big waves', proclaimed that Mao's swim on 16 July across the Yangtze River, which had lasted one hour and five minutes, was exciting news for the nation; billions of people cheered Mao's good health and wished wholeheartedly that he would live forever. There were reports of Mao's precious sayings during his swim and more calls for people to follow him forever. Some people later calculated that according to the propaganda, the 73-year-old Chairman Mao had swum faster than a steamer.

On 20 July, the party central committee announced the setting up of a committee to compile Mao's collected writing and on 1 August the *People's Daily* carried an editorial urging that 'the whole country should become a vast school of Mao Tse-Tung Thought.' A week later the *People's Daily* announced 'the great happy event for all Chinese people', the central committee's decision to print Mao's collected works. Four days later, the first batch of Mao Tse-Tung's selected works, in four volumes, was issued to several universities, where large meetings were held to receive the 'treasure books', which were given out free of charge.

Newspapers began to dwell enthusiastically on Mao's guiding principles for the Cultural Revolution, which had been 'approved' by the party central committee on 8 August. Meanwhile reports appeared daily about the breathtaking sales of Mao Tse-Tung's selected works. All the Xinhua bookshops, nearly 70 of them in Peking alone, were decorated with red lanterns, large posters featuring the character for 'double delight' and slogans reading 'Make a big effort to study Mao Tse-Tung Thought', or 'Carry out Mao Tse-Tung Thought loyally, disseminate Mao Tse-Tung Thought enthusiastically, protect Mao Tse-Tung Thought bravely'. Noisy drums, gongs and firecrackers helped to create a festive mood and long queues moved slowly and patiently towards the huge piles of treasure books.

The *People's Daily* reported that the four volumes of Mao Tse-Tung's selected works in paperback were selling at just two yuans, so that every Chinese person could have a set and almost overnight 98 per cent of Chinese homes were adorned with the great leader's portraits and sayings.

Millions of Red Guards, spellbound by the Maoist cult, made their way to Peking, the revolutionary Mecca, hoping to get a glimpse of the great leader, their 'reddest, reddest, reddest sun' and Mao did not disappoint his worshippers. The first meeting, organised by the Central Cultural Revolution Small Team, was on 18 August 1966. Beginning at one o'clock in the morning, a million people collected in Tiananmen Square and finally, at dawn, Mao himself appeared, wearing a PLA uniform, standing on Tiananmen city wall with other senior Communist officials. Chan Bor-Da, leader of the Central Cultural Revolution Small Team and a member of the politburo, delivered an opening speech in which he referred to Mao as 'the great leader, the great tutor and the great helmsman'. The next speaker, Lin Biao, said that Mao was the highest commander of the Cultural Revolution and it soon became accepted practice throughout the country to add the prefixes 'the great leader, the great tutor, the great commander and the great helmsman' before every mention of Mao's name.

After inspecting the parade, Mao received a Red Guard's armband from a secondary schoolgirl who placed it around his left arm. He went on to meet Red Guard representatives from Shanghai, Tianjin, Wuhan, Guangzhou (Canton), Harbin, Wulumuqi and other cities and group photographs were taken.

On 31 August, Mao inspected a further half million Red Guards in Tiananmen Square. On this second occasion his official heir, Lin Biao, wore a Red Guard armband and openly extolled the Red Guards to the skies. Again on 15 September Mao Tse-Tung inspected a further one million Red Guards. On this third occasion, Lin made a speech praising the Red Guards and their struggle. Chairman Mao and the party supported them fully, he said and their revolutionary action had shaken the whole society and the dregs left behind by the old world. 'You have achieved glorious results in the fight for destroying the four old things and establishing the four new things. You have confounded the ruling clique who have been going down the capitalist road; you have confounded the capitalist class and the reactionary authorities, those bloodsuckers and parasites. You have done the right thing. Well done!'

This speech took place shortly after the massacre in Dasinzhung and the beatings to death of school teachers and a fortnight or so after the Minister for Public Security, Sher Fu-Jee, had told his staff to ignore the law and constitution and to give the Red Guards a helping hand.

From 18 August to 26 November, Mao ascended Tiananmen city wall eight times to inspect gatherings of Red Guards. In that period he saw some 11 million impressionable, naive and frenetic youngsters, firing them with enthusiasm and giving them licence to terrorise the nation. He encouraged them with sinister words, saying that his party, his government and he himself were unable to solve the problems of the class enemies; only the Red Guards could do so. In return the Red Guards offered him their boundless loyalty. They would swear that their hands would not let go of Mao's books, their mouths would not stop talking about Mao's sayings, their actions would not stray from Mao Tse-Tung Thought and their hearts would not be separated from Mao's teaching.

Red Guards were often heard telling their victims, 'We have the backing of Chairman Mao, it means nothing if we beat you to death.' They also knew that ransacking private homes and helping themselves to their victims' property were also endorsed by the great chairman. Often after a parade, gold nuggets would be found on the ground of Tiananmen Square, left behind by absent-minded warriors; some were even found on Tiananmen city wall.

Lin Biao was at the forefront to flatter Mao and to encourage his personality cult. Back in March 1964, he had instructed the PLA propaganda workers to use Mao's sayings whenever possible and in May the PLA political department compiled and published the Little Red Book, *The Quotations of Chairman Mao*. When the Cultural Revolution erupted in 1966, studying Mao Tse-Tung Thought and Mao's sayings seemed more important than water and air and the Little Red Book became world-famous. On 28 September, the *Kwang Ming Daily* reported how three Red Guards, of various ages and from different schools, had appeared on buses to recite Mao's quotations to passengers. During the 40-minute bus ride, each of them had recited nearly 100 of Mao's quotations by heart and the youngest could even recite them in reverse.

Meanwhile, members of the Political Consultative Conference, which included many famous people such as the last emperor, Pu Yi, distinguished scholars, senior Nationalist defectors and veteran democracy fighters from the eight small parties, regularly spent their time in political study groups, reading and discussing papers about the Cultural Revolution; they met twice a week for three hours each time. Feeling uneasy about the unfathomable situation and worrying that they might say something wrong, they all declared their support for the Cultural Revolution. The meetings were often very quiet and the leader of each group would often read out long articles to kill time.

In the small hours of 24 August, a group of Peking Red Guards delivered 'ultimatums' to all the small parties, ordering them to place announcements in the newspapers within 72 hours that they had dissolved. The Red Guards reckoned these parties represented all the quintessentially bad things from old China. The following day all the offices of these small parties duly closed, displaying posters explaining that they accepted the Red Guards' ultimatum and would therefore dissolve themselves. They would request the CCP central committee to decide their future.

In the afternoon of 24 August, 13 members of the Industrialists' and Businessmen's Democratic Party were taken to face struggle meetings and during the next few days about 100 senior people, equivalent to one third of all the members of the small parties' central committee in Peking, were put through struggle sessions and their homes ransacked. Before long it was the turn of the Political Consultative Conference, whose members arrived one day to find the front door of their office sealed. Their political study groups were forced to come to a halt and instead they 'studied' at home.

Madame Soong Ching-Ling had been helpful to the Communist Party for decades and had once been deputy chairman of the People's Republic of China. She lived in a Qing Dynasty palace in central Peking. The Cultural Revolution reached her in the form of a warning letter from Red Guards, ordering her to cut her long hair, which she had been wearing for a long time in the traditional Chinese style with a bun at the back. Ignoring the letter, she did not change her hairstyle and contented herself with replacing some of the paintings on her walls with Mao's sayings. She was furious when her parents' graves in Shanghai were destroyed and she complained bitterly to Chow En-Lai, who immediately ordered the Shanghai revolutionary committee to repair the damage. Photos were sent to her afterwards to prove the job had been done, but she was still more upset when news came from Nanking that the Red Guards intended to smash the bronze statue of her late husband, Sun Yat-Sen, in his mausoleum. On 1 September Chow En-Lai had told the Peking Red Guards:

Sun Yat-Sen was a capitalist class revolutionary, but he had merits as well as faults. His wife, Madame Soong Ching-Ling, has never given in to Chiang Kai-Shek since she started cooperating with us. When the revolution suffered a setback she rescued our party's workers. She cooperated with us during the Sino-Japanese War and was on our side during the War of Liberation. She has worked with the party for a long time and has never changed her mind and we ought to respect her. We are going to commemorate Sun Yat-Sen's 100th birthday this year. Her writing would have great influence internationally, so it would be counterproductive to put up wall posters at her home. She is the only revolutionary among her three sisters and we should not attack her simply because her sister is Chiang Kai-Shek's wife. Her house has been allocated to her by the nation. Some people have said that they want to take action against her, but this is not right; we must, no matter what, dissuade them from doing so... Sun Yat-Sen's merit was confirmed by Chairman Mao a long time ago and his name was inscribed on the Monument to the People's Heroes. We disapprove of the Nanking students' idea of destroying Sun Yat-Sen's statue. It was Chairman Mao's decision to put Sun Yat-Sen's statue in Tiananmen Square on 1 May and 1 October every year.

During the Cultural Revolution, Madame Soong Ching-Ling wrote to Mao and the central committee seven times to voice her disapproval of the situation and she refused to attend meetings and festival activities, using illness as an excuse but saying too that she had no wish to become a political decoration.

In late August, Chow drafted a list containing the names of people who he suggested be given protection, subject of course to Mao's approval. The list contained a few dozen people, with Madame Soong Ching-Ling's name at the top, followed by celebrated Communist fellow travellers and the chiefs and deputy chiefs of the National People's Congress, the Political Consultative Conference, the State Council, the ministries, the small democratic parties and the Legal Department. On 1 September, Chow ordered the exclusive Hospital No. 301 to take in some of these people to shelter them from the Cultural Revolution and on 3 October he told the Red Guards: 'We need to retain the Chinese People's Political Consultative Conference. Chairman Mao is still its honorary chairman and I am its chairman too.'

While Chow was trying to protect this handful of lucky people, countless numbers of Chinese people were living at the mercy of state-sponsored terrorism. On 29 August, an editorial in the *People's Daily* headed 'Salute our Red Guards' praised the Red Guards for shaking up Chinese society, the old world, so quickly. Their fighting prowess was unstoppable and they were sweeping away all the old customs and habits of the exploiters as if they were discarding garbage. None of the old parasites hiding in dark corners would be able to escape their sharp eyes, as the bloodsuckers and enemies of the people were dragged out one by one. Their hidden gold, silver and treasures had already been taken and put on display, as well as their hidden account books and murder weapons. These were the Red Guards' great achievements.

In late August a party of Red Guards went to the home of Cheng Ber-Jeun. After being accused by Mao of forming an anti-party alliance with Lor Lone-Gi in the anti-rightist campaign, Cheng had been sacked from his government positions, but he had been allowed to remain on the standing committee of the Political Consultative Conference. Following the party decision and Chow's instructions, he was allowed to keep his large house and car and he still enjoyed privileged living standards.

Wang Tung-Lin, a writer and government cadre, who had worked for the Political Consultative Conference for several decades, described two incidents he had seen concerning Cheng Ber-Jeun. Around 29 August 1966, office workers at the Political Consultative Conference, who had heard that Cheng's home had been ransacked by Red Guards, were surprised to see Cheng's car drive into their office compound. Three Red Guards, two girls and one boy, all dressed in yellow army uniforms with red armbands and black boots, got out of the car. They asked loudly, 'Where are your bosses?' By then the people of Peking were all frightened of these posses of teenage rogues and since these CPPCC workers did not know their visitors' intentions, they dared not make a sound.

One of the girl Red Guards yelled, 'Are you all deaf?' She proceeded to give them a lecture. They should let the whole Conference know that Cheng Ber-Jeun, the arch rightist, had committed heinous crimes, but despite this they were still providing him with a private car, a large detached house, a private secretary and a cook. Such capitulation was disgraceful; it caused every cadre in the country to lose face. 'Let me tell you,' she screamed, 'that ever since we, the Red Guard little fighters, seized Cheng's old lair, several schools have already denounced him at struggle meetings and made him stink. In just a few days we have achieved the great task of proletarian dictatorship which you couldn't achieve in ten years [Cheng had been condemned as a rightist in 1957]. We have just been to the Department of United Front Work to show them our fighting achievements, warn them to forget their ideas of capitulation and to wash away the dirt from inside their brains. We have come here for the same purpose. Where are your bosses?'

A brave man among the staff answered, 'Our bosses have all gone out to meetings, but we will definitely pass on the message from you, the Red Guard little fighters, to them.'

'All right, we are very busy and we don't have time to chat,' said the boy. Then he shouted harshly, 'Cheng Ber-Jeun, you old bastard, crawl out quickly.' The staff were all puzzled. They could only see a driver in the car; there was no sign of Cheng anywhere. But the boy warrior marched up to the car, opened the back door and roared once more, 'Get out!'

Now the staff could see Cheng, wedged in the footwell in front of the back seat. He crawled out slowly, covered in dust and looking lost. There were obvious injuries on his face. One girl warrior shouted, 'Cheng Ber-Jeun, do you admit your guilt?'

'I do,' Cheng answered in a feeble voice.

'Speak loudly.' It was a sharp command.

'I do. I have committed enormous crimes,' Cheng cried with all his strength.

The boy was now prepared to leave and told Cheng to crawl back into the car. Cheng crawled back into the same footwell, his obese body just managing to squeeze in. The three warriors settled on the back seats and three pairs of feet trod on Cheng's body. The car drove away, leaving the onlookers speechless.

A few days later the senior cadres at the office of the Political Consultative Conference told some of their staff to call at the ransacked homes of the senior members. They were to express full support for the Red Guards' revolutionary actions and at all costs avoid any clash with them. They could try discreetly to find out the situation and ascertain whether any government property had been taken away or destroyed.

Wang Tung-Lin joined the group calling at Cheng's home, which had been taken over by Red Guards from the August The First Secondary School (August the first was anniversary of the PLA's foundation). As most Red Guards were out at the time pursuing the revolution, only a few were left behind to keep watch. The handful of callers found the house in a sad mess, with torn books, rags, socks and shoes strewn everywhere and furniture turned upside-down. Antiques, paintings, scrolls, old books, clothes, bedding and other valuables had all been taken away in trucks while

Cheng and his wife had been evicted from the main building and forced to live in a small house in the compound.

Wang Tung-Lin and his colleagues heard yelling noises coming from where Cheng now lived. Dashing across the compound, they saw Cheng and his wife being confronted by three Red Guards, who had ordered Cheng to crawl out from his 'dog's den' and recite some of Mao's sayings. The couple, clutching their Little Red Books, stood trembling in front of the door of their small house.

One Red Guard read out a sentence and told Cheng to recite the rest. The nervous Cheng made a small mistake, whereupon the Red Guard instantly lashed out at him with a broad leather belt, shouting, 'You bastard, how dare you misrepresent Chairman Mao's saying.' Cheng fell down backwards into the small house, giving the Red Guards a good laugh.

His wife grabbed hold of the leather belt and said hastily, 'He is an old fool. I will recite on behalf of him. I will do it.' Without waiting for an answer, she quickly recited the saying, 'Reactionary things will not tumble down if you don't attack them. It is like sweeping the floor; if you miss a spot, the dust there will not disappear by itself.'

Wang Tung-Lin's group was standing at a distance. Laughing, the Red Guards turned round; one of them said, 'Have you opened your eyes yet? The Red Guards' power is invincible!' Walking away, he shouted to Cheng, 'You had better do as I say and study Chairman Mao's saying intently. Memorise ten of them every day and remember: I may come back any time to check on you.'

Many other members of the Political Consultative Conference, like Cheng, were in trouble too. Among them were Doo Yu-Ming, the deputy commander of the Chinese Army in the Burma War and two senior generals, Soong Shi-Len and Jeng Tin-Jee; all three had been captured in the civil war and belonged to the first group of people released in December 1959 from the war criminal labour reform camp.

Civil servants of 'noble pedigree' from the Political Consultative Conference office soon formed their own group of Red Guards. On 24 August they announced that Doo Yu-Ming's group would not be allowed to stay in their offices to study political lessons. Instead they were to work as office cleaners and their work was to include cleaning all the lavatories and doing other manual work; even the old and sick had to do their best. From then on many committee members of the CPPCC spent their time sweeping floors, cleaning toilets, loading or unloading coal or furniture and pulling carts.

The next day, 25 August, on their return from work the three ex-generals noticed a wall poster at the entrance of their alley, declaring that several Nationalist war criminals were living in big houses in the alley, they were all parasites and bloodsuckers of the new era and so on.

Doo Yu-Ming, Soong Shi-Len, Jeng Tin-Jee and another senior Nationalist army commander, Tang San-Ming, were sharing the same compound. Tang had been a defector in the civil war, so he was in a better situation than the reformed war criminals. He was living comfortably, with no need to go to work.

Nevertheless, they were all worried. The following day the three ex-PoWs obtained permission from their employers to wait at home for the time being. In the afternoon three boy and two girl Red Guards, about 15 or 16 years old, appeared. Ordering the four men to stand in the centre of the big courtyard, the youths began to lecture them. The leader, one of the boys, began by announcing, 'We are the Red Guard little fighters from a secondary school. You all listen to me. You bullied and exploited people in the past and you are enemies of the people. Today you are still living in big houses, eating well and dressing well. We cannot tolerate this. Now we only have orders to come to inspect you and find out what you look like. Our Red Guard headquarters will issue an order tomorrow, so you had better behave yourselves and wait for our order.'

The four men replied that they would definitely follow the Red Guard little fighters' guidance and obey their orders. Tang added a few words to explain his situation: 'I am a defected Nationalist army officer, Chairman Mao has laid down a policy about us.'

One Red Guard snarled: 'We understand policy. You need not talk out of your arse!'

The following morning a directive issued by the Red Guard headquarters of a secondary school was posted on their front door, as follows:

27 August 1966

To the goblins, demons and scum of the Nationalist Party.
1. We order you to reduce your salaries voluntarily. You should live at the same standards as ordinary working people.
2. You are not allowed to employ home help and are forbidden to live the life of a parasite.
3. You are ordered to sweep your alley clean every day, starting from tomorrow. Delay is not permitted.
Anyone who disobeys this directive will be punished severely.

After putting their heads together the three ex-PoWs decided the best thing to do was to write a wall poster to explain that their salaries had already been cut by one third by the Political Consultative Conference. They expressed their wholehearted support for the Red Guards and pledged themselves to obey all their decisions. Tang wrote a separate wall poster denoting his different status. It was similar to the others, except that he was the only one who had been using home help for years, but he wrote that he planned to dismiss his home help immediately. In the afternoon more than 20 Red Guards arrived and the four men were told to stand together and listen to the leader's speech. 'We have seen your wall poster reply,' said the leader. 'That is the correct response. Don't forget that all of you are Nationalist war criminals who owe an enormous debt of blood, so it is reasonable to enforce even the most exacting proletarian dictatorship over you. Now, people have treated you broad-mindedly and given you a new life. But is it right that you should still live a more comfortable life than working people, sitting on the heads of the people? It is nothing more than daydreaming. In the past the bosses of the United Front Work Department gave you too high a living allowance; they were capitulationists and were totally wrong. We have now amended your allowance. From now on you must behave yourselves; talking and acting improperly are not allowed. If any one of you dares to make trouble, he is asking for destruction.'

The speech ended with a noisy chanting of slogans such as 'Long live proletarian dictatorship' and 'Destroy the enemy who does not surrender.' Then the leader announced that they would now start to look for the 'four old things' and any evidence of reactionary crimes.

The compound was shared by the families of the four men. Both Soong Shi-Len and Jeng Tin-Jee had acquired all their belongings after their amnesty, so they had few possessions; even their furniture belonged to the CPPCC. It did not take the Red Guards long to search their two houses, but they found nothing worthy of their attention. Tang, who had returned to China from Hong Kong, lived in a big house with many high quality household goods. The Red Guards turned the house upside down, confiscating everything regarded as a luxury. Any fashionable clothes they found were cut into pieces with scissors on the spot.

When Doo Yu-Ming was released from his labour reform camp, he had been in the same situation as Soong Shi-Len and Jeng Tin-Jee. Later on, his wife had returned to join him from America and it was helpful too that their daughter and son-in-law, the Nobel prize-winning physicist Professor Young, lived in America. Doo's standard of living had consequently improved in recent years and the couple had some nice things at home. When the Red Guards cut up the old lady's favourite dresses, she made a mild protest, only to be slapped in the face. In the end the Red Guards failed to find any criminal evidence and only took away their valuables.

From then on, at 5 a.m. every day the four men started sweeping their alley for half an hour before beginning their day's work at the Political Consultative Conference. Some days they swept the alley twice. By early October many local Red Guards had left Peking, taking the revolution to other parts of China. The alley sweepers were forgotten until the chairman of the local residents' committee kindly released them from the job.

In early September the four men got a pleasant surprise. At the time many cadres working for the Political Consultative Conference and the Department of United Front Work had their salaries reduced or even suspended, but the four men, together with others of similar status, had their salaries paid in full again. The accounts office even planned to compensate them for the 30 yuans which had been deducted from their pay packets the previous month. According to informed sources a telephone call had come from Chow En-Lai's office forbidding the Political Consultative Conference office from deducting money from the salaries of the democrats and ex-PoWs.

As time went by, the Cultural Revolution dealt out increasingly merciless blows. The three ex-PoWs were forced to do more hard manual work and before long Tang and his wife, the well-known actress Xu Lai, were thrown into jail, where Xu Lai died.

Even impeccably Communist organisations soon came under attack. In the afternoon of 23 August, the day after the *People's Daily* had extolled the Red Guards' actions as excellent, a group of girl Red Guards entered Peking city's Cultural Bureau and the nearby Literary Association, singing a song entitled 'Revolutionary Rebellion'. They began by tearing up manuscripts and publications in the editorial department, before barging into the conference room, denouncing those people as mental aristocrats and proceeding to cut holes in the leather sofas. Later on, they drove more than 40 people, among them famous writers and artists, into the sweltering courtyard, where the temperature was more than 40°C. The victims were forced to stand in a circle and ordered to bend down at a right angle. Wooden boards were hung on their necks bearing words such as 'black gang', 'reactionary academic authority' and 'goblin of cow and demon of snake'. The girl Red Guards stood outside the circle and started whipping the victims with all their might.

After an hour or so, they were taken to the courtyard of the Temple of Confucius, where they found a small mountain of art treasures – scrolls, theatrical costumes and other stage property collected and preserved by the Cultural Bureau – which had already been moved there by truck. The Red Guards shaved half the head of each victim to make them look grotesque and poured ink over some. They then set alight the small mountain of collection of art and forced their victims to kneel around the scorching fire in the thick smoke, whipping them with the buckle ends of their leather belts.

Among these hapless people was the distinguished Manchu writer Lao She, aged 67. His spectacles were knocked away, blood began to stream down from his head and he fainted. The Red Guards regarded this as bad manners and accused him of the further charge of being an 'active counter-revolutionary'.

Lao She (1899–1966) had been invited in 1924 by J F Johnston of London University to teach Chinese at the School of Oriental Studies for five years. In 1946 he had gone to America on a lecture tour and in 1949 he was invited back to China by Chow En-Lai. In 1951 he was awarded the title of 'people's artist' and by 1966 he had written 23 scripts for plays, several novels and hundreds of poems. He was a supporter of 'new China'. In July 1966 he had started vomiting blood and was admitted into hospital. Chow En-Lai urged him to take his time and not to rush home. On 23 August, the first day after his discharge from hospital, he returned to work at the Literary Association, but it was that very day that the Red Guards came to destroy the 'four old things'. They ordered the senior officials at the Cultural Bureau to attend a struggle meeting to receive criticisms and they wanted people from the neighbouring Literary Association to keep their Cultural Bureau victims company. When the Red Guards wanted to take away some of Lao She's colleagues, Lao She voluntarily went with them, only to lose consciousness in front of the bonfire.

Members of the Literary Association arrived to take Lao She back to the office building, but they had not expected to find several hundred Red Guards already there waiting for him. When they saw him they spat at him, punched him and whipped him. At first Lao She submitted to his ill-treatment, but later on he stopped being submissive and threw away the humiliating wooden board that had been placed around his neck proclaiming that he was an 'active counter-revolutionary'. He was beaten until late at night and then ordered to come back to the office the following morning with the wooden board.

The following morning Lao She did not appear at his office; he was seen sitting by Tai-Ping Lake in Peking's north suburb for most of the day. He was as motionless as a statue, with a peculiar and dreamy look in his eyes. The next day, 25 August, his body was found in the lake. Years later, when he was finally given a memorial service, his box of remains contained just one pair of spectacles, one packet of tea leaves and one fountain pen, but not his ashes, because Jiang's gang and her collaborator, Lin Biao, would not allow the ashes of members of black gangs to be returned to their families.

Another victim was the celebrated translator Fu Lei (1908–66), who had studied art criticism in France. After returning to Shanghai Fu Lei had taught in the art college and had started a newspaper. He had also become a prolific translator of French literature, translating more than 30 books by Balzac, Romain Rolland, Voltaire and other writers. He was a member of Shanghai's Political Consultative Conference and a leading member of the Shanghai Writers' Association. In 1957, he was condemned as a rightist after making what he had intended as friendly criticism of the Communist Party. In 1961, he had been released from the stigma of being a rightist.

On 30 August 1966, Fu Lei's home was ransacked by Red Guards from the Shanghai College of Music. Inside a box they found a small mirror with Chiang Kai-Shek's picture framed on the back, as well as an old picture book with a picture of Chiang's wife in it. The box had in fact belonged to Fu's aunt and had been left with him temporarily, so he denied the box was his, but no explanation could get him out of trouble. The Red Guards gripped his hair and slapped him in his face, insisting that the pictures of Chiang and his wife were evidence of Fu's hostility to the party and proof that he wanted to overthrow the Communist government.

On the night of 2 September, Fu wrote his will. He left money to pay his rent and the expenses of a cremation for two. All jewellery in the house, some belonging to his aunt and sister, had been confiscated by the Red Guards, so he offered his modest savings to his aunt as compensation. He asked his brother-in-law to help in returning things that people had left with them for safe-keeping. After leaving instructions on how to clear up his unfinished business, Fu and his wife hanged themselves. On 26 April 1979, the Shanghai Literary Association and Writers' Association held a memorial service for the couple and their names were cleared.

One man who fared better than Fu was the veteran Communist Shar Yen, who had been a celebrated left-wing intellectual in Shanghai in the thirties. During that period many Communist suspects were arrested by Chiang Kai-Shek's security forces, but Shar was lucky and avoided arrest. In Communist China he held the posts of deputy Minister for Culture, chairman of the Movie Workers Association and deputy chairman of the National Literary Association.

When the Cultural Revolution arrived, the liberal-minded Shar was in trouble. He was paraded around with an insulting placard hung around his neck then thrown into jail. However, he survived the Cultural Revolution with nothing more than a broken leg. He died in early 1995, at the age of 95, leaving three instructions for his funeral. First, he wanted no memorial service; secondly he did not want the ritual of people saying goodbye to his dead body; and thirdly he did not want to be buried in Eight Treasure Hill, the exclusive cemetery reserved for important party members. Instead he wanted his ashes cast into the river which flowed past his home town.

The party disregarded Shar's wishes and instead arranged a grand memorial service for him, attended by nearly 2,000 people. The official report also avoided mentioning Shar's last wish that he should not be buried in Eight Treasure Hill cemetery. Shar was well respected by educated Chinese people and his decision to keep his distance from the cemetery was widely regarded as his final break with the Communist Party, which he had loyally served all his life. He had been very upset about the Tiananmen Square massacre of 4 June 1989, just as he had been disillusioned by Mao's radical policy of continuous liquidation.

Countless staunch Communists who had zealously executed Mao's policies to purge other people were themselves sooner or later purged, among them Shar's old friend, Tian Han, another leading Communist in cultural circles. Tian Han had played a leading role in persecuting the renowned playwright, Woo Joo-Kwang, who had strayed into taboo territory by asking indiscreet questions such as 'What is the difference between the present-day government and past feudal regimes?' and 'Where is the superiority of socialism?' Woo was duly denounced as an arch-rightist in the 1957 anti-rightist campaign, during which playwrights, actors and film makers in Peking held four large meetings in August to denounce him. Tian presided over all four of these meetings and also wrote an essay accusing Woo of harbouring sinister intentions and of being anti-Communist. Tian published in newspapers what Woo had said at the meetings to emphasise his crime of hostility to the party, using his words 'The party should stop dictating to artists how they should work' as a headline. Woo was later sent to a labour reform farm.

Nine years later Tian himself was caught by the Cultural Revolution. He was falsely accused of having once surrendered to the Nationalists and his own son, Tian Da-Wai, attacked him in a poster, calling him a low animal and a traitor. Once, when Tian was eating in a canteen and spat out a bone, he was promptly berated and forced to swallow what he had just spat out. He was ill-treated in prison; although he was a diabetic, he was often refused permission to go to the lavatory and once, when he had urinated into a portable basin, his jailer forced him to drink the urine. He died a lonely death in jail.

The extraordinary Professor Chan Yan-Lor did not oppose the Communist Party but did not praise it either. Chan Yan-Lor was a brilliant scholar of Chinese history, particularly of the Sui and Tang Dynasties (589–906 AD). He had studied in America, Japan and Germany and was fluent in six languages. In 1940, he was invited to teach at Oxford University, but the Pacific war broke out as he was waiting to sail to England, ruining his plans. Instead he taught in Chengdu, Sichuan province, but developed serious eye trouble which caused him to go blind. After the war he sought medical treatment in Britain, but by this time his eyesight was already lost forever. However, he had an extraordinary memory and historical knowledge and he could easily quote by heart a particular line from a particular page of a particular book. He devoted himself to academic writing and teaching postgraduates.

When Mao visited Moscow in 1950, Stalin once asked him, 'Professor Chan Yan-Lor is a remarkable scholar. Where is he now?' Mao could not give Stalin an answer, but on his return to China he instituted an investigation and found that Chan was by then teaching in Chong San University in Canton. Mao immediately promoted him to the post of grade one professor, giving him a monthly salary of 475 yuans, 35 yuans more than the salary of his university president and also provided him with two nurses.

In the 1957 anti-rightists campaign, wall posters appeared in large quantities denouncing Chan. The party committee of Guangdong province wanted to name him as a rightist, but the party central committee overruled this, arguing that he was too famous a scholar.

During the Cultural Revolution, Chan was the first professor to face struggle meetings at his university. Three different gangs of university Red Guards dragged the blind scholar to a meeting, hitting him as they went. The meeting consisted of 3,000 people, including Red Guards from other higher education institutions. Chan's fellow professors at Chong San University were ordered to stay with him as he faced the struggle meeting. First of all, the Red Guard leaders announced Chan's reactionary crimes, next they recited some of Mao's sayings, telling Chan to repeat them once. He was then ordered to repeat all the sayings together and when he could not do so he was compelled to kneel down. The Red Guards brought him a writing brush, ink and paper and told him to write 'Chan has always been hostile to the party and the people' and 'Chan is unlearned and ignorant and is a scum among historians.' Chan said that he did not know how to write these characters, earning himself several heavy punches on the nose.

Calling the great leader Mr Mao Tse-Tung instead of Chairman Mao also caused Chan grievous trouble. Angry Red Guards screamed that he was reactionary through and through and that he needed to be crushed; how could he dare to be so audacious as to call the great leader, the reddest, reddest, red sun in their hearts, a mere 'mister'? 'Chan's every single hair is saturated with poison juice,' they cried; 'down with the reactionary scholar.'

Chan had to endure this shouting for a whole day, at the end of which the Red Guards announced that his salary would be reduced from 475 yuans to 189 yuans and that his two nurses would be withdrawn. They then turned their attentions to the other professors, denouncing them in similar terms and ransacking their homes.

The Red Guards, when they were at work, would often sing songs, with great gusto, consisting of selections of Mao's sayings, such as 'Revolution does not mean giving guests a meal, it does not mean writing an essay, it does not mean painting or embroidering a picture of flowers. It cannot be gentle and cautious,' and 'There are ten thousand rational arguments in Marxism which can all be summarised in one sentence: it is reasonable to rebel.'

Songs such as these were the only music now allowed; all other music was considered to be among the old things which were treated as trash. A famous song 'On Jarling River', written at the time of the Sino-Japanese War by the renowned composer Hor Leu-Din, was now condemned. This song lamented the loss of the beautiful Chinese homeland and tried to rouse the Chinese people to resist the Japanese invaders. But now it was condemned as sounding dejected and of lacking the spirit of the working class, the peasants and soldiers.

Hor Leu-Din had composed 'On Jarling River' in 1941 in the wartime capital of Chongqing, where he had mixed with left-wing intellectuals. He subsequently went to Yan'an to work in the music composition department of Lu Xun Arts College and it was there that he had joined the Communist Party. Hor also wrote the well-known song in praise of Mao Tse-Tung, 'East Is Red'. In Communist China, he became head of the Shanghai College of Music, chairman of the Shanghai Musicians Association and deputy chairman of the National Musicians Association.

Red Guards from the Shanghai College of Music ransacked his home and his precious collection of western and Chinese music was all destroyed. The Red Guards accused him of being the leader of a black gang among Shanghai's musicians and a phoney Communist. He advocated freedom of the arts and opposed the party's leading role in music. He also cultivated gifted people, so he was a capitalist musical scum who was hostile to the party, hostile to socialism and hostile to the people. The accusers pointed out that Hor came from a capitalist and landlord family and that his intrinsic nature had evidently never changed. He was an enemy agent who had smuggled himself into the revolutionary camp. He was an arch-rightist who had slipped through the net.

In August 1966, Hor was taken to his first struggle meeting, where he was insulted and paraded around the Shanghai College of Music with a placard hanging around his neck identifying him as a member of a black gang. His dedicated work for the party over the decades was denounced. By 1968 he was still under attack. On 25 April of that year the Shanghai newspaper the *Wen Hui Daily* published an article entitled 'Crushing the revival plot of Hor's counter-revolutionary cabal'. Written by the revolutionary committee of the Shanghai College of Music, this article claimed that Hor had not succumbed in his struggle meetings and had instead been trying to overturn his conviction since the end of 1967. The article inadvertently disclosed that Hor actually had many more supporters in the college than Mao, asking its readers not to follow the counter-revolutionary old hand. Yet, the revolutionaries never stopped singing 'East Is Red', the adulatory song which had been written by Hor.

Another important victim of this campaign was Deng Toc, the editor in chief of the *People's Daily* and the Xinhua news agency. When Mao was secretly making preparations in 1965 for the Cultural Revolution and making use of a nonentity to attack *Hai Rui's Dismissal* at the Peking opera, the scholarly Deng Toc sensed that this was the beginning of a new storm which was evidently backed by heavyweights in the party. Yet he knowingly took the risk of speaking out at meetings about the importance of treating academic problems and political problems differently and the importance of not being overly critical.

Deng Toc was made redundant in the spring of 1966. He was left with nothing to do, waiting for other people to decide his fate. Jiang was keen to make him, with his colleagues, into the first batch of sacrificial lambs and in May, newspaper headlines such as 'Fighting Deng Toc resolutely to the very end' appeared all over the country, with full-page articles denouncing him. Yet he still believed in his own innocence and kept faith in the party, thinking he would be cleared within a year.

On 16 May, the *People's Daily* carried an article written by Jiang's underling, Chic Bun-Yu, asking rhetorically, 'What is Deng Toc?' The answer was provided at the end: 'He is a traitor.' Deng had previously been arrested twice by the Nationalist government, but the Communist Party had already formally concluded that he had not betrayed any of his comrades or sold out the party, so he thought that the party had now made a new political judgement on him.

On 18 May 1966, he wrote a letter to the party's Peking city committee emphasising that he was making absolutely no complaint against the people who had criticised him. If it was beneficial to the party and to the revolutionary cause he was willing to undergo any pain and sacrifice. He was now going to leave them and he would repeat his praise for the great, glorious and just Communist Party and for Chairman Mao. Deng killed himself, the first, but not the last, senior official to commit suicide in the Cultural Revolution. The party central committee finally exonerated him completely in 1979.

Not even sports were left untouched by the Cultural Revolution. China's top table tennis player, Yung Kwok-Tuen, was born in 1937 in Hong Kong. His family was poor so he left school and started his working life at the age of 13, but before long he had emerged as a brilliant table tennis player. He turned down many lucrative sport contracts offered to him by wealthy businessmen; instead, on 1 November 1957, he decided to go to mainland China to serve the motherland. In 1959 he won the men's singles world title, the first world champion title for China and through his coaching Chinese men's and women's teams both had great successes in subsequent world table tennis contests.

At the beginning of the Cultural Revolution, like millions of other young people who had implicit faith in Mao and the Communist Party, Yung supported the 'revolution'. As time went on, however, he grew puzzled and bewildered. His team-mates, Fou Chi-Fond and Zhan Yun-Lin, who had returned to China from Hong Kong before him, were framed, paraded in the streets, beaten and imprisoned. Both men hanged themselves. Other team-mates were arrested and many of Yung's senior colleagues fell from grace. The head of the National Sports Commission, Marshal Hor Lone, was denounced as a 'big bandit.' He was accused of running the National Sports Commission as his own independent kingdom and pursuing counter-revolutionary and revisionist policies for the past 17 years.

It was not long before Yung himself was in trouble. His interest in books, movies and music was condemned as evidence of corruption and he was banned from attending the world table tennis contests. At a struggle meeting on 20 June 1968 he was accused of being a supporter of Marshal Hor's black activities and a secret agent who had come back from Hong Kong with the task of overthrowing the Communist regime.

In the small hours of the following morning he hanged himself beside a lake, leaving behind a young widow and daughter. A note was found in his pocket, in which he insisted that he was not a secret agent and emphasised his loyalty to the party and to Chairman Mao. After his death, his home was searched thoroughly, but nothing was found to incriminate him. The authorities declared that they had uncovered an organisation of undercover enemy agents from Hong Kong inside the national table tennis team. In little more than two months, China's three top table tennis players all hanged themselves; all were to be exonerated by the National Sports Commission in 1979.

The Cultural Revolution began with wall posters, debates and criticism but progressed inexorably to violent persecution. On 26 August 1966, the number of people beaten to death in Peking daily rose to more than 100, though it went down to double figures after one week. All Chinese people, from members of the politburo down to the humblest people, were required to 'suspect everything and bring down everything' in order to drag out revisionists and class enemies. Revolutionary groups held struggle meetings, sacked people from their jobs, expelled Communists from the party and tortured their enemies. Neither marshals nor ministers, nor even the President of the People's Republic of China himself, were safe in the face of mob rule.

100

The Red Guards (2)

The Red Guards soon turned their attention to religious matters and before long temples, mosques and churches were forced to close down in large numbers, abandoned by their frightened worshippers. Many Buddhist monks and nuns were accused of being landlord parasites and made to give up their faith, while some nuns and monks were forced to marry each other. Several monks from a temple in Harbin were photographed holding a large banner bearing the words 'The sutra is dog shit,' and handbills appeared sporting the headline 'Extirpating Catholicism' and quoting one of Mao's sayings, 'Religious missions are a cultural invasion of imperialist policy.'

On 24 August 1966, Peking Red Guards from more than a dozen secondary schools, backed by the Cultural Revolution central leadership and the Public Security Bureau, broke into a Catholic seminary. Having first placed a portrait of Mao at the entrance and plastered revolutionary slogans over the walls, the Red Guards ordered the nuns to stand in a line in front of the building with their heads bowed. Surrounded by hundreds of Red Guards shouting slogans and punching the air with their clenched fists, the nuns were accused of being secret agents. Two days later, the Peking authorities announced the closing down of the Catholic mission and the appropriation of its Sacred Heart School and on 28 August the Peking Public Security Bureau announced that the mission would be evicted immediately. Three days later, on 31 August, eight Italian nuns were deported from China.

Some Red Guards proposed that they should wipe out Islam, but Chow En-Lai pointed out that since there were 400 million Muslims in the world, 14 million of them in China, the proposition was unworkable. Chow En-Lai had actually tried his best to pursue rational policies, only to find his efforts more often than not undermined. At a 1955 conference in Bandung, in Indonesia, he had openly encouraged the vast numbers of overseas Chinese in southeast Asia to cooperate with their host governments, so as to demonstrate to the outside world that Communist China was a friendly country. But in mid-1967, when the Red Guards were at their wildest, they denounced this as a capitalist policy of compromise and capitulation. Lew Cheng-Gee, the head of the Overseas Chinese Affairs Commission, who had staunchly supported the friendly policy, was later dragged out of his office and paraded through the streets and the commission was closed. In June 1967, Lew Cheng-Gee was denounced as a reactionary counter-revolutionary, one of whose crimes had been carrying out the Chinese Krushchev's reactionary policy of banning overseas Chinese from joining local revolutionary struggles. The foreign minister, Marshal Chan Yi, was accused of having committed the same crime.

From then on, pro-Communist overseas Chinese began to make trouble in their host countries and they were soon joined by Chinese diplomats. Scuffles soon broke out in countries such as Cambodia and Burma between Chinese and local people, with Chinese embassy staff handing out radical revolutionary handbills in the streets and pestering passers-by to accept Mao badges or the Little Red Books. Some people were even assaulted if they refused to accept these Chinese treasures. Some Chinese recited Mao's sayings on buses, stopped veiled Muslim women in the streets to talk about liberation, or barged into Muslim houses to preach atheism and guerrilla warfare.

In early 1967 the Chinese government summoned all overseas Chinese students back to China for six months to play their part in the Cultural Revolution. Among them were 69 Chinese students from France and Finland, who stopped in Moscow for a short time on their way back to China. Arriving there on 24 January, they decided to pay homage to Lenin and Stalin on the following day and the Chinese embassy duly informed the Russian government about the impending pilgrimage. Not long before this, Stalin had been publicly criticised by Khrushchev and Mao was leading the Chinese Communist Party in defence of Stalin; Mao could see only too well that any attack on Stalin-worship might well damage his own personality cult. By then relations between the two Communist parties was near breaking point.

On 25 January, the 69 students, led by officials from the Chinese embassy, made their way to Lenin's mausoleum, only to be confronted on their arrival in Red Square by hundreds of police and soldiers, whose officers forbade the students from laying their wreath for Stalin in Lenin's mausoleum. After laying their wreath for Lenin, the Students began to recite loudly Mao's sayings in praise of Stalin, to the effect that Stalin had been a faithful friend of the Chinese people's liberation struggle, that the Chinese people's respect for Stalin and their friendship with Russia were totally sincere and that anyone who made slanderous attacks on Stalin would be totally useless.

The Russians told the Chinese students to keep quiet in Red Square, but the students broke into loud singing. Immediately each Chinese student was surrounded by three or four Russian policemen or soldiers, who punched and kicked the trouble-seeking students for half an hour.

Two days later, when word of the incident reached China, there were nationwide demonstrations and in Peking effigies of Brezhnev and other Russian leaders were burned in front of the Russian embassy, whose Chinese employees went on strike. When the students finally returned to China on 1 February they were greeted as heroes; after they had been met by the vice premier, Chan Yi, representing the CCP leadership, they were given a grand welcoming party at the Peking Workers' Stadium. They became sensational propaganda material for some time.

At the same time the Peking Red Guards were organising demonstrations at other embassies, including those of Indonesia and India. The walls of the Indian embassy were covered with hostile wall posters, while a screaming crowd carried large banners reading 'Down with the Indian reactionaries'.

On 22 August, Red Guards from Peking University, Peking Normal University, the Chinese Medical University, Tsing Hua University and Peking's First Machinery Factory held a large demonstration, which they called 'the angry Peking proletarian revolutionaries' big meeting to condemn British imperialist anti-Chinese crimes', in front of the offices of the British chargé d'affaires, on the grounds that the Hong Kong Government had persecuted Chinese journalists in Hong Kong. The revolutionaries demanded an answer from the British and when none came they broke into the British diplomatic compound on 28 August, assaulted staff, set fire to cars and then to the office building itself.

Mao had said 'it is reasonable to rebel' and accordingly students all over China imitated the Peking University students in denouncing the bosses and deputies of their own institutions. Local government chiefs often tried to suppress this riotous behaviour, but the students regarded themselves as acting under the guidance of Chairman Mao and many were keen to go to Peking to air their grievances and to seek Mao's support. A group of students from Tianjin decided that they should march to Peking and it did not take long for the authorities to realise that this could be made into a very useful propaganda coup. A train was immediately dispatched to pick up the Tianjin walkers and when they boarded it, feeling suitably grateful and uplifted, they duly burst into shouts of 'Long live Chairman Mao!'

On 10 June 1966, at the party standing committee meeting in

Hangzhou, Mao said that 'students should be encouraged to go to Peking and allowed to travel free of charge, it would be nice to have a big chaotic fracas in Peking'. Following his two successful inspections of Red Guards in Tiananmen Square in August, on 5 September the State Council issued instructions for teachers and students in other provinces to travel to Peking in order to study the capital's Cultural Revolution. Before long a huge human torrent began pouring into Peking, with some people coming from as far away as Tibet in a movement which became known as the 'Great Stringing'. Travel, by train or bus, was free, with all expenses paid for by the authorities and on arrival in Peking the travellers were billeted in schools, colleges, universities, government offices or the houses of families who had been evicted from Peking. The visitors, it was said, were guests of Chairman Mao, only the nation was paying for them.

The Great Stringing enabled millions of devotees to catch a glimpse of the great leader standing high up on the Tiananmen city wall and for many it was the happiest moment in their lives. It also provided them with the chance to learn about Cultural Revolution Peking-style, so that they could implement the same methods back home. At the same time it enabled the Peking Red Guards to travel around the country to direct the class struggle being carried out by Red Guards in the provinces.

Soon the Great Stringing was extended to factories and rural areas, interrupting normal production work. On 15 September 1966, when Mao inspected the Red Guards for the third time, Chow En-Lai tried to restrain the flood of factory workers and villagers, but with Mao's public support the Great Stringing seemed unstoppable. All in all a total of 11 million people travelled to Peking, many of them largely for sightseeing rather than for ideological reasons. Trains were often two or three times overloaded, sometimes with six or seven people packed into a small lavatory. China's transport system was close to collapse.

In August 1966, 15 students started walking from Dalian to Peking. After nearly a month spent trudging over more than 2,000 km, they arrived at the mecca of the Cultural Revolution. The *People's Daily* commented, 'Marching for the Great Stringing, instead of travelling by train, is a very meaningful act... it is to be hoped that other revolutionary students will do the same.' Soon further groups of marchers set out, with the aim of walking not just to Peking, but also to other revered revolutionary sites such as Yan'an, the wartime capital of the Communist Party, Jinggangshan, Mao's mountain hideout in the late 1920s, Zunyi, where Mao had gained power in 1935, Rui-Jin, the Soviet district capital in Jiangxi province in the 1930s and Shaoshen, in Hunan province, which was the great leader's birthplace.

On 16 October, Mao gave his seal of approval to the long distance march of the Great Stringing. By now the Red Guards were marching with large Mao badges or portraits on their chests and with the indispensable Little Red Book in their hands. Their important mission was to propagate Mao Tse-Tung Thought. Many had Mao's sayings displayed on their rucksacks for the benefit of anyone walking behind them.

With winter drawing near, these 'holy places', nearly all of them under-developed small towns, were overwhelmed by hordes of people. The village of Da-Ja, an agricultural holy land, found 100,000 Red Guards descending on it, while the village of Shaoshen was flooded by 10,000 people. During the course of the Great Stringing, a total of as many as one million Red Guards visited Jinggangshan. When a rumour flew around that Mao would inspect Red Guards in Jinggangshan, 100,000 Red Guards congregated there immediately, only to find themselves marooned in the mountains by heavy snow. It was bitterly cold, they were short of food and many of the roads were impassable. The local government, totally unable to cope with the situation, sent an urgent message to the party central office and the army headquarters and troops worked through the night to prepare relief parcels, with helicopters dropping food, blankets and warm clothing to the 'pilgrims'. More than a million catties of dry provisions were airdropped to Jinggangshan, but this did nothing to stop the spread of acute meningitis. In the end more than 200 people caught the illness and six Red Guards died. Several others starved to death after they lost their way in the mountains.

Although the marching movement was expanding, the stresses on the transport system created by the Great Stringing were still steadily increasing. Many Peking students had left to join the Great Stringing, leaving many educational institutions largely empty. The authorities now decided that the Great Stringing had succeeded in its purpose of stirring up the nation's fighting élan; now it was time for the Peking Red Guards to return home and crush any remaining black gangs.

Beginning in mid-November 1966, the authorities began issuing posters urging the wanderers to return home. But their calls were ignored, for the Red Guards had caught the travel bug. Mao was still interested in the marching around, but the marchers were making life very difficult for local authorities and local people. In some areas epidemics erupted. Some local authorities took a hard line and refused to look after the wanderers, in an attempt to force them to go home. Finally, on 19 March 1967, the central committee decided to order an end to the Great Stringing and this movement gradually died down.

Mao had launched the Cultural Revolution largely with the aim of destroying his prime political rival, Liu Shao-Qi. He knew that Liu had many supporters; not only had he been President of the People's Republic of China for eight years, but he had also pulled the country out of the great famine. Mao saw therefore that he had to begin by eliminating Liu's powerful followers; once they were out of the way Liu himself would be easier to eliminate. Consequently, many party bosses and deputies soon found themselves condemned as black gangs. Their children, left feeling insecure and resentful, made use of the theory of blood-lineage to hit back.

In late July, some lines surfaced in a Peking secondary school declaring that 'heroic fathers produce heroes, reactionary fathers produce bastards.' Before long this saying appeared in universities, colleges and schools all over the country, leading to a vigorous debate. In Chinese culture, pedigree was an age-old and accepted concept and it fitted snugly, with unprecedented evil, into Mao's theory of class struggle.

Students of high birth soon formed many groups of their own kind and there were frequent shouts of 'Long live the born red'. Those who did not belong to the five red categories immediately became the Red Guards' targets for suppression. For a time, 'underclass' students were compelled to study political documents together under the watchful eye of the Red Guards; permission was needed to visit the lavatory and if they took a little too long about it they would receive a dressing-down. The non-red students and offspring of the black categories would be given the harshest, dirtiest and heaviest work and had to put up with insults and abuse. They were forbidden to wear Mao badges, read Mao's sayings or sing songs in his praise, because they were too unclean to enjoy such privileges.

In those days of flinty class consciousness, anyone wishing to enter a shop or a hotel, or to board a bus or train, would be questioned about their class status. People who belonged to the wrong classes would be turned away; hospitals also refused to treat people from the wrong classes and many died as a consequence. Twenty years after the Communists had won power, most descendants of landlords and rich peasants were still the poorest people in the villages. Daughters of these families would try very hard to marry someone with a better class background, while many sons of such families could not find a wife. Only disabled girls or girls with other problems would marry them.

The famous lines, now dubbed the 'theory of blood lineage', spread swiftly throughout the country. Class status determined healthcare, education, jobs, marriage prospects – in short, everything. Many young people, crushed by their class background, felt the injustice deeply and a young Peking man, Yue Lor-Ka, decided to speak up for them.

Yue Lor-Ka, born in 1942, had been disqualified from attending university in 1960 because his parents were rightists. Instead he went to work in a people's commune and later in a factory. During this time he tried his hand at writing, but his efforts were rejected because of his family background. In late 1966 he wrote an essay entitled 'the Theory of Origin', in which he pointed out that the children of landlords and capitalists were now working people, or would be when they were adults. They had not lived through any exploitation. Society – in other words schools, teachers, education, political lessons, current affairs and other such influences – had a greater influence on young people than their families and therefore people could be improved. To classify people by their family background instead of their actual economic status, to put them in an underclass and treat them differently, both politically and socially, was totally unreasonable. He maintained that supporters of the theory of blood lineage who used abusive language, carried out body searches and beat and detained innocent people were seriously infringing people's rights.

No publisher dared to accept Yue's 'Theory of Origin', so he mimeographed his essay onto wall posters which he pasted up in public places. Millions of people from the silent 'underclass' shared Yue's grievance and anger and they scrambled to copy the essay. Students from Peking's 4th Secondary School were moved by the argument, so they launched a newsletter entitled 'The Secondary School Cultural Revolution Bulletin', whose first edition, which came out on 28 January 1967, reprinted the Theory of Origin in its entirety. A total of 90,000 copies were printed and were sold out almost immediately. The essay was also reprinted in other areas, including the remote provinces of Yunnan, Guizhou and Xinjiang and the organiser of the bulletin, Mau Jee-Jing, recalled how they received sympathetic letters from all over the country, several sacks each day when the bulletin had first appeared.

Yue disapproved of the Cultural Revolution from the very beginning and his diary was full of trenchant comments on current affairs. On 4 May, he criticised the promotion of Mao's personality cult by the senior official, Chan Bor-Da and the Communist Youth League central committee and on 6 June he commented that the masses were fanatical and blind followers. The so-called first Marxist wall poster in Peking University which had fanned the Cultural Revolution was nothing but a confidence trick covering up the real political power struggle. On 17 June, he wrote about a primary school teacher who had committed suicide and a headmaster who had been beaten by his pupils, commenting that 'primary school children have no ability to analyse, but their blind impulse was praised by the Peking Party committee as "lovable". Was it really lovable?' On 23 August, he wrote about the Red Guards who had wanted to burn all books in the Peking Library which did not accord with Mao Tse-Tung Thought. This reminded him of Emperor Qin, who had burnt books and buried scholars alive 2,000 years earlier.

At a time when the whole nation had sunk into a state of confusion and fanaticism, the young Yue Lor-Ka, a simple apprentice with only a secondary school education, was one of the few people who had managed to keep a cool head. But on 14 April 1967, a member in the Cultural Revolution leading team, Chic Bun-Yu, publicly announced that the Theory of Origin was reactionary. In the same month, the Secondary School Cultural Revolution Bulletin was forced to close down and Yue was followed by groups of young strangers, his letters intercepted and opened and his friends interrogated. In early 1968 he was finally arrested and accused of making vicious attacks on Mao and the party, of organising a counter-revolutionary bloc and of writing ferocious counter-revolutionary propaganda.

On 5 March 1970 a public trial, attended by 80,000 people, was held in the Peking Workers' Stadium and Yue, now 27, was sentenced to death. He was shot immediately after the trial. Anyone who had had contact with him following the publication of his Theory of Origin found themselves persecuted as members of his counter-revolutionary bloc. Eventually, in 1980, Yue was finally exonerated.

Red Guards from the early period, known as the 'old Red Guards', focused on persecuting those who had been 'born black', believing that most senior figures in the party, government and armed forces were good and that only a small number had made the mistake of sheltering the class enemy. The theory of blood lineage provided the old Red Guards with great moral support, a situation which made Jiang uneasy. She could foresee that the theory might cause inconvenience and she therefore attempted to change the attitude of the Red Guards.

On 18 November 1966, the Peking city party committee issued an important circular stopping unauthorised interrogation, beating, detention and jail. The following day the leader of the Central Cultural Revolution Small Team, Chan Bor-Da, visited the labour reform camp of Peking's 6th Secondary School. Expressing his disapproval of the camp, he ordered the school's West City picket team to close it down immediately. Later on the authorities claimed that the picket team had been used by bad elements to strike at the revolutionaries.

Neither Chan Bor-Da nor Jiang can have been worried in the slightest about the horrific crimes perpetrated by the Red Guards; they, after all, were the very people who had incited the violence in the first place. They were only worried that the Red Guards' rampage was missing many of the intended targets, particularly the senior Communists who were the 'heroes' of the by-now famous line and they therefore wanted to steer the Red Guards quietly in the correct and undivulged direction. Accordingly their speeches now began to criticise the 'reactionary policies of the capitalist class' and so the 'important circular' did nothing to mitigate the situation; on the contrary, the level of atrocities increased.

Another group of Red Guards emerged to demand equality, arguing that everyone should be permitted to join in the Cultural Revolution. Known as 'the rebels', this group included people who were politically undesirable; some were even termed 'reactionary students'. Such people now turned into revolutionaries; many of them even became extreme left-wing radicals. They mounted their attacks largely on 'people in power following the capitalist line', which meant assaults on the senior Communists in the party, government and armed forces.

To snare many highly placed Communists or the 'people in power', Jiang's gang used smear tactics and made false accusations, using the 'rebel' Red Guards to attack the victims. The old Red Guards, nearly all of them the offspring of senior Communists, now realised that the political positions of their fathers and elder brothers were getting shakier and shakier and they sensed danger ahead. They soon found that the rebels, many of them the 'children of bitches', had the backing of the Central Cultural Revolution Small Team.

On 27 November 1966, Peking old Red Guards from more than a dozen secondary schools founded a 'Joint Action Committee'. Openly hostile to the Central Cultural Revolution Small Team, they now demanded guarantees for the safety of senior party members. After several melees with rebel Red Guards and attacks on the Public Security Ministry, many were arrested by the public security police. They faced severe criticism, but responded with defiant chants of 'long live Liu Shao-Qi' and attacking Jiang Ching. Fights broke out between the two factions and the old Red Guards started to fight the rebels. They also vented their spite by wrecking their schools. By now they were a force impeding the government's plan.

On 17 January 1967, the Minister for Public Security, Sher Fu-Jee, denounced the leaders of the Joint Action Committee as counter-revolutionaries and on 31 January an editorial in *Red Flag* declared that the committee was a counter-revolutionary organisation. Its members, all formerly privileged young people, fled, not before putting up wall posters and slogans asking, 'Is Chairman Mao correct? We will see in ten years.'

Mao decided to compromise with these red princes and princesses and on 22 April he released more than 100 leading members of the Joint Action Committee. Although still branded reactionaries, they organised a meeting as a means of demonstrating their strength. They could no longer attack the central leadership of the Cultural Revolution, so instead they concentrated their anger and hatred on their rivals and on purging people from undesirable classes, chanting bloodthirsty slogans and attacking the children of bitches. After a year or so the Joint Action Committee gradually broke up.

Among the numerous groups of Red Guards, the best-known and most powerful was undoubtedly Tsing Hua University's Jinggangshan Army Corps. In June 1966, when Liu's wife, Wang Quon-Mei, was one of the work unit leaders in Tsing Hua University, this unit suspended the university president and party secretary, Chiang Nan-Chane, from his job and took control of the university themselves, condemning as many as 200 people as capitalist-roaders and reactionaries.

The Jingganshan Army Corps was led by a student of chemical engineering by the name of Quie Da-Fu. Together with a group of like-minded students he had resisted the work unit and this earned him imprisonment, struggle sessions and denunciations as a counter-revolutionary. After Mao had made his attack on the work units, on 4 August Quie was formally exonerated by Chow En-Lai. On 19 August a new group, the Tsing Hua University Red Guards, was formed by the son of Marshal Hor Lone, the daughter of Liu Shao-Qi and the children of other senior officials. They confined themselves to censuring black gangs, avoiding any condemnation of the work units; their main target was the group directing the Cultural Revolution, particularly Jiang.

On 24 September, Quie founded the Tsing Hua University Jinggangshan Army Corps. At the beginning it numbered about a dozen people, who were opposed to the policy of the work units and wished to rehabilitate the victims of the work unit. The Tsing Hua University Jinggangshan Army Corps was Jiang's favourite and with her help it quickly expanded into a group of several thousands. They crushed the Tsing Hua University Red Guards and then proceeded to do Jiang's bidding. Before long the corps became the leading Red Guard group and was considered as a beacon, not only in Tsing Hua University or Peking, but by Red Guards all over China.

Quie became Jiang's trusted follower. In April 1967, when Mao's adherents seized power from the Peking city authorities and replaced the city government with a revolutionary committee, the 24-year-old Quie was rewarded with several important positions. He had a hotline to Jiang, a car at his disposal and dozens of people working for him in the Jinggangshan Army Corps office. He even put up wall posters upbraiding Chow En-Lai and Marshal Chan Yi, to which the two men were powerless to react.

Soon Quie's army corps began to expand its operations. Not content with merely dominating Peking, Quie dispatched hundreds of his guards to more than 30 cities to take command of local rebels and his corps was also behind incidents such as the assault on the premises of the British chargé d'affaires.

In the first half of 1967, the corps' assaults on people in power reached new heights, as they broke up local governments and attacked the regular armed forces. On 29 July, more than 40 members of the corps ransacked the home of Marshal Xu Shan-Chen, taking away many important documents. They also tried to kidnap the Marshal. On 1 August they put the ex-Defence Minister, Marshal Peng De-Huai and the PLA's Chief of Staff, General Lor Rui-Chin, through a vicious struggle meeting. They denounced Marshals Xu and Yip Jan-Ying, as well as the PLA's most senior officer, Marshal Zhu De. From July to September the corps leaders sent out teams to collect information about the army and directed rebels in other areas to attack army units, assault servicemen and loot weapons and army supplies. The intention was to cause increasing chaos around the country, as a prelude to seizing power.

Over the course of these months the Jinggangshan Army Corps split into two opposing groups, the '414' group and the 'Army Corps' group, the latter still led by Quie and before the end of the year skirmishes had broken out between the two groups. In mid-April 1968, the Army Corps detained some university staff who were friendly with the 414. In order to extract confessions the victims were beaten, their teeth were pulled out with pliers and ammonia was poured into their noses. One victim died and another one was seriously injured. When the brother of one of the detainees was implicated, he was captured and suffocated. On 20 April the 414 retaliated by kidnapping a member of the Army Corps and the clashes soon escalated into serious battles which continued for over three months.

One of the big battles took place on 30 May, when 300 members of the Army Corps attacked a bath-house on the campus occupied by 21 members of the 414. The attackers threw into the bath-house any combustible material they could find, from wooden tables and chairs to dried chillies and straw mats, followed by several hundred kilos of petrol to start a fire. When five fire engines arrived, they were forced to stop by the attackers. Finally the 414 were driven out of the bath-house by the fire and surrendered, after a battle lasting 11 hours and involving 300 people from each side. In all, three people died and more than 200 were injured.

By June the battles had evolved into gunfights. On 30 June, ten members of the Army Corps were wounded by hand grenades in a battle during which they managed to seize most of the university buildings. On that occasion four men were wounded seriously, one losing a leg and another suffering severe internal injuries. A few days later, in early July, the 414 was hard pressed defending the university science building against a fierce but unsuccessful attack by the Army Corps using a home-made mortar. After a few more days of inconclusive but bloody hostilities, on 9 July the Army Corps relaunched their attack using an enormous catapult which they had constructed on the top floor of a nearby building, using two steel pipes and the inner tube of a car tyre. With this contraption they managed to shoot stones the size of basketballs over to the science building and later they succeeded in firing Molotov cocktails. The fourth floor of the science building was a wooden structure and it was soon engulfed by a fierce fire. Students wearing wicker hats began to force open the front door of the science building in the face of bricks hurled down from above by the defenders; the 414 radio station inside the building sent out a SOS to Peking's armed forces, but for two hours the fire brigade was obstructed by the Army Corps.

The 414 headquarters tried to rescue their menbers from the science building by digging a tunnel from a neighbouring building, but before it was completed the Army Corps found it and blew it up, flooding it with water. The defenders, over 100 in number, were running short of drinking water and food for more than 20 days. Over 20 of them were injured and without medical attention their condition deteriorated rapidly. Corpses inside the building were decomposing fast in the scorching summer heat.

During this internecine period, the two groups seized university buildings, kidnapping and detaining rivals while continuing their attacks on their opponents' positions day and night. They also ransacked the homes of many university staff who sympathised with their opponents and sabotaged their enemies' broadcasting equipment and telephone lines. They brought in a continuous stream of weapons from outside the university, in addition to producing home-made weapons such as mortars, rockets, bombs, grenades, spears, mines and guns and even tanks converted from tractors and armoured vehicles converted from cars. At the same time both sides appealed to the central leadership of the Cultural Revolution for help, hoping to force the leaders to support their own side. With the seat of learning turned into a war zone, most students and staff fled the campus and by the end of April 60 per cent had left.

By now Mao was at last forced to face the fact that he had lost control of the young people. On the morning of 27 July, the Peking city revolutionary committee sent a group known as the Mao Tse-Tung Thought Propagation Team of Workers and Liberation Army, consisting of over 30,000 workers led by a detachment of soldiers, to Tsing Hua University to put a stop to the fighting between the Red Guards, who numbered around 600 on both sides. The new group arrived at Tsing Hua University without warning and swiftly isolated and surrounded the Red Guards, at the same time confiscating weapons and demolishing roadblocks, barbed wire and electric fences. The Army Corps Red Guards, however, put up a determined resistance which continued for 12 hours, at the end of which the Mao Tse-Tung Thought Propagation Team had suffered casualties including five dead, ten soldiers and 139 workers seriously injured, as well as 30 soldiers and 552 workers with minor injuries. In addition 34 soldiers and 109 workers were captured by the Army Corps, while more than 100 Army Corps Red Guards were detained by the Mao Tse-Tung Thought Propagation Team. Finally, after negotiations, all the Army Corps Red Guards were allowed to leave Tsing Hua University, taking shelter with militant Red Guards from another college.

The following day Mao met the five senior Red Guard leaders, including Quie; it was to be the last time he summoned his 'courageous little warriors'. Mao criticised the Red Guards severely and threatened to use the regular army to quash any further fighting. The Red Guard fanatics who had served him so well at the start of the Cultural Revolution were of no use to him any more; instead he began to ponder on the idea of making all students and educated people into targets of the Cultural Revolution.

Tsing Hua University was not the only educational institution where political arguments degenerated into pitched battles on the campus. Many other universities had already seen violence off and on, if only on a smaller scale. On 17 December 1966, two rival groups from Nankai University in Tianjin fought a pitched battle using rods, spears, bricks, stones or anything else which they could find and they also resorted to arson. In early May 1967, fighting broke out in several secondary schools in Hebei province. On 21 June, fierce fighting at an architectural college in Harbin resulted in more than 20 casualties and two days later a battle at an agricultural university in Hebei province ended with seven dead and 250 wounded. On 10 August, three people were killed and more than 100 injured in a battle fought between rival gangs at Harbin Industrial University.

On 3 June 1968, the Red Flag group of Jon San University in Guangzhou city, Guangdong province, launched a surprise attack on the physics building, which was occupied by the university rebels' committee, the East Wind group. In preparation the Red Flag group had deployed sentries and searchlights around the building, with machine-guns positioned at high vantage points and once these were in place they attacked, using guns, hand grenades, machine-guns, home-made chemical shells and even poison gas. The East Wind group, caught unprepared, was unable to hit back and by late afternoon the Red Flag group had seized the two lower floors, setting fire to the building with the help of bedding, mosquito nets, clothes and petrol; at the same time they sent poison gas up to the floors above with the help of bellows. The East Wind group now retreated to the roof, only to be caught by machine-gun fire from the opposite building.

At midnight, one of the East Wind group descended from the roof using a rope, in an attempt to summon help, only to be captured by the Red Flag students and severely beaten. The following morning, 4 June, the Red Flag attacked again. The roof of the building caught fire, finally collapsing after burning for several hours. Two more East Wind students climbed to the ground using a rope, again hoping to seek rescue, but they were caught and beaten to death on the spot. Finally, at four o'clock, the Red Flag took the building, capturing all 31 East Wind students, who received the usual beating one by one.

The Red Flag went on to blockade the East Wind's headquarters in the central library. They began by cutting off all water, food and electricity; then, after 70 hours the library, with more than 120 East Wind students inside, was set alight. For days, the Red Flag pursued their rivals and their families all through the campus and by noon on 5 June more than 60 East Wind students were locked up waiting to be interrogated and tortured. Prisoners who were seriously wounded were beaten to death and their corpses piled up in the university health centre. Because the university was effectively sealed off by the Red Flag, the East Wind was unable to get help from outside.

Although the Red Flag had triumphed over the East Wind in Chong San University, on 6 June Red Flag students from the 29th Secondary School were ambushed and slaughtered in Guangzhou centre by members of the East Wind. The battered Red Flag students of the 29th Secondary School had twice asked for help from the PLA, but the army was not prepared to intervene, the commanders replying bluntly, 'We have come here to propagate Mao Tse-Tung Thought, not to deal with such matters.'

On 7 August 1967, the Minister for Public Security, Sher Fu-Jee, called publicly for the destruction of his own ministry, as well as all judicial departments and courts in the country, on the grounds that they were all capitalist institutions. Rebels throughout China were quick to respond and law and order departments were attacked, files were looted and their staff condemned as enemy agents, traitors and counter-revolutionaries. According to incomplete statistics, approximately 34,400 people were denounced and tortured throughout the country, of whom 1,100 died and 3,600 were permanently maimed. In Shaanxi province alone in a period of a few months starting from April 1968, 281 public security offices, 111 judicial offices and 61 courts were ransacked and more than 141,000 files, 5,800 guns and 5,000 bullets were seized. The property of eleven of the courts was all lost. The law and order departments made no attempt to control the Red Guards; their only function now, after all, was to enforce the class struggle and they continued to send out special units to arrest people of the wrong background.

The activities of the Red Guards lasted for about two years. They began in 1966 at Tsing Hua Secondary School and the beginning of the end came finally in 1968 when soldiers and workers were sent into Tsing Hua University. From late 1968, all educational institutions were put under military control and many of the Red Guard leaders, including Quie Da-Fu, were arrested and subjected to struggle meetings or killed. Millions of Red Guards from the rival gangs were sent to poverty-stricken villages and, whether they had been born red or black, all received lengthy sentences of hard labour reform, after which they were deprived of further formal education or decent jobs.

Meanwhile the Cultural Revolution rumbled on, but now that the young student Red Guards had been removed from the political stage, their place was taken by party cadres and administrative staff.

101

Deposing a President, Mao Tse-Tung Style

Liu Shao-Qi (1898–1969) was born in Hunan province and joined the Chinese Communist Party in 1921 when he was studying in Moscow. At the important meeting in Zunyi in 1935 when Mao won the position of de facto party leader, Liu was one of his supporters and in 1945 he was the first person to introduce the term Mao Tse-Tung Thought. He loyally took part in Mao's non-stop purges of dissidents; when Mao laid trumped-up charges against the defence minister Peng De-Huai, Liu told the Conference of 7,000 People, which met in January 1962, that Peng had run a long-standing anti-party cabal inside the party and that it had foreign backing.

Liu also wrote a famous book, *The Self-Cultivation of Communists*, which attained textbook status for many aspiring revolutionaries. In it he preached that a Communist should act as a tool of the party and obey the party absolutely. In 1954, when the first Chinese constitution was formally approved by the National People's Congress, Liu used the occasion to make a pungent attack on the hypocrisy of Western-style democracy, claiming that only a socialist country such as China had genuine democracy.

In early 1961 this staunch Communist led a fact-finding team to Hunan, his home province, where his elder sister still lived in a village. He found that although the previous season's drought had not been too serious, many peasants were starving and ill with oedema and although they had salt, they had no cooking oil. He closed down the communal canteens at once and urged the cadres who had been denounced for opposing the Great Leap Forward to return to their old jobs. After visiting Hunan, he went on to investigate the rural areas of Hubei and Henan provinces.

A guilt-stricken Liu later spoke at a meeting to a group of officials behind Mao's back: "We need to warn our party to remember this painful lesson forever. Not only should your generation keep it in your hearts, you should also teach the next generation, so that your children will not make such mistakes again. This is a lesson that deserves to be inscribed on a stone tablet to help people remember this painful lesson forever." Such remarks were duly reported to the intelligence chief, Kang Sheng, who in turn reported them to Mao.

Speaking at the Conference of 7,000 People in January 1962, Liu stated quite openly that in his opinion 30 per cent of the difficulties brought about by the Great Leap Forward had been caused by natural disasters and 70 per cent by human error. The Great Leap Forward had not gone forwards, instead it had gone backwards and it would perhaps have been better if the people's communes had not been launched at that time. Liu wanted to solve China's difficulties through economic remedies, whereas Mao wanted to solve them with political measures, or in other words further class struggle. The opposing views of the two leading men were openly displayed at the meeting and Liu's remark about human errors rankled with Mao. When the meeting was over, Mao flew into a rage, concluding by saying that he was ill.

Mao regarded Liu as a capitalist roader and, perhaps more to the point, as his political rival. By 1965, Mao had decided that he did not have sufficient control over many of the provincial party branches and the propaganda department of the Peking party committee in particular seemed out of control. He told the American writer Edgar Snow, who happened to be visiting China at the time, that although a personality cult existed in China, it still needed to be strengthened. It was in early 1965, according to many senior Communists, that Mao decided that Liu had to go.

Mao now began cautiously on the operation to topple his heavyweight target. In addition to disbanding the work units, the party formally revoked a document issued and signed by Liu, which signified that he had made a mistake. At a series of meetings behind closed doors, Liu was criticised by Mao's supporters for having the nerve to compete with Chairman Mao and he was forced to make self-criticisms.

While the propaganda machine was exalting Mao to the skies, astute observers began to notice hints that Liu was falling from power. When the newspapers carried lengthy reports about Mao's first inspection of Red Guards on 18 August 1966, Liu's name went down to number seven in the party's pecking order. Not one clear image of Liu, President of the People's Republic of China, appeared in nearly 40 photos published by the *People's Daily*, although Jiang Ching, in 24th position, appeared conspicuously in several prints.

During this inspection of the Red Guards, the intelligence chief Kang Sheng wrote a note to the Red Guard representatives of Nankai University from Tianjin, as follows: 'Could your Red Guards please make investigations into traitors who have infiltrated a number of units and departments. Check on the arrest and betrayal of Liu and others.' Kang signed his name on the note.

Kang knew that the accusations of going down the capitalist road and of pursuing reactionary policies were not enough to bring down Liu. Only the fatal charges of traitor and enemy agent would do the trick; then Mao's mobs could be used to lynch him. He would have liked to award this task to Peking's Red Guards, Quie Da-Fu or Nep Yuan-Tze, but he was worried that word might leak out, so instead he decided to use the Tianjin group, away from Peking city.

Overwhelmed by this unexpected favour, the Nankai University Red Guards formed an 80-strong group called the 'Catching-Traitors Fighting Squad', which quickly sprang into action. They were armed with copies of Kang's instructions which enabled them to interrogate any suspects and to search through archives to find evidence that could be used against suspected traitors. Kang gave them the names of 61 suspects and the Nankai Red Guards worked day and night to produce a report.

On 19 August, wall posters hostile to Wang Quon-Mei appeared at Tsing Hua University, defying the ban on wall posters and denunciations of the 'first lady'. Now everybody knew Wang was in trouble and this meant that her husband, Liu, was in trouble too.

Two days later, on 21 August, the 11th edition of *Red Flag* repeated the important message that everyone must obey Mao Tse-Tung Thought; anyone who resisted it, no matter how senior, had to be opposed and sacked. The *People's Daily* also dropped sinister hints which bore Mao's unmistakeable hallmark. The following day, 22 August, a second wall poster appeared at Tsing Hua University, openly accusing Liu of being hostile to Mao Tse-Tung Thought and the next day an editorial in the *People's Daily* encouraged people to rebel against the work units.

Under the discreet direction of the Central Cultural Revolution Small Team, the media and the rebel Red Guards engaged in an unremitting onslaught on Liu, Wang Quon-Mei and "the people in power". The old Red Guards, for their part, took the side of the work units and proceeded to tear up all wall posters they found on the Tsing Hua University campus which attacked Liu and Wang.

Most people found the situation perplexing. Many provincial and local government chiefs all opposed the rebel students, as did the working class and the peasants; people naturally assumed it was safer to stay on the side of the party bosses. The rebel minority soon looked isolated and Mao felt he had to turn the tide round quickly. On 2 September, a new instruction was issued warning people not to oppose the student movement and on

7 September Mao wrote to Lin Biao, Chan Bor-Da and Jiang suggesting that any interference in the student movement should be banned. On 11 September, a directive issued by the party central committee forbade local party bosses from encouraging people to oppose the students.

Although Mao occasionally sounded ambivalent during the early stages of the operation to snare Liu, as time went on he often made vicious attacks on the sinking man. Outsiders tried hard to guess what Mao's real intention was; until he made his decision clear no one dared make a move. The Central Cultural Revolution Small Team was certainly unable to do anything without Mao's patronage.

From the second half of 1966, Jiang's team were hard at work secretly encouraging Red Guard rebels to denounce Liu. In October, Kang's men summoned several leading rebels to a meeting, at which they urged the rebels not to delay in putting up wall posters denouncing Liu; it would be a new contribution to the Cultural Revolution. Certain very senior party leaders might try to dissuade them, but they should be ignored. The rebels should avoid telling people that Kang was involved.

By October the Red Guards had seized all educational institutions; they had terrorised the whole of society and appeared by now to be an unstoppable force. The climate was steadily becoming more favourable for Mao and, with the aim of dispelling the resistance of the middle-ranking cadres, he now summoned leading party officials from all over the country to a conference to begin on 9 October. Originally planned to last three days, it was in the end extended to 20 days, Mao chairing the conference himself.

At the conference, both Liu and Deng Xiao-Ping were forced to make self-examinations. On 23 October Deng admitted that Mao's wall poster inside the compound of Central South Sea, ostensibly aimed at a capitalist command headquarters, was actually aimed at the command headquarters of Liu and himself. Two days later Lin Biao told the conference that Liu and Deng were carrying out policies hostile to Chairman Mao and were aiming for a capitalist dictatorship. This finally made clear who the prime targets of the Cultural Revolution were. While the two men's impending purge was nominally kept from the public, Jiang's group was quietly passing on information of this case to the Red Guard rebels.

On 2 November, wall posters condemning Liu and Deng appeared in Tiananmen Square and the following day Mao inspected his Red Guards for the sixth time. Ostensibly Liu and Deng's positions remained unchanged and they therefore joined other senior officials on the Tiananmen city wall. When photographs of the party leaders taken on this occasion were published in the newspapers, there was no trace of either Liu or Deng, a bad omen for them. Yet while they had stood on the city wall in the full glare of publicity, Mao had walked up to Liu and talked to him for more than ten minutes, a calculated move designed to show that he was a munificent and benevolent leader.

At a politburo meeting on 6 December, Lin Biao accused Liu and Deng of having made serious mistakes over a long period; for the past 20 years they had persistently failed to carry out Chairman Mao's revolutionary policies. Liu was forced to criticise himself again, but he never agreed that he had been hostile to, or had plotted against, Mao.

By the end of December, the streets of Peking were full of slogans denouncing Liu and Deng. One of Liu's alleged crimes was his book *The Self-Cultivation of Communists*, which had been published in 1939 and openly praised by Mao. Now, however, the book was said to contain an unforgivable betrayal of proletarian dictatorship. To launch his all-out attack, Mao wrote the outlines of an essay; two of his underlings, Guan Fung and Wang Li, wrote a first draft, which in turn was amended several times by Chan Bor-Da and Kang Sheng before being presented to the politburo for discussion. Once Mao had approved it, it was published as the work of the editorial departments of the *People's Daily*, *Red Flag* and the PLA newspaper.

Guan Fung wondered who had been responsible for approving the original publication of Liu's book and he asked the chief of *Red Flag* to investigate, only to be dumbfounded when it turned out that Chan Bor-Da and Kang Sheng themselves had amended the book and approved its first publication. It had apparently not occurred to him that an important book such as *The Self-Cultivation of Communists* could not have been published by *Red Flag* without Mao's approval. Yet now, in the spring of 1967, Liu's 'black cultivation book' was submerged by a tidal wave of criticism guided by Mao.

Another of Liu's crimes had taken place in the early 1920s, when Mao had been the party secretary of Hunan province and Liu had worked under him. Mao had sent Liu to the big Oun Yuan coal-mine just across the provincial border in Jiangxi province, where Liu had directed the workers' movement for three years while Mao stayed in Hunan province. In 1922, Liu had led 17,000 miners out on strike for better pay and working conditions. This was five or so years before the Communist Party had set its mind on armed struggle; instead Mao had instructed Liu to act lawfully so that they could openly remain close to the workers.

Liu had represented the miners in negotiations with their employers. After a five-day strike, the employers had given in to most of the miners' 13 demands and from then on Liu was greatly admired by the Oun Yuan miners. More than 40 years later, the negotiations with the capitalists were denounced as selling out the interests of the working class. Red Guards from other cities descended on Oun Yuan and ordered local people to remove all portraits of Liu within 24 hours. A workers' club where Liu had once lived was dynamited; Red Guards seized documents from the commemorative building of the Oun Yuan workers' movement, while its manager was taken to a struggle meeting and accused of being Liu's running dog. A film about the Oun Yuan strike was condemned as poisonous on the grounds that it misrepresented history, obliterating the brilliant contribution of Chairman Mao and giving credit to the Chinese Khrushchev. Although Liu had had nothing whatsoever to do with the production of this film, he still had to suffer for it and the scriptwriter, director, actors and reviewers of the film were all accused of manufacturing poison.

Of all the accusations levelled against Liu, the most vicious was to make him out to be a traitor who was leading a renegade bloc. Back in 1931, about 400 political prisoners had been jailed in Peking. More than 300 had been released after accepting the Nationalist demand that they should place advertisements in the newspapers declaring that they would relinquish their faith in Communism. Some senior Communists refused to give in and as a result they were kept in jail even though they had served their full term.

When the Japanese had seized Manchuria back in 1931, they had killed all the Communists in Shenyang prison. It appeared that they were about to invade north China around 1936 and if they did so the Communists in jail in Peking might well be massacred as well. Liu, then the party secretary for north China, decided it was important that the remaining prisoners should be rescued quickly. Since all the prisoners had used false names, denouncing their belief in Communism in the newspapers was of little real significance, so he urged that they should be told to accept the Nationalist condition in order to get themselves out of jail.

The party office in north China reported the situation and Liu's opinion to the party central leadership and the politburo, including Mao, agreed with Liu. Accordingly, the general secretary, Chang Won-Tian, sent a handwritten message to the 61 men still in Peking jail, ordering them to obey the central committee decision and so the 61 men accepted the Nationalist condition in order to get themselves out of jail.

In a telephone conversation with Chow En-Lai in late November 1966, Liu mentioned that he had not known any of these 61 people before they were thrown into Peking jail; he had only met some of them after their release. Jiang and Kang now alleged that the 61 people freed in 1936 had all been traitors. The two of them calculated that as long as their accusation was accepted, Liu would unavoidably go down with the 61 people. The newspapers were quietly tipped off about the case and the Red Guards were incited to attack the 'turncoats'.

On 16 September 1966 Kang sent Mao copies of the Peking newspapers of August and September 1936 which carried the anti-Communist advertisement of the 61 prisoners, commenting that he had long suspected betrayal. At this stage, Mao did not agree with Kang's accusation.

Before long Red Guards in Xian and Tianjin were investigating Liu Lan-Tao, the first secretary of the northwest party bureau, claiming that he had left jail with the 61 traitors. On 24 November Chow En-Lai in a letter censored and approved by Mao wrote to the northwest bureau explaining that the central authorities were aware of the circumstances of the prisoners' release and that Liu Shao-Qi had represented the party to make the decision. The affair had also later been re-examined by two party congresses and both concluded that the prisoners could not be blamed for their efforts to secure their own release. Chow ordered the northwest bureau to explain the situation to the Red Guards.

On 16 March 1967, Jiang and her group issued a letter to all party members in the name of the party central authorities, asserting that the 61 freed prisoners had belonged to a bloc of traitors and that their release from jail had been planned by Liu. Chang Won-Tian had also agreed with the plan, which had been carried out behind Mao's back. The letter urged the masses to drag out the traitors so that they could be dealt with in a suitable way.

The whole country was soon in hot pursuit of these traitors. Among the 61 people was the vice premier, Bo Yi-Ball, who at the time was having medical treatment in Canton. He was duly brought back to Peking by the Central Cultural Revolution Small Team's revolutionary mobs and a special unit was now set up to investigate the bloc of traitors. Bo Yi-Ball told the interrogator that Mao had known about the business, since he, Bo, had reported it to him in person in Yan'an. The interrogator told Bo that if he were to keep silent about Mao's knowledge of the situation they would consider giving him a way out, but if he repeated what he had said he would be punished. After his interrogation Bo Yi-Ball joined other senior Communists in the Chin City prison in 1966. Twelve years later, in 1978, he was rehabilitated by Deng Xiao-Ping's government and in 1979 he was re-appointed as vice premier.

In January 1967 Jiang's secretary, Chic Bun-Yu, alleged that Red Guard "little warriors" had discovered that Ong Tze-Won, director of the party's Department of Organisation, had also been one of the 61 turncoats.

Furthermore, Chic asserted that Liu had been the biggest organiser of the renegades.

On 12 February 1967 another of Jiang's group, Guan Fung, said at a meeting of the armed forces that Ong Tze-Won, Bo Yi-Ball and Liu Lan-Tao all advocated capitalist dictatorship, even though they occupied important departments and held the reins of power. The "little warriors", said Guan, gained great merit by stirring up the Cultural Revolution, because the three men were traitors.

On 21 January 1968 Ong Tze-Won was sent to prison and he was kept incommunicado. Several people from the special investigation unit persuaded him to make a written statement testifying that Liu was an important traitor; if he did so it would be to his credit and he would have a better chance of returning home to his family. Ong Tze-Won refused to cooperate and his teeth were knocked out by the interrogators.

Another member of the 61 'traitors' was Liu Jeun-Chi, the editor-in-chief and deputy director of the Foreign Language Press. He often acted as interpreter when Mao and Liu Shao-Qi received foreign heads of state. In April 1968, Liu Jeun-Chi was sent to prison. The interrogators demanded to know why, when Mao Tse-Tung's selected works had been translated into English, Liu Jeun-Chi had deleted the great leader's brilliant instructions. Liu Shao-Qi had been responsible for publishing the English version of the selected works and Liu Jeun-Chi had been in charge of the practical work. The Chinese Government had reached an agreement with the British Communist Party that the English version of the book would be sold by a bookshop run by the British Communist Party. When Liu Jeun-Chi checked the book's English version, he discovered an omission in the following paragraph from the essay 'War and strategy':

The highest form and central duty of revolution is to seize political power by arms, it is to solve the problem by war. This revolutionary principle of Marxism and Leninism is universally correct; no matter whether in China or in foreign countries, it is always right.

Liu Jeun-Chi noticed that the words 'in foreign countries' were missing and he wrote to the British Communist Party to ask for an explanation. The reply explained that the party's solicitor had objected to the words on the grounds that they could potentially leave the party liable to a fine, not to mention other trouble. Liu Jeun-Shi asked for instructions from Liu Shao-Qi on how to respond and eventually they agreed to accept the

British decision. Now, Liu Shao-Qi was condemned because of these few missing words and Liu Jeun-Chi spent a long time in prison for misrepresenting Mao Tse-Tung Thought.

Chang Won-Tian, once the general secretary of the Chinese Communist Party, was now under immense pressure from Kang to say that Liu Shao-Qi had arranged the affair of the 61 traitors without the knowledge of the party central committee. Chang insisted that the case had been approved by the central committee and that Mao had taken part in the decision. As a result, Chang and his wife were sent to jail.

Trying desperately to extract damaging testimony against Liu Shao-Qi and Wang Quon-Mei, Jiang's group arrested and imprisoned people in large numbers. Wang was vulnerable because she had worked as an interpreter for the American army in Peking just after the Second World War. Many people, some of whom had never even spoken to her, were detained in an attempt to extract confessions that Wang was an American spy. Among those detained were two professors, both of them very ill, who died in prison as a result of interrogations and torture. Jiang even arrested the Liu family's old cook, How Mel, who was imprisoned for more than six years without knowing what he had done wrong.

A new vice premier was now required to replace the disgraced Bo Yi-Ball and the post was given to Tao Jeug. Tao had spent most of his career working in the provinces away from Peking and he was unaware of the insidious nature of the anti-Liu drive. He openly disapproved of the abuse thrown at Liu and he was also cautious about approving the condemnation of other senior Communists by the rebels. He got in Jiang's way in no time and posters soon appeared accusing Tao of being a royalist and committing the crimes of anti-party, anti-socialism and anti- Mao Tse-Tung Thought, among other crimes.

On 4 January 1967, Jiang, Kang and Chan Bor-Da announced to rebel Red Guards that since Tao Jeug had become vice premier he had completely failed to execute the proletarian revolutionary policy as represented by Chairman Mao and he was in fact a loyal follower of the policy of Liu and Deng. Overnight, wall posters bearing the slogan 'Down with Tao Jeug' appeared all over China. Tens of thousands of people gathered outside Central South Sea, chanting all through the night and demanding that Tao should be dragged to a struggle meeting. At 6 a.m. Chow En-Lai emerged to talk to the hostile crowd, managing to calm them down slightly. Tao was now called a traitor. His name was linked with Liu and Deng and nearly everything he had done during the Cultural Revolution was pronounced wrong.

On 7 January, Jiang and Chan met workers from the Xinhua news agency, who claimed that Tao had tried to persuade some of their colleagues to forge a photograph showing Mao and Liu together. A number of provincial newspapers had used the photo and this had had a bad influence on the whole nation. The following day there was an urgent meeting of the central committee, at which Mao said that Tao's problem was very serious. He had been introduced to central government by Deng and right at the start he, Mao, had realised that Tao was not honest, though Deng had disagreed. Tao had resolutely carried out Liu's and Deng's policies. Images of Liu and Deng had appeared in the newspapers and on TV, purporting to show them among other leaders meeting Red Guards after the inspection in Tiananmen Square and this had all been arranged by Tao. The ministries which Tao had overseen had all collapsed. There were many problems which we could not solve; only the Red Guards could solve them.

After Mao's carefully scripted remarks, the Red Guards did indeed solve the problem of Tao, who now found himself detained and subjected to struggle sessions. Suffering by this time from cancer, he was eventually kept in a secret prison ward in Anhui province which was under Jiang's control, where permission had to be sought before he could be given so much as an injection of painkillers. Soon after Liu's death Tao died in the special prison ward and was cremated under a false name. Many others who sympathised with Liu were to meet similar fates.

While hard at work liquidating Liu's supporters, Jiang and her gang were never distracted from their main target. On 18 December 1966, they received the rebel representatives from Peking's educational institutions in the Great Hall of the People. Jiang urged the rebels to unite in support of the revolutionary teachers and students at Tsing Hua University to attack Wang Quon-Mei and Bo Yi-Ball. Bo in particular had a very serious problem.

Jiang now set up a special team to investigate Wang; if she could have Wang condemned as a traitor and enemy agent, Liu would then naturally become a traitor and enemy agent as well. On the same day, Chang Chun-Chel, Jiang's aide and a member of her 'gang of four', summoned the leader of Tsing Hua University Jinggangshan Army Corps, Quie Da-Fu, to a secret one-to-one meeting in Central South Sea, at which he advised Quie to unite the revolutionary 'little warriors' to strike at Liu and Deng.

Quie knew Chang could not have made such a perilous suggestion without some very powerful backing; Liu, after all, was still the President of China and a member of the politburo standing committee. Quie therefore returned to his university in the western suburbs and began to carry out his mentor's instructions assiduously. One week later, on 25 December at 10 a.m., 5,000 Tsing Hua University students and staff arrived at Tiananmen Square, where they split up into five columns to parade and demonstrate in the bustling city centre. Led by vehicles with loudspeakers, they marched through the streets chanting slogans, putting up wall posters, distributing handbills, holding meetings and making speeches, all of them condemning Liu Shao-Qi and Deng Xiao-Ping as capitalist running dogs and urging that the two men should be removed from their posts. The demonstrations continued for a whole day.

The Jinggangshan Army Corps' own newspaper, circulated across the whole country, printed a series of articles vilifying Liu. One of them, published on New Year's Day 1967 under the heading 'Bombard the Chinese Khrushchev, Liu Shao-Qi', listed 12 serious crimes which Liu had supposedly perpetrated during his long service to the party. The anti-Liu campaign was getting more and more vicious and soon no one dared to utter a dissenting word.

On 27 December 1966, Jiang and Kang met Quie and his Red Guards in Tsing Hua University and urged that Liu should be put through struggle meetings. After all, he was the Chinese Khrushchev, wasn't he? There were the vice premiers and ministers too; all of them were supporters of Liu. Quie was clearly taken aback, he asked:"Can we put him through a struggle session?" Jiang said:"Why not? After all, Chairman Mao himself said that if Liu were not brought down, China would turn to revisionism." Kang joined in to urge the Red Guards not to worry; Liu's case had already been confirmed by the party central committee.

Quie, daunted by the task ahead of him, said that Liu was inside Central South Sea, so how could they reach him? 'Just march in,' replied Jiang, 'and drag him out.'

In addition to working on the rebel Red Guards, Jiang's gang, claiming to represent Mao and the party central, paid a visit to Liu's daughter Liu Tao; a daughter from a previous marriage, she was now a student at Tsing Hua University. They told the girl to distance herself from her sinful father; if she failed to do so, it would show that she too was a counter-revolutionary. In the face of this coercion, Liu Tao produced a wall poster with the heading 'Looking into Liu's ugly soul'. Three copies of the poster were made and on 3 January they were displayed at the university.

Chow En-Lai did try to protect Liu. He advised the couple not to leave the heavily guarded Central South Sea; as long as they remained inside they should be relatively safe. The Red Guard rebels among the Central South Sea cadres were keeping quiet at that time, but on the morning of 13 December Jiang's secretary, Chic Bun-Yu, phoned the rebel leaders and railed at them for not producing wall posters attacking Liu and Wang. In the afternoon the first batch of wall posters openly attacking the couple duly appeared inside Central South Sea. Now there was no place for Liu and his family to hide.

At dawn on 1 January 1967, two men knocked loudly on the door of Liu's residence. When the door was opened they elbowed their way into the forecourt, sticking slogans on the walls and daubing slogans on the brick floor reading 'Down with the Chinese Khrushchev, Liu' and 'Anyone who opposes Mao Tse-Tung Thought will definitely be crushed'. In the evening of 3 January, around 30 Central South Sea rebels marched into Liu's home and criticised Liu and Wang for over 40 minutes, Liu was also made to recite some of Mao's sayings.

Three days later, Liu received a telephone call reporting that his young daughter Liu Ping-Ping, a student at Tsing Hua Secondary School, had been injured in a serious traffic accident and that the hospital needed to amputate her leg. The anxious parents, ignoring the danger of venturing out of Central South Sea, rushed to the hospital, only to find the Tsing Hua University rebels waiting for them, with the couple's two other daughters as hostages. The rebels had comrade Jiang's support, they said, to play this trick to entice Wang out of Central South Sea and they wished to take her to a struggle meeting back at Tsing Hua University. It seemed there was no way out for Liu and Wang, so Wang told her family to leave, saying that she would go with the rebels alone. Liu Ping-Ping was uninjured, but was detained in her school as a hostage; she was later released unharmed.

Chow En-Lai soon heard what was happening and, disregarding Jiang's frequent attacks on him, he immediately rang Quie and asked him to release Wang immediately. Quie was not worried about Chow's intervention, since he knew that he had Jiang's backing. He took Wang to the struggle meeting, but Chow sent his secretary to Tsing Hua University to seek Wang's early release. She finally went home before dawn.

On 10 January, the Xinhua bookshops in Peking collected together all their portraits of Liu and Deng, which were taken to Tiananmen Square and burnt there. Soon other Xinhua bookshops did the same and all over China Liu's and Deng's portraits went up in flames. It was sensational propaganda and a nationwide insult to the two men.

On 12 January, Chic Bun-Yu summoned the cadres of Central South Sea to a meeting and urged them to deal harshly with Liu, Deng and Tao. 'There are things which the central authority finds inconvenient to talk about,' he said darkly. 'You, though, can do it for us and bring them into the open.' That evening, around 80 people from the central office secretariat went to the homes of Liu, Deng and Tao and the three men were put through struggle sessions.

The following day, late at night, Liu was summoned in secret to see Mao in the Great Hall of the People. Liu said that he was responsible for all the mistakes of which he had been accused and he asked Mao to set all other condemned cadres free. He offered to resign from all his posts and take his family either to Yan'an or to his home village to work as peasants, hoping this would at last bring the Cultural Revolution to a swift end and minimize the damage to the nation. Mao seemed friendly, though he avoided accepting Liu's resignation offer and his duplicity gave Liu hope.

A couple of days later, the Central South Sea rebels again turned up at Liu's home. New wall posters were pasted around his courtyard and he and his wife were subjected to a second struggle session. On 17 January, rebels from the telephone department marched into Liu's home to remove his telephone. Liu insisted that they had no right to take away the telephone of a politburo member without the permission of Chairman Mao or the prime minister and the rebels left empty-handed. They were back the following day, seemingly having obtained approval from the highest authorities. Paying no attention to Liu's protests, they removed the telephone and Liu was now left in complete isolation.

By late March, many other senior Communists had also been purged and rumours of Liu and Deng's alleged misdeeds were snowballing. On 6 April the rebels again forced their way into Liu's office, where he was upbraided about his crimes, including the case of the 61 traitors. He was to produce written answers relating to all the charges and from now on he was to do his own cooking, laundry and cleaning.

The following day Liu had produced his written answers to the charges on a wall poster, which displayed inside Central South Sea. Within a few hours it was torn to pieces. Whenever he opened his mouth to speak at the struggle meetings, the rebels instantly hit his face, nose and mouth with the little Red Book and said:"stop poisoning the minds of other people." He had lost the right to defend himself. Wang, meanwhile, was faring just as badly. On 10 April, the Jinggangshan Army Corps organised a struggle meeting against her at Tsing Hua University, which was attended by 300,000 people.

During April and May 1963, President Liu and his wife had made state visits to Southeast Asia and the Foreign Ministry's protocol office decided to make new clothes for the couple and their entourage. Wang was equipped with traditional long gowns, silk stockings and high-heeled shoes, but she sought advice from Jiang about a suitable dress code for her foreign visit. Jiang's opinion was inscrutable: 'No brooch'.

When the graceful Wang appeared in the limelight on foreign television, elegantly dressed and wearing a string of pearls, Jiang's jealousy knew no bounds. In July 1966, she mentioned Wang's foreign visits in 1963 at a Peking University meeting, speaking as if she had been deeply insulted. She had told Wang not to wear a necklace, she said, but Wang had not listened to her advice. The Red Guards were duly incensed by this obvious sign of wickedness.

On 10 April, the day of the enormous struggle meeting, Red Guards drove into Central South Sea before dawn to take Wang under guard to Tsing Hua University. There she was forced to put on the costume she had worn on her visit to Indonesia: the silk stockings, the high-heeled shoes and the long gown which was already too small. The Red Guards had prepared her a special necklace in the form of a string of table tennis balls. After receiving a vicious kicking and punching, she was taken to the struggle meeting, together with around 300 other senior Communist capitalist roaders, including the vice premier Bo Yi-Ball, the mayor of Peking Peng Zhen and the Tsing Hua University President Chiang Nan-Chane.

Large caricatures and photos of Wang attired by the Red Guards were displayed in the streets of Peking and printed in Red Guard newspapers circulated all over China. On 1 June, *Red Flag* and the *People's Daily* reprinted Mao's wall poster about firing at another command headquarters to remind people that the primary aim of the Cultural Revolution was to topple Liu and establish Mao's absolute authority. Then on 3 June, Jinggangshan Army Corps, together with another 18 Red Guard groups, formed a 'Frontline Command Headquarters to pursue and struggle against Liu Shao-Qi,' which proceeded to set up a camp outside the west entrance of Central South Sea. By early July about 700 rebel groups had taken up positions covering a huge area outside the west and north entrances of Central South Sea. Displaying red banners of different groups, they were accommodated in tents or improvised straw huts, or simply under tattered pieces of cloths. Some groups used loudspeakers to hurl abuse at Liu Shao-Qi.

On 4 July, Jiang sent Chic Bun-Yu to meet the students of the Frontline Command Headquarters. Chic told the students that he represented the Cultural Revolution central authority to give the students their support and best wishes. By then, Liu was ordered to make a self-examination in front of the Red Guards at an architectural college where he had been working at the start of the Cultural Revolution. He was too exhausted to write anything, so instead Wang wrote on his behalf, declaring his obedience to the great Chairman and admitting that he was responsible for making all the mistakes at the time when Mao had entrusted him with the job of running the country and saying furthermore that he was quite willing to be criticised.

The sentence 'Mao had entrusted him with the job of running the country' brought Liu more trouble. On 9 July, hundreds of loudspeakers blasted Central South Sea day and night, accusing Liu of pointing his spear in his self-examination at Chairman Mao and the Central Cultural Revolution Small Team and proclaiming that Liu was a felonious counter-revolutionary.

The architectural college Red Guards replied to Liu's self-examination on 15 July with a 'directive' calling Liu 'a pile of dog shit disdained by all mankind' and declaring their determination to drag him out of Central South Sea to a public trial. The diatribe ended by ordering Liu to bow his head, admit his crimes submissively to Chairman Mao and produce a second self-examination before 25 July.

In the afternoon of 13 July, Mao called a politburo meeting in the Great Hall of the People to review the progress of the Cultural Revolution. As far as he was concerned, everything was going well and he announced at the meeting that he had decided to visit south China and go swimming in Wuhan, as the water was nice there. He promptly left Peking that same night, leaving Liu at the mercy of Jiang.

By mid-July 1967, several hundred thousand Red Guards, many of them from other parts of China, camped outside the perimeter walls of Central South Sea. This vast palace compound, situated beside the Forbidden City, had originally been built in the 12th century, but most of its existing buildings dated from the Qing Dynasty. The whole complex, which had five entrances, stood in a park of 250 acres, half of which consisted of the lakes of Central Sea and South Sea. The site was now surrounded by a sea of shanty-town structures covered with big red slogans and red banners. On 18 July, the Red Guards held a meeting at which they swore that they were determined to drag Liu out of Central South Sea to a struggle meeting. To show their determination some even went on hunger strike. The party's many provincial first secretaries and central government ministers were taken to struggle meetings outside Central South Sea's west entrance to show an example to Liu. By now any officials still in power had moved out of the palace complex and only a few families, including Liu and Chow En-Lai, were still living there. Chow's office was close to the perimeter wall and he found himself harassed non-stop by the loudspeakers.

After a further speech by Chic Bun-Yu urging the rebels to drag Liu out of Central South Sea, the mobs started to force their way into the palace compound. The guards at the gates held them back with difficulty, telephoning Chow to report the tense situation and Chow immediately dashed around to one gate or other in an attempt to reason with the crowd. Sometimes before he could placate the crowd at one gate, Jiang and Chan Bor-Da would appear at another to incite the Red Guards to try to break into the compound. Before long, a mob of over 100 screaming people had broken through one gate, but Chow rushed there as fast as he could and told the crowd sternly that Central South Sea was the seat of the party central authority and that they were forbidden to enter; if they did so it would be over his dead body. The crowd faltered; Chow's prestige had for the moment checked their attacks.

Jiang, who had long wanted to hand Liu over to the rebels, had once urged the leading rebels inside Central South Sea to gain permission to struggle against Liu face to face. Mao had once said to Jiang, 'Don't do this to Liu!' But now he was sightseeing in south China, in effect giving Jiang a free hand.

Jiang and Kang now arranged a big struggle meeting against Liu inside the palace compound. She ordered the special unit which was dealing with Liu's case to ransack his home when the struggle meeting was in progress and seize all his diaries and documents, because she had still not secured sufficient evidence to incriminate him. Chic Bun-Yu asked what they would do if the struggle meeting ended before they had finished searching his home, to which Jiang replied that the struggle meeting would have to continue until they had finished their search.

On 18 July, Liu and Wang were taken to separate struggle meetings in two different canteens inside the compound. When they were over, Liu was locked up in the office of his home, while Wang was locked up in the couple's bedroom in the rear courtyard; neither knew the other's whereabouts. Their children remained in their own bedrooms in the middle of the house, but were forbidden to have any contact with their parents; in addition they were told to watch and report on each other as well. To be on the safe side Jiang gave orders to post extra guards in the house.

On 5 August, the first anniversary of Mao's famous wall poster, the *People's Daily* reprinted the poster and called for more intense attacks on the capitalist roaders inside the party, while Jiang organised three big struggle meetings against Liu, Deng, Tao and their wives to be held in their own homes. On the day of the anniversary, Liu and Wang were escorted to the meeting. Liu was forced to bend down and his arms were twisted back and raised up high in the notorious 'jet style' torture posture; then he was kicked and punched. Someone grasped his thin white hair to lift his head for photo sessions. The leaders were keen to film the proceedings so that they could be shown to the nation. The couple's children, the youngest one a six-year-old girl, were forced to attend the meeting to see their parents insulted and beaten. This struggle meeting lasted two hours. Whenever Liu tried to answer or defend himself, he was interrupted by the noisy shouting of slogans and the rebels repeatedly hit his face and head with their Little Red Books. The couple were made to bow to a large picture showing a group of Red Guards. By the end of the meeting, Liu's face was bruised all over, he had lost his shoes and could hardly walk.

After he was escorted back to his prison-office, taking out a copy of the constitution of Communist China, he summoned his private secretary and protested:

"I am the President of the People's Republic of China. How you people treat me as a person is unimportant, but I have to defend the dignity of the president. Who has dismissed me as President? If you want to put me on trial, you must go through the NPC. The way you people behave is insulting our country. I am also a citizen. Why forbid me to speak? The constitution protects every citizen's human rights. People who breach the constitution will be severely punished by law."

His secretary was very upset and made a written report the same night to the party central authority. Liu also wrote to Mao on August 7, but there was no reply.

When Liu was in power, he did not hesitate to trample on the constitution and other people's human rights. He had done his share to extinguish these two ideas in China; now he remembered that he should have been protected by the constitution and that he had human rights. It was too late!

Long after the end of the Cultural Revolution, Chan Bor-Da, who had been Mao's trusted political secretary and the nominal head of the Central Cultural Revolution Small Team, said: 'In reality, no important decisions in the Cultural Revolution could be made without Mao's support and acquiescence. For example, there were struggle meetings on 5 August 1967 against Liu, Deng and Tao. Ostensibly Mao was not in Peking, but in fact he was watching the progress of the struggle meetings closely. He told Chow, Lin Biao, me and some other people that it appeared as if Liu, Deng and their supporters were not afraid of us. They were afraid of the Red Guards and the revolutionary masses and at the appropriate time they should be handed over to the masses to receive criticism. If they were not handed over, there would probably be no way of settling the affair. The Red Guards were more versatile than we were and they could not avoid surrendering to the masses.'

In accordance with Mao's instructions, Jiang's clique encouraged the actions of the Red Guards and the revolutionary masses. After Mao had been given details of the struggle meetings in Central South Sea, he had said to Chang Chun-Chel, 'It is good to struggle against them this way. Don't let the masses drag them out, there is no safety guarantee in dragging them out. Show the pictures on television; we will educate more people that way.' Later on, concerned about their international image, the leaders decided not to broadcast the pictures of Liu's struggle meeting.

On 5 September 1967, the Chinese media reported the exciting news that Mao had returned to Peking after an inspection tour of more than two months and that he thought the progress of the Cultural Revolution was very good.

But the news of Liu and his family was not very good. On 13 September, his children were told to pack their bags and go to their schools to receive investigation and criticism; they were not even to be allowed to return home during the school holidays. The youngest daughter was kicked out of Central South Sea with her nanny that very afternoon and in the evening Wang was thrown into jail. Liu knew nothing about what was happening to his family. Some days before, he had managed to exchange a few words with his children and was told Wang was locked up in the rear part of the house. He often limped to the wall separating him from the rear court, hoping to hear his wife's movements, but he never heard anything. Before long a high wall was built overnight to prevent him from approaching the rear court again.

One day some soldiers arrived to search Liu's room, taking away, among other things, his leather belt. When he protested, he was pinned down on the floor and his belt was removed by force. His former bodyguards now became his warders.

The struggle meetings injured both his legs and made an old war wound in his arm worse; he was not given enough sleeping pills so was often short of sleep. It would take him 50 minutes or more to walk the 30 metres to the dining room and though he would often nearly fall none of the guards dared to give him a hand. Eventually he could not walk at all and his meals had to be brought to him; but since anyone who performed this job would be called a 'royalist soldier', none of the guards wanted the job. Often his food was kept for several meals, by which time some of the food had gone bad; sometimes guards would spit into it. Liu had stomach trouble and soon began to suffer from diarrhoea. His hands began to tremble violently and at meal-times he often spilled his food.

Medical staff dared not treat him well. Any consultation would be preceded by criticism, while a few doctors would hit him with their stethoscopes and some nurses would jab him roughly when giving injections. The medicine he took for his diabetes was withheld, but when he fell into a confused state of mind it was held to be just a cunning pretence.

On 26 February 1968 Sher Fu-Jee, the Public Security Minister, sent a note to the special investigation unit making it clear that Jiang was in charge of Liu's case. From now on, when asking for instructions or reporting any important information Liu's warders should turn first directly to Jiang.

In the summer of 1968, Liu fell seriously ill with pneumonia and other complications. Jiang did not want him to die yet and so she gave orders that he should be given urgent treatment. The party was about to hold an important meeting and they wanted to keep him alive so that he could see himself being expelled from the party.

The doctors suggested sending Liu to hospital, but this idea was rejected. They then asked to be allowed to remove the slogans covering his bedroom walls so as to give him some peace of mind, but this request was turned down as well. When Liu's pneumonia at last cleared, he had no energy to get up and no family to wash him, change him or help him to go to the lavatory, so he became very dirty and the muscles of his legs gradually withered away. A nurse recorded that he did not have one good blood vessel because he had had so many injections. All day long he lay in bed. To stop him "becoming violent or committing suicide", his legs were tightly bound to the bed. Soon he could not swallow food and had to be fed through the nose, while by now both his hands were suffering from uncontrollable non-stop convulsions.

From 13 to 31 October 1968, Mao chaired a meeting of the party central committee, which passed a resolution approving all Mao's instructions during the Cultural Revolution and asserting that Liu was a traitor, an imperialist, a revisionist and a running dog of the Nationalist Party. It had been a great victory of Mao Tse-Tung Thought to uncover him and the meeting decided to expel him from the party.

The Cultural Revolution leaders picked 24 November 1968, 24 days after the resolution had been passed, as the day on which they would inform Liu that he had been expelled from the party. It was Liu's 70th birthday. He never spoke again.

By mid-October 1969, Liu was dying and Lin Biao decided to move him secretly out of Peking. On 17 October, Liu was carried on a stretcher to an aeroplane and flown to Kaifeng city, Henan province. There he was locked up in a secure building with thick steel doors, high walls and electric fences; the small courtyard outside Liu's room was guarded by two platoons with four machineguns.

Now without any proper medical care at all, Liu died on 12 November 1969. When the time came for his cremation, instructions were issued to wrap up his head so that he could not be recognised. The small crematorium to which he was taken was cordoned off and Liu's body was cremated in the dead of night, at 3 a.m. The incinerator operator was totally unaware that the body wrapped in white cloth that he had sent into the incinerator had been the President of the People's Republic of China. The authorities tried to keep Liu's death a secret, but somehow the news leaked out. His wife, meanwhile, was being kept in solitary confinement in a dim prison cell. She spent 12 years in jail before she was finally rehabilitated. Liu's eldest son had been persecuted to death before his father died and his second son and two teenaged daughters remained behind bars for years.

While Mao was alive, he succeeded in securing his trophy scalp. It was only in February 1980, after his death, that the party formally cleared Liu's name.

102

Mao Tse-Tung's Birthday Wish

On 8 July 1966, shortly after he had unveiled the Cultural Revolution, Mao wrote to Jiang predicting that great chaos in China would be followed by good order. But the country, he claimed, would need another Cultural Revolution after seven or eight years.

On 11 January 1967, the central authorities sent a telegram of congratulation to 32 groups of rebels in Shanghai, signed in the name of four separate bodies – the Communist Party central committee, the State Council, the Central Military Commission and the Central Cultural Revolution Small Team. The fourth name, the Central Cultural Revolution Small Team, had been added by Mao. With a stroke of the pen Mao had elevated his wife's team to the same level as the three most important institutions in the country and from then on for several years the central authority's documents were issued in these four names. On 17 February, Jiang's underling, Chang Chun-Chel, told Chow En-Lai that on Mao's orders, from now on the Central Cultural Revolution Small Team should be treated as the Central Secretariat. Lin Biao, the Deputy Chairman, also issued instructions that from now on all important business concerning the party and the nation had to be sanctioned by the Central Cultural Revolution authority.

Now an unaccountable ruler had put his wife's unaccountable team above the party and the central government, but no one dared challenge the golden mouth. Mao told his followers that it was reasonable to rebel and urged them to grab the power from the "people in power". This meant the party apparatchiks were now the targets. By December 1966, most of the party and government offices were under attack day and night and were paralysed by student and worker Red Guards. All lessons in schools were suspended and industrial production was suspended or stopped.

Jiang regarded Shanghai as the stronghold for her political power struggle where her three top aids Chang Chun-Chel, Yel Won-Yuan and Wang Hong-Won started their high-flying careers. Later on they became known as the "gang of four".

Wang Hong-Won had recruited two million workers to form a rebel group while working as a security worker in a textile mill. Backed up by student Red Guards, they accused the local party's *Liberation Daily* of going down the capitalist road. A pitched battle ensued between the Red Guards and the newspaper workers which lasted for nine days, resulting in many casualties. In the end Wang Hong-Won succeeded in taking control of the newspaper.

Feeling threatened by the rebel Red Guards, the Shanghai city party committee founded its own group of worker Red Guards for self-protection. Chang Chun-Chel ordered Wang Hong-Won to deploy more than 100,000 rebel Red Guards to surround the 30,000 or so Red Guard supporters of the Shanghai city party committee near its office in Hong Ping Road. As early as 1927, Mao had defined revolution as 'when one class overthrows another class with violence' and this became the most popular slogan of the Cultural Revolution. And so at 2 a.m. on 30 December 1966, the fighting started. The following day, the Shanghai party committee supporters were crushed and their leaders captured; 92 people were seriously injured. The battle marked the beginning of large-scale fighting in the country.

The Shanghai rebels had the full backing of the Central Cultural Revolution authority in their campaign to bring down the Shanghai party secretary and mayor, Tso Di-Chil and the first secretary, Chan Pei-San. The rebels distributed handbills and plastered the streets of Shanghai with posters denouncing the two men. On 6 January 1967, Wang Hong-Won's followers held a struggle meeting against several hundred senior Shanghai party officials headed by Tso Di-Chil and Wai Won-Bor, the secretary of the party's East China Bureau. The rebels grabbed power by force, closing down the Shanghai party and local government. On 8 and 9 January, Mao praised the Shanghai rebels' action and recommended their tactics to the rest of the nation.

On 5 February the new ruling power in Shanghai, headed by Chang Chun-Chel, was formally approved by Mao and it was renamed the Shanghai City Revolutionary Committee.

Mao had decided to destroy his own party machine and people for and against what was happening were inexorably sucked into frenzied fighting. Whenever a rebel group succeeded in grabbing power, the *People's Daily* would unfailingly publish an enthusiastic editorial. This state of affairs continued for a year and a half, during which rebels established new regimes in a total of 21 provinces, 5 autonomous regions (Guangxi's Zhuang minority area, Inner Mongolia, Xinjiang, Tibet and the Ningxia Muslim area) and the three major cities (Peking, Shanghai and Tianjin).

On 22 May 1967, the *People's Daily* published an editorial, amended and sanctioned by Chow En-Lai, headed 'Stop armed fighting immediately'. Two months later, on 13 July, the central committee issued a directive carrying the following message:

Recently a small number of 'people in power' who have gone down the capitalist road in Jiangxi, Sichuan, Zhejiang, Hubei, Hunan, Henan, Anhui, Ningxia and Shanxi provinces have incited peasants who do not know the truth to join in armed fighting in cities and lay siege to the factories, mines, offices and schools of the revolutionary masses. Some areas have even submitted reactionary slogans such as 'using villages to beset cities' and have organised peasants to go to the cities to purge the revolutionary rebels. The party central authority deems such actions as very wrong.

Fighting was by then out of control. Although the People's Liberation Army stationed around the country was still in relatively good order, as early as late January 1966 Jiang had begun to meddle in its affairs; she had summoned senior officers in charge of the PLA cultural and propaganda affairs to a meeting where, in a raging monologue, she attacked their work as not being politically correct. By October 1966, rebel cadets from military academies had begun putting up hostile posters in the streets denouncing several marshals; clearly someone was planning all these actions and supporting the cadets behind the scenes.

Soon after New Year's Day in 1967, several underlings of Mao's heir apparent, Lin Biao, carried out a highly secretive nocturnal operation, putting up posters in the Peking army district calling for a purge of the Peking army commander, Young Yung and its political commissioner, Leu Han-San.

In November 1966, when Peking was packed with millions of Red Guards who had descended on the city, around 100,000 military cadets tried to break into the defence ministry. On 10 January 1967, the sustained attack by the Gang of Four on the People's Liberation Army reached new heights when they began openly calling for 'dragging out the small batch in the armed forces'. Jiang's secretary, Chic Bun-Yu, went to the Chinese People's University to tell the rebels that they were free to attack Marshal Zhu De, the most senior soldier in the People's Liberation Army and the university rebels duly wasted no time in putting up posters full of vitriolic denunciations in Peking streets.

On 14 February 1967, at a meeting chaired by Chow En-Lai in Wei Yan Hall inside Central South Sea, the leaders of the Central Military Commission and the State Council, including Marshals Chan Yi, Yip Jan-Ying, Xu Shan-Chen and Nep Yung-Gin, General Tan Jan-Lin and several vice premiers, confronted Jiang, Kang, Chan Bor-Da, Chang Chun-Chel and Yel Won-Yuan, the members of the Central Cultural Revolution Small Team. The officers accused the Gang of Four of turning a blind eye to the harassment of senior soldiers by Red Guards and of trying to bring chaos to the armed forces. It was a heated row.

One upshot of the meeting was that Marshal Yip Jan-Ying, secretary-general of the Central Military Commission, approved an open letter to the worker rebels of Chengdu city and the Sichuan University Red Guards. On 18 February military aeroplanes dropped copies of the letter in the Chengdu area and shortly afterwards copies were dropped over the whole of Sichuan province. The open letter pointed out that the rebels were effectively pointing a knife at the People's Liberation Army, with their demonstrations against military institutions and their slogan 'smash up the black headquarters of Chengdu military district', their picketing of military organisations, their harassment of military staff and their attempts to break into military compounds. The letter cautioned the public not to be taken in by the troublemakers and it warned the rebel leaders that they would be held responsible for the consequences.

In the night of February 18, Mao, in a rage, summoned both sides from the Wei Yan Hall meeting and insisted that he was opposed to anyone who took sides against the Central Cultural Revolution Small Team. He threatened to take Lin Biao and Lin's wife with him and leave Peking, leaving Jiang and Kang to them. They could behead Jiang and banish Kang for all he cared. Chow En-Lai managed to smooth things over and in the end only General Tan Jan-Lin was denounced as a 'black warrior'.

From April onwards, Red Guards started to mount attacks on army units which supported Liu and Deng; in May, as many as 42 different army bases were attacked in Jiangxi province alone. After a two-month siege the rebels managed to break into the provincial army headquarters and seized weapons and confidential documents, kidnapping senior officers and assaulting troops, over 400 of whom were wounded.

In early February 1967, as Jiang and Lin Biao were quietly encouraging rebels inside the armed forces to seize power from the local military authorities, some of the Peking army rebels marched south to join the army rebels of Wuhan city, in Hubei province. The strengthened rebel forces in Wuhan quickly succeeded in taking over by force one of the city's main newspapers, in which they announced that the whole of Wuhan and Hubei provinces needed to be put into a state of thorough chaos, adding that their seizure of the newspaper had the support of the People's Liberation Army.

The violent and anarchic situation quickly deteriorated further. The headquarters of the Wuhan military district put out a public statement declaring that the army rebels represented nobody but themselves; they did not represent the Wuhan military and certainly not the People's Liberation Army.

The many different groups of Red Guards, some set up by students or government cadres from court officials to cooks, others set up by workers on the railways or in shipping companies, factories or mines etc. in Wuhan, were split into two camps. The Headquarters of the Workers' Rebellion consisted mainly of students but also included military cadres, while their rivals, the Division of a Million Courageous Fighters, consisted largely of industrial workers and demobbed soldiers, backed by the Wuhan district army.

During the first half of 1967 fierce fighting quickly spread from Wuhan city to the rest of Hubei province, continuing for several months and involving as many as half a million people. Meanwhile the workers, peasants and students went on strike. From 19 April to 30 June, there were more than 256 cases of armed fighting, with hundreds of people missing or killed and more than 2,000 injured and between 29 April and 30 June production at Wuhan's 2,400 factories and mines stopped completely.

By the middle of 1967, the Division of a Million Courageous Fighters, with help from the local army, had succeeded in crushing the rebel camp and arresting the rebel leaders. Jiang openly supported the rebels, accusing the Wuhan military district commander, General Chan Jai-Dow and his political commissioner, Lt. General Jone Han-Hua, of having committed political mistakes. The situation in Wuhan was instantly turned upside down, with Jone Han-Hua arrested and taken to a struggle meeting by the rebels. The slogans denouncing Chan Jai-Dow started to appear in the streets of Wuhan.

On 14 July, a group of prominent supporters of Mao and Jiang arrived in Wuhan representing the Central Cultural Revolution authority. It included Wan Li, Guan Fung and the minister of public security, General Sher Fu-Jee and they brought with them a group of Peking Red Guard leaders. On 18 July, the group attended a meeting of the rebel camp, which was attended by several thousand people. Sher Fu-Jee assured the audience that they had the full support of Mao, the party central committee and the

Central Cultural Revolution authority in their struggle against the oppressors.

Wan Li's speech became known as the 'four-point instruction'. He started by saying that the Wuhan military district was wrong in its political direction. Secondly, the Headquarters of the Workers' Rebellion had to be reconstituted. Thirdly, the rebels were revolutionary left-wingers and fourthly, the Division of a Million Courageous Fighters was a conservative organisation which was protecting the capitalist roaders inside the party, government and armed forces.

The following day, 19 July, the rebels paraded through the streets in dozens of vehicles equipped with powerful loudspeakers to broadcast recordings of the speeches of Sher Fu-Jee and Wan Li. The rival camp was furious and within a few hours Wuhan was submerged in anti-Wan Li slogans. In the evening, the Division of a Million Courageous Fighters brought in several thousand soldiers from two local divisions, together with thousands of government cadres. They proceeded in a massed convoy of over 100 army trucks and fire engines, their sirens at full blast, to the local army headquarters in order to question Wan Li about his speech. They were followed in turn by a huge crowd of Division supporters and the surrounding streets were jam-packed with people chanting slogans and demanding to see Wan Li. Soon they found out that Wan's party was staying next door in the East Lake Guesthouses.

There were nearly 30 detached villas dotting the extensive grounds of the East Lake Guesthouse complex, a beautiful park with a labyrinth of paths and roads. It happened that Mao had secretly arrived in early July to direct the Cultural Revolution in Wuhan and he was staying in the most secluded and most heavily cordoned off villa, the No.1 East Lake Guesthouse.

The crowd broke through the well-guarded entrance to the guesthouse complex to look for Wan Li, but it was not an easy job. Chan Jai-Dow and Jone Han-Hua knew where Mao was, but they also knew only too well that if the situation got out of hand, the angry mob might catch the great helmsman as well. By now it was the early morning of 20 July and at this point Chan Jai-Dow just happened to pay a visit to Sher Fu-Jee. As soon as he walked into Sher's room, hundreds of people, mainly his soldiers, rushed through the door after him. They found Wan Li in a bedroom on the same floor and took him back to the 29th Division, where he was locked up. Soon the streets were full of workers, soldiers and peasants from the conservative camp, all shouting slogans denouncing Wan Li, Sher and the central Cultural Revolution authority.

With his presence in Wuhan still a secret to its inhabitants, Mao decided to flee the city and he hastily flew to Shanghai, giving Chow En-Lai the job of dealing with the turmoil. Chow accordingly ordered a fleet to sail up the Yangtze River as far as Wuhan, where they trained their guns on the city. He also ordered armies from the Nanking, Chengdu, Canton and Peking military districts to carry out 'military exercises', moving toward Wuhan from all sides. Paratroopers landed in some of the city's universities to establish bases, from which, with the help of the air force, they succeeded in capturing the Yangtze River bridge. Before long they had taken the cable office, radio station and a number of schools and within 24 hours the local troops and the Division of a Million Courageous Fighters had been disarmed; Wan was soon released and on 22 July he flew back to Peking with Sher.

Both Chow and Mao were keen to play down this incident, mindful perhaps of Chan Jai-Dow's many former colleagues who had served with him in the West Route Army in the 1930s and who were now powerful, high-ranking officers in other military districts. On 23 July the Central Cultural Revolution authority summoned Chan Jai-Dow and Jone Han-Hua to a meeting in Peking, at which both were denounced and it was also hinted that Marshal Xu Shan-Chen had been behind the incident. On 27 July, Lin Biao and Jiang wrote an open letter, in the name of the central committee, the State Council, the Central Military Commission and the Central Cultural Revolution authority, calling the incident of 20 July a counter-revolutionary mutiny. Chan Jai-Dow and Jone Han-Hua were both dismissed by Lin Biao. This was the end of what became known as the '7.20 Wuhan Mutiny'.

Lin Biao had many enemies. Craving the pinnacle of power, he was trying to destroy his foes. There were many who could not accept him as Mao's heir apparent and in particular there was strong opposition from the powerful group around Chan Jai-Dow.

By now fighting and unrest – or rebellion, revolution and mutiny, as the authorities preferred to call it – was everywhere in China. Some of the worst fighting was in Guangxi, an autonomous region with large numbers of minorities. This province is on China's south coast, part of it bordering Vietnam. From the early spring of 1967, Red Guards appeared in Guangxi in large numbers and fighting soon gripped the region. The two main factions in the province were known as '4.22' and 'Joint Command'. The former, 4.22, consisted of worker and student rebels backed by the Central Cultural Revolution authority; their aim was to take over government. Joint Command's members were students, workers and peasants who were all close to the local "people in power'.

Clashes between the two factions were frequent. On 25 March, the official newspaper, the *Guangxi Daily*, was attacked and occupied by the 4.22 faction, but soon afterwards several hundred people from another group known as the '5.25' broke into the newspaper premises and demanded that the 4.22 leave. Fighting soon broke out with stones and wooden rods and by 8 p.m. numbers had swelled to five or six thousand fighters. The Guangxi military authorities dispatched seven propaganda vehicles to appeal for an end to the fighting, but they were ignored; all the army could do was to send ambulances to treat the casualties. Finally, in the early hours, the fighting died down.

A few days later, on 30 March, 400 people paraded in the provincial capital, Nanning, calling for crushing "the restoration of counter-revolutionary capitalism." Representing a total of 16 different groups, with names such as 'Guangxi No.1 Command Headquarters', 'Guangxi 831', 'Storm', 'Jinggangshan' and 'East is Red', they organised two demonstrations at the regional party committee offices, where a melee of fist fighting broke out with members of the office staff. Then a few months later, on 12 July, fighting broke out in Northsea city and over two days more than 100 people were injured, over 30 of them seriously.

In the course of 1968 the fighting escalated in Guangxi, as it did in the rest of the country. On 3 May of that year, an army battalion caught members of the Joint Command attempting to loot some of its weapons. The Joint Command opened fire, killing five soldiers and wounding 31. The following month, on 19 June, 62 people died in fighting in Nanning, after which the corpses were thrown into the river. On 23 June Joint Command requested the assistance of heavy guns to support their attack on a quay occupied by the 4.22 faction. The bombardment went on until after three o'clock the following afternoon, by which time more than 40 ships in the river had been set ablaze.

Wuzhou city, in the east of Guangxi, saw ferocious fighting between 4.22 and Joint Command between 13 April and 5 May 1968, in which more than ten main streets, representing half of the city, were destroyed; 4.22 suffered around 7,000 casualties and 3,500 captured. Several hundred others broke out, some fleeing to Peking to complain to Jiang, others joining the rebels in Canton. Many of the dead bodies thrown into the river in Wuzhou were carried downstream to Zhaoqing city, in Guangdong province, where more than 8,000 corpses were fished out of the river.

By the middle of 1968, the 'people in power' and the army had united to destroy the rebels. By early July, 73 out of the 86 counties in Guangxi province were free of rebels and more than 50,000 had been killed.

The senior official representing the party, the government and the armed forces in Guangxi was Wai Kwok-Ching, who was from the Tong minority. Many of his former colleagues in the army, including Deng Xiao-Ping and the fallen defence minister, Peng De-Huai, had been purged by Mao and Wai Kwok-Ching himself had once been condemned by Red Guards and had narrowly escaped being denounced as a counter-revolutionary. Like many others in his position, he could see that his best protection was to strengthen his own military power and he not only supported the Joint Command in their fight against the 4.22, but he even allowed them to intercept a trainload of military aid passing through Guangxi on its way to North Vietnam. Mao, Lin and Chow were deeply shaken by this. They asked the Joint Command to return all the military aid destined for Vietnam, promising not to investigate, but they received no response.

Whereas Wuhan was surrounded by other provinces and could be intimidated by military strength, Guangxi was on the south coast and could receive outside aid easily. This left the central government in a dilemma. It was left to Chow En-Lai to summon Wai Kwok-Ching to Peking and ask whether he had backed the correct left-wingers. Wai did not give an answer. The central government dared not punish him severely for killing members of the 4.22 and stealing the weapons destined as aid to North Vietnam; instead he was allowed to return to Guangxi, where he continued in his fight against the 4.22.

The Cultural Revolution began with verbal attacks, then moved on to punching, kicking and fighting with stones, staves and knives. Soon it escalated to tear gas, machine-guns, tanks (in Shenyang) and cannons (in Yunnan) and the number of participants increased from tens, then hundreds to tens of thousands. In the early stages, the regular army was simply onlookers, although they covertly supported the rivals of the rebel Red Guards. As time went on, the army began to join in the fighting openly and sometimes regular troops fought on both sides. In the Wuzhou clash in April and May 1968, the troops of the Guangxi military district and its branch in Wuzhou military district fought on the side of the Joint Command against more than 10,000 members of 4.22, who in turn had the support of the People's Liberation Army's 6908 unit, fighting on their side. The 4.22 managed, at the end of this particularly bloody 22-day battle, to cling on to half of Wuzhou city. It was, effectively, civil war.

When Mao denounced Liu's work units, which were soldiers sent to control the wild students, he was giving his unequivocal backing to the rebel Red Guards. After the power-grabbing hurricane of January 1967, the disorderly rebel groups were incapable of forming a new and functioning

795

administration; instead they usually plunged into inter-factional fighting for position and power. According to Mao's instructions, his new ruling bodies, the revolutionary committees, were to be a union of three partners – the army, the revolutionary cadres and the masses (or in other words the rebel Red Guards). Since nearly all the cadres were or had been in disgrace, their authority carried hardly any weight. The rebels' contributions were negligible and the army was therefore virtually the only operational force. In effect the country was under military rule.

The army promptly meted out severe punishments to the Red Guards, many of whom were beaten savagely. In February and March 1967, more than 20,000 Red Guards in Chengdu, more than 3,000 in Wuhan and more than 2,000 in Guangzhou were arrested. The army in Qinghai province even shot resisting rebels, causing dozens of casualties. Red Guard groups were dissolved and their membership recorded. There were 16,000 Red Guards in Guangzhou alone. Large numbers of radical rebel groups were crushed.

The leaders of the Central Cultural Revolution authority could not allow their shock troops to be eradicated and they now called for a counter-attack on the 'adverse current'. There was a swift response from the rebels and for several months they fought hard against the army. But the central authority did not make any blanket denunciation of the armed forces, whose powers were only weakened slightly and temporarily.

On 6 April 1967, the Central Military Commission issued a series of orders forbidding troops from opening fire on rebel Red Guards or arresting revolutionaries and ordering them to stop their purges of rebel groups. All groups which had been suppressed by the army were rehabilitated and instead the army was ordered to support the left-wingers. The situation was highly confused; because every group proclaimed itself to be pro-Mao, the army often found itself supporting the wrong side.

In March 1968,Mao and Jiang purged three senior soldiers, Young Cheng-Wu, Fu Shon-Bi and Yue Li-Gin. At the same time they launched a new campaign to liquidate the 'three rights and one wind', that is, right-leaning opportunism, right-leaning schism, right-leaning capitulationism and the right-leaning wind to overturn convictions. A second campaign was known as the 'three investigations and one cleansing', or in other words investigations of traitors, spies, capitalist roaders and the cleansing of class enemies. The first campaign's targets were mainly senior cadres and leading figures among the Red Guards.

The end result was that fighting escalated for self-protection, with battles increasingly organised on a large scale. In many cases, such as the

May 1968 battle in Wuzhou, they involved tens of thousands of people, while in the small county of Bok Bai in Guangxi province, several thousand rebels were attacked by 30,000 militiamen.

Already in possession of large quantities of weaponry, the armed gangs launched campaigns to seize even more. The rebel Red Guards, backed by the Central Cultural Revolution authority, were increasingly daring in attacking military bases. They even went so far as to drag senior commanders to struggle meetings, in turn driving the latter to arm the rival Red Guards (such as the East Wind group in Guangdong, the 823 group in Yunnan, the Big United Command in Tibet and the Red No.1 HQ in Xinjiang). For their own self-protection, local armies were now united in opposition to central government.

A few months later, the aforementioned '7.20 Wuhan mutiny' took place and after it had been suppressed a shocked Mao tried hard to tread carefully and placate the armed forces. On 5 September a directive was issued in the names of the party central committee, the State Council, the Central Military Commission and the Central Cultural Revolution authority, banning the revolutionary masses from seizing either guns, ammunition, other weapons or documents, ordering the return of all such items to the armed forces and threatening to arrest all who resisted. In addition, all leading rebels and senior commanders of the various military districts were summoned to Peking to attend classes in Mao Tse-Tung Thought.

By early September 1968, after grabbing power, out of 29 new heads of revolutionary committees, 20 were professional soldiers and nine were revolutionary cadres; not one rebel had managed to obtain a senior position. Contrary to what Mao had expected, real power had fallen into the hands of the armed forces.

After all the local governments had been replaced by revolutionary committees, the authorities in Peking announced that 'the whole nation has now turned red.' In other words, the new Mao regimes had been installed. On 14 September 1968 the *People's Daily* reported that Guangdong province was already one big sea of red, since revolutionary committees had been established in 98 per cent of the people's communes and in all the 106 counties in the province.

Yet the chaotic situation in Guangdong province was not getting any better. There were numerous Red Guard groups pursuing their own struggles in Guangzhou. Some had reprinted Jiang's denunciations of rightists, while others claimed that the revolutionary committee now stood opposed to the people. In Guangzhou, just as in other provinces, Jiang's rebels were assaulted mercilessly. In one battle at a secondary school, on 1 June 1968, when the attackers – the offspring of senior officials and worker pickets – were getting the upper hand, the rebels appealed for help from the local army, but when the troops arrived at the scene they joined the attackers to assault the rebels and in the end more than 62 of the rebels sustained broken ribs and other injuries. One girl complained in the 7th bulletin of the *Secondary Schools' Red Guards Magazine* that the soldiers had punched and kicked her, pulling her hair and hitting her with rifle butts, landing blows on her abdomen and she fainted many times.

However, the revolutionary committee had many splits of opinion. Some wanted to quash the rebels, while others claimed that suppression would only incite more fighting and create more chaos which might spiral out of control. Some wanted to protect themselves, calculating that although they were now being told to suppress the rebels, they might well be denounced the following day for making mistakes. It was only too true. Many people did the bidding of the leaders of the Cultural Revolution, only to become culprits when the leaders changed their minds.

On 10 July 1968, the revolutionary committees in Guangdong province and Guangzhou city issued the first of a number of joint orders informing the Red Guards that they were to congregate at a series of meeting points, from where the local revolutionary committee would take them back to their homes in other parts of Guangdong province or other provinces. But these orders were ignored. One month later, from 9 August, the Guangdong revolutionary committee repeatedly publicised an order from the central authority which dissolved all the civilian fighting groups. This order too was disobeyed.

As a result of the armed fighting, dead bodies appeared in the streets of Guangzhou every day and some of them were hanged from the branches of trees. The terrified residents dared not go out at night. Some of the defeated Red Guards escaped to the surrounding villages, where they behaved like fleeing bandits, robbing and murdering the villagers. Anyone who was seen as an anti-Mao bad element would be seized by the Red Guards, often to be bound and thrown into a river. The Sea Pearl Bridge across the Pearl River, in Guangzhou city centre, was a favourite spot for Red Guards to carry out murders. One Hong Kong visitor reported seeing Red Guards push more than 20 people from the bridge into the river; most of the bodies were washed out to sea, but others were swept to Hong Kong by the tide. The Sea Pearl Bridge had until recently been guarded by troops armed with machineguns to prevent sabotage, but since the Red Guards were not saboteurs, the soldiers simply looked on.

The differences of opinion which emerged in the Guangdong

revolutionary committee were mirrored in other provinces, hampering the ability of the provincial authorities to deal with the Red Guards. The authorities in Peking felt that they could not rely fully on the revolutionary committees so had to adopt other measures. In early August 1968, Mao instructed the 'Workers' and Peasants' Mao Tse-Tung Thought Propagation Teams', supported by the People's Liberation Army, to take over the running of all schools permanently (later on these new bodies were renamed the 'Workers' Mao Tse-Tung Thought Propagation Teams'). This new policy, which appeared on the front page of the *People's Daily* on 8 August, instructed workers to take control of all institutions ruled by the intelligentsia, such as universities, secondary schools and primary schools and departments of art, science, law, propaganda, medicine and health and so on.

On 30 August Guangzhou's radio station reported how 'comrade workers have gone into Chong San University (Sun Yat-Sen University) to put down the turmoil with brave determination. It is the first time in their lives they have walked into a university and although they do not understand the situation fully, they can still drag out the enemy one after another.' The first enemy to be dragged out of the university and paraded in the streets, adorned with a dunce's cap, was the 77-year-old Shee Shon-Ching, the university president. He was accused of being an American spy and a spy for Chiang Kai-Shek. The workers forced students to do manual work day and night and normal lessons came to a halt; the intelligentsia was rife with antagonism towards the workers.

Fighting often reflected the power struggle at the highest levels of the Communist Party. On 26 January, 1968 in Xinjiang, a rebel group known as the Red Second Command Headquarters tried to grab power from an army corps. Fighting broke out and all the officers and men of an artillery regiment stationed in the Shek Hor Tze area, together with 10,000 people from another group called the August 1 Field Army, formed by demobbed servicemen, attacked the rebels with machine-guns and grenades, resulting in heavy casualties. This rebel group was under the direct command of the Central Cultural Revolution authority and so, under pressure from Mao and Jiang, the army corps concerned was forced to surrender and the August 1 Field Army was dissolved.

A few months later, another group, the Red First Command Headquarters, was formed with the support of Wang En-Mou, the commander and political commissar of Xinjiang military district. The new group launched a counter-attack on the Red Second Command Headquarters, with open backing from the troops of Xinjiang military district and they arrested and killed many of the rebels. It was a reflection of the power struggle between Mao, Jiang and Lin's army faction in Xinjiang.

Keen to suppress the fighting and the opposition to the rebels from within the army, Mao decided to use force. On 10 June 1968 he created a new body known as the Central Support to Left-Wingers' Troops, which he immediately sent to the military districts to seize power from the recalcitrant local armed forces.

Anti-Mao sentiment was openly revealed by Liu Lan-Tao, the first secretary of the Communist Party's North West Bureau and the most senior official in Shaanxi province. Liu Lan-Tao had once criticised Mao's policy of Three Red Flags as petit-bourgeois fanaticism, he had also said that Mao was not God and did not have a golden mouth. Showing his contempt for those who chanted 'Long live Chairman Mao!' he quipped, 'Chairman Mao will see Marx soon. When you are 73 or more, even the god of the underworld does not summon you; you will go to see him of your own accord'. Instead, he suggested another slogan: 'We should propagate Liu Shao-Qi Thought'. For his blasphemy and bad management, Liu Lan-Tao and his four sons suffered brutal persecution in the Cultural Revolution and he spent eight years in jail.

The most serious problem in Liu Lan-Tao's territory was an armed group of peasants near Xian city which broke up the local 4.22 rebel group and shot dead 500 Red Guard activists. The situation in Shaanxi was extremely tense. Liu's close aids defended him publicly, denouncing the Red Guards' atrocities as worse than those of the Nationalist Party.

In July 1968 two important bulletins were published, after they had been approved by Mao. The first, issued on 3 July, aimed to stop armed fighting in Guangxi province. It began with the cliché: 'The proletarian Cultural Revolution, launched and led personally by our great leader, Chairman Mao, is now advancing forcefully to outright victory. The situation in the country is excellent and the situation in the Guangxi Zhuang minority Autonomous Region is, like the rest of the country, excellent as well.' Totally devoid of any sense of irony, the bulletin went on to discuss problems in Guangxi province. The railways had been sabotaged and train services could not be resumed. Mobs had robbed the military aid to Vietnam and had refused to return the plunder. PLA institutions and troops had repeatedly been attacked, their weapons looted and troops killed and the locals were still refusing to obey the urgent 6.13 telegram sent by the central authority.

The second bulletin, issued on 24 July, began in almost the same way, except that it substituted Shaanxi for Guangxi. After proclaiming how excellent the situation was in Shaanxi, it went on to talk about the problems in that province. People were breaking into and stealing from banks, warehouses and shops. National warehouses, public buildings and ordinary people's homes were being destroyed; railways, ships, cars and other transport were being attacked, mail and cable services were being disrupted and radio stations were being set up without permission; PLA institutions and troops were being attacked, with weapons seized and troops injured and even killed; and the locals were refusing to obey directives, orders, circulars and announcements issued by the party central committee and the Central Cultural Revolution authority. As in Guangxi, the people of Shaanxi were also accused of attempting to break into prisons and steal national secrets. Both bulletins ended by threatening to punish the counter-revolutionaries who had committed these heinous crimes. Similar bulletins were in due course sent to all other provinces; the situation in the rest of the country was evidently similar to that in Guangxi and Shaanxi.

Beginning in early 1967, large-scale armed fighting broke out along many railways from Changchun city in Manchuria down to Nanking, south of the Yangtze River and into Guangxi. Many sections of railway were forced to suspend operations, or at best to provide a very intermittent service. In addition to robbing trains, some gangs sabotaged water-towers and even dug up rails. In Guangxi rival gangs set up machine-gun posts along the railways, bringing traffic to a complete halt and leading to chaos in the neighbouring Guangdong and Hunan provinces.

The chaos had dire consequences for industrial production. On 5 March 1968, the Chongqing 102 Steel Mill, in Sichuan province, was forced to stop production completely for the third time because of fighting. In 1968 it produced just 33,000 tons of steel, equivalent to only 18 per cent of its output in 1966. In Manchuria the situation was just as bad. China's biggest vehicle factory, in Changchun, Manchuria, employed 50,000 workers, but as many as 30,000 stopped work frequently to join in the fighting. The unrest spread to Sichuan province, where in September 1967 fighting broke out in Loozhou; several hundred people were killed and 21 ships destroyed.

On 2 October, Chow En-Lai telephoned the Amoy military authority to complain that the harbour and customs offices in Amoy appeared to be so busy fighting that nobody was attending to their proper jobs. A British cargo ship was currently unable to enter the harbour to load and unload; such behaviour was harming the motherland's reputation and could not be tolerated.

While Chow En-Lai was trying desperately to maintain some order in the country, Jiang and her group were openly inciting unrest, urging the

Red Guards to arm themselves for defence. On 16 August 1967, Kang Sheng acknowledged a group in the Ningxia Muslim Autonomous Region as rebels and ordered the local army to provide them with guns. Later that year he accused a rebel group of preparing a counter-revolutionary putsch, sending the army in to Bronze Gorge, Ningxia, to suppress them in a bloody encounter which left 101 people dead and 133 wounded. Jiang and Kang were only pursuing Mao's dictum, 'The more chaotic the better'. For most Chinese people, however, chaos had produced only hardship and disaster. By the end of the Cultural Revolution, huge numbers were left without either work or food. Even in a province with rich natural resources such as Sichuan, destitute people were reduced to selling their children for a pittance.

On 18 December 1970, Mao told an American visitor, the writer Edgar Snow, that fighting had broken out everywhere, they had split into two groups. 'It has happened in every factory, school, province, county, ministry. There are two groups in the foreign ministry too. There is no way we can refrain from this, because of the counter-revolutionaries and the capitalist roaders.'

Fighting continued for a long time, until after 1970 while, aside from the fighting, fanatical class-hatred consumed human decency. To demonstrate their implacable detestation of the class enemy, the 'revolutionaries' dumped soil in their victims' rice bowls at mealtimes. In Tam city, Shandong province, the corpses of 18 people who had been killed in fighting were tied up on trees and used for shooting practice. In Wuxuan county, Guangxi province, the politically-motivated cannibals ate the livers and flesh of their class enemies.

On 26 December 1966, on Mao's 73rd birthday party, he made a wish loud and clear:"I want there to be civil war throughout the country!" His wish certainly came true.

103

The Non-Stop Purge

When Mao's Cultural Revolution struck at the 'people in power', nearly all the top Communists soon plunged into disgrace. Seemingly endless campaigns with names deriving from Communist jargon – 'three rights and one wind', 'three investigations and one cleansing', 'catching the 5.16', '5.7 cadre schools', 'cleaning the class troops' and 'going up mountains and down to villages' (this was aimed at students) – were all pushed through during the Cultural Revolution with the aim of casting bigger and bigger nets to catch all the undesirables.

In the early stages of the Cultural Revolution, Jiang and Lin Biao formed a partnership of convenience. For Lin it was a means of ingratiating himself with Mao and Jiang, while Jiang was using Lin to extend her influence in the People's Liberation Army. Lin responded by awarding her a new title, 'Cultural Adviser for the People's Liberation Army'. They cooperated on striking out at each other's enemies, but later, when they were vying for the top job, they launched vicious operations to purge people who might get in their way. Their victims included many top soldiers who had fought for the party all their lives, such as Marshal Hor Lone.

At a high-level meeting of the Military Commission in early January 1967, Lin launched a tirade against Hor, to the astonishment of those present. Lin said that nobody in the armed forces had attacked Hor Lone and this was odd given that Hor was an evil two-faced man, a big bandit and big plotter who was opposed to Chairman Mao. He had sneaked into the party for his own gain.

Hor's face turned ashen and cold sweat appeared on his forehead. The ill-feeling in fact went back a long way. Hor's wife, Sed Ming and Lin's wife, Yip Cheun, were old schoolmates and the private feud between the two families had started in the 1930s when the party headquarters had been in Yan'an. The problem was that Hor and Sed Ming knew too much about Lin and Yip Cheun's past and with this knowledge they could jeopardise Lin's bid for power.

As a preliminary move Lin had arrested and tortured cadres who had worked for Hor in order to extract 'confessions' and he had spread rumours about Hor, urging people to write to Mao with false accusations against him. With the cooperation of the Central Cultural Revolution authority of Jiang and Kang Sheng, he claimed that Hor was planning a military coup. Jiang now announced at a meeting that Hor Lone had problems and must be exposed.

Hor's home was duly under siege and ransacked by the rebels. Chow En-Lai tried to protect Hor and his wife by inviting them to stay temporarily at his own home. Jiang rejected Chow's invitation to a meeting with Hor and vice premier Lee Fu-Chun inside Central South Sea to talk things over. Instead she steered a crowd to a spot outside the perimeter wall near the meeting place, where they used loudspeakers shouting abusive slogans at Hor. When rebels appeared inside Central South Sea, Chow felt it was not safe for Hor to stay, so he made secret arrangement to move him with his wife to a mountain area near Peking.

By the summer of 1967, Hor had gradually fallen into the grip of Lin and Jiang. He and his wife were seized and held under virtual house arrest. Their windows were covered up to exclude the sunlight and they were even deprived of bedding for a few days. Soon the warders claimed it was difficult to obtain water and they were given only a small pot of drinking water daily, making washing impossible. They were reduced to collecting water from the eaves on rainy days. In September Hor was placed formally under investigation and any contact with Chow was cut off completely. At the same time Jiang replaced Hor's physician with a nurse pretending to be a doctor. By now he was completely at her mercy.

Hor was one of the vice premiers and since 1952 he had also been the minister in charge of sports. On 12 May 1968, in the name of the central authority, Lin's group condemned the national sports institution as an 'independent kingdom'. Hor became the 'number one counter-revolutionary revisionist' in sports circles and many athletes were either purged or killed themselves.

By the winter of 1968, Hor, now 73 years old and a diabetic, was getting no proper food or medicine and he and his wife were forced to patch and repatch their clothes, socks and shoes, since they had no others. One day a doctor came to take away whatever medicine they had managed to save for emergencies and before long they were told that the central heating was out of order and there was no guarantee they would be able to keep warm. From then on their room temperature was usually no more than 6°C.

Hor's diabetes worsened and on the morning of 8 June 1969, after two and a half years of virtual house arrest, he became seriously ill. It was only at dawn on the following day that he was taken on his own to hospital, but, still denied proper treatment, he died six hours later. His widow was informed coldly that he was dead. The news of his death was suppressed and his body was cremated in secret, without his family present.

Another senior victim of Jiang's plotting was General Lor Rui-Chin. Lor was not only a vice premier, but also Minister of Public Security and Chief of Staff of the People's Liberation Army. Ever since the Long March he had been Mao's loyal personal security chief and he was highly regarded by Mao. Lor disapproved of Lin's sycophantic propagation of the Mao personality cult and his hyping politics and reductions in military training. He also declined to help Jiang interfere in the PLA and he refused to give Lin's wife, Yip, a more senior rank in the army. These were just some of the many differences between him and the group of Lin and jiang.

On 2 December 1965, Yip presented Mao with a report containing trumped-up charges against Lor. Mao accepted Yip's back-stabbing report. Lin dismissed Lor from all his posts and pressured him to admit the accusations levelled against him. On 18 March 1966, Lor attempted to commit suicide by jumping from a roof, but he survived, with a broken leg. He was detained under guard in a sunless, barely furnished cell. Before his broken leg had had time to heal, he was carried in a wicker basket to a series of brutal struggle meetings, one of them attended by as many as 36,000 people. At some of these meetings his wife and other senior Communists appeared beside him as victims. Sometimes Yip was an amused spectator; at other times she sat on the platform.

Censured by the *People's Daily* and now suffering from a lingering high fever, Lor was persecuted day and night, his hospital ward turned into a makeshift interrogation room and his medical treatment left at the mercy of his enemies. When Lin wanted to intensify the interrogation, he rejected the hospital's advice that Lor should undergo an operation on his leg and eventually, after nearly three years of ill treatment and unsuccessful operations, it had to be amputated. Eventually complications caused by his leg trouble led to the death of this old-timer. In May 1967, Jiang's chief assistant, Chang Chun-Chel, commented that 'the Cultural Revolution is intended to strike down all the old-timers, leaving not a single one behind.'

As the senior officials were coming under suspicion one after another, millions of ordinary people who had been condemned in past years were now brought forward to face the music again. Among them was Dr Shel Kwong-Yan, an overseas Chinese from a capitalist family. Shel had gained his PhD in chemistry from Chicago University in December 1945 and had worked as a researcher there and subsequently for the Mobil Oil Company. With patriotic enthusiasm Shel wanted to help his motherland develop its own petroleum industry and so after spending a year collecting technical papers, he returned to China in November 1950 with his new wife and was given a research job in Dalian by the petroleum ministry. Within nine months of his arrival, the 'mind reform' campaign began and Shel was picked as a prime target. He was accused of having the mind of a reactionary and a collaborator and of having a corrupt capitalist mentality. The papers he had brought back with him were merely intended to help him crawl upwards.

Shel began to suffer from serious bouts of insomnia and for a long time he was unable to work. In 1956, his bosses decided that they had been treating intellectuals unfairly, so they expressed regret to Shel and amended their unfavourable appraisal of him. A relieved Shel regarded the experience as a simple misunderstanding, so he plunged himself into his work, trying to make up for the five lost years. But he was not left in peace for long. Late 1958 saw the start of the 'pulling out white flags' campaign and the hapless Shel found himself in trouble once again, although he had no idea why. The corridors were all of a sudden covered with posters condemning Shel, the 'old white flag' and containing accusations of all sorts: 'You have no feeling at all for our motherland', 'You brought back tatty papers for crawling upwards', 'You have a high salary, yet you have achieved nothing for several years' and 'If you joined the party you would be defiling it'.

He went to his research institute's New Year's Eve party, which contained a satirical show. At one point a clown made up to look like him appeared on the stage and said: 'I am Dr Shel. Using my parents' dirty money, I muddled along in America and managed to get a foreign doctorate. I heard the Communist Party was ruling China, so I stole some information and sneaked into China in an attempt to get myself an official job.' He complained to his boss that humiliation was not the best method of reform, only to be replaced by a younger person as the head of his unit. Feeling dejected, Shel lost his drive; from now on he spent much of his time sitting silently in a corner of his room, while at meetings he did not utter a word.

In 1961 party policy altered to become more lenient towards scientific research work. Shel's new party boss made another official judgement on him, to the effect that his return to China had been motivated by patriotism. His important contributions at work were acknowledged; he was given assistants and assigned to a new job.

Shel's hopes for a bright future were rekindled. He believed that the party was fair and just and that its shortcomings were only temporary. A few years later the Cultural Revolution began, showing Shel just what a Communist regime could do. On the night of 5 October 1968, when he was lying ill in bed, more than 20 burly, armed revolutionaries from his workplace went to his home, where they arrested him and confiscated all his valuables. He endured hours of interrogation and torture, his interrogators asking: "You had a good life and made a lot of money in America, why did you come back to China?", "If you brought American information to China, you would certainly be able to send information on China to America. How much intelligence have you gleaned?"

Amid beatings, insults and curses, he was forced to write one confession after another. But even after he had written 26 the interrogators were still not satisfied; they continued to berate him, even threatening to flay him alive. During one interrogation on 10 December, he was given another severe whipping. The following morning when members of the proletarian dictatorship team ordered him to get up, they found that he had taken an overdose of barbiturates.

The revolutionaries asserted that Shel, the counter-revolutionary spy, had killed himself from fear of punishment for his crimes; it was a great victory for the proletarian dictatorship. A big poster promptly appeared reporting this 'great and delightful news' and the resulting decision to press forward on the strength of this triumph and dig ever more deeply to destroy all class enemies. That afternoon, Shel's wife Zhen Shu-Fei, an English teacher who by then was in a labour reform farm, was taken to his workplace and told that Shel was an enemy of the people and that she had to confess his crimes.

She cast a glance at her husband's body, but did not cry. Instead she asked for two days' leave to go home and make arrangements for her child, a request which was granted. Ever since Shel and his wife had got into trouble, their 15-year-old daughter had been scorned and bullied and she lived a lonely life. Two days after Zhen Shu-Fei returned home, mother and daughter both killed themselves, also with an overdose of barbiturates.

A special unit was now formed to investigate the important spy ring of which Shel had been the central figure. A total of 26 people were implicated, including Shel's neighbours, an old couple who had looked after their young daughter, an old barber who had exchanged tropical fish with Shel and a nurse who had given him an injection. No tangible evidence was found. As in other liquidation campaigns, those who were condemned had no right of appeal. Trying to overturn a conviction amounted to another crime. The dead Shel was luckier; on 11 March 1978, two years after Mao's death, a memorial service was held for him in Dalian, at which he was

807

praised as a talented scientist who had clearly loved Chairman Mao, the party and socialism. His death, according to his eulogy, was a great loss to science research.

Shel's "death in difficulty" had implicated 26 people, which in comparison with other cases was a very modest number. In the Cultural Revolution, confessions extracted under torture often produced spectacular results. The underground party in Guangdong province implicated 85 people, while a case in Hebei province implicated 2,955. In the Yue Mon oilfield in Gansu province, more than 2,000 out of 30,000 employees were condemned as enemies and there was supposedly also a 247-member spy ring in the oilfield. Even this, according to the spy catchers, was only the tip of an iceberg. The Zhao Gen-Min spy ring in Yunnan province, by contrast, involved 14,000 victims.

As the party eventually admitted, the worst injustice happened in the Inner Mongolia Autonomous Region. When the 'Lin Biao and Jiang Ching counter-revolutionary bloc' was put on trial in November 1980, during the post-Mao era, 48 counts of criminal offences were listed in the indictment papers, the last of which related to the case of the Inner People Party in Inner Mongolia. The prosecutors pointed out that Kang Sheng had issued instructions to purge this party. A total of 340,000 cadres and ordinary people were framed, of whom 16,222 were killed. The official source also disclosed that some half a million people had been jailed and tens of thousands more permanently disabled. Of the total, three quarters were Mongolians, at a time when the Mongolian population was around two million.

The Inner People Party (Its full name was the Inner Mongolian People's Revolutionary Party) had been founded in 1924 by a group of young, left-wing Mongolians, with the aim of securing autonomy for the province. It was later disbanded by the Comintern, but regrouped after the Second World War. To suppress its independend tendencies, Woolanfu, a Mongolian senior member of the CCP, was sent to control it, but in 1946, worried that it might get out of control, the Communist Party disbanded it. Taking into account the fact that the Mongolian people lived a nomadic life in widely scattered communities, Woolanfu instead assumed a softer policy. There were no struggle meetings, no dividing of land and property, no designations of people as belonging to different classes, no communal canteens and no satellite from the steel mill in Hohhot city.

Because of this suspiciously non-conformist policy, Woolanfu was purged in the Cultural Revolution and instead Mao sent his own man, a Peking army deputy commander by the name of Tun Hai-Ching, to Inner

Mongolia as an army district commander. Kang Sheng and the public security minister, Sher Fu-Jee, urged Tun to purge members of the Inner People Party and, with the support of Red Guards, Tun began a brutal 18-month-long operation to catch them. His group claimed that their victims belonged to a reactionary organisation which wanted complete autonomy. Many nomad villagers had been forced to register as members of the Inner People Party and as the witch-hunt went wild, whole families killed themselves.

After the 9th CCP National Congress in April 1969, Mao admitted that the Mongolian purge had been unduly extensive. To protect his man, he transferred Tun to Shandong province and blamed a Mongolian CCP activist, Woolanbargon, for engineering the trouble. The unfortunate scapegoat, in fear of being lynched by his own people, was forced to flee Mongolia. Finally, in 1978, the Inner People Party was formally rehabilitated. Before the Cultural Revolution the Mongolians and the Hans had in fact got on well together. Most Mongolian cadres could speak the Han language and there were a lot of mixed marriages, but the Cultural Revolution seriously poisoned race relations in Inner Mongolia.

Such collective liquidations aside, numerous ordinary and innocent individuals were also caught in the gory storm. Among them was Chang Jee-Cin (1930–75), who had joined the Communist Party in 1955 and had worked in the party propaganda department in Liaoning province. In the early stage of the Cultural Revolution, Chang Jee-Cin's elder brother was condemned as an active counter-revolutionary for trimming a newspaper photo of Mao in order to fit it into a smaller picture frame. Chang Jee-Cin herself disapproved of the Cultural Revolution and the lack of democracy. In September 1969 she was arrested, but refused to give in. She was given a life sentence and her husband was forced to divorce her. On 3 April 1975 she was sentenced to death and the following day, after her windpipe had been cut to stop her from shouting out slogans, she was taken to the execution ground and shot.

Another victim, Mao Yin-Sing, was condemned as a rightist in 1957 and sent to a labour reform farm on the edge of a desert. When the Cultural Revolution arrived, she was condemned as a counter-revolutionary; her home was ransacked and several hundred old stamps belonging to her brother were found. The fact that they contained portraits of famous foreigners and of Chiang Kai-Shek was used as evidence to prove that Mao Yin-Sing was an international spy. Arrested in January 1969 and jailed for five years, while in prison she penned attacks on the Cultural Revolution's leading figures. She was later sentenced to death.

Chang Jee-Cin and Mao Yin-Sing were educated dissidents, even though educated Chinese people had been subjected to non-stop re-education. At the beginning of the Cultural Revolution, all intellectuals were compelled to attend political study groups, which were usually directed by people who were not well-educated. Professor Chen Jar-Cheu recalled that his group had to study two of Mao's essays every afternoon. They had been written for the Nationalists during the civil war and were now being used to drop hints to the capitalist intellectuals that they were beleaguered by the revolutionaries and had to surrender. Their group leader, who was the teenage office boy, would read out one sentence at a time and the group of well-educated people, most of them in their fifties, had to recite the sentence loudly as if they were still in primary school. Chen Jar-Cheu later discovered that the young leader did not actually understand some of the words in the essays.

Because of the intellectuals' low standing in the society, academics could often find themselves arraigned by simple young rebels, as happened to Professor Yu Ping-Bor. Yu's research paper on *The Dream of the Red Chamber*, a great Chinese novel written by Tso Sher-Chin during the Qing Dynasty, had been savaged by Mao in 1953. With such a blot on his personal history, Yu had no chance of escaping being paraded in public in a dunce's cap during the Cultural Revolution. On one occasion he was being interrogated at a public meeting inside the Academy of Literature and one of the Red Guards asked:

'What poisonous articles have you written?'

'I wrote *The Dream of the Red Chamber* research paper,' stuttered the professor.

The interrogator did not catch the last two words, 'research paper' and he said, 'Oh! So it was you who wrote *The Dream of the Red Chamber*!'

'No, no, no, I wouldn't dare to appropriate another person's great achievement.' His stutter grew worse.

'You have just said you wrote it and then you deny it in a flash. What kind of game is this?' The young philistine hit Yu Ping-Bor on the head.

After Mao had discarded the Red Guards, the country was placed under military rule and soldiers belonging to the Military Mao Tse-Tung Thought Propagation Team presided over the reform of the intellectuals. Most soldiers were simply peasants wearing army uniforms, but it was they who oversaw the re-education of the intellectuals in numerous '5.7 cadre schools'. These schools derived from a letter written by Mao on 7 May 1966 in which he had urged that everyone should learn a second trade; this letter was henceforth known as the '5.7 Instruction'. Two years later, Jiang and Lin made the instruction serve their own purposes when they banished potential opponents to labour reform farms, which they called 5.7 cadre schools.

In northeast China, large numbers of cadres, particularly educated people, were forced to go and live in villages. Amid the festive sound of drums and gongs, these people, their families and their household goods, were thrown onto trucks, taken to villages and dumped there before they had time to prepare for their new life.

From 1968, nearly all the big organisations sent their staff to 5.7 cadre schools. These 'students' usually went with their work colleagues. Many departments had already been forced to reduce or even stop their work as a result of the Cultural Revolution, so they set up their own 5.7 cadre schools. There were as many as 106 such schools in 18 different provinces, catering for 100,000 staff of the central government and State Council alone, plus 30,000 of their dependents. Although the 5.7 Instruction had included a clause to the effect that old, weak, sick and disabled people could be exempted, in reality this was ignored. One of Jiang's gang, Wang Hong-Won, said bluntly, 'Send all these undersirables to work in the 5.7 cadre schools'.

When a group of literary workers arrived at their 'school', their soldier boss spoke at the reception meeting: "You must all take a good look at the situation. There are labour reform prisoners on your north side, Rightists on your south side. If you don't do as you are told and dare to talk or behave badly, I only have to make a telephone call and you will be sent over there!" The 'students' would only now realise that they were not there to study anything; instead they were political pariahs kicked into the penal system. The schools were usually situated in very harsh and remote areas; some were indeed former labour reform farms. Often male and female students lived in separate 'barracks' and were organised into regiments, battalions and so on, as in the army.

The first three years (1968–70) were the most difficult, as many of them had to start from nothing. First they had to build huts to live in and then they had to try their best to achieve self-sufficiency in grain, cooking oil, meat and eggs. They spent long hours every day on hard manual work. Political study and struggle meetings occupied their evenings and even the ten-minute rest they were supposed to have while working in the fields was often used as a struggle session against someone.

In February and March 1971, Mao approved a new national campaign to catch members of a counter-revolutionary organisation, the secret '5.16 bloc'. This campaign gripped the entire country, including all the 5.7 cadre schools. The proportion of 5.16 criminals exposed in the 5.7 cadre schools belonging to the Culture Ministry and the Chinese Social Science Academy reached between 25 and 30 per cent, while 200 out of 300 'students' in the 5.7 cadre school belonging to the Chinese Children's Theatre of Art were identified as 5.16 members. It was said that there was a complicated and formal procedure to apply for 5.16 membership, similar to the procedure for joining the Communist Party.

The authoress Wei Jeun-Yi recalled that 5.16 suspects in her 5.7 cadre school were interrogated day and night and were often forced to go without food or sleep for three days; the record was seven days and seven nights. Many once overbearing Red Guard rebels were now humble 'students' too and even they were identified as members of 5.16. Some were beaten late into the night; their screaming brought protests from residents nearby. Many of the confessions were literally incredible and when the Cultural Revolution was over, the 5.16 episode was officially discredited.

Wei Jeun-Yi wrote that 'All the 5.16s in our unit were university students. Why were they denounced? Only because the authorities were determined to identify more criminals and capitalist roaders. Yet they could not find any grounds for charges of incorrect thinking, so this nonsensical 5.16 organisation was fabricated. The scheme nevertheless swept through the country and harmed many young cadres. After millions had suffered indescribable torments, at last it was said that the entire thing had been spurious. This volte-face made these 5.16s think deeply. They now felt they had been wronged and had responded to the call of the great revolution with confused minds. They had actually been fooled.' The campaign to purge 5.16s continued until 1976. It finally died down after the fall of Jiang's Gang of Four.

Even in such a bleak atmosphere, there could still be amusing moments. At one art workers' 5.7 cadre school, a slogan composed of several big characters reading, 'Never forget the class struggle', was displayed on the wall. A strong gale one night blew away the word 'never' and the slogan became 'Forget the class struggle'. The soldier boss called an emergency meeting and claimed that the slogan had been sabotaged by class enemies. An intense investigation followed, but the culprit, the wind, was never caught.

The peasants and the working class were not required to go to 5.7 cadre schools, whose students were all intellectuals and included many distinguished academics. All books, even books relating to professional knowledge, were banned and offenders would be criticised at meetings. The only acceptable books were Mao's writings. Professor Qin Jon-Shu, a brilliant writer, took a dictionary with him to read while hiding inside his mosquito net, hoping that a dictionary would not be deemed politically incorrect. Now the professor's job was that of boiler attendant; it was not an easy job in winter as, when bitterly cold winds kept blowing at his boiler, the water just would not boil.

The director of the Literary Research Institute, Ho Chi-Fong, was responsible, with a colleague, for looking after pigs, which they kept on a patch of land surrounded by a water-filled moat. They were unaware that pigs could swim and so the pigs would often run away at night, leading to frantic torchlight searches. Another old professor, Yu Ping-Bor, lived with his bound-footed wife in a ramshackle house, where he was given the comparatively easy job of making hemp rope by hand.

All these intellectuals now lived under the thumb of their inexorable soldier bosses. A successful French translator, Xu Shao, who was in his 50s, once accidentally trod on some wheat seedlings while working in a field. The soldier boss immediately snarled at him, 'You have sabotaged production, I could shoot you!'

These 5.7 cadre schools pointedly made life harder for their students. Some schools limited their expenditure on food, saying that being well fed could breed capitalist thought. Professor Chen Jar-Cheu was in the Commerce Ministry's 5.7 cadre school, where they had enough rice but never any meat and they were only ever allowed to buy between a half and one small piece of bean curd when shopping. In 1970, Chen had one month's leave in Peking and invited two 'schoolmates' to a famous restaurant to enjoy a Peking duck feast. The soldier boss heard about this episode and when they got back to their school all three had to make self-criticisms. Chen was accused of dragging his comrades with him down the capitalist road and his two guests declared that their class consciousness was not sufficiently high and that was why they had allowed Chen to drag them down the capitalist road.

On another occasion, Chen brought back some white sugar, fried flour, broad bean sauce and dried vegetables from his Peking home. His food was found, so he had to face a criticism and struggle meeting where he was told that he was still craving the way of life of the capitalist class. Some of his 'schoolmates' brought back scented disinfectant and medicinal ointment to treat their plentiful mosquito bites. Such items, like face cream, were treated as offensive goods enjoyed only by the capitalist class; poor, low and middle peasants did not use such things. The scented disinfectant and Chen's food were put on show to demonstrate the seriousness of the class struggle. After the exhibition, Chen was ordered to send all his food back to Peking, even though the post office was nearly 6 km away and he had to make the trip there and back on foot. Chen also got into trouble after his son sent him an atlas of China and the soldier boss asked, 'Is an atlas useful in helping your mind reform?' The professor had had to admit that no, it wasn't and his atlas was duly confiscated.

It was very difficult to obtain leave to visit anyone sick in the family. The wife of Ho Si-Lai, a literary researcher, suffered from heart trouble which often caused her to faint at the factory where she worked. One day, as she was carrying her sick daughter to hospital, she collapsed in the street. Her factory cabled Ho in his 5.7 cadre school to ask him to go home immediately, but the soldier boss refused to let him go. In protest he went on hunger strike for two days and he was then given four days' leave. He spent three days travelling, managing to spend just one day with his wife. But when the distinguished writer Bar Gin put in a request for a few extra days' leave at home to look after his wife, who was seriously ill, his soldier boss replied 'Bar Gin is not a doctor. What is the use in him staying at home? Staying at home is not good for his reform.' Bar Gin therefore had no choice but to return to his job of cleaning latrines at the school.

Several academics, including the famous playwright Woo Joo-Kwang, had the same job as Bar Gin's, which was to scoop out the contents of all the indoor, outdoor and open-air latrines. Woo had been denounced as a big rightist and was therefore banned from attending meetings or studying political documents with the other students. Sometimes they were ordered to go out during snowstorms and collect dung in the fields. In 1970 Woo fell ill with appendicitis, but the soldier boss forbade people from informing his family. He was forced to leave hospital before his wound had healed properly and was made to resume his normal work. After a second operation his wound became infected, but still he was compelled to stand evening after evening until late at night to face struggle meetings.

The attitude of the authorities to the 5.7 cadre school students, who included many of China's top intellectuals, was encapsulated by one military ruler who compared them to rotten tomatoes; nobody wanted them even if they were sold in piles. Chinese people traditionally regard number one as the best and number nine the worst and intellectuals were now known officially as 'the stinking number nine'. In those days, a hospital consultant's salary was lower than that of a nurse, while professors' salaries were stopped; instead they were given only living expenses, which were less than the wages of a cleaner.

The staff of the two elite universities, Tsing Hua and Peking, were sent to Jiangxi province where they set up a 5.7 cadre school around the huge Poyang Lake. First of all they had to build huts to give themselves some shelter, after which they began to bring virgin land into cultivation. Families were broken up, with men and women separated by curtains in their dank dormitories. Everything, including bedding, clothing and shoes, soon became mouldy and started to rot. Hygiene conditions were poor, food was bad and the physical labour was hard and intense. Sometimes hurricanes would capsize boats on the lake and blow down their huts.

When the soldiers of the Mao Tse-Tung Thought Propagation Team arrived at this 5.7 cadre school to supervise the reform of its stinking number nines, sometimes the students would find themselves being dragged out of bed late at night to attend political lectures, march in the rain, run to political study meetings or just to watch a film. When an old engineering teacher refused on one occasion to go out to work in the fields, he was dragged to a struggle session in the rice field. Afterwards he protested at this ill-treatment by going on a hunger strike.

The two groups of people, from Tsing Hua and Peking Universities, were sent to parts of the lake known to be infested with bilharzia, but the Tsing Hua group was not told of this hazard. They lived a primitive life, depending on the lake for their drinking water, as well as washing and swimming in it. It was over two years before Chow En-Lai at last heard of their whereabouts, he recalled them immediately and within a week they were back in Peking.

About a million intellectuals were sent to 5.7 cadre schools, with no prospect of graduation and no escape even for veteran Communists or lifelong Communist sympathisers. The schools in effect were used to punish a whole generation of people who were guilty of being educated. Jiang and Lin glorified the project and tried to make it into a permanent system. However, Lin's death in 1971 marked the beginning of the end and from 1974 to 1976 these schools started to collapse. The students began increasingly to flout the penal system, often going on home leave and failing to return, while those still in schools spent their time fishing, cooking, playing chess, reading for pleasure or studying. The soldier bosses were losing control. After Mao's death, the Communist Party admitted that the 5.7 cadre schools had been one of the Cultural Revolution's wild products, yet Mao had said again and again that China needed two, three, four or even more Cultural Revolutions. Since this first one had plainly been aimed at destroying culture, the message was that China did not need culture, knowledge or education. Many intellectuals sold their books cheaply, by weight, before they moved to the villages to start a new life as manual labourers.

By 1968 nearly all educational institutions in China had been moribund for three years. This meant that the 15 and 18-year-olds who had finished junior or senior secondary school had no way of receiving further education and therefore very little chance of getting a decent job, possibly for the rest of their lives. Mao's answer to this problem was contained in his instruction published in the *People's Daily* on 22 December 1968, which urged educated young people to go to the villages to receive re-education from poor, low and middle peasants. People in the cities should send their children to the villages and the villagers should welcome them.

Educated young people duly set out to settle in villages, prompted by the realisation that they would be judged insufficiently revolutionary if they did not volunteer to become peasants. It was a huge mass movement, involving many millions of young people over a period of ten or more years. On 8 December 1973 the Xinhua news agency reported that in the previous five years a total of eight million teenage students had settled in villages and by 1978, according to official documents, the figure had risen to 16.23 million.

The poverty and hardship in rural China soon broke the young people's rosy dreams, stranded as they often were far from home. One of Mao's famous sayings was 'Although peasants' hands are black and their feet have cow dung on them, they are still cleaner than those of capitalist intellectuals.' Many of these young people married peasants in order to seek family support, though in many cases lonely young girls were coerced into such unions, or even raped by their bosses. In 1970 and again in 1973, documents issued by the central government emphasised that forcing girls into marriage was strictly forbidden, implicitly admitting just how widespread the practice was and that the authorities had failed to stamp it out.

The Cultural Revolution rulers went to great lengths to protect their reputations. Jiang, back in the 1930s, had led a scandalous life as a second-rate actress in Shanghai struggling to make her name. Her former fellow inmate Zee Kwei-Ying, who had been sent to the same Shanghai prison in late 1934 for her involvement in left-wing politics, testified in 1976 that Jiang had often gone drinking at night with the senior Nationalist warders. It was a story that would be highly damaging to Jiang, the 'great and valiant standard-bearer of the proletarian Cultural Revolution' and she needed desperately to erase her past, even if it meant liquidating her former colleagues and friends who knew too much.

In October 1966, a group of Jiang's henchmen pretending to be Red Guards searched the Shanghai homes of five well-known people, four of whom had belonged to the same amateur actors' association as Jiang in

Shanghai in the 1930s. Among them was Jeng Jeun-Li, who had previously been summoned to see Chang Chun-Chel, one of the gang of four and ordered to hand over all material concerning Jiang, including any photographs and letters. Jeng and his wife, understandably worried, put together a big package and sent it to Chang and so by the time his home was searched most material concerning Jiang had already gone. The Red Guards had started ransacking homes in August 1966 and in Shanghai their activities peaked in late August and early September. When Jiang's henchmen came to search the five homes in October, every one of them had been ransacked already.

Jeng's widow, Wong Sun, recalled in May 1977 that one night, after Chang had had a second talk with Jeng, a group of people had broken into their home. They did not come from Jeng's workplace, a film studio and they forbade the family from asking which department they belonged to. There were more than a dozen young men led by an older man and all wore surgical masks, so that only their eyes were visible. The leader ordered them to hand over all their material to do with 'the big boss' (that is, Jiang). When told the family no longer had any such things, the intruders refused to believe them; instead they sealed up the building and started a methodical search, examining everything, including all the books, carefully. They even prised open picture frames on the walls to check that nothing was hidden.

Since all the material about Jiang had already been handed over to Chang Chun-Chel or taken away in previous ransackings, the October search did not uncover anything of importance, though the searchers took away diaries, notebooks, letters, even small notes, in fact anything with writing on it, in case Jiang was mentioned in them. They were all sent to Jiang in Peking and burnt, often under her personal supervision.

The search of Jeng's home, which included body searches of all the family, lasted from ten o'clock one evening to after five o'clock the following morning. When it was finished the leader warned Jeng menacingly that if he was found with any material relating to Jiang at home from now on, he would be held responsible. 'If you were in Peking,' the leader added for good measure, 'you would have been shot already.' Soon afterwards, Jeng was arrested and locked in a small cell. His family was not even permitted to ask what had happened to him or where he was. It was only when he was dying, after more than two years of continuous torture, that his family saw him again. He died in April 1969.

The other four people, including Koo Er-Yee, met a similar fate. Back in 1936, three couples in the Shanghai drama circle had held a joint wedding ceremony in nearby Hangzhou city, at which a group photo was taken. One of the brides was Lan Ping (later Jiang), who was marrying her second husband, a scriptwriter. Koo, who was one of the bridegrooms, had kept the group photo until it was seized in one of the 17 searches carried out at his home and it brought him a great deal of trouble. By now he had become a film director in the Shanghai Tianma Studio and every day when he entered and left the studio he had to crawl under the crotch of Jiang's rebels who were guarding the entrance. He was forced to do heavy physical work even when injured or ill. In early June 1970, when he was ordered to report to a 5.7 cadre school, Koo remarked to his family that Jiang would not give up until he was dead. He viewed the future with foreboding. On 8 June he reported at the school and just ten days later he was found hanging in his room. His family, when they arrived, noticed that his body was covered with injuries.

The fifth person in the group, Tong Gee-Ling, was a Peking opera singer who had arrived in Shanghai only in 1940 and so had not known Jiang well; she had had contact with Jiang only in the 60s while she had been rehearsing a drama. Jiang nevertheless hated her, although neither Tong nor anyone else could understand why.

Jiang presented herself as a leader on cultural matters. She had produced a total of eight shows, including Peking operas and musicals, insisting that no one was allowed to alter a single word or movement of these sacred examples. In fact, all the productions were originally the work of other people and all of them had been performed before. Jiang and her team had merely altered the characters to create rigid, stereotyped revolutionary heroes. In other words, she stole other people's work, tampered with them and called them her own. At that time, Chinese people had nothing to watch except her 8 politically correct shows. While rehearsing one of Jiang's dramas, Tong had dared to disagree with Jiang, who had sacked her as a result. Later, when Jiang began to eliminate her old colleagues and friends in performing arts circles, it seems, she decided to deal with Tong at the same time.

When Jiang had been living in a small first-floor room in Shanghai in the 1930s, the landlord's maid, Qin Kwei-Jing, had lived on the second floor. The two young women got on well and Qin often helped Jiang with domestic chores and money. Jiang said at the time she was grateful and hoped to repay Qin in the future. Years later, in February 1968, when Qin received a visit from a group of Shanghai Red Guards who were attempting to find out about Jiang's past, Jiang sent an aeroplane to fetch Qin from Shanghai. Qin, who by then was retired, was told only that a leader from central government had asked her to go to Peking. Once there, Qin was kept in an air force guesthouse and forbidden to leave her room. Jiang had already told the air force chief, Woo Fa-Shan, to lock Qin up; she had no intention of seeing her. Qin was beaten and then thrown into prison. Her hair was shaved off and she was tortured, in an attempt to make her admit that she was a spy and counter-revolutionary. Qin was finally released in 1975, after spending seven years in jail.

Since Jiang had also spent time in the provinces of Shandong, Zhejiang and Jiangsu as well as Shanghai and Peking, a number of local public security departments possessed "dirty" files on her. Shortly after the start of the Cultural Revolution, she claimed that certain people in the public security system were collecting black material to malign her. This was the signal for a thorough purge of the public security departments in all provinces where she had lived. As many as 26 members of the Shanghai public security bureau were locked up, some of whom were persecuted to death.

The Shanghai Library had a collection of newspapers and magazines from the 1930s which included stories about Jiang and some also contained politically incorrect articles written by Chang Chun-Chel. Identifying this as another possible danger, Jiang closed down the store-room housing all the 1930s material and all librarians without express permission from the Gang of Four were banned from entering the room. Nine people who had worked in the room, including handymen and temporary workers, were investigated and persecuted, as were large numbers of readers. One young librarian, Yuan Jar-Si, who had done nothing more than speak to some readers looking for material from the 1930s was imprisoned for more than two years.

104

The Promotion of an Emperor

In one of his poems, Mao claimed that he was smarter than many successful Chinese emperors. In reality he had finally attained a status which no Chinese emperor had achieved. The Chinese people had been forced into a situation where any disagreement with Mao was against the law, while Mao's personality cult was legalised by the Chinese Communist Party.

Mao's personality cult went through ups and downs inside the party. In 1956, when Khrushchev first voiced criticism of Stalin and attacked his personality cult, Mao was keen to avoid a row with the Russians and with the majority of the Chinese Communist Party. Accordingly he accepted a number of resolutions intended to eliminate personality worship and he agreed to delete the words 'Mao Tse-Tung Thought' from the new party constitution and to ban the practice of treating Mao Tse-Tung Thought as on the same level as Marxism and Leninism.

When a chill wind started to blow over from Russia, Mao wasted no time in stamping out all these unwelcome ideas. In March 1958, at the party's Chengdu conference, he commented that communism in China would not work without personality worship; he was all for personality worship. People who objected to personality worship were really just objecting to worshipping another person and wanted to be worshipped themselves.

This sinister accusation managed to silence all the opponents of a personality cult, because the only person who could possibly be the object of personality worship was Mao himself. If being against a personality cult meant wanting worship for oneself rather than for Mao, this would clearly be a deadly crime. Mao's private secretary, Lee Yui, recorded in his memoir of the Lu Mountain Conference that when the American journalist Anna Louise Strong told Mao that he had surpassed Marx, Engels, Lenin and Stalin, Mao swallowed the compliment without a word.

In 1966, at the beginning of the Cultural Revolution, Mao personally amended an essay in the *People's Daily*, adding and underlining the following sentence: 'We should accept unconditionally the correct guidance of the party central authority headed by Chairman Mao'.

When the Mayor of Peking, Peng Zhen, tried to find out why the Three Red Flags campaign had failed, he organised a group of more than 20 important cadres from the Peking party committee, led by the editor-in-chief of the *People's Daily*, Deng Toc, to make a systematic examination of central government documents. Deng told his team to speak out freely but to make certain that they kept everything private. To protect their party, family shame should not be made public, but in order to ascertain the truth they had to ask questions.

Deng discovered that in 1958 and 1959 all sorts of important policies had been implemented without proper study by specialists and without any debate by the central authorities. They had simply been signed by Mao and issued to the party to be carried out as national policies. People's communes had never been put on trial and had no rules or regulations. They had been ineptly launched without any preparation.

Deng's team produced a long report, concluding that the calamity of the Great Leap Forward had been caused by errors of leadership, not by natural disasters. Mao's orders had frequently been contradictory and had been changed too often and too fast. The report concluded that Mao was getting old and becoming arrogant; he wanted to surpass other international leaders, yet his haste had led to disaster. Deng's team, who worked in a building named Panorama Pavilion, eventually met with big troubles which became known as the Panorama Pavilion Incident. There was of course no chance of the team surviving Mao's Cultural Revolution. Peng Zhen went to jail and Deng Toc killed himself.

The elevation of Mao and of Mao Tse-Tung Thought through studying his writings started as early as 1945, after the 7th Party Congress, but the real drive to create a personality cult came after the 1959 Lu Mountain Conference, after Lin Biao had replaced Peng De-Huai as Defence Minister. At a high-level meeting in September 1960 Lin suggested a resolution that the study of Mao's writings should be put before everything else. The resolution was approved by Mao and quickly conveyed to the whole country. Before long a campaign was launched to promote the study of Mao Tse-Tung Thought and Mao's writings.

Lin disapproved of Mao's Great Leap Forward, which he condemned in his diary as folly based on illusion. He also regarded Mao's anti-revisionist campaign as wrong. But he did not reveal what was really in his mind; instead he publicly and repeatedly lauded Mao to the skies. His duplicity enabled him to gain Mao's favour and in a period of just ten years

Lin overtook Liu Shao-Qi, Chow En-Lai, Zhu De, Chan Yun and Deng Xiao-Ping to become Mao's deputy, the second most important man in China, soon after the start of the Cultural Revolution. His many well-known remarks included 'Chairman Mao's every sentence is the truth. One of his sentences is equal to ten thousand sentences of other people.' 'Chinese people must carry out Chairman Mao's orders, whether they understand them or not.' On 18 May 1966, he told a meeting that Mao was a genius above Marx, Engels and Lenin; in fact he was the greatest genius in the world.

Well before the Cultural Revolution, in April 1961, Lin told the PLA newspaper to print Mao's sayings frequently and conspicuously and so Mao's quotations duly began to appear daily on the front page. The PLA newspaper soon produced a collection of Mao's sayings, the final version of which was the famous Little Red Book, published in May 1964. The book's editor, a woman called Tian Shel-Kwang, later disclosed that as soon as it was launched, one of Mao's subordinates was ordered to telephone her and ask for a copy. This prototype had been compiled for the benefit of the armed forces only, but in 1965 Mao instructed that a longer version was needed for the whole nation.

The many millions of Red Guards were the formidable tools used to propagate Mao Tse-Tung Thought and they contributed their own very special brand of eulogy, including gems such as: 'Thousands of things depend on the sun to grow, Chairman Mao is the red sun' or 'the reddest, reddest red sun', or 'Mao Tse-Tung is the only forever invincible and infallible leader'.

Mao's sayings quickly appeared on the front pages of all newspapers, calendars, envelopes, writing paper and even maps. Any letter or telephone call had to begin with paying great respect to Chairman Mao and wishing him to live forever. On 2 July 1967, the Xinhua news agency announced 'Great news for people of the world – rapturous cheers for the worldwide publication of Chairman Mao's sayings'. Long and moving stories would often appear in newspapers reporting that people all over the world loved Chairman Mao dearly and supported the Cultural Revolution and working-class people in other countries had risked their lives to hide their precious portraits of Mao and books of his sayings. A docker in an African port had asked for a Mao badge from a Chinese seaman and had pinned it on his bare chest without hesitation before raising his arm and crying 'Long live Chairman Mao!'

These stories indicated that a new world order was rising in China where the reddest, reddest red sun rose and the lucky Chinese had started their new life ahead of the rest of the world. In 1969, the Xinhua news agency and the *Kwang Ming Daily* reported a new type of wedding ceremony. Wan Chu-San, a poor peasant from the Dajone commune in Yiyang county, Hunan province, decided to marry off his daughter without presents or a feast, following Mao's teaching to be frugal. He gave his daughter a dowry consisting of a set of Mao's selected works, one Little Red Book and two Mao badges. The bride, accompanied by her family, had walked to the bridegroom's home where, after a volley of clapping, they sang:

> The sky is immense, the earth is immense,
> they are not as immense as the party's loving kindness!
> My father is dear to me, my mother is dear to me,
> they are not as dear to me as Chairman Mao!

After singing, the newly-wedded couple exchanged presents. The bride gave her groom Mao's Little Red Book and the groom pinned a Mao badge on his bride. Then followed a study of Mao's sayings with the guests and the wedding ceremony ended with a criticism of Liu Shao-Qi's revisionist and counter-revolutionary policies. Another story concerned a group of very lucky people who had shaken hands with Mao and refused to wash their hands afterwards, while other people had fought to shake their hands to acquire some reflected glory.

The leaders directing the Cultural Revolution vigorously promoted a new code of conduct, demanding three loyalties and four immensities from all Chinese people for Mao. These were: loyalty to Mao, to Mao Tse-Tung Thought and to Mao's policies and immense love, trust, worship and devotion.

From time to time, casual remarks by Mao were made public by Lin's gang, often in broadcasts by the central radio station at 8 p.m. People were expected to react immediately; they would organise themselves in groups to parade through the streets, beating drums and gongs to cheer for the latest holy instruction, sometimes parading for several nights running. Even in atrocious weather no one would dare refuse to take part in them. It was said that Mao's sayings and Mao Tse-Tung Thought could help people overcome difficulties and even achieve miracles.

Most people were forced to perform a twice-daily ritual in honour of Mao. Every morning and evening they would stand to attention or kneel down in front of portraits of Mao and repeat this extravagant homage to the leader:

We wish with great respect the great leader, great teacher, great commander, great helmsman, the reddest, reddest red sun Chairman Mao to live forever, forever, forever!

We wish with great respect the close comrade of Chairman Mao, our deputy Commander, Lin Biao, to be healthy, forever healthy, forever healthy!

Then they would wave their Little Red Books above their heads, recite some of Mao's sayings, sing either Mao's quotation songs or *The East Is Red* and dance the loyalty dance. In the most hysterical period, those who had failed to perform the loyalty dance were forbidden from boarding the train in Shenyang railway station.

Mao's sayings, portraits and statues were everywhere and in every home. One did not say 'buy a portrait of Chairman Mao'; the correct formula was 'invite with great respect the treasure-portrait of Chairman Mao to one's home'. Mao's Little Red Book was now China's bible and Mao himself was now the Chinese people's god.

Any unwitting profanity could bring untold misfortune, as vast numbers of people knew to their cost. On one occasion a peanut hawker unwittingly wrapped his goods in an old newspaper which happened to have the great man's photograph in it and as a result found himself condemned as a counter-revolutionary. A teacher of Peking No.2 medical college inadvertently cut off part of a photograph of Mao in a copy of newspaper, for which crime he was subjected to a whole series of struggle meetings. Another man sat on a chair forgetting that he had put the Little Red Book on it and as a result was severely beaten for the crime of sitting on the treasure-book. One man was branded as a counter-revolutionary when he sat on a copy of *Red Flag* magazine containing a photo of Mao, while a worker in Nanking got into trouble when, annoyed by the black smoke blown in his face by the east wind, muttered to himself, 'It would be nice to have a west wind.' He was denounced for contradicting Mao's famous saying, 'East wind overcomes west wind', which signified that the Communist bloc in the East would triumph over the Western world. This worker was sent to jail for seven years.

A villager who had once been chairman of a peasants' association went down the hill to a market to 'invite' a treasure-bust of Mao to his home. Since he had to trudge up the narrow and rugged mountain path, he tied the big, heavy plaster bust on his back. Before he could walk out of the market, he was arrested as a counter-revolutionary in action, because he had wrapped a rope around the neck of the bust. He was not allowed to go home and was sent to prison for five years.

On another occasion a village teacher told his pupils a story he had read about Mao. Once when Mao was being pursued by Chiang Kai-Shek's army, he had hidden in a culvert to avoid being captured. The teacher's intention was to praise the great leader for being clever and astute, but he was accused of insulting Mao. How could the great leader hide in a lowly culvert? He could not remember the names of either the author or the story book and so he was thrown into prison. His illiterate wife took their young son with her to pick up scraps of paper everywhere, begging people to read the words out for her in a desperate attempt to find the story or the author's name so as to save her husband. Eventually, after spending eight years in jail, he was released, but by then his wife and son had died in a house fire. One day, quite by chance, he found the story again and discovered that it had in fact been written by Sher Ger-Jai, the deputy Minister for Public Security.

Mao's writings were published with the enthusiastic support of central and local government and of Mao himself. Soon no other books were being printed, because all the paper was needed for printing Mao's works, but even so there was a paper shortage. The paper industry underwent a terrific expansion, the *Workers' Daily* in Peking reporting on 3 December 1966 that the machines in a Guangzhou paper mill, bought ten years previously from abroad, were already rotating at a speed which far exceeded the maximum speed recommended by the foreign experts, in order to increase production. On 29 December the *People's Daily* reported that any machine which could possibly be adapted to produce paper was being used, including machines in the sugar factories of Guangdong and Sichuan provinces. In 1966 there were a total of 18 paper mills in China, in 15 different provinces. By the end of 1967, the number had increased to 105 new and reconstituted paper mills, in 27 provinces.

In early 1967, when millions of Red Guards were milling around to take the Cultural Revolution to other parts of the country, the authorities ordered all Red Guards who worked in publishing and printing houses to return to their workplaces immediately in order to speed up the publication of Mao's writings. In 1967 there were a total of 181 printing houses in the country which specialised in printing Mao Tse-Tung's selected works, but the following year their numbers increased to 300.

Many other trades abandoned their normal work to devote themselves to China's new national priority. On 26 December 1968 the *Inner Mongolia Daily* reported that all the goldsmiths in Inner Mongolia had joined in producing Mao badges and the radio station reported that the treasure-books produced in other provinces were being sent to Nanking and Suzhou to have their covers gilded. On 20 January 1969, the *People's Daily* disclosed that whereas formerly the gold powder used to gild book covers had always been imported, now a Nanking factory had succeeded in producing it to international standards. This was surely good news for the treasure-books! The authorities stressed repeatedly that all the treasure-books were not simply free propaganda; people were queuing up to buy them, although poor and middle peasants were given the treasure-books free.

In Jiangsu province, 5,000 workers from more than 1000 cooperative stores in the villages were used as door-to-door salesmen to sell the treasure-books. In the inland province of Gansu, which had a population of 1.3 million, two million sets of Mao's selected works and ten million copies of his sayings were distributed before the summer of 1968; yet the production and distribution of the treasure-books still showed no sign of stopping. The authorities in Hunan province, which had a population of 38 million, announced in September 1968 that 160 million copies of Mao's quotations had been printed in the province, in addition to the books printed in Peking and sent to Hunan. In all, 220 million copies of the sacred books were distributed in Hunan.

In the same period the authorities in Shandong province, which had a population of 37 million, were going through a period of soul-searching self-criticism. They tried to find out why not a single portrait of Mao or a set of Mao's selected works had been printed in the province before the Cultural Revolution. Still, the province soon began to mend its ways. At the start of the Cultural Revolution, as many factories as possible were mobilised to help the province's 30 printing houses to produce seven million sets of Mao's selected works, 60 million copies of the quotation books, two million copies of Mao's poems and 76 million portraits of Mao.

By March 1968 Mao's Little Red Book had been translated into over 20 foreign languages and around ten million copies had been printed, because the whole world was waiting impatiently for liberation. Books of Mao's quotations were reportedly on sale in 117 foreign countries and by September 1968 Mao's selected works had been published in about a dozen foreign languages. Shockingly, however, the sale of these foreign-language treasure-books was a gigantic flop and years later huge quantities of them were still to be found stacked up in warehouses. Nobody knew what to do with them, but nobody dared get rid of them.

In 1991, a Cultural Revolution researcher, Song Hua, gave the following figures in a Peking magazine. Between 1966 and 1971, at least two billion Mao badges were produced, in more than 10,000 styles. Over

500 compilations of Mao's writings were produced in more than 50 languages, amounting to some five billion copies in all, although this figure excluded books produced by the myriad groups of Red Guards. A record produced during the same period featured singers demonstrating the amazing feat of singing 'Long live Chairman Mao' no less than 130 times.

The Chinese economy was devastated by the Cultural Revolution, as the authorities demanded that the nation economise, reducing people's food rations and increasing their workload. At the same time resources were poured into China's only thriving industry, that of worshipping Mao Tse-Tung.

The number of Chinese-language treasure-books greatly exceeded the Chinese population, even if babies were included. This begs the obvious question of how many people could read them. The boastful declaration made at the time of the Great Leap Forward that illiteracy would be eliminated had long been forgotten. On 1 November 1968, the *People's Daily* carried a letter from a peasant-soldier which claimed that in his village most young people had never been to school. On 17 November, the *Jiangxi Daily* carried a report about peasants who had never heard Chairman Mao's voice because there was no radio in their village and nobody was able to read Chairman Mao's writings. The peasants were condemning Liu Shao-Qi for the way he ran the country, because only a very few children were able to go to school. In other words, most people were illiterate. The situation in Kwang Jone county, Hebei province, was not as bad; 69 per cent of its children went to school. This meant, however, that 30 per cent were illiterate. On 16 December 1967, the *People's Daily* carried a report of a survey of several streets in Changsha, the biggest city in Hunan province, which found that out of 18,000 people only a few could read. On 29 November 1968, the *People's Daily* reported that literacy in minority areas was even worse. The best-selling author of all time was sitting on top of a protection racket, as frightened Chinese people were trying to buy themselves some safety and peace.

Although Lin was the driving force behind the craze to deify Mao, Mao's tacit approval was abundantly clear. When Lin's coup to topple Mao failed in 1971, his death caused billions of Little Red Books to disappear abruptly.

105

Different Ends for the Gang of Five

Lin Biao, 13 years Mao's junior, was born in 1906. In September 1959, Lin replaced Peng De-Huai as defence minister and first deputy chairman of the Central Military Commission. From then on he ardently propagated Mao's personality cult, particularly in public gatherings. It was his shortcut to the pinnacle of power. His adulation produced considerable antipathy, leading many people to complain about him to Liu Shao-Qi. During a speech at a meeting of the Central Military Commission, Liu overtly lampooned not just Lin, but even Mao himself, saying, 'Everybody can make mistakes. Marx, Engels, Lenin and Stalin all made mistakes, Chairman Mao made many mistakes too. I used to advocate worship of Mao, but not any more. I now advocate worship of Deng Xiao-Ping.' The offensive remark was reported to Mao by General Young Cheng-Wu.

Although Mao enjoyed his own deification as promoted by Lin, he was not prepared to allow Lin to control the army, laying down a rule during the Cultural Revolution that any transfer of troops, even a platoon, had to have the signature of the chairman of the Central Military Commission, in other words Mao himself. As a result of Lin's close cooperation with the Cultural Revolution leadership, Mao's policy triumphed in the 11th session of the Eighth CCP National Congress in August 1966. Lin, the opium-addict, was publicly chosen as the second most senior person in the pecking order of the party. However, he still had to work hard to strengthen this newly-acquired position. Working closely with the other pretender, Jiang, he encouraged his supporters to smear other senior communists who were potential obstacles, such as Liu Shao-Qi, Deng Xiao-Ping and Marshal Zhu De and ransack their homes.

In April 1969, at the Ninth CCP National Congress, Lin was written into the party constitution as Mao's 'close comrade and successor'. His position as the heir apparent had been formally confirmed. Although the Chinese people were kept in the dark about President Liu's death, it was an open secret within the ruling clique. Lin wanted Liu's job, but Mao had different ideas. On 8 March 1970, Mao set out a proposal to revise the constitution, abolishing the post of president completely. Lin and his supporters made a sustained effort to retain the post. Lin's wife, Yip Cheun, asked privately, in a confidential conversation with the air force chief, Woo Fa-Shan, 'If there is no president, what will Lin do? What position will he occupy?' Lin's supporters began to sell the idea that Lin was an exceptional genius and a brilliant assistant to Mao.

However, Mao doggedly refused to change his mind and Lin could no longer cover up his displeasure. In August 1970 he began spending most of his time in Beidaihe resort, pretending he was ill. On 1 May 1971, the Labour Day festival, Lin joined the national leaders in the morning to inspect the Tiananmen Square parade, but he was unwilling to go to the Tiananmen city wall for the evening firework display and only appeared after an anxious Chow En-Lai had telephoned him repeatedly, urging him to attend. When he finally arrived he did not speak to or shake hands with Mao; instead he stayed for a few minutes, looking sulky and left without telling anyone, leaving behind an empty seat. His absence was noticed by the Cambodian guest of honour, Prince Sihanouk. It gave an impression of disunity in the CCP central leadership and it was bad for government publicity.

Lin cultivated supporters in the armed forces, while his men in the navy brought about the death of the navy chief of staff. In March 1967, he asked Woo Fa-Shan, the air force chief, to find his 23-year-old son, Lin Li-Gol, a job in the air force. Later, in the first half of 1969, Lin and his wife, Yip Cheun, kept dropping hints to Woo about granting their son quick promotion and on 17 October 1969 Woo obliged by giving Lin Li-Gol the job of deputy director of the Department of Military Operations. He also issued an order giving the young man a free hand to run the air force. Lin and Yip knew very well that their son was too young and inexperienced to be given such authority and their solution was to instruct Woo to arrange a meeting at which Lin Li-Gol delivered a nonsensical day-long lecture on Mao's writings. Lin Biao and his supporters then proclaimed that Lin Li-Gol was a genius, arranging the printing and distribution of 700,000 copies of his lecture.

Lin by now saw himself as the emperor-in-waiting and his heir therefore needed an exceptional beauty as consort. In June 1969, Lin and Yip used their Shanghai supporters to form a recruiting team which fanned out to search for beautiful girls all over China, ostensibly for the purpose of selecting staff for the office of the military commission. In early 1970, after the girls assembled in Shanghai, mother and son went to vet them. The girls had no idea that they were part of a selection process for an imperial consort. The recruiting team was later reformed as the Shanghai Small Team, all of whose members were required to be completely loyal to the Lin family.

Lin's moves did not escape Mao's attention. In late August 1970, Mao questioned many of Lin's senior followers repeatedly about their activities, ordering them to make self-criticisms. It was obvious that they were already under surveillance and that the net was closing in. Lin therefore decided that if he could not get what he wanted by persuasion he would have to get it by force. On 21 March 1971, Lin Li-Gol and his senior army supporters held a secret meeting in Shanghai to discuss Lin's ideas for a military coup and immediately afterwards they embarked on special training, collecting intelligence, establishing a secret communications network, storing weapons, ammunition, bugging devices and other useful equipment.

On 16 August 1971 Mao left Peking on a special train to inspect the provinces and cities of south China. During his tour he met many senior army officers and officials from both party and government and talked about someone who wanted to be president and seize power. On 10 September his train stopped at Shanghai. The plotters expected him to stay in the city for a few days and were intending to attack his train with cannons and rockets; their back-up plan was to blow up a nearby railway bridge. But in the event Mao left Shanghai unexpectedly early the following day. He did not allow the train to stop at any station on the way back north and he arrived back in Peking on the evening of 12 September. Lin, Yip and their son were panic-stricken. At midnight they took off in a military aeroplane bound for Russia, but in the small hours of the following morning the aeroplane crashed in Mongolia, killing all nine people on board.

There was a time when Jiang and Lin had formed an unholy alliance to help purge each other's enemies. Chang Chun-Chel, a member of Jiang's Gang of Four, said frankly in May 1967, 'The intention of the Cultural Revolution is to get rid of all the old folk (the communist veterans), leaving not one behind.' In those days Jiang was attentively served by Lin's gang, who took photographs, played poker, went for outings and meals with her and more importantly, plotted to snare their prey together. Lin's ignominious end put Jiang in an awkward position. She promptly claimed that Lin had persecuted her for years and had even tried to kill her.

After Lin's death, Jiang's group turned their attentions to attacking Chow En-Lai and Deng Xiao-Ping. In November 1973, Jiang's writing team in Shanghai produced a critical article about a Qin Dynasty prime minister which alluded to Chow and in January 1974 Jiang organised several meetings of the Peking armed forces and many government institutions. She launched a campaign to criticise Lin and Confucius, in which her real target was certain unnamed senior communists; the clear implication, though, was that Confucius was code for Chow. Using her own name, Jiang wrote to the armed forces in Nanking and Guangzhou to expand her campaign across the country and posters bearing slogans such as 'Down with the contemporary Confucius' and 'Down with the political director of Whampoa Military Academy' appeared in Anhui province. These pointed directly at Chow. On 15 February, Mao declared that he supported the campaign to criticise Confucius and Lin.

One of Jiang's main targets was Chow's chief assistant, Deng Xiao-Ping. At the 1968 Party Congress Lin, Jiang and their gang proposed that Deng should be expelled from the party, but this was rejected by Mao, although Mao regarded Deng as a follower of Liu Shao-Qi and condemned him as the party's number two arch-capitalist roader. On 20 October 1969, Deng and his family were sent to Jiangxi province, where they were put under house arrest. For more than three years he worked every morning in a tractor factory as an ordinary worker and in the afternoons tended the vegetable plot at his home. After Lin's death Deng twice wrote to Mao making self-criticisms and accepting Mao's term that he should never denounce the Cultural Revolution. By then, Chow was ill and many heavyweight party apparatchiks had been purged; even Mao's long-time political secretary, Chan Bor-Da, once the head of the Central Cultural Revolution Small Team, was in prison. In February 1973, with Chow's support, Mao allowed Deng to return to Peking and appointed him vice premier.

Jiang tried very hard to install her underlings into important positions in preparation for her succession. She was not pleased to see Deng back in power and made frequent derogatory comments about both Chow and Deng, most notably during the *Fung Chin* affair. Back in 1964, Chow had made the decision to buy and build ships at the same time and Mao had agreed with him. By 1970, Chow wanted China to build its own ocean-going ships, with the hope that within a few years the country would no longer need to rent or buy foreign ships and Deng faithfully carried out this policy. In May 1974, the newly-built vessel *Fung Chin* went out on sea trials, sailing back to Shanghai on 30 September. The Gang of Four made a great deal of propaganda out of the *Fung Chin*'s success, claiming that those responsible for the Chinese shipbuilding industry were worshipping Confucius, flattering foreign countries and selling out China. On 17 October Jiang wrote to the politburo to declare her overwhelming proletarian indignation, asserting that some people in the State Council were subservient to foreign countries and she urged the politburo to deal with the collaborator problem.

The following day, Wang Hong-Won, one of the Gang of Four, was secretly sent to Changsha, Hunan province, to report to Mao on Chow's activities. Wong alleged that although Chow was ill in hospital he was still busily meeting Deng and other senior officials, the insinuation being that they were similar to Lin's cabal. That same evening, the Gang of Four sent for Wang Hai-Yung and Tang Won-San, Mao's official interpreters and asked the two woman interpreters to inform Mao about the *Fung Chin* dispute and about Deng's policy of subservience to foreigners. On 19 October the two interpreters reported everything to Chow, who was still in hospital. Chow commented that the Gang of Four had long tried to make trouble for Deng and that Deng had tolerated them all the time.

In late 1974, with Chow seriously ill with cancer, Mao decided to give Deng a number of important jobs, but this did not stop Jiang's group from continuing to make vicious attacks on him, culminating on 2 March 1976 when she summoned the leading officials of 12 provinces and autonomous districts to a meeting in Peking, though she did not have any authority to do such a thing. She announced that Deng's policy of exporting goods to capitalist countries and importing machinery were the actions of a traitor.

Deng, meanwhile, turned his hand to sorting out some of the chaos into which the country had been plunged by the Cultural Revolution. He began by rehabilitating large numbers of condemned cadres, giving many their old jobs back. Now Jiang could make her most damaging attack, complaining to Mao that Deng did not truly appreciate the Cultural Revolution. Mao regarded the Cultural Revolution as his most glorious achievement and he would not allow anyone to question it. As a result, in September 1975 his attitude to Deng began to change. He had, he said, been paying close attention to comrade Deng's speeches and was starting to feel that there was a problem. Deng rarely talked about the achievements of the Cultural Revolution and he rarely criticised the revisionist policies of Liu Shao-Qi. The politburo accordingly did as Mao wanted. Deng was duly sacked and the country was gripped by another national campaign to criticise the capitalist roader Deng and to attack the right-leaning trend of overturning convictions.

When Chow was in hospital, Jiang would often tell Mao that Chow was a malingerer, or alternatively that he was using the opportunity to liaise with the 'old folks'. In addition the Gang of Four would use any excuse to disrupt Chow's treatment and stop him having peace and rest. On 8 January 1976 he died.

All through the Cultural Revolution the media were effectively under the control of Jiang and her gang. On 9 January Yel Won-Yuan, a member of the Gang of Four, instructed the *People's Daily* to print only a short report of Chow's death. They should not give foreign condolences too much space, they should not suggest wearing black, sending wreaths or setting up memorial halls and they should use only small headlines. He also made clear that words like 'revered' or 'beloved' prime minister should be avoided. Jiang's gang banned the huge crowds gathering to mourn in Tiananmen Square.

On 14 January about a million people gathered around the Martyrs Monument in Tiananmen Square to mourn Chow, even though his name only appeared on the fourth page of that day's copy of the *People's Daily*. The headline on the front page of the day was about an obscure education debate. The *Xinhua Monthly Periodical*'s edition of January 1976 carried news of people at home and abroad expressing their sorrow at Chow's death; all copies of the magazine were promptly confiscated. Jiang regarded Chow as Deng's backer and therefore they would not withdraw the trumped-up charges on him.

The Chinese people had endured unspeakable suffering during the Cultural Revolution and they were rancorous. In mourning the seemingly decent Chow their hatred against the Gang of Four finally came to a head. From late March 1976, beginning in Nanking and spreading to other cities, huge crowds gathered spontaneously to mourn Chow, at the same time openly displaying their hostility towards the Gang of Four. A poster appeared in Nanking with the blunt words 'Down with Jiang' and slogans such as 'Down with anybody who opposes prime minister Chow' were everywhere. Jiang's gang in Peking sent their people to Tiananmen Square late every night to remove wreaths and tear down posters, poems and other inscriptions and the public were told not to go to Tiananmen Square so as to avoid being used by troublemakers. However, this failed to stop people from pouring into the square in their tens of thousands.

On 4 April the politburo, by now under the control of the Gang of Four, concluded that a counter-revolutionary movement was attempting to assault the party leadership and sabotage the campaign to criticise Deng; their conclusion was endorsed by Mao. At around 9 p.m. the following evening 10,000 public security men, supported by 20,000 militiamen, were sent to seal off Tiananmen Square. By that time there were only a few hundred people left in the square, all of whom were arrested after violent confrontations. On 6 April, Mao's confidant and nephew, Mao Yuan-Sien, reported to him that 168 people had been injured in the operation to clear the square, 15 of them seriously. The militia had remained out of sight nearby and there had also been four army divisions waiting in the suburbs. Mao replied: 'Good, good, good. Good for morale!' The Tiananmen Square gathering, he added, had been the biggest counter-revolutionary incident since the founding of Communist China and behind the scenes Deng had been its organiser.

It took the public security men many hours to wash away the bloodstains in the square and they spent a further two months forcibly confiscating ten million copies of the condolence writings and photographs of the protestors. Of these they selected some 600 items to compile an album entitled 'Criminal Evidence of the Tiananmen Square Counter-Revolutionary Incident'. Around ten thousand people were investigated in Peking alone, with nearly 400 arrested.

Deng again lost his freedom. On 7 April, the party announced his dismissal from all his posts. Hua Guo-Feng was appointed as the new prime minister, causing great anger to Chang Chun-Chel, Jiang's aide, who had wanted Chow's job for himself.

Many people, especially the more educated Chinese, felt that Chow had tried to protect them and that he had treated them better than Mao. When Chow himself was bullied by Mao and the Gang of Four during the Cultural Revolution, he gained a lot of sympathy. People overlooked the fact that he had fawned on the evil tyrant, excusing it as an act of self-preservation performed in order to protect other potential victims. Many were therefore genuinely grief-stricken over his death. Later, it became clear that actually the inscrutable Chow had in fact acted as Mao's loyal and cold-hearted servant, whose overriding principle was to protect himself. When Liu Shao-Qi and Lin Biao fell foul of Mao, Chow helped Mao liquidate them. The special unit that had investigated Liu's case and confirmed Liu as a traitor had been headed by Chow, athough it was Mao's deliberate and evil act to appoint him to the job. In the post-Mao era it was discovered that nearly all of the warrants to arrest the senior victims of the Cultural Revolution had been signed by Chow. Although many had supposed that he had protected large numbers of veteran communists, it now transpired that many more veteran communists had been arrested using warrants signed by him.

During the worst period – the 'Red August' and September of 1966 – when the high-birth Red Guards were freely torturing and killing the 'five black categories' and their families, Chow supported the Red Guards because it helped soften the pressure on his authhourity. He used to praise the Red Guards lavishly for their success in taking their campaign of criticism and reform into society at large, instead of just confining it to their schools, adding how much he admired their great work of destroying the four old things and establishing the four new things.

When some of the red princes and princesses were arrested after they began to oppose the Cultural Revolution leadership, it was Chow who persuaded Mao to set them free. Chow was wily, always making sure that Mao's desires were fully catered for. Back in 1938, when most senior party officials opposed Mao's proposed marriage to Jiang, Chow alone gave Mao his support, realising that Mao was determined to marry her. For a long time Chow and Jiang remained on good terms and when Jiang came to prominence during the Cultural Revolution, Chow would praise her extravagantly at public meetings.

As far as his own image was concerned, Chow preferred to remain in the background. When Mao's personality cult was at its height, his family home in the village of Shao-Shen-Chung, Hunan province, began to attract large numbers of pilgrims. Chow, after Lin's death, had become in effect the second most important person in China and the party secretary of Jiangsu province was keen to encourage tourists to come and visit Chow's family tombs in Jiangsu. Chow came from a privileged family and his grandfather had been a senior official in the Qing Dynasty. The family graveyard, where Chow's grandparents, uncle and aunt and his parents were all buried, was well maintained and planted with fine old trees.

Chow rejected the party secretary's idea angrily. The careful Chow could not afford to compete with Mao for glory, so, he sent his wife there to secure himself safety and peace. She employed some workmen to dig a very deep hole and rebury the six coffins down there. After filling the hole, a bulldozer was used to level the ground and the big trees were all chopped down. His family graveyard disappeared without trace.

Chow was the leader of a large and powerful group within the party. Jiang's political ambition soon swept her into a whirlpool of power struggles, which unavoidably led to conflict between her and Chow and they soon became implacable enemies. When Jiang attended Chow's funeral, millions of television viewers noticed, with fury, that she did not remove her hat or bow to his body.

Even though he enjoyed Chow's loyalty, Mao, as he became increasingly paranoid, regarded Chow with increasing enmity. In early 1974, he issued vague instructions to redouble the campaign to denounce Lin and Confucius. Years later, Wang Hong-Won, one of the Gang of Four, confirmed that Mao had encouraged them to attack Chow. Mao had tried to groom Jiang for the top job and this was obvious to his inner circle. In an interview given after Mao's death, Chan Bor-Da commented that Mao had often criticised Jiang. In retrospect his criticisms had demonstrated his unfulfilled expectations of her; he had actually tried to remind her how to act.

Another member of the politburo, the vice premier Chan Yun-Kwei, said in a interview after Mao's death, "During the Cultural Revolution, the really important business was decided by Jiang and her group in advance and then taken to the politburo to be rubber-stamped. They did not really listen to our opinions. I reported this to Chairman Mao and he came to the politburo meeting and told Jiang, "I've warned you many times, you mustn't do things in your own name. You should speak in the name of the politburo and party central. It is not wise to put yourself at the front; you should emphasise the influence other leading comrades have had." To Chan Yun-Kwei it seemed that Mao's criticism of Jiang was a result of his desire to protect her. Mao absolutely did not want to bring her down; all his politburo colleagues could see that.

Gee Dun-Fei, also a member of the politburo, voiced similar thoughts in the post-Mao era. Chairman Mao, he said, trusted Jiang and her group such as Chang Chun-Chel very much; he worked hard on their behalf and was very close to them throughout the Cultural Revolution. To claim that he did not see through them was empty talk. How could he not understand them? He swept away obstacles of all sorts for them and nearly all those who were purged were regarded as bad by Jiang.

In early 1975, Chow once told Gee Dun-Fei: 'Chairman Mao wants to hand over supreme power to Jiang's group, so they must try to unite the majority of the people. If they constantly cling together in a small clique, how can they shoulder this heavy historical responsibility?'

With Mao's help, Jiang's political status rose quickly and in April 1969 she became a member of the politburo. All through the Cultural Revolution she stood at the forefront stirring up the fighting and she was involved in nearly all the purges of senior communists. Mao knew she must have incurred widespread resentment and after Lin's death he frequently warned her that she should be less exposed; it was better, in other words, to be the power behind the throne. He repeated the advice many times at politburo meetings, publicly praising her for leading the fight in the all-out civil war of the Cultural Revolution and praising the Gang of Four for their excellent understanding of Mao Tse-Tung Thought.

It was obvious to the more astute onlookers that Jiang was destined to become a powerful figure. Hua Guo-Feng, the future party leader, swore undying loyalty to Jiang in fulsome terms in front of Chang Chun-Chel, vowing that he would be her loyal assistant forever and that every generation of his family would be loyal to Chairman Mao's family.

As Mao's health deteriorated steadily, Jiang began a major propaganda campaign in her bid to succeed him. She had articles printed in the newspapers extolling matriarchy and in particular the greatness of two of China's empresses, openly comparing herself with them. Both empresses had been very able and great stateswomen, but neither had possessed any historical knowledge; Jiang, on the other hand, had both historical knowledge and progressive class-consciousness and so obviously she was much better than either of them.

On 26 August, two weeks before Mao's death, Jiang attempted to insert a news item in the *People's Daily* following a visit she had made to a factory and two universities; the article was to say that 'Comrade Jiang represents Chairman Mao and the party central authority on a visit to the people of Peking'. But the piece was vetoed by Hua Guo-Feng. By then Chow was dead and Deng had been sacked and Hua now became her rival in the power struggle. Her cabal began to incite people to write open letters expressing their loyalty to her and urging her to go for the top job.

Soon after Chow's death, Mao realised his own end was near. For some time he had had difficulty in speaking clearly, he had been suffering from insomnia and had become very bad-tempered. Even when supported, he could only manage to walk a few steps and before long he was bedridden, unable to eat and even finding it difficult to breathe. He was still mentally alert, though and had no intention of giving up his power. The politburo dutifully reported all its decisions to him and he would write down his instructions.

Mao spent the last few years of his private life with young female companions. His so-called secretary Chang Yue-Fung recalled in the post-Mao era, that after 26 March 1976 most of the reports sent to Mao concerned the spontaneous gatherings of condolence for Chow in Tiananmen Square, where people vented their hatred for the Gang of Four and the Cultural Revolution, often with negative comments aimed at Mao. In addition many letters full of grievances came from veteran communist cadres and the armed forces. The politburo tried to protect Mao by forbidding anyone from reading hostile news to him, but when he realised that the briefings were being curtailed, he angrily demanded to know who had decided to keep him in the dark.

Towards the end of his life, Mao was deeply worried that after his death Deng and other senior communists would criticise him and denounce the Cultural Revolution. He told Jiang and his handful of confidants to remember to kick these potential detractors out of the politburo and the Central Military Commission after his death.

At the end of 1975, a campaign against Deng and the capitalist roaders was launched with the aim of preserving Mao's political legacy and building up Jiang's political capital. The film industry, under Jiang's supervision, produced seven films with suitably anti-capitalist-roader themes, of which 7,832 copies were made. The Peking film studios were also ordered to make newsreels and documentaries attacking Deng and other leading figures; seven of these were also made, with a total of 1,072 copies produced. The films were duly screened around the country, together with ballet shows on the same theme.

At Mao's last politburo meeting, held in his study on 11 June 1976, he said they had told him that 95 per cent of the people supported him, but this was superficial. In January a million people had joined Chow's funeral procession and in April another million people had gathered to protest and he knew that their target was himself. He had the added worry of picking his successor. In the past he had chosen first Liu Shao-Qi, then Lin Biao and Wang Hong-Won, only to abandon each of them later.

At one point he asked Wang Tung-Chin, his trusted bodyguard and later the deputy chairman of the party, whether he should designate Jiang as his successor. Wang remained silent. Mao said: 'This is not my decision, only a proposition of mine. You have worked for me for nearly 40 years and I trust you.'

'If Jiang becomes party chairman,' replied Wang, 'I am afraid the party and the armed forces will not be happy. Perhaps comrade Hua Guo-Feng should take the job.' Mao now admitted that he was considering making Jiang the chairman, while Wang Tung-Chin, Hua Guo-Feng and three other trusted people would form a group to work with her. If this didn't work, it could be rearranged.

Hua Guo-Feng, therefore, was not Mao's first choice. Mao certainly knew that Jiang was not a popular character and shortly before he died, on 9 September 1976, he chose Hua Guo-Feng as his successor. Later, in September 1980, some people openly criticised Mao for appointing a successor, saying it was feudal and illegal. Mao had behaved like an emperor in choosing his own heir.

Mao's death left behind a hierarchy split into two implacable groups. The pro-Mao Cultural Revolution group, led by Jiang, dominated the party machine and controlled the media, through which they had issued Mao's instructions over the head of the dysfunctional government. But although they had seemed to have the upper hand all through the Cultural Revolution, the only area they effectively controlled was Shanghai. Mao's death immediately cut the ground from under their feet.

The other group within the party hierarchy was composed of veteran communists who had been sidelined by the Cultural Revolution. Their leaders were Deng, in charge of the party and civil service bureaucrats and Marshal Yip Jan-Ying, who was head of the armed forces. Although the army had played an important role during the Cultural Revolution it had not escaped the terrible purges and many officers hated Jiang. With the backing of the army, Marshal Yip Jan-Ying and his colleagues were effectively out of reach of the Gang of Four, Hua Guo-Feng and their followers.

As soon as Mao had died, Marshals Yip Jan-Ying, Nep Yung-Gin, Xu Shan-Chen and other senior officers moved immediately, with their families, to the heavily guarded offices of the Military Commission in West Hill outside Peking, for safety and for secret discussions. Yip ordered his secretary to report the current situation to him every 20 minutes. Deng, still under house arrest, had managed to have two short and secret talks with his old friend Yip. In the first half of September a group of generals had secretly moved into the exclusive PLA 301 Hospital pretending to be ill. They all hated and were wary of Jiang and her gang.

As Mao was dying, the members of the Gang of Four were already quietly arming their Shanghai power base. Beginning on 15 August, several hundred machine-guns and mortars were issued to the militias, together with 80,000 rifles. They also attempted to procure tanks and armoured vehicles. In addition Mao's nephew Mao Yuan-Sien, a middle-ranking political commissar who supported Jiang, secretly summoned two divisions from Manchuria. As the troops were on their way to Peking, Marshal Yip Jan-Ying simply ordered Mao Yuan-Sien's boss to recall the two divisions back to Manchuria immediately. Yip also transferred the 28th Army from Tianjin to seal up all routes leading into Peking.

On 5 October, a meeting of the politburo, but without the Gang of Four, was held in West Hill, the offices of the Military Commission. By now Hua Guo-Feng, Mao's successor and Wang Tung-Chin, Mao's powerful security chief in Central South Sea, had already abandoned Jiang and gone over to Yip, partly because of Jiang's arrogant and arbitrary behaviour which had made her so many enemies. The meeting decided unanimously to arrest the Gang of Four and the following day all were duly detained, as well as their close allies including Mao Yuan-Sien. The tense situation in Shanghai was defused without bloodshed.

Within one month of Mao's death, the upstarts he had groomed to run China had all been arrested. Hua survived by defecting to the military. As Mao's hand-picked successor, he was now the chairman of the party and the Central Military Commission, as well as prime minister. Hua was now officially known as 'the brilliant leader', but Mao's policies still ruled supreme. On 8 October, the new rulers decided to publish an edition of Mao's complete works and it was also decided to build a memorial hall in Tiananmen Square to house his corpse. It was now that Hua first put forward the rules of "Two Whatever". He said: "We have to protect whatever policy made by Chairman Mao and whatever words and actions that harm Chairman Mao will have to be stopped. It can not be tolerated."

Accordingly, on 7 February 1977 the new Two Whatevers were circulated widely in the *People's Daily*, the *Red Flag* and the PLA newspapers and at the same time the party began a campaign to blacken the names of the Gang of Four and to attack any right-leaning attempt to overturn their convictions. Any criticism of the Cultural Revolution or of previous campaigns was banned and anyone who breached these rulings was to be arrested as a counter-revolutionary. As late as 30 April 1978 a young woman by the name of Jone Hai-Yuen was sentenced to death and shot in Sienjan county, Jiangxi province, for criticising the Cultural Revolution.

Deng, meanwhile, was rehabilitated in July 1977. On 24 May 1978 he publicly rejected the Two Whatevers, arguing that it was nonsensical to say that every sentence that someone uttered was always absolutely correct. The liberal veteran communist Hu Yel-Bound initiated a debate about the nature of truth and criticised the Two Whatevers group, to the intense irritation of Mao's diehard follower Wang Tung-Chin. Only after General Lor Rui-Chin had spoken out to support Hu Yel-Bound was the debate allowed to continue. Hua, the political upstart, was no match for the able Deng. By 1982 Hua had been forced to resign and Deng's reign began.

In December 1978, the party formally put an end to the central plank of Mao Tse-Tung Thought – the policy of permanent class struggle – and admitted that the ten-year Cultural Revolution had been a mistake. In January 1981, the members of the 'Lin and Jiang counter-revolutionary cabal' were put on trial. Jiang and Chang Chun-Chel were given suspended death sentences and sent to prison, while the other members of the Gang of Four were jailed for between 15 and 20 years. Two years later, in 1991, Jiang hanged herself.

The party still purposely avoids pointing a finger at Mao, for it cannot afford to damage the glorious icon which justifies and protects its right of one-party rule. The official line is that Mao was a great and infallible leader bamboozled in his old age by the Gang of Four – although Jiang declared in court: 'I was Chairman Mao's dog, I bit whoever he told me to bite.'

The Cultural Revolution turned China into an anarchic state and it took people away from their workplaces to pursue the reign of terror. With nobody really in charge of the workplace work slowed down or came to a standstill. Even the government was unable to function properly. On one occasion in 1967, Chow summoned his departmental heads to a meeting of the State Council only to find, to his dismay, that many of them were absent, some because they had been taken to struggle meetings and others because they had been purged.

In the Great Stringing, the millions who travelled freely up and down the country caused immense disruption and when large-scale fighting erupted the whole traffic system was paralysed. The harbour offices along the Yangtze River were repeatedly destroyed and the staff all ran away. The Red Guards fought not just against the Chinese but also against foreign seamen. It was hardly surprising, therefore, that foreign ships were reluctant to enter Chinese ports, with the result such as Sino-Russian trade in 1967 was as much as 60 per cent lower than in 1966 (according to figures issued by Moscow in August 1968).

As production was disrupted, black markets mushroomed and prices rose dramatically. The State Council issued circular after circular to stress that the fundamental task of economic institutions was production and Chow tried very hard to maintain production and the transport system. On 5 June 1967, the *Liberation Daily* in Shanghai, controlled by the Gang of Four, carried the first of five articles attacking the State Council's circulars, claiming that they wiped out the class struggle and that they put production first and politics second.

From 1967 the Chinese economy was seriously in the red and the party blamed counter-revolutionaries for the economic trouble. The economic damage caused by the 10-year Cultural Revolution was in the region of 500 billion yuans.

More importantly, the human suffering was immeasurable. Among the documents which came to light during Jiang's trial was a highly confidential letter written by Kang Sheng. On 21 July 1968 Kang, a member of the powerful politburo standing committee, had reported to Jiang, who was then not even a member of the party central committee, that he was enclosing a list which Jiang had asked for and which named 88 members and alternate members of the current party central committee as traitors, collaborators and enemy agents, a staggering 76 per cent of the total membership. This figure surpassed even Stalin's big purges of 1937 and 1938, in which 73 per cent of the Russian politburo was eliminated.

According to statistics submitted by the special prosecution service after the Cultural Revolution, a total of 744,554 people were purged during the Cultural Revolution, 34,766 of whom were killed, including 22 members of the politburo, 96 members and alternate members of the central committee, 13 vice premiers, 60 members of the National People's Congress standing committee, 74 members of the Political Consultative Committee standing committee and 11 heads of the small democratic parties. Among the armed forces, 80,000 people were purged and 1,100 were persecuted to death, including eight marshals and 25 senior generals.

Countless ordinary people were purged unjustly, many of whom killed themselves, but none were included in the prosecution service statistics. In Guangdong province alone nearly 40,000 people were killed and a million people imprisoned or put through struggle meetings. It was estimated that one in nine people in the country was affected, meaning that in all there were some 100 million victims.

When Lin and six other members of the politburo, all of them very powerful during the Cultural Revolution, were named as traitors, it produced widespread shock. Lin had been personally picked by Mao as his heir apparent and his privileged status was written into the party's constitution. Under the new public security rules people could be condemned as active counter-revolutionaries if they dared criticise Lin. After Lin's death in 1971, a letter claimed to have been written by Mao in July 1966 was published to protect Mao's infallibility; in it the judicious leader had expressed his distrust of Lin. But the letter begged a very obvious question: if Mao had seen through Lin Biao well beforehand, then why promote him?

To demonstrate that Lin was an enemy, his anti-Mao activities and plan to assassinate Mao were made public. Now people could see the ferocious power struggle at the highest level. They began to understand that the Cultural Revolution had had nothing to do with culture and was never a revolution; it had been nothing more than a scam launched to retrieve the power which Mao had lost after the disaster of his Great Leap Forward. The new world depended totally on Mao's fancy; there were no laws, no principles and no political criteria. Many people were disillusioned enough to realise that they had been fooled and used.

On 15 June 1976, Mao said that he had achieved two things in his life. First, he had kicked Chiang Kai-Shek onto an island after several decades of fighting and had defeated the Japanese after fighting an eight-year war and secondly he had started the Cultural Revolution. Mao's defeat of Chiang certainly benefited Mao himself, but whether it benefited China is a different matter. In 1976, the year he died, the average annual income per head in more than 100 counties around the middle reaches of the Yellow

River was 39 yuans, equivalent to 20 American dollars, or two to three hours' wages of a skilled American worker. In December 1978, two years after Mao's death, his Cultural Revolution was formally denounced as a mistake and the CCP at the same time decided to abandon his policy of perpetual class struggle and instead concentrate on developing China's economy.

Mao's policy on the Sino-Japanese War was recorded by his private secretary Lee Rui in his book *The True Record of the Lu Mountain Conference*. It was: 'The more land the Japanese occupied the better'. Much later, on 27 September 1972, Mao openly thanked his visitors, the Japanese prime minister Kakuei Tanaka and foreign minister Takeo Fukuda, for the Sino-Japanese War, because without it the CCP could not have come to power. Hence it was difficult to see that he was very keen to fight the Japanese. The Nationalist troops fought well in Burma and west Yunnan but they did not send the Japanese home and Mao's poorly equipped Red Army certainly did not do so. It was the British in Burma and the Americans in the Pacific who inflicted devastating defeats on the Japanese, while American bombers paid daily visits to Japan to bring the war to the warmongers' motherland and it was the two atomic bombs which finally kicked the Japanese home. It is astonishing to say the least that Mao felt fit to claim the credit, but many Chinese people still believe him today.

Mao ruled China for 27 years. He brought China nothing but poverty, trauma and endless fighting. It was 20 per cent Mao's fault and 80 per cent the fault of the political system. The faults of the system remain and that is why, 13 years after Mao's death, the Chinese government felt free to slaughter students on 4 June 1989 in Tiananmen Square.

Mao's portrait is still hanging high on Tiananmen city wall. Dishonesty and the narrow self-interest of a political party are the reasons why it is there. Sooner or later, China must face the truth that no one, not even Mao Tse-Tung, can rewrite history.

844